# AFRICAN PEOPLE IN THE GLOBAL VILLAGE

*An Introduction to Pan African Studies*



**John K. Marah**

To Dr. Stuart-Appelle
Dean
in Appreciation
John K. Marah
6-25-98

**University Press of America,® Inc.**
**Lanham • New York • Oxford**

**University Press of America,® Inc.**
4720 Boston Way
Lanham, Maryland 20706

12 Hid's Copse Rd.
Cummor Hill, Oxford OX2 9JJ


Printed in the United States of America
British Library Cataloging in Publication Information Available

ISBN 0-7618-1133-8 (cloth: alk. ppr.)
ISBN 0-7618-1134-6 (pbk: alk. ppr.)

™ The paper used in this publication meet the minimum requirements of American National Standard for information Sciences—Permanence of Paper for Printed Library Materials, ANSI Z39.48—1984

# Chapter I

## African Sensibilities in this Global Village

By anyone's standards Africa has been, and might continue to be the least developed continent in this global village for some years to come. Between the 1970s and the 1990s Africa took a nose-dive into the abyss of poverty, stagnation and the concomitant inferiorization. The debt crisis, starvation, malnutrition, AIDS, the Somalian, Rwandan, Burundian and the then Zairian debacles, African kleptocracies, the ripple effects of the failures of USSR etc. all deeply and negativity affected the African personality. Davidson (1974), Whitaker (1988) and Sandbrook (1985) all wondered whether Africa would survive. According to Davidson (1974:36), African people had 'inherited a situation' in which they seemed powerless, vulnerable and unequal players in the global arena of capitalism. In Davidson's terms, Africa epitomized "the development of underdevelopment" (28).

The 1960s had promised Africa a brighter future than that which actually came about in the 1980s and the 1990s. In the 1960s universities proliferated in Africa; nation building, Pan-Africanism, Authenticity, African Socialism, Afro-Marxism and other ideologies promised to advance Africa. The slogan 'forward forever, backward never' pervaded the African air. "...a hefty $225-Million independence gift to Nigeria in 1961" from the U.S.A... went into "capital investment in roads, water supplies, and education. Three Nigerian universities...were started at that time..." (Whitaker, 1988:65). Other African nations also began to expand their own educational and national road systems, health services and the Africanization of their bureaucracies. "Several independent (African) countries adopted names which evoke(d) the magic and glory of past African civilizations: Ghana, Mali, Benin, Zimbabwe–though these original societies had a tenuous or non-existent geographical link to the contemporary (African) state(s)" (Sandbrook, 1985:47). In 1966 Kwame Nkrumah was overthrown and while in Guinea he wrote his *Dark Days in Ghana* (1968), in which he lamented the vulgarization of the African revolution. What would have happened to Africa had African leaders agreed with Nkrumah in 1963 that Africa must unite? What have Africans accomplished since the 1960s? Are Africans more enlightened today than they were fifty, or hundreds of years ago? What is the position of African people in the contemporary global village? Is there a panacea to the contemporary African economic, political, social, and technological problems? How do African people, those in the United States as well as those in Africa, depict themselves in their literature, religion, history and political economy? Aside from their 'brave' political speeches, how really do African people feel with regards to their place in this global village?

Even the most illiterate and the blind African knows that Africa is backward at the moment and might continue to be so for a while, but not forever. Because African people are a living people, who think first and foremost, feel and have imaginations, they will stand to the challenges of the times. Africans are more conscious now than ever before of who they are, of their past and what they must do for the betterment of the African continent and its people within and without it, in the diaspora. They are aware of the African diaspora's social, political and economic conditions in the west and their contributions to the ideology of Pan-Africanism, Negritudism and Liberation Theology, all of which continue to be effective instruments in defining the African moment.

As it is well-known, African people have had a long history, have influenced western civilizations in the areas of theology, philosophy, science, writing, education and other fundamental endeavors (James, 1976; Ben Jochannan 1971; and even Lefkowitz, 1995). For a people who have been denigrated for thousands of years this self-knowledge is not for nothing. Contrary to the now, almost, anachronistic view that whatever of noteworthy in the African continent's past had been brought by outsiders, we can now unequivocally challenge that notion. It has even become mundane to state that people migrated from Africa and spread, like a fan, into the northern continents of Europe and Asia. Furthermore, Africans have had well-established political, economic, social, and higher educational institutions that any race or ethnic group could be proud of; Africans have had expansive empires, kingdoms, nations, chiefdoms and states, of multi-ethnic compositions that were well-organized on the basis of humanism, equality, respect for individuality, the ancestors, the gods and monotheism. Africans have built monuments, exploited and explored rivers and the oceans; they have mined minerals and engaged in long distant trade; they have produced great poets, groits, and orators.

Like any other group, Africans have made wars, traveled out of curiosity to see what laid beyond the Atlantic Ocean (Van Sertima, 1981); they have learnt and borrowed institutions from foreigners, made laws, produced scripts and have imagined creativity. They have produced leaders with charisma, in the most basic sense of that word, as well as others less charismatic, more despotic, autocratic, exploitative, egocentric and even kleptomaniacs down to the present time. Africans have had glorious as well as inglorious times in their historical experiences. They have participated in trickery, democracy, falsehood, deceit, exploitative mechanisms, slavery, communalism, socialism and other-isms.

Thus in 'all' human endeavors African people have made their mark directly and indirectly to fundamental ideas and institutions in the past as well as in the present day global village, and will continue to do so because they are not going to evaporate; African-Americans are not going back to Africa enmasse and disappear into the Congo forest. As the world becomes truly a global village, Africans are not going to remain at the periphery; they are going to mingle into the stream of humanity as equal members, with their heads held high. They are going to be proud of their color (which has been used against them for centuries); they are going to modify their institutions, ideas, and feelings just as other ethnic or racial groups have had to do when they've come into contact with 'strangers,' this time within the global village.

Nonetheless, one must never understate the tremendous handicaps and problems African countries have inherited from African traditions, European colonialism and Arabic domination in Africa. Furthermore, African people today, globally, are comparatively poorer, more illiterate, more unsophisticated about modern technology, are disease stricken, dependent on outside sources for techniques, economic advancement, textbooks, political ideas and vocabulary, modernizing concepts and foodstuffs. The list could be as long as the reader wishes.

To a large measure, this must make African people experience a taint of uneasiness and inferiority. They have one foot in modernity, the other steeped in tradition and superstition; they go to modern churches, come home and make libations to their ancestors (Appiah, 1992:9-120). They obtain advanced degrees and skills in the modern economy, but keep their wives as second class citizens (Emecheta, 1974). They see that the masses of their people are afflicted with diseases that have been obliterated elsewhere in the world, but seem powerless to radically change the health conditions of their people; they can write eloquently against the west, but feel more comfortable living in London, Paris, New York or Washington D.C. They also see clearly that some of their people are starving to death, while others are malnutritioned, inhabit overcrowded shanty towns in Nairobi, Freetown, Lagos,

Kinshasa and elsewhere, but seem unconcerned or unable to bulldoze these disease afflicted 'habitations.'

The few that are educated enough cannot fail to see that they have not made much dent on the path of African development and know that they are often not taken seriously by their western counterparts. They might have received their degrees from Oxford, Harvard, Yale, or Princeton, but they are still of the African race, and that negatively categorizes them at once (Cose, 1993: 28; 55; 78; 87). African diplomats in the United Nations do not often speak with one voice, are influenced and dictated to by non-Africans in times of crucial votes. If they want western aid, their sons and daughters to be admitted at elite western schools, they must speak the language of their benefactors; they know that their black leaders in Africa and the United States are not totally free.

Educated Africans know very well that their countries have become too dependent on the World Bank and other international monetary institutions that suggest to them the path of development that Africa must take; they are asked to become like the west. Rather than being a force after independence, African countries became, literally, beggars in the global market; they've remained balkanized and easy to be manipulated, even by the smallest European country.

On the other hand, it is not too hard to see that Africa has not lacked strong-willed leaders, interested in Africa's rapid economic development. A case in point is that of Kwame Nkrumah of Ghana, who was one African patriot adamant about African unity, one African citizenship, one African currency, etc. as a panacea for African development; but the west was not too pleased with such an African patriot (Rooney, 1988: 166-169).

It must also not be too hard to see that those African leaders who have been selfless about the improvement of the social and economic conditions of their people have often been discredited and painted negatively by unfriendly propaganda media. One must not also forget those selfish African leaders who sold their birth right for a mess of pottage (192-193). This group of African leaders aligned themselves with the forces of exploitation and selfishness in the midst of appalling poverty. They advanced themselves as a group at the expense of the illiterate African masses and other working class people. They live today in expensive houses, drive overly expensive cars from Germany, France, Japan, and America in the midst of absurdity and hopelessness (Kaplan, 1994:44; 48). These African leaders have their supporters in their governments and in the West as administrators, civil servants, heads of departments and even some professionals in the military, police and educational institutions. They have, and continue to perpetuate themselves in houses and offices built on sand that might soon erode. One wonders what the West says behind the backs of this group of African leaders? They, this group of Africans, might have received the highest, or a higher western degree, or training, in Europe or in Africa, but have been impotent in terms of African development. They go to numerous conferences on behalf of African development, where they end up blaming the West for most of Africa's socio-economic ills.

There are specific African attitudes that must at once be addressed. That the educated African should not soil his hands is dangerous for African development; that African elders should be respected, even when they are dead wrong must be challenged. African elders have made numerous foolish mistakes that contemporary Africans are now paying for dearly.

African people's attitudes towards work and nature must also be challenged. The African worker who takes too many breaks, and is not punctual at work must be made to bear the consequences of his own actions. Africans must know, as they should have learned from the western man, that there were no devils in the evil forest around Okonkwo's village; they must be confident that Africa is their special gift from 'god' to conquer and subdue. African people's attitude that the white man is superior because he has produced so much technology must also be challenged. The fact seems to be that black people have also been technological, and are aware that technology develops from the interaction of various group talents from various regions and people; technology can also be bought. Because Africa is technologically backward in the 21st century does not mean Africa will be so forever. The Anglos were once upon a time so technologically behind the Arabs that the latter thought of the former as too stupid even to be made into slaves; "the Greeks did not carry culture and learning to Egypt, but found it there, and wisely settled in that country, in order to absorb as much as possible of its culture (James, 1976:47).

There are African students, scholars and researches all over the world today, 'wisely' learning and 'absorbing' modern technology. These men and women will transfer western technology to Africa. To a great extent, western technology is already in Africa in the industries of South Africa, educational and research institutes in Nigeria, Kenya, Ghana, Egypt and elsewhere on the continent. African American engineers and scientists could also be a valuable resource for African technological development. These dispersed resources must, however, be centralized for Africa as a whole to obtain a maximum harvest.

Black Africans must take an eclectic attitude towards Islam and Christianity. These two major religions, despite their affinity to Africa, have historically manhandled African people within and without Africa. For those who are inclined toward Islam uncritically, simply observe that the Arab practitioners of Islam cannot wash their hands of black African blood. Bernard Lewis (1971:7; 66), tells us that even "though the Qur' 'an' expresses no racial or color prejudice," practioners of Islam associate slavery with blackness. Thus, black slaves

> consisting principally of slaves imported from East Africa, and numbering some tens of thousands ... lived and worked in conditions of extreme misery. They were fed, we are told, on a 'few handfuls' of flour, semolina, and dates. They rose in successive rebellions, the most important of which lasted fifteen years, from 868 to 883, and for a while offered a serious threat to the Baghdad Caliphate. The leader of these black rebels was a white man.

"There were also white slaves but the black ones were far more severely restricted in their social and occupational mobility" (64-65). The legacy of black slaves in Arab/Muslim lands continues to this day, despite the fact that Africans themselves helped perpetuate the Islamic faith into Western Europe (Spain), where they were expelled in 1492 (Lewis, 1993:42). Some Africans may boast of "Libya's strongman, Colonel Muammar El-Gadhafi ... with his Chief of Army staff, Brigadier Abubakar Yornis Jabar ...who is black" (El Mahmud-Okereke, 1983:48), but this hardly explicates the socio-material conditions of black Africans in Libya, Mauritania and other predominantly Arab-ruled North African countries.

Without a doubt, the Arabs are also now confronted by western technology, education, feminism and secularization that are challenging traditional Islamic beliefs, practices and attitudes; Africans cannot afford to be further balkanized by religious demarcations, religions that are anti-black African Animism. As Black African civilizations have been challenged by 'westernization,' so also have the Arabic civilizations. Lewis (1993, 39-40) goes on to tell us that traditional Islam has been enraged by its confrontation with the modern world dominated by the west:

> Schooled in a religious culture in which, from the beginning, rightness has meant supremacy, he has seen that supremacy lost in the world to Western power; lost in his own country to foreign intruders, with their foreign ways and their western protégés; lost in his home to emancipated women and rebellious children. Brought up in a complex but functioning system of social loyalties and responsibilities, he finds those loyalties, defined by faith and kin, denounced as sectarian and nepotistic, and those responsibilities divided and abandoned in favor of capitalist acquisitiveness or socialist expropriations. ... he does not fail to notice that the way of life of the rich and

> tyrannical–their homes, their clothing, their style, their food, their amusement–are modeled, at least in appearance, on those of the infidel west.

Thus, the Islam that was brought to Africa in the 6th century A. D. is not the same Islam of the 21st century. As Africans must creatively respond to the process of globalization, so also must Islam in Africa, "France, Germany, Sweden, Italy, the United States and other western countries" (Lapidus, 1993:8). Like Christianity, Africans cannot continue to regard Islam as an absolute and sacrosanct, without African blood on its hands. In practice, Islam has not only enslaved black Africans, but also continues to dominate them in Sudan, Mauritania and Saudi Arabia, Libya and Morocco.

For Western Christianity, one only needs to observe how Europeans used it against black people in South Africa and in the United States, just to take two examples. White South Africans believed that it was their manifest destiny to Lord it over Black South Africans indefinitely, or so they wished. In their belief in Herrenvolk (Fredrickson, 1982:154-155), they saw Africans as kaffirs, pagans, or animists whose god given duties had been inscribed in the bible–to be hewers of wood and drawers of water; they forgot about the Exodus story in their myopia. David Walker (1829) elaborated on how Western Christianity was used to contribute to the wretchedness of the African-American. However, it was the same theology that Nat Turner used to attempt to liberate his people (Aptheker, 1966). Frederick Douglass (1968:121) pinpointed the contradictions inherent in Western Christianity relative to the African slaves in America; in his own words, he elaborates with particular reference to the U.S. South:

> The man who wields the blood-clothed cowskin during the week fills the pulpit on Sunday, and claims to be a minister of the meek and lowly Jesus. The man who robs me of my earnings at the end of each week meets me as a class-leader on Sunday morning, to show me the way of life, and the path of salvation. He who sells my sister, for purposes of prostitution, stands forth as the pious advocate of purity. He who proclaims it a religious duty to read the Bible denies me the right of learning to read the name of the God who made me. He who is the religious advocate of marriage robs whole millions of its sacred influence, and leaves them to the ravages of wholesale pollution. The warm defender of the sacredness of the family relation is the same that scatters whole families,-sundering husbands and wives, parents and children, sisters and brothers,–leaving the hut vacant, and the hearth desolate. We see the thief preaching against theft, and the adulterer against

> adultery. We have men sold to build churches, women sold to support the gospel, and babes sold to purchase Bibles for the *poor heathen! all for the glory of God and the good of souls!* The slave auctioneer's bell and the church-going bell chime in with each other, and the bitter cries of the heart-broken slave are drowned in the religious shouts of his pious master.

These explications do not, however, imply that African people should not be Christians or Muslims; they must not, however, permit these two major global religions to further balkanize them into competing, antagonistic groupings. Africans already have too many variables fragmenting the continent to add two more lines of demarcation to divide and subdivide them. Africans have far more exigent problems to attack within the continent to further add fighting amongst themselves over religions that really do not think too much of them; religions that 'enslaved' them and told them that they were doomed to hell if they remained animists, unchristian or non-Islamic.

In addition to 'alien' religions balkanizing Africa, tribalistic attitudes continue to disintegrate African countries. The Hutus and the Tutsis (Lorch, 1993:3) in Rwanda-Burundi, have been at each other's throats for centuries. Though most African countries have been able to 'nationalize' their various tribal groupings, it still seems to be the case that Africans feel much more at ease marrying Europeans than doing so intertribally, or inter-regionally; Africans are still suspicious of each other based on tribalism and regionalism; they want to be modern/global, yet they are still confocal and parochial.

Tribalism, like racism, classism, regionalism, ethnocentricism and Europeanism, views other people not belonging to the tribe as 'strangers,' untrustworthy, of less ability, less desirable and even less competent. One is treated as an outsider by a tribe he/she does not belong to; one's own tribe has all the desirable qualities that one can think of; it is needless to say that such an outlook is detrimental to African development. Contemporary Africa needs tribalism as it does starvation or a plague; Africa must transcend tribalism as it should attack poverty, ignorance and disease; tribalism has added its own to Africa's economic, social, and political underdevelopment:

> The problem is compounded in Africa by the prevailing economic culture, where ties to tribe and family still rule most economic exchange. Because of this, people put the good of local and economic communities before whatever the government may declare as national goals: a job is probably not worth doing unless you're doing it for a family or ethnic group. When 'everybody' feels this way, there will not be a lot of pressure from below for

> good government. Moreover, it puts the national treasury itself up for grabs. (Whitaker, 1988:23)

In addition to tribalism, class divisions in Africa are entrenching themselves. The traditional village systems of communalism, egalitarianism, and hospitality are under strain in the modern African urban centers. Where we once lived in compounds and farmed or raised cattle, we now live in apartments in Nairobi, Freetown, Lagos and elsewhere where the extended family system is not conducive. "...in the villages of Africa it (was) perfectly natural to feed at any table and lodge in any hut. But in the cities this communal existence no longer holds. You must pay for lodging and be invited for food" (Kaplan, 1994:46).

The highly educated ones, and those others who have made it in the modern market place, are 'delinked' from the illiterates and others who are not armed with skills to flourish in the modern African cities and economies; those Africans who have not 'made it' are pitiably the most wretched of the earth, and most of these can be found in mostly African countries, south of the Sahara (The World Bank, 1997:108-109).

With western education, modernization and urbanization, the traditional African family has also been negatively affected. It used to be that the larger one's family, the more respect/prestige the individual obtained from his peers, the clan or tribe; that is no longer the case; monogamy and the nuclei family's time have arrived; quality of children, not quantity has come into vogue; individualism, not communalism; individual success, not group success; yet the successful individual in the family is expected to shoulder the less fortunate ones. Nkrumah (1963:100), states that

> Thrift has not been a characteristic of our people, largely because they have not enjoyed enough income to make the question anything but academic. How to instill a need to spend and save wisely among them has become a major preoccupation now that they are beginning to enjoy higher incomes and the taste for amenities. Our family system actually discourages family heads from saving, for the system, in effect, penalizes the man with initiative in favour of the lazy and the weak. The indigent members of the family live upon the more fortunate ones. A praiseworthy and useful practice in our past, more or less stagnant society based on subsistence farming, it acts today as a break upon ambition and drive. At the present time, the man who makes a reasonable living finds his money eaten up by his relatives (and this includes the most extended members reaching to the -nth degree of relationship), so that he simply cannot meet his personal obligations, let alone save anything. But save we must, if we are to build up

> the hard reserves of capital necessary for our development. Side by side with the family hindrance to saving, there has been a real and developing increase in expenditure upon a vast miscellany of imported goods.

It is not only the traditional African family that is under strain; African tribal languages are too, profoundly affected. It is not hyperbolic to state that most of the least prestigious African languages will soon be out of favor and become extinct; they are not only less prestigious, but will also continue to have fewer and fewer speakers; speakers, who would soon become polyglots in western and the major African languages. Anthropologists and interested linguists should attempt to rescue some of these African languages for the scientific, religious or medical potentials they might contain.

Thus, the African continent has entered the global village with a lot of disabilities stacked against her, but can not afford to continue epitomizing "the development of underdevelopment" (Davidson, 1974:28). Western languages and consumer goods have penetrated the thickest African jungle and the smallest African tribe; western ideas and manufactured goods tantalize and impact the most illiterate African man, woman and child.

> The 1980 movie "The Gods must be Crazy" humorously portrays the impact a coke bottle, a symbol of western technology, could have on a remote African tribe of bush people. The bottle falls from a passing airplane and a member of the tribe picks it up. He brings the unfamiliar object to his village, where the people are delighted by it. ... The villagers begin fighting over it and discovered it can also be used to hit each other. ... The movie effectively dramatizes the impact a single western object could have on the people of the Third World. (Rohr, 1989:12)

Klitgaard (1990:32) observed in 'deepest' Equatorial Guinea that "the (African) villagers' clothing was western, though ragged; there was no sign of African costume or distinctive clothes. The huts were also western in appearance, only smaller and dirtier: they were rudimentary rectangular houses made of wood planks with tin roofs and shutters: no beehive huts or adobe structures." Though the Africans themselves do not produce the clothing and the 'tin roofs,' they are participating in the economics of the global village. But what is this global village? And what is the place of African people in this global village dominated by western ideas, manufactured goods, and 'technopoly'? (Postman, 1993).

## The Contemporary Global Village

The contemporary global village is headed by the U.S.A., Western Europe, Canada, and Japan, put under the rubric of the first world. The other regions of the world have too had their days of grandeur and splendor. Asian and African regions had had their days of sophistication and 'unequaled' civilizations at times when Western Europeans lived in caves and worshipped several gods, engaged in tribal warfare and practiced cannibalism that might have put African practices to shame. The western man then was not only a polytheist but he could also have been appropriately labeled a barbarian of no mean disposition.

Looking at the western man today, however, one would think that he has always been civilized, that he has never been enslaved, has never practiced barbarity, that he was never once perceived by Egyptians to be at the lower levels of humanity (Diop, 1974:46-49). Nonetheless, that Africa developed sophistications thousands of years before Europe can no longer be disputed. It was the ancient Egyptians who left us the sacred *Book of the Dead* in which we find the negative confessions: "I have not committed theft; I have not slain man or woman; I have not uttered falsehood, ....", Budge (1989:367), the Egyptian fashion of the Ten Commandments, that could be profitably used in today's global market. It was the Egyptian Ikhnaton, unquestionably black (Rogers, 1972:57-66) who, in 1360 BC., instituted monotheism, to worship the only God, Amon-RA, Amon, or Amen, who judged the soul against a feather to determine its fitness to enter the underworld, heaven. Our own current alphabet can be traced back to Egyptian characters, hieroglyphics, which were taken over by the Semites, Hebrews and the Arabs, later improved upon by the Greeks who added letters for vowels; from the Greeks, the Roman alphabet has come to our present civilization from Western Europe, from which, of course, the United States, Canada, Australia and South African whites have come. From the Egyptian papyrus has come paper; the Egyptian civilization also gave us the pen and ink that have been improved upon. The idea of monotheism, the Ten Commandments, the twelve month calendar, the three-hundred and sixty-five days a year, the thirty days a month, math and engineering, dentistry, architecture and medicine, commerce and democracy have all had African contributions. Other world civilizations, including the west, have added to these African contributions to human civilizations, as America has built upon European industrialization, as Japan has built upon American and European civilization, which is now globalized.

Paradoxically, despite these African participations, African people remain one of the most underdeveloped, illiterate, powerless and not surprisingly, the least respected. Graphically, Africa's current position in the global context, as can be seen below, is at the bottom of all other world regions and people, excluding the American Indians and the Australian aborigines, a non-European people themselves.

1)U.S.A., Canada, Western Europe, Japan, etc.
2)Australia, Eastern Europe, China, India, etc.
3)Latin America and the West Indian Islands, except Haiti (the least advanced in the Western Hemisphere);
4)Africa (the second largest continent in the world is at the bottom in this global village).

This is undoubtedly an oversimplification for we are aware that even within the first world, there are pockets of poverty and third world people and conditions in terms of longevity, lifestyle and life chances; in the third world, there are also first world classes of people and conditions in terms of education and other first world amenities. Nonetheless, Wiseman (1990:13-14) states that

> Of all the continents, Africa is much the least developed. Most of the world's poorer states are African and the bulk of its people are among the most poverty stricken. Standards of living, measured by all the usual criteria of health and welfare, life expectancy, infant mortality and so on are extremely low. Its economics, predominantly agrarian and non-industrialized, are among the most vulnerable and least developed in the world.... In a distressingly large number of African states the post independence era has ... been of economic decline.... The terminology that places African states in the category of 'developing countries' is, for many, simply misleading: all are under-developed but only a few are developing.

Very few black African nations can realistically boast that, since independence, their citizens have enjoyed more economic, political or psychological security than when they were under their former colonial powers. The few African countries that do boast are often heavily dependent on western technology, technical personnel and western businesses; these countries often neglect to critically examine the living standards of the African masses, but boast about their tall buildings and freeways. Thus, we hear that the Ivory Coast, Cameroon and Kenya have done better than those African countries that embraced Marxism, or Communism; democracy is viewed as the panacea for African development; non-governmental intervention in private enterprises is suggested as the corner-stone that would unleash the entrepreneurial spirit of African businessmen; if only African leaders were democratic, non-dictatorial, and concentrated their efforts in agricultural development, etc. their countries would be well on the road to an overall development. But the case of Ivory Coast is hardly one that black Africa should boast of; Kaplan (1994:48) tells us that

> though Sierra Leone is widely regarded as beyond salvage, the Ivory Coast has been considered an African success story, and Abidjan has been called 'the Paris of West Africa.' Success, however, was built on two artificial factors: the high price of cocoa, of which the Ivory Coast is the world's leading producer, and the talents of a French expatriate community, whose members have helped run the government and the private sector. The expanding cocoa economy made the Ivory Coast a magnet for migrant workers from all over West Africa: between a third and a half of the country's population is now non-Ivorian and the figure could be as high as 75 percent in Abidjan. During the 1980s cocoa prices fell and the French began to leave. The skyscrapers of the Paris of West Africa are a facade. Perhaps 15 percent of Abidjan's population of three million people live in shantytowns like Chicago and Washington, and the vast majority live in places that are not much better.

African countries that pursued the socialist as well as those that followed capitalist paths (Ghana and Zaire, for an example) have all not faired well. Ethiopia was plagued by civil wars through the 1970s and 80s; Tanzania's African Socialism succeeded in educating the masses, but was not able to radically improve their material conditions; Ghana's socialist experiment that was so promising 'ended' with the overthrow of Kwame Nkrumah in 1966. African socialists alternated between the east and the west when it was most opportunistic. In the final analysis, however, neither model has greatly improved the material conditions of the African masses, who have been left at the very bottom in the global market economy, technology, and technopoly.

Nkrumah's Pan-Africanism in the 1950s and 60s was diluted by conservative African leaders and their western counterparts, who feared that their national positions would be undermined, and rationalized that Nkrumah was too adamant about becoming the first president of his proposed union of African states. Thus, a close examination of the 1963 OAU charter would reveal the anti-Nkrumah sentiments running through the OAU principles that emphasize non-interference, a sacrosanct territorial integrity and a definite stance against subversion on the part of any African nation, or leader, desirous of spreading his ideological influence. Nkrumah's stance for the political, social and economic integration of the African continent was diluted to emphasize a nebulous co-operation between African states that, in no small measure, left Sub-Saharan Africa at the periphery of the global market.

Supporters of the 1963 OAU charter have gone to lengths to point out the success of the organization with respect to its stated purposes, but none can deny, retrospectively, that Nkrumahism could easily be the most profound renascent African ideology. At least Boswells as well as enemies of Nkrumahism are now in a better position to realize that a divided Africa is an impotent Africa; a divided Africa is an underdeveloped continent, and an 'underdeveloped' African-Americans and other African people in the contemporary global village.

West European unity, institutions, ideas of democracy and economic systems have pervaded the globe. Western technology, communication systems, transportation, capitalism, individualism, systems of organization, the western concept of individual liberty, the emphasis on private property and the insistence on the scientific method have enthralled non-western societies. Africa is an epitome in this zeitgeist of enthrallment. The Russian alternative has been discredited for its failure to produce diverse material goods for the Russian populace. Furthermore, Russian restrictions on individual liberty and western propaganda about freedom of thought, worship and the pursuit of happiness challenged the status-quo in Eastern Europe, and that propaganda is undoubtedly infectious in Africa. Chinese students rose up to challenge their government and pictures of the confrontations were reported world-wide. The ANC in Southern Africa became bolder, more deviant and uncompromising with the Apartheid regime. Women, minorities and other traditionally disadvantaged populations have increasingly become aware that they are aware. As the French bourgeoisie benefited from the western enlightenment period that challenged the old regimes in Europe, so also has the global village learnt from the west European emphasis on individual freedom and the insistence that governments be accountable to the governed. West European technology, industrialization, patterns of organization, culture, etc. have become the yardsticks by which to measure one's economic, social, political and individual development.

The ideological 'defeat' of Marxism left little room for Africa to attack westernization. "The West is now at an extraordinary peak of power in relation to other civilizations" (Huntington, 1993: 39). Now that western ideas have shown their efficacy, the western man has become confident and supremely self-assured. Ellul (1978:3-7) has abundantly appraised the western mind. In his view, irrespective of the incontestable brutality of the west, including the spread of European diseases to Indians, opium to the Chinese, the advocacy of 'Eugenics' to abate population growth in third world countries, slavery and colonization of Africa, Ellul still prefers the west; he begins to 'cleans' his western mind by comparing western atrocities to that of non-westerners', including the Arabic invasions of North Africa, the Turkish empire, the Chinese expansions and other inhuman atrocities before the advent of Europeans into Africa and elsewhere. "The Arabs," for instance, "built splendid cities, but they used slaves to build them" (14). To Ellul, was it not the western man who

> invented the 'rights of man'? The same holds for the elimination of exploitation. Where did the move to socialism originate? In Europe, and in Europe alone. The Chinese, like the Algerians, are inspired by western thinking as they move toward socialism. Marx was not Chinese, nor was Robespierre an Arab. The whole of the modern world, for better or for worse, is following a western model; no one imposed it on others, they have adopted it themselves, and enthusiastically. We exported our rationalist approach to things, our 'science,' our conception of state, our bureaucracy, our nationalist ideology. ... the essential, central, undeniable fact is that the west was the first civilization in history to focus attention on the individual and on freedom.... we have committed crimes, but we have also caused the whole of mankind to take a gigantic step forward and to live its childhood behind. (16-17)

Apart from science and technology, the west, according to Ellul, has given the rest of the global village 'freedom and the individual' which are concepts that have revolutionized the entire world, pervading the tiniest corners of the globe. Certainly, Ellul speaks for the rulers of west. Implicitly or explicitly, westerners have come to believe that without them the rest of mankind, especially the non-Europeans, will be in a sea of ignorance and barbarism; westerners therefore carry about them an air of superiority. This feeling of superiority is currently subdued, but explicit enough, and shows in how the western man treats the rest of the world, and especially the African.

The United States, France, Great Britain, Germany, Canada, Italy, and Japan are currently the masters of the global economy and can economically and technically 'control and dictate' to other world regions such as Africa, Latin America, India, China and even the former U.S.S.R. With the power of western media, Europe, Canada and America have been able to change the tastes of African peoples and others who now, more than ever before, aspire to look, consume, think, and recreate like westerners. Some Japanese now undergo cosmetic surgery to appear western; Japan adopted the western parliamentary-democratic process of politics and, for all practical purposes, she seems to be beating the West at its own game. Japanese can successfully undergo cosmetic surgery, but Africans may have to pump a lot of 'white' blood into their veins to approximate European physical features.

But Africans have too been affected by western standards of beauty. Some African men are now more comfortable in western tailored suits, while educated African women spend quite sometime 'burning' their hair to make it a bit more manageable, they claim.

M'bow (1984:388) has re-emphasized the impact of western media and technology in bringing peoples of the world closer together. People of different religions, cultures, stages of development, and world regions are today in more frequent contact than ever before, and these contacts will continue to grow rather than diminish. Many more people are being hired outside of their countries of birth, and have not become rootless. The world's religions are becoming more 'similar' than different; the world is becoming more westernized in numerous ways; western products can now be found in the remotest of villages. The concerns for water and air pollution are no longer the sole prerogatives of the west coast of the United States or New York City in the northeast, but have become global concerns. In no small measure, the globe is irrevocably in the process of being westernized, or made more compact.

But contradictions in the west are also being transported worldwide. For instance, "the west has always claimed to be on the side of David against Goliath, and it continues to make this claim. The difficulty is that the west is now a Goliath, one of the mighty of the earth, yet it cannot but still judge itself according to its old values" (Ellul, 1978: 109). Through western information media, magazines, films, newspapers, and textbooks, these contradictions have been propagated worldwide. How can the west be the Goliath and faithfully police itself?

Nonetheless, there is hardly any question about western technological, economic and institutional superiority. But is this western global dominance to be absolutely perennial and cantankerous? What is the position of African people in this western dominated global system? Are Africans to remain at the bottom of this global village as they have been for the last five-hundred years?

In this book, we examine the position of African people in Africa and the United States with particular emphasis on some of their salient predicaments in the present global system, the place of African unity and some reflections concerning Africans and African-Americans with respect to what they must do to have a decisive impact on the west so that they become actors in this global system as opposed to being merely subjects and insignificant members of this impending, new, global system. African people do not only have to adapt to this new global system, but they also must change it in their own image and resolutely oppose racism, exploitative classism, brutal capitalism and the resurgence of naked Marxism.

In African eyes, the global system must be a village that is radically changed to accommodate and appreciate the darker races from the lightest mulatto to the darkest Senegalese or southern Sudanese, where the African point of view is not simply swept aside, as has been customary with Westerness, but accepted as a valid constituent of the global system. Africans now understand the west more than ever before, having been subjected to western ideas, religions, economies, fantasies and contradictions. Above all, Africans are now aware that they are aware and western bulldozers cannot bury that academic and intellectual achievements away, no matter how much westerners wish for such a thing. In the final analysis, it is with African peoples that western technology, religion, ideas about freedom, equality, individual liberty, private property, democracy, etc. face their greatest challenge; African people have, in no small measure, the advantageous right to refute or affirm the West. It is with African people then that the west has its most advantage or disadvantage in its move to be the global leader. In the eyes of the African, the western man is an unbelievable ruler "... who does not live and act according to his declared principles" (52). The western man in the U.S.A. freed himself in 1776, but maintained African slaves for eighty-seven more years; the French bourgeoisie proclaimed liberty, equality, and fraternity in 1789, but would not do the same for Toussaint L'Ouverture; there are other inconsistencies with regards to Africans and the other non-western peoples. The western man proclaimed his civilized laws and institutions globally, but has behaved barbarously toward Africans in Africa and in the Americas. This internal contradictions in the west are Africa's bones of contention. "Western man claimed to be faithful to his wife, but he multiplied his adulteries; egalitarian, but he crushed the poor; liberal, but he favored those in authority; rational, but he surrendered to the desire of power; humane, but he built a world of alienation" (52). Since Africans are not westerners, they may chose to judge the west by not only what is written and codified, but also by that which is practiced daily in their relationships with the west. The European may boast of his Christianity, emphasize the brotherhood of man in Christ, liberal democracy, evolutionary socialism, one man–one man vote and all the other seemingly utopian ideas with respect to the African, but these will all fall far too short with the white man's continued racism, institutional as well as personal, obstacles against social, residential, economic and institutional integration of the African. The African insists upon the eradication of racism against blacks and other colored people globally.

Because blacks are different from whites in all things that shouldn't really matter but do, the African poses the greatest challenge to the western man in addressing those issues that shouldn't matter but really matter in the western man's repertoire. For hundreds of years the West insisted that he is superior, but really he is not, for a tiger does not boast in the jungle. In no small measure, the western man insisted on the separation of the races, but this too has not worked. The white man lynched, imprisoned and flogged the black man for even allegedly going near the apple of his eye, his white woman, but the twain have met and have even grown fond of each other. The white man said, in so many ways, that the black man was ugly, but the African turned around and said black was beautiful, and the white man knew it too. Since the 1960s some thorny conflicts between Africans and Europeans have simmered, but a substratum of suspicions and envy remain. History can be accommodated for mutual progress, but it cannot be forgotten. The western man has his own story recorded in his own books, but the world is much more literate today than ever before. There are now highly educated Africans who have been intimately familiar with western culture and have seen that it no longer is the bogeyman that frightened a multitude of Africans by firing its pistol in the air to cow thousands of Africans into submission. His mighty guns are nowhere now as potent as they used to be; his insistence on his superiority is no longer as daunting as it used to be; his institutions are no longer sacrosanct! His scientific method to arrive at or approximate the truth is now an open book that the Japanese, Koreans and others have used very well. All the 'hidden' intentions behind colonialism, the White man's Burden, the British Commonwealth, the French Community, etc. have all been brought into the open and are now subject to numerous interpretations to the limits of one's interest, outlook and talent.

Therefore, the western man of today is not the European of yesterday. He too has learnt from his errors, failures and successes. He graves, however, to continue to maintain his civilization, direct it, and make the world into his image under his control; but these efforts and desires are no longer left to him alone to decide upon. The Japanese, Indians, Latin Americans, and Africans have already challenged western hegemony in the political and technical domains, and there is hardly any reason to suggest that that process will be reversed. Of all the non-European peoples so far, the Japanese have been the most able to challenge the European on his own grounds. "As Emperor Meiji put it in a poem that became a motto for the" ... renascent Japan, the Japanese were going to modernize willfully:

> May our country,
> Taking what is good,
> And rejecting what is bad,
> Be not inferior
> To any other. (Taylor, 1984:772)

Africans, too, can do the same; they can eclectically organize and develop their own societies in their own way with particular understanding of their place in the modern global village. But what is this Africa? Have Africans not always been members of the global village? If so, what have they already contributed to this modern global village? It is these questions that chapter two attempts to address.

**References: Chapter I**

Appiah, Kwame Anthony. 1992. *In My Father's House: Africa in the Philosophy of Culture.* New York: Oxford University Press.

Ben-Jochannan, Josef A.A. 1971. *Africa: Mother of Western Civilization.* Baltimore, Maryland: Black Classics Press.

Cose, Ellis. 1993. *The Rage of a Privileged Class.* New York: Harper and Collins Publishers.

Davidson, Basil. 1974. *How Can Africa Survive: Arguments Against Growth Without Development.* Little, Brown and Co.

Douglass, Frederick. 1968. *Narrative of the Life of Frederick Douglass.* New York: New American Library.

Ellul, Jacques. 1978. *The Betrayal of the West.* New York: The Seabury Press.

Emecheta, Buchi. 1974. *Second Class Citizen.* New York: Braziller.

Fredrickson, George M. 1982. *White Supremacy: A Comparative Study in American and South African History.* Oxford University Press.

Gregg, N. Taylor. 1984. "Hagi: Where Japan's Revolution Began." *National Geographic.* 16516:751-772.

Huntington, Samuel P. 1993. "The Clash of Civilizations." *Foreign Affairs.* Summer, Vol. 72, No. 3 (Summer), pp. 22-49.

James, George G.M. 1976. *Stolen Legacy.* San Francisco, California: Julian Richardson Associates, Publishers.

Kaplan, Robert D. 1994. "The Coming Anarchy." *The Atlantic Monthly.* Vol. 273, No. 2 (Feb.) pp. 44-46, 48-49, 52, 54, 58-60, 62-63, 66, 68-70, 72-76.

Klitgaard, Robert. 1990. *Tropical Gangsters: One Man's Experience with Development and Decadence in Deepest Africa.* Glenview, IL: Basic Books.

Lapidus. 1993 "A Review of Islam and the West." *New York Times Book Review*: May 30:8.

Lewis, Bernard. 1971. *Race and Color in Islam.* New York. Harper and Row Publishers.

______. 1993. *Islam and the West.* Oxford University Press.

M'bow, Amadou-Mahtar. 1984. *Where the Future Begins.* UNESCO.

Nkrumah, Kwame. 1963. *Africa Must Unite.* New York: International Publishers.

______. 1968. *Dark Days in Ghana.* New York: International Publishers.

Postman, Neil. 1993. *Technopoly: The Surrender of Culture to Technology.* New York: Alfred A. Knopf.

Rooney, David. 1988. *Kwame Nkrumah: Political Kingdom in the Third World.* New York: St. Martin's Press.

Sandbrook, Richard. 1985. *The Politics of Africa's Economic Decline.* Cambridge University Press.

Van Sertima, Ivan. 1976. *They Came Before Columbus.* New York: Random House.

Whitaker, Jennifer Seymour. 1988. *How Can Africa Survive*? New York: Council of Foreign Relations Press.

Wiseman, John A. 1990. *Democracy in Black Africa: Survival and Revival.* New York: Paragon House Publishers.

The World Bank. 1997. Global economic Prospects and the Developing Countries. Washington, D.C. The International Bank for Reconstruction and Development.

# Chapter II:

## Ancient and Modern Africa

To study Africa and African peoples is a complex phenomenon. We are at first confronted with 'What is Africa?' Secondly, we are dealing with a continent and a people who have been, until perhaps most recently, one of the most abused, misrepresented, misjudged, mistreated and subjected to countless other negativities. Furthermore, Africa and African peoples have been called several things: they were the Ethiopians, the Dravidians, the Cushites, Egyptians, the Moors and, again, countless other names that give different pictures other than perhaps the contemporary African. One historian (Brunt, 1974: 36) states that "The large population of Rome and later Constantinople was fed with grain imported from overseas, especially from Africa and Egypt." We must also state that African people have been globally dispersed and have shared similar, mostly negative experiences, under different regimes, cultures and various nationalities.

In addition, in comparison to other world regions and people, Africa and Africans have been Romanized, Arabized, Anglicized, Americanized, etc. religiously, culturally and educationally, in language, political ideology and the market economy, while Africa's contributions to these global variables have not been termed as, say, the Africanized Roman, or Greek, except of course the Afrikaners who, despite their Africanized name, oppressed the native Africans for more than two hundred years. The presence of Europeans, Arabs, Indians and other peoples in Africa makes it singularly difficult to operationally define the African. Are the Moors, the Dravidians of ancient India, the Aborigines of Australia, and the North African Africans? Are white South Africans Africans? Is Africa an extension of Europe, or Saudi Arabia an extension of Africa? If Saudi Arabia is not an extension of Africa, why should Madagascar, which is much farther away from the African continent, be considered

African? Ali Mazrui (1967: 42-58) attempted to grapple with the concept of 'we are all Africans!' There are those who are in Africa, (have been in Africa for hundreds of years) who do not have an emotional attachment to Africa, or think of themselves as Africans. An Afrikaner in the West could be most readily accepted as a European over the native African of the same class, education and economic status.

> Contemporary Europeans named Africa and associated South of the Sahara with Blacks. The new West European racial thinking implied that the 'real Africa' is south of the Sahara, that Africans are Black, that Africa is a race, that the northern boundary of Africa is the Sahara. On the other hand, European geographical thinking came to assume that Africa is not a race but a continent, that the northern boundary is not the Sahara but the Mediterranean, thereby including in Africa the Berber and Arab lands north of the desert. (Mazrui, 1986:25)

These racial and geographical African definitions, however, must include the historical Africa. Who were the North Africans before these contemporary North Africans? What do we know of the historical Africans to substantiate that, despite the historical events that Romanized and Arabized North Africa, Africa was originally a Black African land, that these Black Africans contributed, in no small measure, to the now fundamental globalized institutions of science, education, religion, literature and philosophy?

This chapter also examines some of the major forces that contributed to the demise of African civilizations, leading to the contemporary unenviable African zeitgeist in the global context. Cognizant of the paradigm that macro-studies are often too sweeping, we submit that looking at the big picture often enlightens us about our own peculiarities, or provincialisms. Furthermore, if Europeans are 'ecstatic' about the origins of <u>their</u> own civilizations, Africans, the victims and recipients of western civilizations, must too continuously attempt to ascertain where they fit into this historical drama of the rise and fall of human civilizations. For African people, too much can not be made about their unabating interest in world civilizations that, until the early 1900s, nearly wiped them off the slate of human institutional developments, and even relegated them to a different human species. African people's interests in their histories then are attempts to know who they are in this cosmic drama of science, politics, economics, and the development of human communities and identities.

## What is Civilization?

From the evolutionary point of view, civilization is a more recent phenomena, and has been achieved only by man, not an ape, despite, perhaps, our common ancestry with that animal. Civilization is supposed to be on the higher scale of human development from his gathering and hunting days when he maintained no permanent settlements, but roamed in small groups in search of food, shelter and safety. He didn't believe in any higher supreme power and, compared to our current living standards, lived a short and brutal life. Gradually, he came to believe that he must have a soul; he began to have high regards for his ancestors, several gods, and magic before he finally embraced monotheism. Generally, man has passed through the ages of magic and religion and is today fully in the scientific-post-industrial age. He is done with worshipping the solar systems, heroes, vegetation gods and the seasons; he has formed communities, made laws, built educational institutions, research facilities and communication systems to transmit ideas, goods and services to millions of people within a short period of time (Wright, 1990:83-94).

Clearly then, for a people to be considered civilized, they would first of all have to live as a community with laws and regulations about land and human behavior. Agriculturally, they would have to grow enough food to feed a large population (at least 5000), maintain a differentiated population to carry out the different functions of the community. These different functions would include persons as tillers, harvesters, tax collectors, administrators of justice, and scholars to do research and keep records; the whole community does not have to be literate, but there has to be scholars, scientists, teachers and educational institutions to experiment, keep records and transmit the cultural values of the community. One of the most significant cultural values of a community is a belief system, a religion that attempts to conciliate superior powers believed to direct and control nature and human existence.

A civilized community is not a static community; its scientists are engaged in research on vital issues of health, politics, and the economics of the community so that the group can continue to progress; its scholars teach and keep records; its workers produce adequate food supply, use 'iron' to construct buildings, roads and make tools; its leaders, religious or political, see to it that the community is smoothly run, including the keeping of armies, guards or other means of control or restraint. Like organisms, civilizations are 'born, grow and die.'

Taking into account our basic definition of a civilized community, it can not still be entertained that Africans have not had any civilizations of their own except those which were inspired by the Romans, Greeks,

Arabs, the British, or the French. And yet Lyon, Rowen and Hamerow (1970:6) state that "All that can be said about the inhabitants of Egypt is that they were part of the Mediterranean group of the Caucasoid (white) race." These western writers go on to credit the Hyksos for conquering Egypt and bringing light to a darkness (7). Lady Lugard (1965: 14-15) states that "speaking in roughly general terms, the Berbers are a white people. One among many stories (is that) of their original introduction from Arabia Felix by a certain leader Ifrikiah, or Afrikiah, who gave his name to the continent; and that from these are descended no less than six hundred clans of Berbers." Lady Lugard goes on to insist that "Equatorial Africa...represented... only barbarism and obscenity" (16). In her paradigm, even the Hausas and the Fulanis are of the white race, "absolutely distinct from the pure Negro type" (22). The pure Negro type represents "...the inferior races in the southern portions of the fertile belt" (22). Discounting the Moors as Africans, Lady Lugard goes on to credit white Arabs for transmitting eastern science and medicine to medieval Europe at a time when even "Charlemagne, the greatest monarch of the west, couldn't write" (47). Mrs. Lugard does not seem able to make up her mind about differentiating between a Moor and an African, an Arab-African and a Negro, but seems confident that the pure Negro is of "...wholly a different race" (69). Lady Lugard is not alone in attributing much of the west African empires of Ghana, Mali and Songhai to alien-inspired civilizations; but even Mrs. Lugard could not be oblivious to the historical fact that "the ancient civilization of Egypt spread, as we know, from south to north" (219), that is, from the current day Uganda, Ethiopia, and Sudan, the sources of the famous Nile River, that empties itself into the Mediterranean Sea through Egypt; therefore, there was an Ethiopia before Egypt.

## There was Ethiopia Before Egypt

Scholars from the Gloriana School of Africana Studies (Mazrui, 1986), or the African vindicationist school (Drake, 1986 and Bernal, 1987) have pointed out African people's contributions to western civilizations in religion, science, philosophy, math, law and other fields of endeavor contemporarily 'accepted' as western derived. The efforts of these scholars, European and African alike, have often been termed polemic and particularistic. Rather than dismiss the efforts of the African vindicationists as particularistic, one must note that had western scholars been inclusive, the Gloriana School of African Studies would not have had much to restate or reinterpret. For a people whose history, education, psychology and peoplehood have been defamed in the global arena, one should expect no less than those people's attempts to view themselves from their own particularistic point of view.

Luckily for African people, their historical counter-factuals are being uncovered everyday by all sorts of scholars and researchers, including paleontologists, historians, linguists and even geneticists. Though there seems to no longer be much debate about African people's peoplehood and humanity, there is still much more to be derived from studies progressively confirming African contributions to this nowaday global village.

Some historians have traversed ancient African monuments and documents to reveal that Africa (Alkebu-Lan) had had well established civilizations thousands of years before Europeans emerged, as it were, from darkness (Ben-Jochannan, 1988). Hansberry and Johnson (1964:32) state that according to the Kushites, Egypt had been buried beneath the sea before it finally emerged into land in the mid continent by the river Nile from its varied sources of the present day Sudan, Ethiopia and Central-East Africa where human civilizations originated. It was the Kushites who then brought civilization into Egypt and taught the natives "the fundamental elements of civilized life." It was from the Kushite colonialists that the primitive Egyptians learned how to make statues, practice writing, to give their dead proper burial, to deify their kings as gods and many other working practices which were established in their land. The Kushite prince Osiris and his princess Isis, including their son, Horus, were instrumental in civilizing the Egyptians, and are now part of Egyptian mythology. Many other writers have designated tropical Africa as the birth place of mankind and that Blacks have greatly contributed to world civilizations through Egypt, before Europeans designated that portion of Africa as the Middle East. These African vindicationist writers go beyond claiming Egypt to assert that the original color of man was black and that the human family was derived from the Black ancestral parent stock through physical modifications induced by responses to different types of cultural and environmental influences (Hansberry and Johnson, 1964:32, 34). Paleontologists, linguists and even geneticists (Allman, 1989:52-59; Allman, 1990:60-70; Wilson and Cann, 1992:68-73) have all joined the debate with respect to the origins of human civilizations. John G. Jackson (1970:93), a radical African-American historian, has too observed that Egyptian civilization had a Black African origin from the south of the present day Egypt, at the dismay of the traditionalists' belief that Egypt was it and nothing more or less.

Even Lady Lugard (1965:218-219), perhaps notorious for making Berbers and Fulanis Caucasians, could state that "The ancient civilization of Egypt spread, as we know, from the south to the north...there is seemingly no doubt that the earliest seat of civilization in Africa was the country watered by the Upper Nile, which was known by the name of Ethiopia to the Ancients....The principal state of this Ethiopian country bore the well-known name of Meroë." In the city of

Meroë the ancient Africans began to worship Ammon and the building of temples and pyramids that were later 'perfected' in lower Egypt. Thus, before Egyptian civilizations, Meroë triumphed in the arts and sciences. "The worship of Ammon and his attendant gods would seem to have spread to Egypt, and through the Oasis of Siwah to Carthage and the Mediterranean coast" (220). Hansberry (1960:365) also tells us that

> When Diodorus Siculus was traveling in Egypt in the first century before the Christian era, he was informed by 'envoys from Ethiopia' that it was in their country and among their remote ancestors that mankind first learned to practice the arts, to create laws, and to render worship to the gods. It was also from their country, the envoys contended, that ancient Egypt's oldest cultures' earliest civilized peoples, and most ancient kings were derived. ...It is true that long after the 'glory that was Greece' and the 'grandeur that was Rome' were no more, it was still widely believed in learned circles that it was the Ethiopians of remote antiquity who laid the foundations upon which all subsequent civilizations were built. ...'Ethiopia was the earliest established country on earth and the Ethiopians were the first to introduce the worship of the gods and to establish laws.'

Wilson and Cann (1992:70) assert that Mitochondrial DNA studies can reveal an individual's maternal ancestry and they seem to be convinced "that Africa was the ultimate human homeland before people began to move to other world regions, such as Asia, New Guinea, Australia, and Western Europe, perhaps 200,000 years ago. Multiregional evolutionary theorists challenge this mono-regional evolutionary position, but there seem to be not much evidence to nullify that Africa is the original home of mankind." Furthermore, "...The light skin color of many whites is probably a late development that occurred in Europe after that continent was colonized by Africans" (71). Linguist Allman (1990: 60-70) seem to support the geneticists that "...the human family based on genetic evidence closely mirrored the language groupings laid out independently by historical linguists. The oldest split occurred between Africans and other world populations, reflecting the migration of homo sapiens out of Africa" (69). As Africans followed the Nile 'down' into Egypt, they left monuments along that river and brought into the Mediterranean coast cultural institutions that had developed thousands of years. As linguists and geneticists would argue, from Egypt, Africans migrated and colonized other would regions; these other world regions gained from Africa as Rome was to gain from Greece; other European countries from Rome; Holland, Germany, France, etc. from the British industrial revolution;

America from Britain, Germany and the then U.S.S.R.; and more recently, Japan from the United States and France and Korea, from Japan, China, and the United States. Africa, the victim of contemporary western civilizations, will too gain modern technology and other institutions within the global village, from the other world regions.

## Some Egyptian Contributions to the Global Village

If western civilizations cannot be dislodged from their Greek and Roman 'foundations' (Lefkowski, 1995), so also cannot Egyptian civilizations be from black African civilizations. When Pericles, the Athenian, boasted in 430 BC. that the Athenian "...system of government does not copy the institutions of our neighbors" (Wiesner, Ruff and Wheeler, 1989:25), he probably was being hyperbolic; about 1400 years later, Britain also boasted concerning the 'limitlessness' of her possessions; is it not about time that Africa, too, acknowledges its own contributions to this historical patriotism?

From the numerous contributions of African people to the global village, it is of interest to note that Akhnaton (Aton Devotee), a black man, was the father of monotheism. "A thousand years before Moses wrote the Second Commandment banishing graven images of God Akhnaton did so" (Rogers, 1972:59). Wallbank and Taylor (1942:43) write that "The most beautiful surviving piece of Egyptian literature is Ikhnaton's 'Hymn to the Sun'. A few lines will suffice to give some idea of its poetic beauty and its conception of one all–powerful and beneficent Creator and Heavenly Father":

> Thy dawning is beautiful in the horizon
> of the sky,
> O Living Aton, beginning of Life!
> When thou risest in the Eastern horizon,
> Thou fillest every land with thy beauty.
> Thou art beautiful, great, glittering, high
> above every land,
> Thy rays, they encompass the Lands, even all
> that thou hast made.
> How manifold are thy works!
> They are hidden from before us.
> O sole God, whose powers no other possesseth.
> Thou didst create the earth according to
> thy heart
> While thou wast alone.

In his, and even in contemporary times, Akhenaton was a man among men; he remained monogamous and insisted on respect for women. "As for his mother, the great Queen Tiyi, a coal-black woman, his affection for her stands out as one of the great examples of filial love" (Roger, 1972:60). Not surprisingly, Akhenaton "...was to learn, like others who try to create perfection, that mankind was not ready for it" (61). Like most rare men, Akhenaton remained steadfast in his monogamy to his sister, monotheism and 'respect for women,' ...till his death at the age of thirty-one" (61).

Jackson (1970:111) tells us that "although the monotheistic Aton cult was crushed in Egypt, it did not perish altogether for there was a young Egyptian priest named Moshe (Moses), who had received his theological education at Heliopolis, and who became a disciple of Ikhnaton." After Moses' graduation from the Temples of Egypt, where he had learned all that he could, he came out opposing the worship of various gods. It was this Moshe who led a group of people out of Egypt into Palestine when Atonism was viewed as a mystery religion.

The path to knowledge in the Egyptian mysteries, we are told, was a difficult one. The temples were monopolized by a few who had the courage, ability, stamina and will to go through the various stringent stages to acquire knowledge at extreme cost. Students were accepted from various countries, and the first symbol or lesson to master concerned the genesis of the world and the sole creator of the universe. The student then progresses, after passing various rites, into priesthood and prophethood. The initiates into the Egyptian mystery system were introduced to the concept of purgatory and of heaven, including the trinity of Osiris, Isis and Horus, the concept of virgin birth and, at certain levels in their education, they may experience a glowing light, such as that which Moses saw on the mountain and fell to his knees. '"He had seen the sun of Osiris"' (Weiser, 1988:134). In the Egyptian mystery system (challenged by Lefkowitz, 1996),

> ... initiation into the Highest Knowledge was not open to just anyone (much like the Ph.D. of today), not even to any Egyptian priest. Before they were ready for the Highest Initiation, priests had to fulfill a number of tasks and pass a number of tests to be allowed to go through to the next level. ...Those who did not pass the test with flying colors the first time were denied once and for all the chance to try to fulfill the entrance requirements for higher levels.
>
> If the candidate was a stranger to the mysteries, an extremely strict inquiry would first be made into the candidate's ancestry, and...the college of magicians would convene...to determine admission or rejection.
>
> The Greek philosophers–Thales, Pythagoras, Plato and Eudoxus–were the best-known foreign scholars to successfully pass the various tests. Pythergoras was assigned the prophet Sonchis as his mentor. ...Plato was trained for fourteen years....the brilliant teachings of Plato, who had an enormous influence on the

> development of Christian philosophy, originated in the sacred places of Memphis, the city of Menes, and in Heliopolis, the city of the Sun. (Weiser, 1988: XXI, XXII)

As Nkrumah and other African students went to the United States in the 1930s to study so also did these Greek students studied in Africa, took their educations to their respective nations and improved on what they had gained elsewhere. By the twenty-second symbol in the Egyptian mystery system, we are told that the young student should have by then "...received an answer to the question: where do we come form, where are we going, what do we live for?" (151). To be aware of where one came from, where one was going and what one lived for formed the fundamental basis of the Egyptian mystery system.

The ancient Africans in Egypt believed that death was not the end of life. *The Book of the Dead* (Budge, 1923:CCXI), "was intended to teach immortality. ...The fundamentals of the Egyptian religion were":

> I. Belief in the immortality of the soul, and the recognition of relatives and friends after death.
> II. Belief in the resurrection of a spiritual body, in which the soul lived after death.
> III. Belief in the continued existence of the heart-soul, the Ka (the double), and the shadow.
> IV. Belief in the transmutation of offerings, and the efficacy of funerary sacrifices and gifts.
> V. Belief in the efficacy of words of power, including names, magical and religious etc.
> VI. Belief in the Judgement, the good being rewarded with everlasting life and happiness, and the wicked with annihilation. (CCXI)

When the individual died, he faced the Judgement day on which he confessed his actions in life; he accounted, in the negative confessions, that he had "not committed theft; slain man or woman; acted deceitfully; uttered falsehood; uttered evil words; set (his) month in motion (against any man); defiled the wife of a man; committed sin against purity; made (himself) deaf to the words of right and truth; committed acts of impurity, neither have (he) lain with men; increased (his) wealth, except with such things as (justify) (his) own possessions", etc. (367-371). Thus, in *The Book of the Dead*, we have the genesis of Moses' Ten Commandments; the negative confessions also make plain the Egyptian stance against homosexualism, exploitation of man by man, and the bearing of false witness against one's neighbor. For the deceased to enter the kingdom of everlasting life and happiness, his accounts of his actions in life are weighted against a feather to assure his purity and admissibility. Budge (CCXI) reminds us that

> *The Book of the Dead* contains beliefs of all periods gathered together from every part of Egypt and the Sudan, and its gods, though perhaps under different names, were well known throughout the country. The forms of the beliefs and the attributes of the gods changed from time to time, but the principal doctrine which *The Book of the Dead,* as a whole, was intended to teach, i.e., the belief in immortality, never changed.

It could be clearly deduced from *The Book of the Dead* that Africans were Christians before Christ, or in the words of John G. Jackson, Africans practiced *Christianity Before Christ* (Jackson, 1985).

In the above mentioned book, Jackson sees a lot of similarities between the Egyptian Horus and Jesus Christ: They were both conceived by virgins; both were brought up as one of five children, stayed with their mothers for twelve years before venturing out, the accounts of their lives between ages twelve and thirty remain obscure; Horus and Jesus were baptized by Anup and John the Baptist respectively at age thirty; the holy spirits of Horus and Jesus are represented by a bird and a dove respectively, including the perennial pair of the Black Madonna (Isis and Horus), and Mary and Jesus Christ. Importantly, what happened to both Horus and Jesus Christ between the ages twelve and thirty? "The Egyptian influence on Orthodox Christianity is far more profound than most people realize. The whole Christian bible was derived from the sacred books of Egypt, such as: *The Book of the Dead*, The Pyramid texts, and The books of Thoth" (Jackson, 1985:115-116). To the Egyptians, the world of the hereafter was a place of plenty, where the deceased had to cross a river to reach that place of plenty in terms of food, blessings, and a delivery of gifts for the dead person's Ka, his dynamic force, or personality. "...We are told that the food and drink placed in the tombs were not meant for the body of the dead person, but for his **Ka**, his dynamic force, his personality. The **Ka** lived in one tomb" (Manniche, 1987:6).

In addition to Bal of Babylonia, Prometheus of Greece, Mithra of Persia, and Krishna of India, Osiris of Egypt was an ancient savior-god that greatly influenced 'western' Christianity (Jackson, 1985:41). To ignore Africans' contributions in the development of western Christianity is to ignore African history, to ignore one of the contributions of Africans to one of the fundamental institutions in this global village.

After the Romans, Africans were the second people to accept the new, westernized Christianity as a state religion and provided popes and bishops who helped propagate the 'New' Christianity to lands within and without Africa. Scobie (1982:85-95) discusses three African popes who helped institutionalize western Christianity. Pope Victor I, AD. 189-199, was the fourteenth pope after Saint Peter. This African pope insisted that Latin be institutionalized as "the liturgical language of the Roman Catholic Church" and "that Easter Day (be) always celebrated on a Sunday" (85). Pope Victor is reported to have convened the earliest Roman Synod on record and the first to celebrate the holy mysteries in Latin. This Romanized African 'globalized' the celebration of Easter on Sunday. In insisting that the language of the Catholic church be Latin, he helped propagate Latin culture and civilization. Like Akhenaton before him, his insistence on the celebration of Easter on Sunday brought him into conflict with other Roman constituencies. Nonetheless, "Victor I was an energetic and zealous pontiff who served the Church of Rome with unswerving faith, even though his firmness in certain issues...made him somewhat unpopular with certain bishops; he died in 199 AD. and was buried in the Vatican near St. Peter's" (88); fourteen hundred years later, his people would be bought and sold by European Christians and non-Christians alike.

The second African pope, Miltiades (88-92), also contributed in firmly institutionalizing western Christianity. Becoming pope in AD. 311, he is said to have worked tirelessly in defending Christians with respect to their freedom to practice their religion without fear of persecution. "...They could come out of the catacombs where they used to live" (89). Miltiades also helped mitigate the problems "of the Donatists schism in Africa" and "although (he) ruled the church for only three years his pontificate witnessed one of history's turning points–the coming of Constantine and the end of the era of persecution" (89, 90). Miltiades is described as "an excellent pontiff, a true son of peace and father of Christians" (92).

The forty-ninth pope after Saint Peter, Gelasius, was also an African "born in Rome of African parents" (92). Gelasius, whose people were to be later termed paganistic, bitterly opposed and denounced Roman pagans who desired to continue their paganistic, ritualistic, practices of the Lupercalia, believed to bring good luck. "Gelasius forbade all Catholics from having anything to do with the affair, and this pagan rite soon ended. He replaced the Lupercalia by the feast of the purification" (95).

From the Temples of Egypt, Akhenaton, *The Book of the Dead,* African popes and their contributions to western Christianity, must be added other African "gifts" to the contemporary global village, the following: embalming; circumcision; stress on life after death, and "solar calendar of 365 days; pen; ink; surveying and irrigation" (Belasco, Reilly, and Bump, 1967:13). Other contemporary African 'gifts' to the west include the following to Britain, France and Germany in 1957 (Nkrumah, 1965:2):

| | |
|---|---|
| tin ore and concentrates | 19% |
| iron ore | 29% |
| Manganese | 80% |
| copper | 46% |
| bauxite | 47% |
| chrome ore | 50% |
| asbestos | 66% |
| cobalt | 82% |
| antimony | 91% |

French imports from Africa included:

| | |
|---|---|
| cotton | 32% |
| iron ore | 36% |
| zinc ore | 51% |
| lead | 85% |
| phosphates | 100% |

To Germany, Africa provided:

| | |
|---|---|
| copper imports | 8% |
| iron ore | 10% |
| lead ore | 12% |
| manganese ore | 20% |
| chrome ore | 22% |
| phosphorites | 71% |

Nkrumah (2) goes on to assert that "if Africa's multiple resources were used in her development, they could place her among the modernized continents of the world. But her resources have been, and still are being used for the greater development of overseas interests."

To take the area of religion alone, African contributions to one of the major religions in the global village cannot be underestimated, and will never be obliterated. Ironically, however, by the 1600s AD. Africans were being labeled primitive and fit to be slaves on the plantations of South and North America, the Caribbean Islands and elsewhere.

In the other fields of endeavor such as science, architecture, mathematics, government and military science, Africans have not been without their own contributions. Wallbank and Taylor (1952:44) tell us that "...the Egyptians were the first people to develop real science of mathematics. Precise measurements were needed to build the pyramids, and the constant obliteration of field boundaries by the inundations of the Nile necessitated frequent land measurement." In medicine, the "Egyptian physicians...were alone among the nations of antiquity in the development of specialty medicine. In the old kingdom, the diseases of each organ were under the care of a specialist" (Finch, 1982:9). Finch goes on to elaborate that

> A study of ancient Egyptian diagnostic methods reads disconcertingly like a modern textbook on physical diagnosis. A physician summoned to examine a patient would begin with a careful appraisal of the patient's general appearance. This would be followed by a series of questions to elicit a description of the complaint. The color of the face and eyes, the quality of nasal secretions, the presence of perspiration, the stiffness of the limbs and abdomen, and the condition of the skin were all carefully noted. The physician was also at pains to take cognizance of the smell of the body, sweat, breath, and wounds. The urine and feces were inspected, the pulse palpated and measured, and the abdomen, swellings, and wounds probed and palpated. The pulse taking is worth noting because it indicates that the Egyptians knew of its circulatory and hemodynamic significance. (9)

The Egyptians also dissected, bandaged wounds and broken bones, used animals, plants, and mineral products to treat various types of illnesses (14). "The Egyptians were...quite knowledgeable in handling obstetric and gynecological problems. ...They even had an effective pregnancy test" (15). Later on, Africans (Moors) were to transmit 'eastern' science and medical knowledge to Western Europe through Spain; the dark continent's gift to Western Europe also include scholars, warriors and emperors. deGraft-Johnson, (1986:32) tells us that "the Emperor Septimus Severus was an African, and the Emperor Caracalla was half African and half Syrian." Born in Tripolitania in AD. 146, Septimus Severus was a well educated Romanized African, who became emperor of the Roman Empire in AD. 193. Despite being a Romanized African, Septimus Severus is said to have retained some of his African idiosyncrasies:

> All historians are agreed that the Emperor Severus retained the imprint of this African birth and education all his life. He was bilingual, and so were all his compatriots. When Severus was Emperor, his sister came to see him in Rome. He quickly packed her off home again because she made herself ridiculous at court by her absolute ignorance of the Latin language. Septimus Severus himself, though he grew to like Latin literature...retained all the habits acquired in his youth, and it is recorded that throughout his life he never lost his taste for African cooking, and that special foodstuffs, including fruits and vegetables, had to be brought from Africa to Europe to supply his table. (34)

Again, about 1400 years later Emperor Severus' people would be termed tribalistic and said to be living in stateless societies by West Europeans, especially the British, whom he had defended against Scottish tribes. "Three years of active campaigning by an African unaccustomed to the climate of Britain was too much for his health and the Emperor Septimus Severus died in York on a cold day in February AD. 211" (35). It seems ironic that this African died defending a Britain that was to later colonize much of Africa and call its inhabitants primitive and fit to be enslaved.

The great African warrior Hannibal "...defeated the Romans in battle after battle...was appointed dictator or sole ruler of Carthage" even when he had been at last defeated (21). Furthermore, the Moors of North Africa who dominated Southern Spain for close to eight-hundred years were Arabized Africans. Even though they were eventually driven out of their last stronghold in Granada in the 1400s, their impact on Western Europe as scholars, medical doctors, chemists, educators and transmitters of Eastern science and culture to Western Europe can not be underestimated; they made

> ...Cordova...the intellectual center of the western world. Scholars from Christian Europe came to Muslim Spain to study, and through them much of learning of the Arabs eventually passed to France and Italy. Cordova had the first paper factory in the west for bookmaking, and chemistry, pharmacy, and mathematics made notable advances. (Wallbank and Taylor, 1942:419)

Like Christianity, Islam, the 'newest' global faith, claims monotheism as the central tenet and posit that "every good Muslim adheres implicitly..." to the following:

1) Belief in one God, Allah
2) Belief in Angels who intercede for men
3) Belief in the Koran.
4) Belief in the prophets of Allah.
5) Belief in judgement, paradise and hell.
6) Belief in the Divine decrees. (237)

Muslims are also expected to fast, give to the poor, turn to Mecca in prayer and if possible, pilgrimage to pay homage to "...a wonderful black stone (El Ka' aba)–the remains of an immense meteorite. Side by side with the worship of this stone was the worship of the goddess named Allat" (deGraft-Johnson, 1986:61-62). deGraft-Johnson goes on to tell us that 'Allat' came to be 'Allah,' the masculine form of the goddess 'Allat', who had attracted worshippers to the El Ka' Aba. But Mohammed, like Akhenaton before him, insisted on his monotheism, claiming to be the last of the prophets. Of interest to us here is that

> Hadzrat Bilal Iba Ratlab, a tall, gaunt, bushy-haired Black Ethiopian slave, was the first high priest and treasurer of the Mohammedan empire. After Mohammed himself, that great religion which today numbers upwards of 300,000,000 souls (most of whom are in Africa) may be said to have begun with Bilal. He was said to be the prophet's first convert. (Rogers, 1972:143)

Bilal continued to be a faithful Muslim and lived for a hundred years propagating the Islamic faith beyond Mecca. Thus, the Islamized Moors of North Africa, it could be said, joined the great legacy of Bilal in the propagation of Islam to West Europeans. Between 762-1100 the Moslems in Spain translated Greek and Indian texts on medicine, physics and chemistry, astronomy and mathematics and made these available to European scholars.

> Learned Jews translated Arabic treaties on Greek and Moslem science into Latin. Beginning about the eleventh century and continuing for the next 150 years, scholars gathered at Narbonne, Marseilles, and Toledo for the all-important task of translation. During these years they made available to Europe the scholarship and the scientific writings of the Moslems. Aristotle was introduced to Europe in Latin through Spain. The great diffusion of Greek and Arabic knowledge, more or less completed by 1300, was a tremendous factor in the revival of classical learning and the coming of the Renaissance. (Wallbank and Taylor, 1942:251)

Thus, through Spain, eastern science was transmitted to Western Europe. It is of import to note that Greek students and "philosophers Thales, Pythagoras, Plato and Eudoxus" had all attended "the sacred places of Memphis, the city of Menes, and in Heliopolis, the city of the sun" (Weiser, 1981: XXII) in Egypt, taking their educations with them to their homelands, and by the 10th century AD., Arab scholars were transmitting Greek knowledge to Western Europe via Spain, which had originally come through continental African educational institutions in the name of Temples, or sacred places in Memphis and Heliopolis. Africa and Africans have not been without their own contributions to science, papermaking, architecture, medicine, the alphabet, religion, documentation, the calendar, philosophy of life and death, ethics and law. Perhaps the global village still needs to take full heed to the negative confessions in the Egyptian *Book of the Dead* that so eloquently addresses some of the modern day problems even though written thousands of years ago by Africans in Africa, denouncing homosexualism and the exploitation of man by man, now depicted in the religion of Jesus Christ.

## From Dust to Dust

Recent scholars, both European and African, have described significant African civilizations in West, South and Central Africa (deGraft-Johnson, 1986; Jackson, 1970; Williams, 1974; Davidson, 1967; Webster and Boahen, 1970). At the outset, it is important to note that Africans, like others, have been interested in learning, trading, borrowing, and synthesizing that which they have borrowed to fit their own climate and temper. Furthermore, they have resisted domination and fought back as best they could to keep at bay usurpers. As it would be shown, however, Africans have not been saliently successful in defending themselves against invaders and usurpers, Arabs and Europeans. Nonetheless, African civilizations did not end in Europe and north Africa; in western Africa, African descents can claim that their ancestors had had empires and rulers of international fame, respectability and repute.

Africans in the Western Sudan were able to establish expansive kingdoms and empires before the Europeans penetrated West Africa through the coastal plains. deGraft-Johnson (1986:109), has organized the following West African empires and their most salient rulers:

**WEST AFRICAN EMPIRES**
The Ghana Kingdom and the Ghana Empire AD. 300-1076
The Mali Empire 1238-1488
The Songhai Empire 1488-1591

**IMPORTANT RULERS OF THE MALI EMPIRE**
Sundiata, Mari Jata (who was ruler of the Mali Kingdom in 1230 and in1238 became the founder of the Mali Empire 1238-1255
Sakura 1285-1300
Mansa Musa 1307-1332
Maghan and Sulayman 1332-1359
Mari Jata II 1359-1374
Musa II 1374-1390

**IMPORTANT RULERS OF THE SONGHAI EMPIRE**
Sonni Ali (who mounted the throne of the Songhai Kingdom in 1464 and in 1488 became the founder of the Songhai Empire)1488-1492
Bakari Da'a 1492-1493
Askia Mohammed I, Askia the Great 1493-1528
Musa 1528-1531
Askia Ismail and Askia Ishak I1531-1549
Askia Daud 1549-1582

> Askia Ishak II (during the latter part of whose reign Moroccan forces invaded the Songhai Empire)1582-1591

According to Lady Lugard (1965:21), the Ghana empire was foreign inspired. In her view, whites dominated the Ghana empire and the finer black races ruled the Negroid type of blacks and pushed the latter further and further into the tropical belt. Thus, even in the Ghana empire, for an instance, "...twenty-two white kings...reigned...before the year of the Hegira" in AD. 632. She categorizes the Fulanis as partly a white race, distinct from the typical West African Negro, who is, in contrast to the Fulani, an inferior type of black. In Lady Lugard's paradigm, "The Hausa and the Songhey are other races which, though black, are absolutely distinct from the pure Negro type" (22).

Despite Lady Lugard's scheme of splitting up Africans into superior/inferior races, which her husband practiced so effectively in British Africa in the name of divide and rule, she still acknowledges that "when the Arabs first visited Negroland by the western route in the eighth and ninth centuries of our era, they found the black kings in the height of their prosperity" (82). She goes on to relate that "...the black women of one of the kingdoms of the Sudan, ...too proud to allow themselves to fall into the hands of white men, preferred to commit suicide" (87). Additionally, she describes

> The King of Ghana as 'one of the most just of men', whose custom it was to ride once daily into the poorest and most wretched part of the city, and there to disperse justice to all who had ground for complaint. On all other occasions he rode with great pomp, magnificently dressed in silk and jewels, surrounded by guards preceded by elephants, giraffes, and other wild animals of Sudan, and no one dared to approach him. (111)

As the Ghana Empire declined, as all organisms and civilizations do, the Mali Empire rose up to take Ghana's place. The Story of Mansa Kanka Musa has been told by almost all historians dealing with West African civilizations. In addition to Mansa Musa's famous pilgrimage to Mecca, after which he returned with Muslim scholars and architects, Lady Lugard tells a sobering incident about a white judge in Mansa Musa's employ; on Mansa Musa's pilgrimage to Mecca,

> a characteristic little incident occurred. There was in the Sultan's train a white judge to whom he had given four thousand ducats that had been stolen. Mansa Musa sent for the governor of the town, and ordered him, on pain of death, to produce the robber. The governor caused the town to be vigorously searched, but he found no robber, 'because in that town there were none.' He went to the

> house occupied by the judge and cross-examined the servants. A slave of the judge then confessed: 'My master has lost nothing; but he himself hid the money in this place.' He showed the place to the governor, who took the ducats, and reported the circumstances to the Sultan. Mansa Musa sent for the judge, and, after trial, banished him to the country of the pagans 'who eat men.' He remained there, the historian states, for four years, at the end of which time the Sultan allowed him to return, not to Melle, but to his own native country. 'The reason,' it is added, 'why the cannibals did not eat him is that he was white. They say that the flesh of white men is unwholesome because it is unripe. Black flesh alone, in their opinion, is ripe.' (Lugard, 1965:123-124)

Mansa Musa, the Alhaji, brought back scholars and the University of Sankore boasted of African scholars in law and Islamic religious studies. Based on the 1300s, Mausa Musa must have been a leader of foresight in his emphasis on scholarship, university education and peaceful relations with other rulers. He embraced Islam and gave scholars a peaceful environment in which to work; he saw what was beneficial in Islam and borrowed and synthesized from other cultural contributions to improve his own people and society. deGraft-Johnson (1986:98), further writes that

> Mansa Musa developed Timbuktu as a commercial city having caravan connections with Egypt, Angila, Ghadamer, Fez, Sus, Sijiilmasa, Tuat, Dra'a and Fezzan. Side by side with trade and commerce came the encouragement of culture and learning. The scholars were mainly learned theologians well versed in Koranic theology and law, who made the mosque of Sankore in Timbuktu their center of instruction and also laid the foundations of the University of Sankore. The university was to bring learning not only to Africa but also to the whole of the Middle East.

While Mansa Musa prided himself on pilgrimaging to Mecca, his brother, Abu Bakari recruited shipbuilders from afar to prepare for his sojourn beyond the Atlantic Ocean; his dream was not to replicate that of Mansa Musa's impressive journey to Mecca. He had more 'fantastic' ideas of his own; "the most ambitious of all campaigns" (Van Sertima, 1976:45) was to see what laid beyond the Atlantic; even though Abu Bakari and his fleet never returned to Mali, Mansa Musa's brother cannot be said to have been a man without imagination or courage. Abu Bakari

> specified that each boat built for the ocean voyages should be accompanied by or attached to a supply boat, which stored gold and other items of trade, along with dried meat and grain and preserved fruit in huge ceramic jars to last its company in the master boat for at least two years, four times as long as the stocks of the trans-Saharan caravans from Cairo to the Sudan. Two hundred master boats were built, and two hundred supply boats. As the task neared completion Abu Bakari left his palace at Niani and encamped on the seacoast to watch the final stages of the operation. ...He called the captains of the boats together and issued this order: 'Do not return until you have reached the end of the ocean, or when you have exhausted your food and water.' (45)

Abu Bakari's imagination and desire to see beyond the Atlantic Ocean had been encouraged by competition with his brother Mansa Musa, Malian scholars' knowledge about the shape of the globe, navigation and wind currents, and by Malian resources, which were diverse and centralized enough so as to be directed to accomplish the feat entertained by the Malian leaders in the early 1300s. "Like the Meccan pilgrimage, Abu Bakari's expedition was done in a grand style, involving perhaps as many vessels as the caravans of Kankan Musa thirteen years later, but leaving only ripples on a very far shore, an enigmatic chain of artifacts and influences, which, like the resuscitated mummies, are beginning at last to haunt us with questions" (67). As a characteristic of a civilized nation, state or empire, Abu Bakari and his brother Mansa Musa were able to use their nation's resources to explore, discover and establish relationships with peoples and cultures beyond their own boundaries. Thus, the presence of Africans in Honduras, Costa Rica, Columbia, the Dravidians in India, the Aborigines in Australia, and New Guinea, and elsewhere no longer astonishes.

The West African empires and kingdoms of Songhai, Kanem-Borno and others before the advent of West Europeans, to enslave and colonize Africa, also produced daring leaders, governments, institutions and artistry that denote a civilized people improving their economic and political conditions in their own geo-political confines. Solanke (1982:20) tells us that

> Like Ghana, Mali and Songhai, Kanem enjoyed the economic benefits of her situation at a crossroads of the Saharan trade. The people of Kanem had also mastered the techniques of iron smelting. Under the dynasty of Kanem....a feudal form of rule was established, reinforced by military conquest and held together by skillful administrative overlordship. Islam...introduced in the

> eleventh century, was another unifying factor in Kanem. From its emergence around the ninth century until its decline in the eighteenth...Kanem and its succession Kingdom of Borno...remained an important power, achieving greater sophistication of government and a higher degree of stability than had been evident in West Africa up to this time.

African civilizations in Ethiopia, Egypt, Mali, Ghana, Songhai, Kanem-Bornu, Zimbabwe, and others faced in the 1400s a number of destablizing forces with the advent of Europeans around the West and the other African Coasts. The golden ages of West Africa were to face and be afflicted by mightier powers they could not keep at bay, much less defeat. The destruction of African civilizations began with the advent of the Persians in 525 BC.; this was followed by the Hyksos in 1800 BC. Though the Hyksos were expelled from Egypt in 1580 BC., there were to come the Assyrians, the Greeks, the Romans, the Arabs and the English who, one after the other, defeated and Romanized, Arabized and Anglicized Egypt.

While West Africa looked toward Egypt through the trans-Saharan route, the Portuguese were making 'trading' connections with the coastal areas. At about the same period, the Moors of Spain were expelled; these were to later attack Songhai to inflict destruction on one of the major remaining West African empires. "...Songhai was invaded by a Moorish army led by Judas Pasha, a Spaniard, captured by the Moors in infancy, and reared in the precincts of the Royal Palace. This army numbered only five thousand men, but about half were armed with firearms imported from England" (Jackson, 1970:218). Timbuktu was destroyed and African scholars at the University of Sankore and their books were taken to Morocco, which "...poured men and war materials into West Africa, and squeezed out every particle of gold she could lay hands on" (deGraft-Johnson, 1986:118). The aftermath of the Moroccan invasion included chaos for an Africa that was already engulfed by an 'irreversible' decline. Africans, defeated in Egypt, Carthage, Ghana, Mali and Songhai by 'outlandish' men from Persia, Turkey, Rome, Arabia, etc. could then be subjected to unparalleled hardships, including slavery and colonization. deGraft-Johnson (118), tells us that

> There was chaos where once there had been order. States broke up. There were intrigues everywhere; treachery and corruption became the order of the day. Ordered society gradually crumpled.

People began to feel no qualms about selling each other enmasse. "The sack of Timbuktu was the signal for letting loose of all the evils of lawless tyranny upon the country. From this time (the 1590s), the history of the Sudan becomes a mere record of riot, robbery and decadence" (Lady Lugard, 1965:310). African peasants became victims of creed and the exploitative zeitgeist unleased from Asia and Europe. Thus, while the Moors from Spain and Morocco captured the inland areas of West Africa, the Portuguese and other European powers made headway into the coastal areas; Arabic slave trade was replaced by West European slave trade, for which Black African peasants were the chosen ones, taking them into Brazil, the West Indies and North America. "The Atlantic Ocean became a highway of the world..." (Lugard, 335), taking the place of the trans-Saharan slave trade between Africa south of the Sahara and Iran, Iraq, Egypt and Saudi Arabia.

Before the West African slave trade (Harris, 1971:5), "the principal slave dealers were the Arabs, the Omani Arabs in particular....The Arabs called the Northern Somali Coast RAS ASSIR (the cape of slaves)". In Eastern Africa, Arabs had their Swahili agents to aid them in their raids or purchase of African slaves. Some Africans sold their own children in exchange for food, while others gave themselves up rather than die, say, of starvation. "Another means of acquiring slaves," writes Joseph Harris (13), "was to spread food on the ground and catch hungry children who attempted to eat it." In addition "...pilgrims frequently purchased one or two domestic slaves to take back with them" (30) to Kuwait, Baghdad, Basra, Turkey, Tripoli or Alexandria. Up to the 1800s, and even much later, African slaves were bought and sold "...in the bazaars of Mecca and other Arabian cities" (38). African female slaves were used as domestic servants and "the greatest demand by affluent Arabs was for concubines..." (40). Bernard Lewis (1971:66-67) states that Arab Muslims obtained slaves from Eastern Africa and took them into Iraq and Basra where they numbered up to

> ...Some tens of thousands...lived and worked in conditions of extreme misery. They rose in several successive rebellions, the most important of which lasted fifteen years, from 868 to 883 AD., and for a while offered a serious threat to the Baghdad caliphate. The leader of these black rebels was a white man. Even religious groups with...radical and progressive ideals seem to have accepted the slavery of the black man as natural.
>
> A common explanation of this status, among Muslim authors is that the ancestor of the dark-skinned peoples was Ham, the son of Noah (according to Muslim legend) who was damned black for his sin. The curse of blackness, and with it that of slavery passed to all black peoples who are his descendants.

When Blacks and Asians are mixed, the off-springs, being of lighter-skin color, are often preferred over the 'typical' Negro. Thus in North

Africa, as elsewhere in the world, darker skinned Africans are comparatively disadvantaged, despite the Islamic doctrine of the brotherhood of Muslims. Even in Ancient Egypt, Williams (1974:75) tells us that "...Afro-Asian offsprings were given preferential treatment, positions of authority, wealth according to the status of their patriarchal family, and an education that could draw on Asian culture as well as the highly advanced African civilization in upper Egypt and Southwards to the 'Land of the Gods'."

As slavery was not condemned by Islam so also was it not by Christianity. The Portuguese, and later other West Europeans, came to Western Africa with a mixture of motives; they wanted to trade with Africans; to search for the legendary Prester John; to Christianize pagans, and to counteract the Islamic influence of the Moors from whom the Portuguese had gained much knowledge about the African continent. Furthermore, writes Peter Forbath (1977:17),

> The Niger...was a river of abiding fascination. Although no European actually laid eyes on it until the early nineteenth century, it was part of Europe's mythology from earliest middle ages. For the Niger was the river of Timbuktu, the fable golden city from whence the Saharan Caravans brought the precious merchandise of Bilad al-Sudan, the land of the blacks, to the Barbary shore and the courts of the European kings. And for this, if for nothing else, it was a river to be sought, a lure compelling enough to have tempted adventurers on daring voyages of discovery for hundreds of years.

Thus the European 'adventurers' around Africa in the early 1400s had many reasons to leave their native lands: The development of scientific instruments to sail long distances; curiosity about foreign lands; the religious zeal to convert pagans and economic interests all combined in varying degrees to 'compel' Europeans out of their national confines. The 'discovery' of America by Christopher Columbus brought into existence the last signal for the devastation of Africa, which became the victim as a labor supplier to Brazil, the Caribbean Islands and North America. The condition of African-Americans in the United States has been documented, and there does not seem to be much need to deal with that here. It might only suffice to state that the mass enslavement of African people in the West represents the epitome of the exploitation of man by man.

With the abolition of slavery by Britain in 1808, expeditions into the West African interior was vehemently begun by missionaries, adventurers and merchants; new items of trade and for exploitation other than human beings came into vogue. British and American Christians, notably the Quakers, began to practice the religious dictum that all men were created equal in the eyes of God. Furthermore, the slogans of the French Revolution of 1789, the Haitian ascendancy in 1804, voices of vehement philanthropists, and the political competition between the U.S. and Great Britain after 1776, all contributed to the zeitgeist of human liberation. But while Haiti, the U.S.A. and the French masses were liberating themselves, a new form of domination in the name of colonialism was entrenching itself in Africa. As a liberated nation, the United States joined other western powers to colonize non-Europeans directly and indirectly, in the cases of the Philippines and Liberia respectfully. In the United States, Africans are still a captive people for whom there is no major power or institution to defend them beyond the integration process machine in which they remain unmeltable.

Europeans who once favored slavery and went to lengths to capture their human cargo, came to 'despise' the trade in favor of more 'humane' economic exploitation of Africans and the other non-European people. Slave catching and raiding were no longer as profitable as the exploitation of Africa's raw materials. With the promises and confidence of the industrial revolution and the efficiency of the factory system, goods could be rapidly produced, railroads laid from the coasts to the interior and African products could be shipped to Liverpool for processing for the global distribution of manufactured goods. Kup (1975:161) observes that

> Adam Smith's *The Wealth of Nations* attacked slavery...not on humanitarian grounds, but because it denied the sacred principles of a free labor market. His book came out when the American Revolutionary War was driving the first nail into the coffin of protectionist mercantilism. Thus, some have seen abolition as the logical outcome of economic development.

In the scramble for Western economic expansion and development, Africa became the victim for cheap labor and raw materials. Benjamin Disraeli, Cecil Rhodes and Joseph Chamberlain, as spokespersons for colonial expansion, urged for the acquisition of more lands to provide employment for Europeans and markets for British goods. Furthermore, enlightened Britain assigned itself the 'sacred' duty to civilize the backward races of Asia and Africa. Perhaps more importantly,

> The area of the United Kingdom was only 120,000 square miles; the area of the British Empire was over 9,000,000 square miles, of which nearly 500,000 were to be found in the portion of Africa. ... If tomorrow it were possible, as some people apparently desire, to reduce by a stroke of a pen the British Empire to the dimension of the

> United Kingdom, half at least of our population would be starved.... (McKay, Hill and Buckler, 1991:180)

In the western psychic, social Darwinism was also in vogue, which strongly held that the stronger and the more superior had the manifest destiny to civilize and develop the so-called weaker races by force. "You cannot have omelets without breaking eggs; you cannot destroy the practice of barbarism, of slavery, of superstition, which for centuries have desolated the interior of Africa, without the use of force..." (181). In addition to force, Christian missionaries could also carry out the task of perpetuating western religion and values to the African natives. Thus,

> By 1855...much of the interior of West Africa was known to Europe. Directly or indirectly the discoveries of the explorers were to lead to an increase in missionary activities; active trading contacts between Europeans and peoples in the interior; and European imperial expansion and colonization. ...The most heavily Christianized area was the freed slave colony of Sierra Leone around the port of Freetown....The Christianized Creoles of Sierra Leone played the major role in spreading the gospel to Southern Ghana, Yorubaland and the Lower Niger. (Kwamena-Poh, 1982:34)

The 'Freetown' of Eastern Africa was Freretown where freed slaves from Bombay, India, had been settled and used to perpetuate Christianity to the natives of the interior of Kenya, Uganda and Tanzania. By 1884-85, Africa's fate was in the hands of Europeans who parceled Africa out to themselves without even consulting the Africans. By the early 1900s West, East, South and Central Africa were completely dominated by several European powers. Africans became British, French, German, Spanish or Portuguese Africans (it now seems that Africans are most unlikely to rid themselves of the impacts of western colonialism and imperialism). In South Africa, where the Zulus and others had been defeated, "The first diamonds in the Kimberley area were discovered in 1867, and the gold of the Witwatersraand was revealed in 1886. As a result, competition between British and Boers became intense, while the whites in general were placed at an overwhelming advantage in relation to the Africans" (44).

In relation to the African the European obtained the best lands in Southern, Eastern, Central and Western Africa; he came; he conquered, and he exploited African labor, mineral resources, practiced unequal economic, political, social, psychological relationships with the natives and declared that the African was his junior brother who needed him, the bigger brother, to guide the African through the proper rites of passage to full manhood, equality, economic, political and technical developments. Since the domination of Egypt by non-Africans to the collapse of the African empires in East, West and Central Africa, Arabs and Europeans have been religiously, politically, and economically prominent in Africa. Their destruction of African civilizations culminated into slavery, colonization, neo-colonization and the prominence of international monetary organizations dictating to African governments to accept the new world order headed by Europeans and other machine exporting countries. Cities and governments that African people had developed were raised to the ground by aliens: Arabs, Hyksos, Romans, the Portuguese, the British, the French and others. With the defeat and domination of African people came their dispersal into Latin America, the Caribbean Islands, North America and other western countries. As a dispersed people, "disunity and mutual suspicion (became) an African way of life" (Williams, 1974:48). French Africans, British Africans, and African-Americans are educated to be strangers to one another; they are all Africans, but some have become lighter in color, Islamized, or Christianized. Lighter skinned Africans in Egypt and Haiti began to think of themselves superior to their darker brothers and sisters (53, 78); James (1963:37-38). With the conversion of Africans to Islam and Christianity, Africans became non-Africans; those who remained traditionalists are labeled pagans and backward, and savage-like. The 'anointed' Africans were required to change their names, and "...if their black Emils, Johns, Muhammads, Samuels, and Abdullahs happened to achieve greatness in some field, the assumption would be that it was Caucasian achievement, unless a special effort was made to identify the race of the persons in question" (Williams, 1974:59). For instance, how many would readily accept that Septimus Severus (deGraft-Johnson, 1986:38), Victor I, St. Miltiades and Gelasius I (Scobie, 1982:84-95) were Romanized Africans?

Educated mostly in the western paradigm Africans have been 'schooled' to be suspicious of their ancestors, who are said to have invented nothing, not even an alphabet or anything of value to add to the contemporary global village. Contrary to that Euro-centric bias, Williams (1974:136) tells us that Africans did have their own alphabet that consisted of 4 vowel signs, 17 consonants and 2 signs of syllable "which were mastered by only the view" and that "the religious belief in sacrifice for the remission of sins was an African belief and practice for at least 2000 years before Abraham." Van Loon (1972:17) states that the earliest ancestors of Europeans

> Who lived in the great European wilderness were rapidly learning many new things. It is safe to say that in due course of time they would have given up the ways of savages and would have developed a civilization of their

> own. But suddenly there came an end to their isolation. They were discovered.
>
> A traveler from an unknown southland who had dared to cross the sea and the high mountain passes had found his way to the wild people of the European continent. He came from Africa. His home was Egypt.
>
> The valley of the Nile had developed a high civilization thousands of years before the people of the west had dreamed of the possibilities of a fork or a wheel or a house.

There is already enough on record to claim that the original inhabitants of Egypt were Black. In fact, "according to Homer and Herodotus, the inhabitants of the following territories were Ethiopians: 1) Sudan; 2) Egypt; 3) Arabia; 4) Palestine; 5) Western Asia; and 6) India" (Jackson, 1970:75). Jackson goes on to state that

> Men of almost every shade of color can be found in modern India; but the early inhabitants of India were black. Their descendants survive in Central India today. They have Negroid features, dark skin, and woolly hair. The ancient Indians are described by professor Lynn Thorndike as 'short, black men with almost Negro noses.'

Despite African contributions to western and Asian civilizations, Africans are today the wretched of the global village, and are asked to be grateful to the Arabs and Europeans for bringing them monotheism, a monotheism first advocated by Akhenaton. But we shall not belabor the point that contrary to what most Africans, Europeans and Arabs have been taught, African people did not sit idly awaiting the Europeans' religion, science, education and forms of government. Archaeologists, linguists and geneticists have now refutably illustrated African people's humanity and primariness in world history and development. To a large measure then, African people should claim their rightful place in this global village in which they must ascend above hewers of wood and drawers of water, or the dumping ground for 'cheap' consumer goods and western industrial wastes.

On the other hand, however, Africans should not blindly call for 'drumbeats' to celebrate their golden past, which was followed by disintegration and defeats by Arabs and Europeans who had superior military weapons, a better military organization and a uniform world outlook with regards to other peoples unlike themselves. Though Africans could be said to have smelted iron, they maintained no vast armies to deter the onslaught by the Arabs and Europeans who proved themselves to be far more/better organized, aggressive, and determined to subdue Africans. Though Africans knew their terrain, they were unable to repel their invaders on their own African territories. The invaders used technology, Christianity, Islam and science to defeat Africans not only in Africa but also in Iran, Iraq, Latin America, India, Australia, the United States and in Western Europe. Africans were so disorganized that they could even be used against one another and be recruited to fight for the Arabs and Europeans in outlandish wars and countries and even in Africa.

The Atlantic slave trade was officially declared open on "August 8, 1441" when some Africans were captured by the Portuguese and shipped to Europe to labor like animals (Forbath, 1977:50). The story of western slavery is fairly well-known, including the most wretched treatment of blacks, that was even more vicious than the mass elimination of African slaves in Iraq (Lewis, 1971:66). With respect to western slavery, the ordeal of the 'peculiar institution' started during the capture of Africans and continued through the match to the waiting ships, across the Atlantic, onto the plantations and beyond; the ugly scars of African enslavement have not been obliterated and might not be. Indeed, the Atlantic slave trade epitomized the destruction of African empires and carried away the most productive segment of the African population; the healthiest, the strongest and the most fit of the Africans were shipped away to labor on the West Indian Islands and the Americas. There, they were subjected to some of the most vicious forms of brainwashing and cultural destruction. They were taught that they had been uncivilized in Africa and needed Christianity and European tutelage. Phillis Wheatley (1971:34), in one of her most famous poems, celebrated, albeit subversively, her being brought from Africa to America. African-Americans were miseducated not to have been educated that their ancestors had contributed to the very western Christianity that was used to justify their enslavement; they were miseducated not to have been taught that the so-called western science and religion had some of their beginnings in Africa and spread to Greece, Rome and the rest of Europe during the Moorish domination of Spain, where African scientists, in the Moorish city of Cordova, showed that the world was spherical, long before Magellan did so in 1519.

Under slavery, African-Americans were indoctrinated that Christ was a white man and that Ham, instead of his son Canaan, had been cursed and damned black for a father's nakedness in his drunkardness; that Blacks, being descendants of Ham were, by divine providence, to be slaves forever. The historical claim that Christ and the Virgin Mary were black (Jackson, 1985:151-152), that monotheism had its recorded beginnings in Africa, and that Africans were in the west before Columbus (Van Sertima, 1971), that Africa had had its golden past (Hansberry and Johnson, 1964-65), all seemed inconsequential to the Europeans who were, by the 1700s, practically intoxicated with their own feelings of superiority. "The idea that Africans were in the new world (more than) three thousand years ago is hard for many people to believe, even among the educated classes, for old stereotypes die hard" (Jackson, 1970:254).

As if to add insult to injury, barely twenty years after slavery was abolished in the United States in 1865 than western countries took it upon themselves to divide Africa up as though it were a cake in 1884-1885. By 1918, Africans were being recruited to fight in outlandish lands; this was repeated in the 1940s; African-Americans and colonized Africans were to fight for their alien fatherland's wars of independence and imperialism. With the demand for independence by some Asian countries in the latter part of the 1940s, African countries too began to demand independence. By the end of the 1960s most African countries were politically free from their ex-colonial masters. As though to materialize that African people should perennially remain hewers of wood and drawers of water for the western man, neo-colonialism, or the economic domination of Africa's resources, was put in place by multinational corporations interlocking themselves over Africa's raw materials (Nkrumah, 1965). In the United States, outspoken African-Americans against American imperialism were assassinated, branded subversive, or publicly discredited. As we enter the 21st century, the IMF, derisively called the International Ministry of Finance (Ngugi, 1986:2), we see the prominence of that monetary organization in the affairs of African governments; with the 'death' of Russian Marxism, western multiparty political systems and capitalism are upheld for African countries to adopt. Of all the above means by which African people have been made the wretched of the earth (Fannon, 1968), "The excesses of the slave trade must never be forgotten, for in them lie much of the horrors of the African continent" (deGraft-Johnson, 1986:153).

As all organisms must be 'born', grow and 'die', so also do civilizations; ancient African civilizations, the empires of Ghana, Mali, Songhai and others began to 'die' with the advent, first, of the Hyksos, then the Persians, Greeks, Romans, Arabs, the British and the French and other West Europeans. From dust to dust then did African civilizations crumple under the weight of mightier powers and civilizations. In all these, however, a thorny question seems to emerge: Why could Africans be enslaved and colonized enmasse, and for more than four-hundred years? It is this question then that the next chapter attempts to examine.

## References: Chapter II

Allman, William F. 1989. "The First Humans: Scientific Detective Work Yields a Radically New View of Early Man." *U.S. News and World Report.*. February 27:52-59.

______. 1990. "The Mother Tongue." *U.S. News and World Report.* November 5:60-70.

Belasco, Milton J. et. al. 1967. *Basic Review of World History.* N.Y. Bronxville: Cambridge Book Company, Inc.

Bernal, Martin. 1987. *Black Athena: The Afroasiatic Roots of Classical Civilization.* Vol. I. New Brunswick, N.J.: Rutgers University Press.

Ben-Jochannan, Josef A.A. 1971. *Africa: Mother of Western Civilization.* Baltimore, MD. Black Classic Press.

Brunt, Peter A. 1974. "Work and Slavery," pp. 36-46, in Allan Mitchell and Istvan Deak (eds.) *Every Man in Europe: Essays in Social History; The Preindustrial Millennia Vol. I.* Englewood Cliffs, N.J.: Prentice-Hall, Inc.

Budge, E.A. Wallis. 1923. *The Book of the Dead.* New York: Viking Penguin Inc.

de-Graft Johnson, J.C. 1986. *African Glory: The Story of Vanished Negro Civilizations.* Baltimore, MD. Black Classic Press.

Davidson, Basil. 1969. "Africans Before Columbus?" *West Africa.* June 7:641.

Drake, St. Clair. 1987. *Black Folks Here and There, Vol. I.* Los Angeles, California: Center for Afro-American Studies.

Fanon, Franz. 1968. *The Wretched of the Earth.* New York: Grove Press, Inc.

Finch, Charles S. 1982. "The African Background of Medical Science," pp. 8-24 in Ivan van Sertima (ed.), *African and African-American Science and Invention.* New Brunswick, N.J. Rutgers University Press.

Forbath, Peter. 1977. *The River Congo: The Discovery, Exploration and Exploitation of the World's Most Dramatic River.* Boston, Mass: Houghton Mifflin Company.

Hansberry, William Leo and E. Harper Johnson. 1964. "Africa's Golden Past: Part I." *Ebony,* Vol. XX, No. 1, Nov., pp. 30-32, 34, 36, 38-39.

Hansberry, William Leo. 1960. "Ancient Kush, Old Aethiopia, and the Balad Es Sudan." *Journal of Human Relations.* Vol. 8, No. 3 and 4 (Spring and Summer), pp. 357-387.

Harris, Joseph. 1971. *The African Presence in Asia: Consequences of the East African Slave Trade.* Evanston, Illinois: Northwestern University Press.

Jackson, John G. 1970. *Introduction to African Civilizations.* Secaucus, New Jersey: The Citadel Press.

______. 1985. *Christianity Before Christ.* Austin, Texas: American Atheist Press.

James, C.L.R. 1963. *The Black Jacobins.* New York: Vintage Books.

Kup, Alexander Peter. 1975. *Sierra Leone: A Concise History.* New York: St. Martins Press.

Kwamena-Poh, et. al. 1982. *African History in Maps.* Longman Educational Books.

Lefkowitz, Mary. 1996. *Not Out of Africa: How Afrocentrism Became an Excuse to Teach Myth as History.* Basic Books.

Lewis, Bernard. 1971. *Race and Color in Islam.* New York: Harper and Row Publishers.

Lugard, Lady. 1965. *A Tropical Dependency.* New York: Barnes and Nobles, Inc.

Lyon, Bryce, Herbert H. Rowen, and Theodore S. Hamerow. 1970. *A History of the Western World, Vol. 1: Prehistory to 1715.* Chicago, Illinois: Rand McNally and Company.

Manniche, Lise. 1987. *City of the Dead: Thebes in Egypt.* Chicago, Illinois: The University of Chicago Press.

McKay, John P, Bennett D. Hill, and John Buckler. 1991. *A History of Western Society, Vol. I.* Houghton Mifflin Company.

Mazrui, Ali. 1967. *Towards a Pax-Africana: A Study of Ideology and Ambition.* Chicago, Illinois: The University of Chicago press, pp. 42-58.

______. 1986. *The Africans: A Triple Heritage.* Little, Brown and Company.

Ngugi, James. 1986. *Decolonizing the Mind: The Politics of Language in African Literature.* Heineman Educational Books.

Nkrumah, Kwame. 1965. *Neo-Colonialism: The Last Stage of Imperialism.* New York: International Publishers.

Rogers, J.A. 1972. *World's Great Men of Color, Vol. I.* New York, New York: Collier Books.

Scobie, Edward. 1982. "The African Popes," pp. 84-95, in Ivan van Sertima (ed.) *African and African American in Science and Invention.* New Brunswick, New Jersey: Rutgers University Press, 1982.

Solanke, Julayemi. 1982. "Internal African Migrations and the Growth of Cultures." pp. 13-37, in Richard Oloniyan (ed.) *African History and Culture.* Lagos, Nigeria: Longman Nigeria Limited.

Van Loon, Hendrik. 1972. *The Story of Mankind.* New York: Garden City Publishing Company, Inc.

Van Sertima, Ivan. 1976. *They Came Before Columbus.* New York, New York: Random House.

Wallbank, Walter T. and Alastair M. Taylor. 1942. *Civilization: Past and Present, Vol. I.* Scott, Foresman and Company.

Webster, J.B. and Boahen, A.A. 1970. *A History of West Africa: The Revolutionary Years - 1815 to Independence.* New York: Praeger Publishers.

Wiesner, Merry E., et. al. 1989. *Discovering the Western Past: A Look at the Evidence, Vol. I to 1715.* Boston, Mass: Houghton Mifflin Company.

Wiesner, Samuel (Translator). 1988. *Egyptian Mysteries.* York Beach, Maine: Samuel Weiser, Inc.

Wheatley, Phillis. 1971. "On Being Brought from Africa to America," p. 34, in Ruth Miller (ed.), *Black American Literature 1760 - Present.* New York: McMillan Publishing Co., Inc.

Williams, Chancellor. 1974. *The Destruction of Black Civilization: Great Issues of a Race From 4500 B.C. to 2000 A.D.* Chicago, Illinois: Third World Press.

Wilson, Allan C. and Rebecca L. Cann. 1992. "The Recent African Genesis of Humans: Genetic Studies Reveal that an African Woman of

200,000 Years Ago Was Our Common Ancestor." *Scientific American.* 3:68-73.

Wright, Karen. 1990. "The Road to the Global Village." *Scientific American.* 3:83-94.

# Chapter III:

## Why Africans Could be Enslaved and Colonized

> I am the Lord, your God, which brought you forth out of the land of Egypt to give you the land of Canaan, and to be your god.
>
> Both they bondmen, and thy bondmaids, which thou shall have, shall be of the heathen (pagan nations) that are around about you; of them shall ye buy bondmen and bondmaids.
>
> And ye shall take them as an inheritance for your children after you, to inherit them for a possession; you can use them as permanent slaves.
>
> (Leviticus 25:38; 44, 46)

Throughout history, man has wronged another man for many reasons; people have been 'enslaved' because of their age, color, sex, nationality, weaknesses or religious beliefs. Throughout history, people have made slaves of their own people, of others, or both at the same time as well as at different times. In Athens, persons became slaves for failure to pay their debts. Greek culture condoned slavery for "The Greeks as a people disclaimed to soil their hands in manual labor. Slavery was tolerated in all the city-states, and it proved a costly handicap to a well-balanced and contented society" (Wallbank and Taylor, 1942:144). In ancient India "The menial tasks were performed by slaves-captives, debtors, and members of the Dravidian group" (74). The Romans, Persians, Russians, Arabs, and Africans have all practiced slavery at one time or the other in their historical developments. At its heights and splendor in the Seventh and Eighth Centuries, Baghdad boasted of "...white slaves from Scandinavia and Russia... and black slaves from Africa"(243). In medieval Japan, there were two types of slaves: the public and private. "The public slaves worked on the land, from which they received a food ration, or were engaged in such menial tasks as scavenging and grave-digging. The private slaves belonged to the households of wealthy nobles and could be sold or given away" (297).

Much of these localized slavery could also be termed 'domestic' in the sense that the people being enslaved were not radically different from their enslavers, except in class, social standing and other 'inherited' syndromes of disadvantage. External slavery also existed as the case of whites in Baghdad, Koreans in Japan and Africans in Rome, Baghdad or Saudi Arabia. In Egypt, Iran, Iraq and elsewhere African people were enslaved enmass, abused and misused, Romanized, Arabized and de-Africanized to a large extent. In the popular mind, however, slavery seems to be synonymous with Africans; literal translators of the Bible also associate blacks with slavery. Some African people have, too, been convinced that slavery is synonymous with blackness.

It is certain that Africans practiced both domestic and trans-Saharan slave trade before West Europeans arrived on the west coast of Africa in the 1400s. The Arabs had been trading with Africans in slaves hundreds of years before west Europeans arrived in eastern Africa. As in other world regions, African domestic slaves consisted of prisoners of war, captives, those born into slavery, imported from other tribes or clans, or those captured to work on state-owned farms. The liabilities to domestic slaves were many; they could be sold or be sacrificed to the gods, but they also 'enjoyed' many rights in terms of their freedoms to marry, own property, inherit their master's property, etc. As 'domestic' slaves, they knew the terrain and could therefore runaway into a 'warm' climate where their physical wants were few as compared to the western world. All things being equal, the African slaves in Africa "... at least knew they would live among people like themselves, in a country like their own, and would do work such as they were accustomed to" (Lisitzkey, 1947:116). Forbath (1977:109), tells us that

> The African's slave was of course not a free man and his status certainly was inferior to that of a free man. But he was not a chattel slave as that term came to be understood in the subsequent centuries; he was not stripped of his property or human dignity or all his rights. He was rather what might more appropriately be called a serf or vassal or perhaps an indentured servant, a condition common enough to Christians during the Middle Ages. And it was a status to which he fell in much the same way Christians did in feudal Europe: in punishment for a crime–thieves, murderers, and adulterers were usually enslaved–by being taken prisoner in a war, or by being

offered as tribute from a subjugated tribe to a dominant one.

Outside Africa, however, African slaves were subjected to numerous inhumane treatments. They could be eliminated en masse as in Iraq (Lewis, 1971:70); they could be separated from their offsprings without qualms about the sanctity of familihood; the men could be castrated and the women could be made into bedwenches; all of these and more could be done to African people partly because they were and remain too different in terms of their epidermis, culture, language, religion, stage of technical, political and economic development, lacked and still lack a powerful nation or leader to talk or pose a threat on their behalf. In addition to these are of course the European's own explanations as to why he could so unabashedly enslave millions of blacks who had caused him no harm, except resist their enslavement. As David Walker remarked in 1829 (Aptheker, 1965:76), what have black people done to Europeans that they should treat blacks so awfully?

## Color and Cultural Differences

It might seem tolerable to the soul to oppress, discriminate against and even enslave some one who does not look or behave like oneself. The enslaved are always someone else in terms of class, color, age, sex, nationality or ability. The enslavers are always better off in terms of wealth, power, technology, lifestyle, life chances, and belief system. With respect to Arabs and Europeans, African people's dark complexion differentiated them greatly from the other humans, making them so vastly different that they were to be enslaved with sumptuous explanations and rationalizations, using the 'Koran' and the 'Bible' to justify the extreme exploitation of black people. To the European and the Arab, the African was a brother, but a junior brother who had been marked by the great one to be enslaved. It was not only the African's color, but his cultural attainments which also showed that he could be made into a beast of burden, a chattel, a human slave. After all, black Africa had been militarily defeated by the Arabs in North Africa in the seventh century; the Islamized Moors destroyed the remaining black empires in the western Sudan, so that by the fourteen-hundreds, when the Europeans arrived on the west coast of Africa, African civilizations were already 'dust to dust.' As a 'disorganized' people, African communities were classified as stateless, tribal kingdoms, clans or extended families. These types of social or cultural organizations did not pose a threat to the Arabs and Europeans, whose Caliphates or kings and queens directed them thousands of miles away from their metropols to explore, conquer and civilize those who looked and worshipped differently. In the European as well as in the Arabic mind, and up to this day at that, the African is the junior, inferior brother, the black sheep of the family, so to speak. And the "inferior races of a different faith did not count in the ranks of free human beings. They were little better than cattle, and as such might be hunted and taken without any denigration from the laws of humanity" (Lugard, 1965:409). To be of a different color, faith, culture and be at a lower stage of technical development all at the same time seemed to be the needed ingredients for a whole group of African people to be subjected to slavery; Africans were generally perceived by non-African peoples as "... a people at a low order of humanity" (333). Thus, the French, the Danes, Dutch, Portuguese, etc. used Africans and the African continent as they saw fit without any feelings of quilt or remorse for, after all, Africans are too far removed from the Europeans themselves, in all things that mattered to them. Soon, the Europeans were competing amongst each other in terms of which European nation should Lord it over which African people. Europeans, "intending on making quick profits" (324), rushed into the African scene with all manner of rapacity. "The Portuguese government... used the west (African) coast from a very early period as a place of deportation for convicts" (324). Members of the European ruling classes were convinced that 'fortunes' could be made in the buying and selling of Africans. The English Queen, Elizabeth, and others saw that Africans were good commercial items; the Christian god condoned the buying and selling, especially of Africans who did not look like them, or think, behave and pray like them. Furthermore, after Britain's Industrial Revolution, the English man began to think of himself as the incarnation of perfection; next to him, African peoples and their culture represented depravity.

> ... in Brazil, the Caribbean, and the Southern American colonies, Africans were known only as slaves. In these societies, and ultimately in Europe as well, Negro skin color, hair texture, and facial features were associated with the status of slavery. Prejudice based on culture and that based on social rank were blended together and expressed as a 'Racial Prejudice'. (Bohannan and Curtin, 1988:51)

Despite Snowden's (1983) position that the ancients were not racists, there is a stronger stance that the ancients were nonetheless not color-blind (Lewis, 1971; Be'teille, 1968); by the 1800s Europeans and Americans were already convinced of their own racial/biological superiority over the Africans. "In the period following the American Civil War the wretched position of the American Negro and the triumph of colonialism in Asia and Africa pushed the question of equality between Europeans and non-Europeans so far from the realities of politics that it was not a very lively topic of discussion in the west" (King, 1971:121-122). European and American scholars and other men of ideas advanced the doctrine of social Darwinism that saw non-Western persons as fit for 'Europeanization' and exploitation. Thus, the Filipinos and other Asians and Africans were fit material for colonization and outright exploitation and enslavement. The Australian aborigines provided another example of how the superior white man dealt with the inferior, non-white races; colonies had to be obtained and there was no condemning the aggressors who had been endowed by the great one to Lord it over the weaker races of mankind. In short, by the late 1800s Africans were at the mercy of the Europeans in both Africa and abroad. Some Europeans opposed colonization, as some had slavery, but the material, political and psychological benefits of the domination of the non-White Africans were too much to be laid aside as yet. "Other cultural qualities" of the African, writes Winthrop Jordan (1974:53)–"the strangeness of (the African's) language, gestures, eating habits, and so on–certainly must have contributed to the English colonists' sense that (the African) was very different, perhaps disturbingly so." If the African was so culturally different, he could indeed be enslaved by whites without much compunction; after all, he was a strange African. As Wright (1996:76) has observed, "...humans don't naturally deploy (their) 'moral' impulses diffusely - showering love and compassion on any needy homosapiens in the vicinity. (Humans) tend to reserve major doses of kindness either for close kin ... or for non-kin who show signs of someday returning the favor."

## Technical and Military Strength

In addition to African peoples epidermic and cultural differences contributing to the 'ease of conscience' with which they were enslaved, for they were simply too different from their Arab enslavers in the seventh and eighth centuries and the Europeans in the fifteenth, sixteenth, and seventeenth centuries; the Arabs and Europeans were more technically advanced and militarily much stronger in comparison to the Africans. With respect to one of the major defeats of one of the major African empires, Jackson (1970:218) writes that:

> ... Songhay was invaded by a Moorish army led by Jordan Pasha, a half were armed with firearms imported from England. The superior numbers of the Songhay army were no match for the gunpowder of the Moors. In 1591, both Gao and Timbuktu fell to the invaders from the north. From that moment on everything changed. Danger took the place of security; poverty of wealth. Peace gave way to distress, disasters and violence.

Thus, while the Moors pounded away at the remaining large African political centers, the west Europeans were already nibbling away at the African Atlantic Coast. Though Africans had been in South America and Hispanola before Columbus (Davidson, 1969:641; Sertima, 1976), the European Atlantic slave trade took Africans to work the lands of the west, not to visit out of curiosity about what laid beyond the Atlantic. By this time, the western world had "discovered the power of industrial technology, which made it possible for people to produce and consume material goods on a scale completely unprecedented in the world's earlier history" (Bohannan and Curtin, 1988:16). As though these historical epochs were mere accidents, the African became the victim of the Moors from North Africa, who had been driven out of Spain, and West Europeans who prowled the African Atlantic Coasts; they were to soon nibble at the East African Coasts as well. Africans became the chosen people in this drama of the European Atlantic slave trade because they were defeated by western technology; Western technology in terms of science, administration, and military might, were far too advanced for African people to challenge with any success. To a large extent, these are still Africa's weaknesses; Ali Mazrui (1980:118) acknowledges that African countries are not only politically weak, but also administratively, militarily and technologically underdeveloped; most contemporary writers on Africa would concur that Africa's lack in technology has indeed left her fragile and weak in the face of any sort of determined challenge or adversity from within and without.

It was partly due to the Europeans' technological achievements that gave them the confidence in the first place to venture out into the oceans and to the other outlandish places. By the time Gustavus Vassa was captured in 1756, Europeans were already 'masters' of the sea and navigated 'complex' ships over unknown waters to distant lands, cultures and peoples. The first two chapters of Vassa's narrative (Gates, 1987) depict a technologically simpler African society as compared to that of Europe. As he was separated from his native culture, environment and people, Vassa's life became more technologically complex; he was fascinated by the ship, a watch, and a picture for "... having never seen such things as these before" (39). Upon his arrival in England in 1757, Equiano was impressed by books and churches, for such things were not in his African village. After many trials and tribulations in the hands of Christian enslavers, Mr. Vassa desired to return to Africa to replace slavery with legitimate commerce and promote the technical development of Africa; he saw that Africa could benefit from western science, religion, and other more advanced European institutions that would develop Africa commercially and industrially. Perhaps more than most Africans would admit publicly, Olaudah Equiano was quick to practically realize the technical power of

Western Europe; more than two hundred years later, Western Europe's technical superiority still loom over Africa and Africans. Africans in north, south, west, east and central Africa were all militarily defeated. Africans continued to fight against their domination at all costs, took any opportunity that presented itself, anywhere, anytime, but as Harding (1981:23) remarks, "'... what could they do against firearms?'" On board ship Africans rebelled against their captors; in west, east and south Africa, African nationalists fought the European as hard as they could, but what could they really do against firearms with bows and arrows, hoes and machetes? Thus, west Europeans' military superiority and technical know-how greatly put African people at a disadvantage, in their attempts to defend themselves and hold on to their dignity.

In North and South America, African people could run, but they could hardly hide. They were unfamiliar with the terrain, in contrast to the Indians who could run-away and band with other Indians. In the West Indies, Africans banded and formed the Maroons of Jamaica and posed a troublesome presence to their European masters, whose military might they knew very well. Due to their lack in military strength and organization, African people in the west adopted covert means of rebellion, including running away, poisoning their masters, feigning illness, etc. in an effort to maintain their inner souls and sense of humanity. The Africans who rebelled, such as Nat Turner and Gabriel Prosser, were all finally militarily and organizationally defeated; they could hardly win against a system bigger and better organized than themselves. The Africans were so poorly organized that some members of the African race reported on other Africans' attempts to rebel against the system of slavery. In this way, some remained slaves for more than four hundred years; after the abolition of slavery, Africans continued to be dominated by Jim Crowism, colonialism, neo-colonialism, The World Bank, The International Monetary Fund, the Euphoria about western democracy and concepts such as The New World Order, Westernization and other western dominated concepts, ideas and institutions to which African people, globally, remain peripheral in terms of political power, economics, technical know-how or the transfer of technology. African people's technological liabilities have been so great that they have been 'totally' dependent on western medicine, media, and technical experts in most human endeavors and institutions. Though African people seem to have consistently rebelled against much of western domination, there have been no large scale institutions erected to effectively counteract the numerous forms of degradations African people globally experience on a daily basis in New Guinea, India, London, New York, and elsewhere. The NAACP, CORE, and OAU have all had their say, but none, or all of these together are of any significant threat to the U.S.A.'s National Guard, for an example; in the face of the military, political, economic and scientific organizations of the western white man, African people's organizations have been ineffective, and have sometimes been wholly subordinated to the white man's international organizations.

The power and sophistication of the western man's military science was certainly a significant factor in the defeat of Africans. Boley (1984:15), in the case of Liberia, states how the white man's "...pointed... pistol at the (African) king's head ... procured a signed 'treaty' giving the American Colonization society rights to Cape Mesurado,' a stretch of land thirty-six miles long and three miles wide'.... By means of the U.S. armed war vessel, 'the tribesmen were 'persuaded' to sell a strip of land on the coast.'" From the Cape of Good Hope in 1652, Europeans, with their military might, carved out lands for themselves and were able to rule Africans for more than three hundred years because of their military and technological sophistication. When the French tested their nuclear bomb in the Sahara in the 1960s, Africans were bamboozled; they 'simply' sat, watched and made certain high level moralistic arguments, but could not prevent the highly technologically advanced France from frightening African peasants and leaders on their own continent.

One 'recalcitrant' East African chief once wrote in 1890 to a Herman von Wissmen, the German who had ordered him to submit to colonialism (Hodder-Williams 1984:22); arrogantly, the African chief replied the German thus:

> I have listened to your words (Macemba wrote) but can find no reason why I should obey you–I would rather die first. I have no relations with you and cannot bring it to my mind that you have given me so much as a *pesa* (a fraction of a rupee) or the quarter of a *pesa* or a needle or a thread. I look for some reason why I should obey you and find not the smallest. If it should be friendship that you desire, then I am ready for it, today and always; but to be your subject, that I cannot be...If it should be war you desire, then I am ready, but never to be your subject...I do not fall at your feet, for you are God's creature just as I am...I am sultan here in my land. You are sultan there in yours. Yet listen, I do not say to you that you should obey me; for I know that you are a free man...As for me, I will not come to you and, if you are strong enough, then come and fetch me. (Cited in Davidson, 1964:357-358).

Unfortunately for chief Macemba, "von Wissman was strong enough. ...whenever there was a direct clash of this kind, which occurred when the European presence was clearly seen as a threat to an African state's power and position, the ensuing fight was one-sided" (Hodder-Williams, 1984:22).

Generally, African responses to European colonialism ranged between outright rejection by some African chiefs such as Macemba and effective collaboration on the part of others; the rest employed 'strategic retreat' knowing that they could not face European weapons of destruction frontally. Regardless of the mode of resistance, by the early 1900s, the 'whole' African continent had been balkanized into French, Portuguese, Spanish, Italian, German, and British colonies, including the gallant Asante of West Africa (Parker, 1955:12).

Thus, despite Africa's ancient contributions to the fundamentals of contemporary science, religion and social organization (Asante, 1987:166), the Africa from the 1400s to the present has not been a spectacular Africa in medicine, military science, agricultural economics and global politics; by the 1800s Africans were already fully at the mercy of western powers, and this western hold on Africa and Africans has not radically changed in favor of the African masses in any appreciable degree. Africans have not been able to transform their food production technology, defend themselves effectively, and have in fact experienced numerous famines that have rendered a host of African youngsters practically helpless in an age of scientific sophistication and global economic competition. Because of Africans' military and technical weaknesses, they were the most easily chosen victims of slavery and colonization, the impacts of which still 'strangle' African people globally. With respect to science, Africans are still dependent on outlandish scientific and research institutions. As Hountondji (1990:6) observes,

> Elsewhere, outside Africa, are located the most fully equipped laboratories, the best universities, the most powerful research centers, the editorial teams and offices of the most prestigious scientific journals, the most complete reference libraries and publishing houses, and... the world's major concentration of practicing scientists. Elsewhere, therefore, are taking place most of the events considered to be important scientific occurrences... Now, how do African scientists react to this situation? They hardly question it. They take it for granted?

## Africans in Islam and Christianity

The two major groups of people that enslaved Africans enmasse are generally associated with two of the world's major religions that do not regard African people too highly. Both Arabs and Europeans, Muslims and Christians, and Islam and Christianity depict black African people derogatorily. Furthermore, both Arabs and Europeans justified the enslavement of African people in Islam and Christianity because of the 'famous' biblical Noah's curse on Ham (Genesis 9:18-27). Lewis (1971:66-67) states that "A common explanation of (the slave) status, among Muslim scholars, is that the ancestor of the dark-skinned peoples was Ham the son of Noah who (according to Muslim legend) was damned black for his sin. The curse of blackness, and with it that of slavery, passed to all the black peoples who are his descendants." Lewis (67) goes on to observe that "Muslim law unequivocally forbids the enslavement of free Muslims of whatever race, and was usually obeyed in this. There is, however, some evidence that the law was not always strictly enforced to protect Muslim captives from black Africa." As late as the 1990s (Masland and others, 1992:32) state that "more than 100,000 descendants of Africans conquered by Arabs during the 12th century are still thought to be living as old fashioned chattel slaves. Aside from the shanty towns and a strip of land along the Senegal River, virtually all blacks are slaves, and they are more than half the population." In the Sudan and other Arab dominated countries, blacks are at the bottom of 'Arabic' society. Muslims are quick to point out that Bilal, the black Ethiopian slave friend of prophet Mohammed, was a honored propagator of the Islamic faith, and that compared to Christianity Islam is not too harsh on black people (Blyden, 1988); nonetheless, it might suffice to observe that Arabs are not, and have not been color blind in their perceptions and treatment of black people in ancient and contemporary times. They did not only take slaves from Africa, but also attempted to 'exterminate' blacks from eastern and northern Africa in Iraq (Lewis, 1971:66).

In the (Christian) bible, "Genesis 9:18-27 has been used by many white-racists to teach that black people had been cursed by Noah to be in utter subjection and slavery to non-blacks. This biblical incident involves Noah, his three sons (Japheth, Ham and Shem) and one of his grandsons, Canaan, the youngest son of Ham" (Salley and Behm, 1988:84). When Noah awoke from his drunkenness, he cursed Canaan instead Ham who had actually seen him naked and drunk: "cursed be Canaan; a slave of slaves shall he be to his brothers" (V. 25). What seems unclear is how Canaan's curse came to apply to all black people; did Noah's curse on Canaan turned him black, while the rest of the family remained white? If Ham is reputedly the ancestors of black people, then blacks were not the ones cursed by Noah, since the curse clearly went to Canaan, the youngest son of Ham, whose descendants settled out of Africa. Nonetheless, Salley and Behm (85) assert that "In order (for the curse) to apply... to blacks the following propositions must be established in the text: (1) Blacks are descendants of Canaan; (2) Noah's words are valid as a curse; (3) The curse applies today; and (4) We should enforce the curse." Of these, propositions 2, 3 and 4 seem difficult; for example, is Noah's curse more powerful than god's blessings? Are the teachings of Jesus Christ not more powerful and override that of Noah? With respect to proposition #1, "It is clear that they are not inhabitants of Africa and were not considered as black-skinned by those of the ancient world" (Salley and Behm, 86).

But even if Canaanites were black (Hamites), which also included a diverse group of people (McCray, 1990:115-17), has the curse not already diluted itself in light of the intermixture of people globally, and especially of Africans and Arabs, and Africans and Europeans? Furthermore, has the world not grown more 'civilized' beyond a drunken grandfather's curse on an innocent Canaan? Finally, what did African people do to Europeans and Arabs to deserve the intense hate that they have had and continue to have against blacks? As David Walker asked in 1829, what have black people done to Europeans to 'deserve' their enslavement and continual negative treatment from Europeans? (Aptheker, 1965:76). In Walker's own words,

> I have been for years troubling the pages of historians, to find out what our fathers have done to the *white Christians of America*, to merit such condign punishment as they have inflicted on them, and do continue to inflict on us their children. But I must aver, that my researches have hitherto been to no effect. I have therefore, come to the immovable conclusion, that they (Americans) have, and do continue to punish us for nothing else, but for enriching them and their country. For I cannot conceive of any thing else. Nor will I ever believe otherwise, until the Lord shall convince me. (76)

Nonetheless, it seems clear that both Muslims and Christians have used their religions to justify their enslavement of blacks globally. Ironically, blacks in slavery used the bible and emphasized the liberation motif in the Exodus story, identified themselves with the despised Jesus Christ in whom they saw their own redemption from bondage, and emphasized that in the Lord Almighty there was freedom for the faithful and a judgment day for all god's children, including the master as well as the bondmen and bondmaids, the possessed and the possessors, the oppressed and their oppressors.

Like blacks, women have also come to realize that they too have been traditionally denounced by the Bible as well as the western and Arabic machoist societies; they too are said to have been cursed to be subservient to the male rulers of the universe. It is interesting to note that the powerless, blacks and women, have been the once cursed in the Bible to carry the white man's load, to plow the white man's fields and to provide the European and the Arabic man with the required comforts to substantiate their rulership. On the other hand, to keep the black man ignorant and powerless, the white man did his utmost, albeit unsuccessfully, to keep the bible, the gun and the white woman from the black man's reach. But both blacks and women have now progressively educated themselves to see themselves, from their own vantage points of views, and cannot accept the white male's ideology that they were forever cursed to be bondmen and bondmaids.

As there have been attempts to change Christianity with the advent of Liberation Theology in the 1960s, the women's liberation movement, and civil rights legislations, so also have there been gestations to adapt Islam to the modern global zeitgeist. Miller (1992:22-26; 38, 40, 42) states that the Shah of Iran in the 1960s and 70s attempted to change Iran's Islamic society in light of the impact of western democracy and technology. Though the Shah was deposed, western secular challenges to Islam and Arabic culture remain formidable, despite Arabs' desire to recapture the good old days of the 8th through the 11th centuries, when they conquered extensively and transmitted eastern science to western Europe. But times have radically changed, and the past glories of Islam's religious and scientific domination of a large part of the world can now be only dreamt of, or wished for, but not recaptured in essence. The Iraqi defeat in the 1992 Gulf war must have been a telling blow to Pan-Arabism and the Arabic male ego of warriorship. Furthermore, the more Arabs become acquainted with western secularism, the more their Arabic culture of male domination, the continued disregard for blacks in Mauritania and Sudan (*Newsweek*: May 4, 1992), will come to be challenged and undermined by the more powerful western notions of democracy and individual liberty regardless of race, sex, nationality and religious belief. Educated Arabs, in and outside of the Middle-East, are going to unrelentlessly demand for more participatory forms of government; for an instance,

> Saudi Arabia, despite its cultural fundamentalism (has felt) compelled to appease the elite with a slight increase in political participation and poorer Saudis with larger subsidies for gasoline, electricity, health care and so on. Jordan has attempted to draw the militants into the government... Egypt is ruthlessly repressing groups that espouse violence, tolerating those that don't and stealing Islamic militants' themes and slogans. 'We are becoming more Muslim than the prophet,' says Mohammed Noah, a popular Egyptian singer and playwright. (Miller, 1992:25-26)

Furthermore, "...the mostly western oriented, secular middle-class, particularly women" (38), are going to continue to challenge an Arabism and Islamism that does not enhance their own image of themselves or their class interests and acquired culture. Islamic laws that purport to restrict and regulate people's dress patterns, laws that inflict primitive forms of deterrents such as "corporal punishments,... amputation for repeated theft, stoning for adultery, lashings for offenses and even crucifixion" (40) are going to be increasingly viewed as anachronistic, inhumane and uncivilized. In addition, other secularized Arabs are going to continually demand political ideals that will challenge Islamic religious ideals of government; educated Arabic women, religious or secular, in cognizance of the Americanization of the globe, are going to continue to challenge traditional Islamic ideas about the ideal Islamic family, roles of women, wives, children, and husbands. It seems clear therefore that Christian and Islamic views that once justified slavery, the lowly treatment of blacks and women, in religious and secular institutions, are no longer in vogue in the impending global village. Certainly, blacks and women are still regarded with some unease and difficulty but they have already challenged the anachronistic notions that they were the chosen ones to be hewers of wood and drawers of water for European and Arabic men.

## Africans and Accidents of History

Various other writers have attempted to explain why Africans were the 'chosen people' for western slavery; these explanations have ranged from the notion that Africans became victims of the accidents of history; a historical accident that caught black people unprepared to deal with the advent of Europeans at that crucial time that the white man arrived in Africa. West Africans, for an instance, had taken it for granted that all things of value, religion, articles of trade, schools, inspiration, etc. came from across the Sahara. African leaders had traveled to Egypt and Mecca in Saudi Arabia and elsewhere to trade and learn from the north. Arabic scholars, architects, schools and administrative styles had been 'imported' from the north. While most Africans were settled in this mode, west Europeans, after ousting the Moors from Spain, became actively interested in the African interior in search "for the legendary kingdom of Prester John (Forbath, 1977:18). Furthermore, Europeans were by the late 1400s sufficiently equipped to attempt a circumnavigation of the African continent to reach the Indies trade, to propagate Christianity, to stop the spread of Islam, look for markets and "to know what lands there were beyond the Canary Isles and a cape, which was called Bojador" (39). To these reasons for venturing into and around Africa was quickly added 'the desire for slaves to work the American plantations,' "and by 1448 more than 50 ships had gone to Guinea and returned with nearly 1000 slaves" (52). Some Africans rebelled against these early European Christians who "...eat human flesh and buy black men only to make a meal of them" (53). The Bakongo Africans were curious about the whiteness of the Europeans whose skin they thought could be rubbed-off (74). Despite these initial gestations concerning skin color and cultural differences, the economic impetus became overwhelming enough to dictate the type of relationship that would ensue between the well-armed Europeans and the poorly armed African natives on the west coast, east, central Africa, and the Cape of Good Hope.

It must always be borne in mind that, in addition to the other variables of the accidents of history, economic motives, religious and color differences, Africans have not only been at a technological, but also administrative disadvantages, say, since the advent of the Hyksos (the white Shepherd Kings) into Egyptian civilization, that began the destruction of African civilizations; the other aliens who came after the Hyksos found a declining African civilization. The Greeks, Assyrians, Persians and Romans all invaded Egypt and transformed it into a near-white civilization long before the Christian era (Williams, 1974:127). The more contemporary Arabs and west Europeans found weakened African civilizations in terms of technology, organizational leadership and the lack of a powerful African state to speak and defend the national, ethnic or racial interests of black people globally. Thus, had Africans had a strong powerful state to fight on their behalf, or even posed a meaningful threat to the Arabs and Europeans, they might not have been the chosen ones for international slavery and colonialization.

## The Absence of a Powerful African State

We must never fail to reiterate that had Africans not been militaristically weak, they might not have been the chosen ones for international slavery and exploitation. The European slave or indentured servant and the African slave or indentured servant did not really have the same status on the American plantations in the early 1600s in at least two major respects: the white man's feelings of superiority, indentured, slave or not, with respect to the African; the fact that the African indentured servant or slave did not have a political center, a religious or political leader, or an African state powerful enough to pose a threat, challenge or intimidate Europeans and even Arabs with regards to how black people were treated globally. Africans did not, and still do not have a political center that poses a threat to any international organization or body with regards to the welfare of Africans wherever they are; for the white indentured servant "America was but an extension of Europe" (Chee-Mooke, 1980:21). For the African villager, or tribal chief, commoner or 'scholar' in slavery, America was a nightmare. The African could not appeal to any international African religious leader to explain to him the treatment of his brethren in the American wilderness. To the African, the pope, the Anglican church, and their bibles were all in cahoots against him, denouncing him as a savage who needed to be civilized anyway. For the African in the American wilderness, in a different culture, climate, environment, and linguistic area, servitude was not a continuity of life, an evolution of his progression; it was the vulgarization of his progression. While some European indentured servants signed up to leave the old country, a good number of Africans jumped overboard ship only to be had by sharks; while Europe got rid of some of its excessive population and some criminals, Africa was 'depopulated' of some of its most able bodied men, women, and children, unprotected by any government, African or European. As Chee-Mooke (1980:22) has correctly observed,

> escape for the white servant was easy. White servants often sued for unlawful detention after they obtained clothes, food, etc., just before the ship's departure. ... the case of a Mr. Peel was more the rule rather than the exception. He took three hundred... white servants with him to Australia. But when he arrived the poor whites whom he had thought were going to work for him simply preferred to work for themselves than for him.

These white servants of Mr. Peel could run and hide among the other Europeans, and be protected with much more ease than black Africans in, say, colonial Virginia. Certainly, some whites provided cover for escaping black slaves to the U.S. north and Canada, but the black man's fear of being recaptured was oppressive in itself. With respect to North Africa and the absence of a powerful black state to intervene on behalf of the black African slaves, Brown (1968:189) states that

> The blacks arrived in Northern Africa as detribalized individuals...scattered over Northern Africa, (they) could easily be absorbed and even ignored.
>
> The wide Sahara made it unthinkable that the blacks would flee or by any other means return to the land of the blacks, which is the meaning of the Arabic word Sudan. Furthermore, no black nation in middle Africa even posed a physical threat to the states of Northern Africa... The Moroccan expedition into West Africa at the end of the sixteenth century that overthrew the declining Songhay Empire furnishes a major illustration of a threat, both political and military, moving from north to south. There are, however, no examples of a threat moving in the opposite direction.

Therefore blacks in North Africa and the other Arab dominated countries are not highly respected or valued beyond the level of military men, domestic servants, concubines, and road builders, etc. Arabic terminologies and proverbs relative to blacks "all reveal a strong prejudice against the black man and the implication that he would usually be close to the bottom of the social ranking" (192). Generally, contemporary North Africans have come to be familiar with seeing blacks at the bottom of the Arabic society, irrespective of Islam's nebulous claim that it is color blind/or not racist. North African writers who go to the extreme to show that Arabs are not anti-black often end up showing how indeed the Arabs are anti-black Africans, Muslims or not. Even during the nationalist movements of the 1960s North African leaders remained split between Arabism and Pan-Africanism; today, Arabs are still enslaving black Africans in Maunitania (*Newsweek*, May 4, 1992), without any fear from the south of the Sahara. In both North Africa and India, the color black is not highly valued, at least not to the same degree that the white skin is. With respect to blacks in India, Beteille (1968:173) states that "In many Indian languages the words *fair* and *beautiful* are often used synonymously. The folk literature places a high value on fair skin color." A dark India girl, all things being equal, has a disadvantage in terms of her opportunities for marrying up. While there is hardly any support globally for Indian Blacks, Muslims in India can expect help from Pakistan and the rest of the Islamic world, should their freedoms to be Muslims be infringed upon; a similar threat cannot be said to exist, within and without India, for the Dravidians in India, or from any black African state. Globally, black skinned people are at a distinct disadvantage in not having a nation, state or a powerful organization that defends them. For several years NATO defended West Europeans, Warsaw Pact, East Europeans; American citizens in Europe and elsewhere are highly protected. A similar thing cannot be said about Africans in Europe, America, and North Africa, or anywhere else. There are European and American Jewish organizations to speak on behalf of the world's Jews; Israel is a Jewish nation to which all Jews can turn to in times of crisis; and Israel is backed by the powerful American nation and numerous Jewish organizations. The same cannot be said for black Americans, blacks in Great Britain, Australia and New Guinea. Within the last hundred years or so, NAACP, Urban League, OAU, CORE, UNIA, ANC and others have been created to speak on behalf of downtrodden African people, but these organizations are no threat, physical, military, economic or otherwise to the U.S.A., Great Britain, or the United Nations; as such, they cannot defend blacks, especially the black masses, who are daily made to feel their blackness in humiliation and powerlessness.

Perhaps the Haitians would not have been so blatantly denied entrance into the U.S. in the earlier part of 1992 had there been 'a powerful black voice' to make the United States feel intimated as to what might happen. The continued absence of that powerful black voice or nation in the past contributed to the large scale enslavement of Africans and the colonization of the African continent. Thus, blacks in Mauritania, Saudi Arabia, India, and elsewhere continue to be the wretched of the earth, because African people, globally, are not a threat to the various nations that keep the masses of African people at the bottom of their respective societies. As David Walker asked in 1829 (Wiltse, 1915:129), "would they fool with any other people as they do with us?" In addition to the Indians of the Americas, the European has been able to manhandle many other peoples, and continues to do so more so the black man. In the early 1900s and the 1980s, for instance,

> ...the San Francisco Board of Education decreed that all Asian children in that city had to attend a single, segregated school. The Japanese government protested, and after negotiations, the United States and Japan reached what became known as a 'gentleman's agreement.' The Japanese agreed to discourage emigration and President Roosevelt agreed to prevent the passage of laws discriminating against Japanese in the United States.
>
> Japanese Americans were subjected to especially vicious mistreatment during World War II.... Many lost their homes and possessions in the process.
>
> In 1988, President Ronald Reagan signed legislation apologizing for this war time action. The legislation moved to 'right a great wrong' by establishing a $1.25 billion trust fund as reparation... Each eligible person was to receive a $20,000 tax-free award from the government. (Tischler, 1990:301-302)

It is important to note that by 1988, Japan was one of the world's leading economic and technological powers; America had nothing to fear from Africa; therefore, when Africans were promised 40 acres and a mule during the reconstruction period (1865-1877), to rehabilitate the newly freed African slaves after the U.S. Civil War, there was no powerful African nation to make sure that that promise was kept. Instead, in the place of reparations for African people, there were instituted the KKK and other forms of Jim Crowisms. There was not a single African state in 1865, powerful enough, to intimidate the United States concerning the improvement of the conditions of the ex-African slaves. There is still not an African state that is capable of intimidating any nation outside the African continent with regards to the mistreatment of African people in say London, Los Angeles, or Moscow.

It was because of this absence of a strong black African nation to defend its own that in part compelled Marcus Garvey to advocate for an

African nation. In his own words, he emphasized the need for that African nation:

> The Negro needs a nation and a country of its own, where he can best show evidence of his own ability in the art of human progress. Scattering him as an unmixed and unrecognized part of alien nations and civilizations is but to demonstrate his imbecility and point him out as an unworthy derelict, fit neither for the society of Greek, Jew nor gentile. (Garvey, 1971:24)

As would be expected of Garvey, he goes on to stress the need for a powerful African organization, military power, "government, industry, art, science, literature, and culture." (24). Before Marcus Garvey, there was Mansa Musa (de graft-Johnson, 1986:99) and Toussaint L'Ouverture (James, 1963:265); after Mr. Garvey, there have been Kwame Nkrumah, George Padmore, W.E.B. DuBois and other African thinkers who have appreciated the necessity of a powerful African nation, state, or organization and leadership for African people's defense and development wherever they are. "On the eve of the partition of Africa," writes OLaniyan (1982:7),

> except for such older states as Egypt, Morocco, Tunis, Liberia and Ethiopia, and the states that were at the height of their power at this time in sub-Saharan Africa, there were no large political entities; and those which did exist could not be compared with England, France or Germany which had achieved a higher level of political integration, demographic homogeneity and national outlook. African states such as Asante, Buganda, Zulu and Sokoto lacked the natural resources and the fairly heavy populations that could be commanded by the large political organizations of Europe or Asia.

The African masses still await that powerful African nation to represent them in the global village.

## Other Reasons as to Why Africans Could be Enslaved and Colonized

The enslavement of people, as we've seen, is not a new phenomenon in history, but the large scale enslavement of African people has had no parallel. Furthermore, the hatred of African people's skin color has too not had any parallel in human civilizations. As we have tried to establish above, the enslavement of man by man in the form of having 'total' control, if that is ever possible, over another person's labor, income, working hours, family and marriage etc. seemed to have occurred in different societies around the globe. It could also be recalled that the weaker ones in some form or another have always been the chosen ones for enslavement in the various societies around the globe.

African people were perhaps enslaved due to historical accidents over which they had no control, such as the 'discovery' of America in 1492, and the Portuguese's routing of Africa in the 1400s, which was about the same time that the destruction of the last major African empire by the Moroccans took place, and left Africa weak in disarray - between the 1490s and the 1590s. As such, Africa was in a crisis when the then major world regions were resolute about the development of their respective nations and the propagation of their religions at whatever cost. While the Arabs and Europeans were 'united' around their race and religion, much of Africa was divided along the lines of the tribe, or believers against infidels (Muslims and non-Muslims). Where religious and racial unity existed, as in North Africa and Northern Nigeria, the French, English and Italians had difficulties subjugating those people as compared to most of the other regions south of the Sahara. The Italians had to wage a long and bitter battle over Libya and Somalia before these countries were finally subjugated. Furthermore, Asian and North African countries were ahead of African countries south of the Sahara in challenging the European colonial powers to set them free due to their consciousness of themselves as a people with a common language, a culture, religion and a common history. Black African people (military men, popes, academicians, etc.) had either been Romanized or Arabized but not Africanized; that is to say, there were Africans defending the Roman Empire and spreading the Islamic faith but not defending or propagating the African nation for the sake of the nation. The Moors of North Africa who dominated Southern Spain and Portugal for close to eight hundred years were African Muslims; these Arabized Africans transmitted eastern science and technology to Western Europe, not to Africa, south of the Sahara, where they continue to discriminate against black Africans (*Newsweek*, May 4, 1992).

The development of European commerce and the industrial revolution are also factors that contributed to the zeitgeist of domination and the feelings of European superiority and racism. In addition to all these reasons, Africa's political and technological backwardness and weaknesses seem to stand salient as to why Africans could be enslaved. The absence of a powerful African state based on technological advancement still holds Africa and Africans as hostage of the contemporary New World order. After all, Vietnam was not just that "...poor isolated little country facing a colossus; the colossus could not set foot on Vietnamese territory because another colossus stood ready to interfere and protect Vietnam. ...the state of Vietnam had a mighty protector, and this made her as powerful as the United States" (Ellul, 1978:101-102). Arabized and Romanized Africans were no longer African enough to even think of defending Africa south of the Sahara; they had been detribalized and often educated to be ashamed of their blackness (Williams, 1974:78). Afro-Asians, a result of the sexual traffic between black women and Arab men, emerged and were soon classified as Caucasians or Asians who vowed to enslave the whole African race and even destroyed the major marks of black civilizations by destroying monuments "...with all African faces (which) simply had their heads knocked off" (79-80).

As these detribalized Africans contributed to the enslavement of African people, so also did African poverty. In extreme poverty people have been known to sell their offsprings to maximize those offsprings' survival chances. In Eastern Africa "famine ... swelled the ranks of volunteer slaves on the Zambezi estates...children (were) sold into slavery by their families in times of need" (Fisher and Fisher, 1971:75). In times like these, the climate of opinion becomes conducive to slavery, not in contradiction to the love parents may have for their children, but in the confirmation of that love; they simply may wish to have their children live even as slaves. The opposite reaction also occurred, where Africans committed suicide rather than live as slaves (Harding, 1983:18-20).

According to Mazrui (1986:224), Africa's ecology may have condemned her to underdevelopment, and by implication susceptible to being dominated, in that the African climate was not conducive

> ...for either the capitalist ethos of anticipation and maximization of returns or for the pre-capitalist stimulus of civil engineering and textile consumerism. The African ecology did not foster capitalist formation. The winter-gap 'condemned' tropical Africa to a pre-capitalist condition.

By this is meant, of course, that Africans could not form the habit of saving for a rainy day or for a winter season of unbearable colds, because their environment did not require the absolute need to anticipate and predict a harsh period of the year. This lack in the culture of anticipation, prediction and planning may have retarded Africa's technical development. Africans may have seemed not to have also reached the stage of development not to have borne in mind "...that economic forces were the prime movers of history" (217). Because Africans were at the pre-capitalist stage when they came into contact with Western Europe, they were at a distinct disadvantage in dealing with the European who knew that buying slaves from as far away as West Africa was an investment, including the risks involved. To the African, the village was his world, the European, the world his village (295).

Certainly, there have been a few African leaders and patriots such as Queen Nzinga, who challenged the Portuguese for forty years in her opposition to the enslavement of Africans; the "...betrayal of Affonso (the African king of the Congo in the early 1500s) came with its steadily diminishing willingness to provide technical aid and material for the modernization and evangelization of the African realm. Affonso year after year wrote in vain requesting priests and missionaries, teachers and technicians, church artifacts and tools" (Forbath, 1977:117). Evidently, the Portuguese were by then more interested in the taking of Africans as slaves (116). Queen Nzinga died in 1663, and three hundred years later in 1975, the Portuguese were still in Angola as colonialists.

Despite the brave efforts of a few African leaders, Africans could also be enslaved in part because

> There were people in West Africa who saw themselves as benefiting from the trade. The export of slaves enabled the powerful to accumulate wealth in the unsatisfactory form of luxury goods hoarded in their compounds. These they could use to purchase local products, reward service and increase their political influence. Coastal traders made profits on the sale of 'trade goods' in the interior; their rulers benefited also from revenue imposed on the trade and from the purchase of guns to defend and expand their frontiers. Powerful rulers of the interior also derived considerable advantage from tolls and taxes imposed on indigenous traders and from the purchase of armaments. ... a ruler of Dahomey was to reply to a British invitation to abolish the slave trade in his dominions that a large British subsidy plus the development of palm oil production could not adequately compensate his slave trade revenues. (Stride, Ifeka, and Ajayi, 1971:215)

If African chiefs and other rulers were willing to sell, European Christians, Kings, Queens, shipbuilders, merchants, adventurers, etc. were also willing beneficiaries in the trade in Africans (de graft-Johnson, 1986:154). Furthermore, African leaders "...neglected to organize standing armies against possible invaders from the seas. The rulers took little thought for the future that was encroaching on them from across the waterfront" (Chinweizu: 1987:54).

The stance that slavery would save the Africans themselves from perdition was at least believed by one educated African at the time. Jacobus Elisa Johannes Capitein, a Ghanaian, who "...crowned his academic career by delivering a Latin oration (which) was published and went through four editions," believed that slavery was not "contrary to religious liberty" (de graft-Johnson 1986:158).

Capitein himself was appointed chaplain to Elmina Castle in 1742. The Europeans at Elmina Castle disregarded his office because he was an ex-slave; his own people in turn ostracized him. He had a short and troubled career, and died at the age of thirty (158-159).

We shall never know for certain how many 'black' souls were uprooted from Africa into the American wilderness, the Caribbean Islands, or across the Sahara into North Africa, Iran, Iraq, Saudi Arabia, and elsewhere, but we are at least certain that attempts were made by the host cultures to dis-Africanize the African diaspora. In the United States in particular, the African family was systematically broken up and vulgarized; African names, religions, customs, and belief systems were bastardized; African languages, recreational patterns, and 'superstitions' were all challenged and denounced by their host environment. In the language of Ali A. Mazrui (1986:111),

> the African slaves ceased to be called 'Africans' or anything related to their geographical ancestry, and rapidly became 'niggers' or 'Negroes.'
>
> This was accompanied by the dis-Africanization of collective pride. The captives' capacity for African nostalgia was undermined or destroyed by a ruthless negative indoctrination... The blacks in the Americas were systematically taught to be ashamed of where they came from.

Even though Euro-Americans did their utmost to 'totally' dis-Africanise the Africans, they were not completely successful. In fact, the more European-Americans were bent on dis-Africanising the Africans, the more, it seemed, the Africans were bent on asserting their Africanity; they began to call their churches African churches; after liberating Haiti, Toussaint desired to sail"... to Africa with arms, ammunition and a thousand of his best soldiers, and there conquering vast tracks of country, putting an end to the slave trade, and making millions of blacks 'free and French,' as his constitution had made the blacks in Santa Domingo" (James, 1963:265). The more the Africans were deprived of their human rights, the more they became racially conscious and began to propose Pan-Negroism and Pan-Africanism to develop themselves.

As though to add insult to injury, as Africans aimed to build a powerful nation of their own, Europeans abandoned slavery for the colonization of the African continent. Thus, by the early 1900s the African continent had been so effectively 'occupied' by west Europeans and Americans, that the Africans were either French, English, Portuguese speaking Africans, or Americo-Liberians. Again, African resistance against colonization was defeated by the mighty weapons of West Europeans. Africans, however, did not give up their struggles against Jim Crowism, Apartheid, and the brutal colonial administrators in the Belgium Congo, Angola, Guinea-Bissau, Kenya, Somalia, Algeria, the Sudan, Senegal, etc.

The African Nationalist and Pan-African movements in the 1960s had their roots in the Atlantic slavery trade. If the Atlantic slave trade was brutal, long, and depopulated and underdeveloped Africa, it also brought various Africans together in a crucible in which they found that, in their relations to the Europeans and European-Americans, Africans were Africans and powerless; the Europeans and Euro-Americans were Europeans and powerful. As Cleage (1987:XXXI) observes in the case of Black America,

> No matter how learned a black man may be, his children find it difficult to get a decent education in a public school. No matter how well-mannered he may be, he finds it difficult to secure a decent house to live in. ...Only a black fool can believe that he is not discriminated against in America. The white man's d*eclaration of Black inferiority* has served to provide for black people a unique experience.... We can sit in the same room, we can live in the same town, we can be neighbors... but we are a separate people because our experience has been different.

Cleage goes on to say what other black nationalists have said and continue to say:

> Black people must secure enough power to protect themselves. A helpless people provoke oppression and brutality by their very powerlessness. There is no known process by which a group with power can be redeemed into giving their power to the powerless. The only kind of world in which overt violence could be reduced to a minimum would be a world in which power was so equitably distributed that no one group dared to move against another. (61)

African people's experience in the west then prepared them with a different outlook; like the master and the slave, the powerful and the powerless, they may live on the same plantation, or in the same global village but see harvesting time radically different. One of the greatest ideological fruits that the western enslavement of Africans gave to African people was the ideology of Pan-Negroism or Pan-Africanism and the appreciation of Africa as never before. Had there not been the western enslavement of Africans, there might not have been the pan-Africanism we know of today. But what is this pan-Africanism? What are some of the other factors that give rise to the ideology and the movement? Of what significance is Pan-Africanism for African people in the modern global zeitgeist? These are some of the questions that the next chapter attempts to address.

**References: Chapter III**

Asante, Molefi K. 1987. *The Afro-Centric Idea.* Philadelphia, Penn.: Temple University Press.

Behm, Ronald and Salley Columbus. 1988. *What Color is Your God: Black Consciousness and the Christian Faith.* Secaucus, New Jersey: Citadel Press.

Beteille, Andre. 1968. "Race and Descent as Social Categories in India," pp. 166-185 in John Hope Franklin (ed.), *Color and Race.* Boston, Mass. Houghton and Mifflin Company.

Bohannan, Paul and Philip Curtin. 1988. *Africa and Africans.* Prospect Heights, Illinois: Waveland Press, Inc.

Boley, G.E. Saigbe. 1983. *Liberia: The Rise and Fall of the First Republic.* London: MacMillan Publishers.

Brown, Leon Carl. 1968. "Color in North Africa," pp. 186-204 in John Hope Franklin (ed.), *Color and Race.* Boston, Mass. Houghton and Mifflin Company.

Chee-Mooke, Robert A. 1980. "White Indentured Servitude and the Atlantic Slave Trade." *Negro History Bulletin.* Vol. 43, no. 1. Jan-March. pp. 20-22.

Chinweizu. 1987. *The West and the Rest of Us.* Lagos, Nigeria: Pero Press.

Cleage, Albert B. 1987. *Black Christian Nationalism: New Directions for the Black Church.* Detroit, Michigan: Luxor Publishers of the Pan-African Orthodox Christian Church.

Davidson, Basil. *The African Past: Chronicles from Antiquity to Modern Times.* London: Longman.

______. 1969. "Africans Before Columbus?" *West Africa.* June 7:641.

DeGraft-Johnson, J.C. 1986. *African Glory: The Story of Vanished Negro Civilizations.* Baltimore, Maryland: Black Classic Press.

Ellul, Jacques. 1978. *The Betrayal of the West.* New York, NY: The Seabury Press.

Fisher, Allen G.B. & J. Humphrey. 1971. *Slavery and Muslim Society in Africa.* Garden City, NY: Doubleday and Company Inc.

Forbath, Peter. 1991. *The River Congo.* Boston, Mass: Houghton and Mifflin Company.

Garvey, Amy Jacques. 1971. *Garvey and Garveyism.* New York, NY: Collier Books.

Gates, Henry Louis (ed.). 1987. *The Classic Slave Narratives.* New York, NY: New American Library.

Harding, Vincent. 1983. *There is a River: The Black Struggle for Freedom in America.* New York, NY: Vintage Books.

Hodder-Williams, Richard. 1984. *An Introduction to the Politics of Tropical Africa.* London: George Allen and Unwin.

Hountondji, Paulin. 1990. "Scientific Dependency in Africa Today." *Research in African Literatures*. Vol. 21, no. 3. Fall 1990, pp. 5-15.

Jackson, John G. 1970. *Introduction to African Civilizations*. Secaucus, NJ: The Citadel Press.

James, C.L.R. 1963. *The Black Jacobins*. New York, NY: Vintage Books.

Jordan, Winthrop D. 1974. *The White man's Burden: Historical Origins of Racism in the United States*. Oxford University Press.

King, James C. 1971. *The Biology of Race*. New York, NY: Harcourt Brace Jovanivich, Inc.

Kwawena-Poh, et. al. 1982. *African History in Maps*. Longman.

Lewis, Bernard. 1971. *Race and Color in Islam*. New York, NY: Harper & Row.

Lisizkey, Gene. 1947. *Thomas Jefferson*. New York, NY: The Viking Press.

Lugard, Lady. 1965. *A Tropical Dependency*. New York, NY: Barnes & Nobles.

Masland, Tom et. al. 1992. "Slavery." *Newsweek*. May 4:30-32, 37-39.

Mazrui, Ali A. 1980. *The African Condition*. Cambridge University Press.

______. 1986. *The Africans: A Triple Heritage*. Little, Brown & Company.

McGray, Walter Authur, Rev. 1990. *The Black Presence in the Bible and the Table of Nations, Genesis 10:1-32*. Chicago, IL: Black Light Fellowship.

______. 1990. *The Black Presence in the Bible: Teacher's Guide*. Chicago, IL: Black Light Fellowship.

Miller, Judith. 1992. "The Islamic Wave." *The New York Times Magazine*. May 31:22-26, 38, 40, 42.

Olaniya, Richard (ed.). 1982. *African History and Culture*. Longman, Nigeria, pp. 1-11.

Parker, George. 1995. "Communication by Gun Powder: The British and the Asante Were Much Alike, Except for the Machine Guns." *New York Times Book Review*. 2/12:13.

Snowden, Frank M. 1983. *Before Color Prejudice: The Ancient View of Blacks*. Cambridge, Mass: Harvard University Press.

Stride, G.T., Caroline Ifeka and J.F. Ade Ajayi. 1971. *Peoples and Empires of West Africa: West Africa in History 1000-1800*. New York, NY: Africana Publishing Corporation.

Tischler, Henry L. (ed.). 1990. *Introduction to Sociology*. New York, NY: Holt, Rinehart & Winston, Inc.

Wallbank, T. Walker and Alastair M. Taylor. 1942. *Civilization: Past and Present, Vol. 1*. New York, NY: Scott, Foresman and Company.

Williams, Chancellor. 1974. *The Destruction of Black Civilization: Great Issues of a Race From 4500 B.C. to 2000 A.D.* Chicago, IL: Third World Press.

Wiltse, Charles M. (ed.). 1915. *David Walker's Appeal....* New York, NY: Hill & Wang.

Wright, Robert. 1996. "Science and Original Sin." *Time*. Oct 28:76-77.

# Chapter IV:

## The Origins and Development of Pan-Africanism

> Pan-Africanism had its origins as a movement of intellectual protest against ill-treatment of blacks all over the world. It was initiated by the blacks of America and the West Indies whose ancestors came from Africa. In the words of Professor George Shepperson 'Pan-Africanism was a gift of the New World of America to the Old World of Africa.' It was an expression of the feelings of the people of African stock about their condition of helplessness and degradation.
>
> (S. O. Arifalo, 1982)

### Some other definitions:

Pan-Africanism is the emotional, cultural, psychological, and ideological movement that began among the African diaspora in the Western hemisphere, for a closer unity of purpose, so that African people could feel secure, attain political, economic as well as psychological power, visa vis other races or world regions. The defeat of Africans on the African continent, the humiliating treatment of African people on the Caribbean Islands, in Latin America and the United States, etc., all went to convince the African diaspora of its utter powerlessness. As an ideological movement, African people believed that the marshaling of their energies, industries, and the sheer number of the scattered people of the African connection could be a phenomenon with which to reckon. It was culturally easy to see that Europeans and Euro-Americans were cultural cousins, or brothers and sisters, who left the African as the distant junior half-brother or sister, who had been left up country, in the village, tilling the soil. He needed to be brought up in the ways of the West, the city, or the metropol. He could be a Christian, but not worship with his white brothers and sisters. His women, mothers and sisters, etc., could be had by the white master at any time of the day, but he could not protect or rescue them, much less know a white woman as Adam knew Eve; he could be shot down, lynched, or castrated but he could not have a gun or other means of defense; he could be preached to but was to be kept illiterate about the Bible from which the sermon was given; he could be acted upon but not act in anyway disrespectful in the American wilderness in which he was in bondage; he had no rights that the Euro-American could respect!

Pan-Africanism then is a psychological response to powerlessness and a desire to act upon the environment in which Africans found themselves, rather than remain the ones being acted upon without any meaningful resistance. It was the psychological desire to have a nation Africans could call their own that gave the Pan-African movement a fundamental ingredient that most African people could identify with in the various world regions and stations in life. Psychologically, African people in the West and Africa became victims of Western domination and were at times forced out, or alienated from the white man's political system or world view. As a group of people barred from the white man's higher places in the United States, the Caribbean Islands, South America, Africa, and elsewhere, a certain racial consciousness began to emerge in the early 1900s that caught the attention of the 'talented tenth' on the continents of Europe, America, and Africa. As early as the 1800s Toussaint L'Ouverture, David Walker, and others began to address African people's international conditions (James, 1963; Wiltse, 1915).

Those who espouse the cultural aspects of Pan-Africanism are convinced that African people, wherever they are, have a common, cultural substratum that distinguishes them from, especially, the Europeans. African people tend to have an affinity to simplicity, ruralness, humanism, expressive art, the extended family, and eclecticism in religious concerns, which are not highly differentiated from the other human concerns, such as marriage, sex, and procreation (Mbiti, 1969; Kenyatta, 1965). In music, literature, and the other arts, African people have exhibited their uniqueness and humaneness in, for an instance, Cubism. Contemporary African-American writers, for another instance, have always had a place for Africa in their works. This cultural Pan-Africanism (negritudism) recognizes an African substratum over and around which have been built Westernisms and modern Africanisms or syncretism.

Continental Pan-Africanists such as Nkrumah (1973:276-309) insist on the continental political unity of Africa in a union government in which all the islands surrounding Africa are included, and the Sahara does not remain as a barrier. "I am not saying that we should spurn foreign trade and reject foreign investment," wrote Nkrumah (288); "what I am saying is that we should get together, think together, plan together, and organize one African economy as a unit, and negotiate our overseas economic relations as part of our general continental economic planning." Even though continental Pan-Africanism would unmask a lot of ideological, racial, and religious tensions, it cannot be simply dismissed as too bombastic (*Africa Research Bulletin*, 1994:11889-11890).

While continental Pan-Africanists would de-emphasize racism and other parochialisms, Pan-Negroists or Sub-Saharan Pan-Africanists are, privately, if not publicly, disturbed about the competition between Pan-Arabism and Pan-Africanism, not only in terms of the Arabic membership in the Organization of African Unity, but also because of the history of discord between Black Africa and the Arabic world. Furthermore, in light of the fact of Israel's historic connection with former Apartheid South Africa, some Black African countries's relationships with Israel and/or South Africa, etc., all could unearth, perhaps, unpleasant relationships between North Africa and the other Africa, south of the Sahara. In his seminal essay, "On the Concept Of We Are All Africans," Mazrui (1971:42-58) attempts to grapple with the concepts of the geographical, racial, and perceptual Africanism. Do North Africans see themselves as Africans as Ghanaians do? What are some of the differences between the feeling of being in Africa and of being African? Was Gabel Nasser as African as Kwame Nkrumah? Could the two have claimed to be equally African? And if they could not, therefore, what? Similar questions cannot be asked of the New Englander and the Southerner of the United States of America, because even though they may be geographically different, they are at least not too culturally, linguistically, racially or religiously different.

As there are continental, sub-Saharan, and cultural Pan-Africanists so also are those who favor regional Pan-Africanism. In regional Pan-Africanism, North, West, East, Central and Southern Africa are viewed as 'rational' units that should pursue the integration of their respective units with the sublime notion that these regional groupings would eventually converge into some form of larger unity. The danger with regional Pan-Africanism might be that the various regions, in their integration process, could become 'unique' and therefore resistant to other forms of larger unities. Would ECOWAS dismantle its organizational apparatus for a larger union with SADCC (South African Development Co-ordination Committee), the Arab League, or the Union of South Africa? Even though regional organizational uniqueness does not in itself preclude compromise, it could deter continental unity, for as nations look at other nations as unique (them) so could African regions regard each other suspiciously. Furthermore, regional groupings could be based on linguistic affinity: French West

Africa; Arabic North Africa; British West Africa; French Equatorial Africa; Lusophone Africa, etc., which could go to complicate the process of a larger African integration. Are French speaking Africans going to be forever suspicious of English and Portuguese speaking Africans? What institutional, financial, and constitutional changes do the various African linguistic groups need to make to mitigate antagonistic differences and suspicions?

According to Nkrumah (1972:87) Africans on the continent and the African diaspora belong to the African nation. This African nation includes a feeling that non-Africans could never have or experience. Elsewhere (Jennings, 1973:142), Nkrumah is said to have remarked that

> In meeting fellow Africans from all parts of the continent, I am constantly impressed by how much we have in common. It is not just our colonial past, or the fact that we have aims in common, it is something which goes far deeper. I can best describe it as a sense of oneness in that we are all Africans.

In this paradigm, Africans are implied to have certain uniqueness about them that goes beyond the Western imprints on Africa and Africans to a substratum of feelings that cannot be quantified. These feelings include an image of oneself in this cosmos that steers one into one direction and not the other. It is this African personality to be one's truest self in a complex of views, ideas, and personalities, to be true to one's ancestors and Islam, at one and the same time that perhaps sets Africans apart. Furthermore, the European, Eric Ashby (1964:3), states that "at the core of an African's loyalty lie his extended family and his tribe. Outside this core his loyalty extends far beyond the frontiers of his nation; it covers the Black African people, their oral traditions and religions, their dance and music, their liberation from foreign control, and their ultimate political unity." But does this political unity include the Diaspora, and in what respects? How would African unity affect the African Diaspora?

Other writers on African culture, economics, politics, and society all seem to be inclined to submit that Africans have a common set of problems that they, as Africans, must solve on their own; Western countries and their global financial institutions and international experts could help, but Africans must do for themselves what no other can do for them. This consciousness on the part of the Africans in the Diaspora compelled them to look toward Africa. As the West had failed them, Africa must not fail them; if the Arabs had failed them, Africans must not fail Africans; and if the whole world looked down on Africans, then Africans must develop, industrialize, and create a powerful state and vigorous institutions based on commerce, science, organization, and industry to elevate the African masses from starvation, illiteracy, malnutrition, ignorance, and from most of the other ramifications of poverty and powerlessness (Garvey, 1971:24).

As it could be deduced, Pan-Africanism is a multifaceted, eclectic, and trans-continental phenomenon that emerged because of the forced and massive dislocation of African people into the West. Prior to African people's Western dispersion, they had had expansive empires and had also had extensive connections with Southern Europe, Asia, and South America (Van Sertima, 1976; Harris, 1971; 1976). However, none of these prior contacts came anywhere close to the massive depopulation of the African continent as a result of the Triangular Slave Trade. Indeed, it could be argued that the Atlantic slave trade deprived Africa (deGraft-Johnson, 1986:153) of its young, the healthiest, and the most active element of the African population. This active element of the African population did not take its dispersals lying down (Harding, 1983); from their African homeland, they began to fight for their liberations, educations, economic, social and political developments.

## From Pan-Negroism to Pan-Africanism

According to deGraft-Johnson (1986:99), "...Mansa Musa was the man who came nearest to building a united West Africa. ...(for) such were the affairs of West Africa at that time (in the early 1300s) that, whether you lived in the Gambia, Sierra Leone, the Ivory Coast, the Gold Coast, Togoland, Dahomey, or Nigeria, you could not help but feel the power and strength of the Mali Empire, the empire which sought to fuse all West Africa into one whole." Other attempts by several African leaders included similar approaches at governing a host of African communities over an expansive geographic area. At certain points during the ancient Nile Civilizations, Egypt and the Sudan were governed as a unit. The name Ethiopia once referred to a more extensive area than that of modern day Ethiopia. Furthermore, Shaka Zulu's attempts to expand his domain to include other African people clearly demonstrates an expansive idea. Samori Touré's attempts to extend and hold to his Mandigo empire against the French were culturally and geographically expansive and could be used as early examples of regional Pan-Africanism in which an African people attempted to 'colonize' and bring into their fold other African people.

The twentieth-century Pan-Africanism, however, began with the Atlantic slave trade. The Saharan slave trade had brought various Africans together before as domestic servants to wealthy Arabs as concubines or soldiers for Arabic and Roman generals, but the Atlantic slave trade was unique. Harding (1983:4) states that contemporary Pan-Africanism actually began among Africans on the West African beaches and the slave ships that transported them to the so-called New World; on the beaches of West Africa and on the ships loaded for the Western

Hemisphere were "Bambara, Malinka, Fon, Dinka, Ewe, Bakongo, Ibo, Yoruba, and hundreds more. In many places, it was probably necessary to break through all the real and fancied barriers of each particular geographic, tribal, and national history represented in these first confused and unlikely Pan-African assemblies." Outwitted by the white man's technology (Gates, 1987:39), the various Africans could not help but graduate from being Mandikas, or Ewes, etc., to become Africans. The Africans, "...an alien, non-Christian, non-white people, (were) easily... identifiable" as totally unlike the European (Harding, 1983:8). The Africans who were, until perhaps before their capture, Mandigo, Fulbeh, Yoruba, etc., became the 'Africans'; their names were changed from Kamara and Kwame to Francis or Johnson, to Peter or Tobey. Attempts were made to denigrate their African background, religion, customs, family life and even their concept of beauty. As properties they could be sold, lynched, castrated, bred, and worked from sun-up to sun-down with impunity; they were mules to be worked and 'dis-Africanized' by the Euro-Americans in the Western Hemisphere.

The more the Europeans attempted to literally 'kill' Africa in the minds of the African slaves, however, the more it seemed the Africans held firmly to the salient characteristics of their African homeland. Africa could not be obliterated from their mental, psychological, emotional, cultural, and religious repertoires. Kunta Kinte reluctantly accepted Tobey, but he never forgot from whence he was abducted; Africa could not be obliterated in him and, following the footsteps of the West African groits, he transmitted his knowledge to his off-springs (Haley, 1977). As late as the 1900s, African-American visitors to Africa still observed cultural similarities between them and the native Africans; they continue to recognize the cultural and psychological similarities that transcend micro-nationalism, geographic and linguistic differences. Africans and African-Americans will continue to be different from the European and the European-American in fundamental ways. Asante and Asante (1983:X) observe on one occasion that African people, globally, immediately acknowledge certain basic similarities amongst themselves:

> Our similarities and commonalities were obvious once those of us who had been colonized by France, England, Portugal, Spain, and Belgium could get beyond our language differences. What evolved during the discussions was the centrality of origin and struggle in the African world view. Africans from the New World met the continentals and saw themselves. We gathered from Brazil, Venezuela, Colombia, Cuba, and North America and immediately built cultural kinship with Africans from the African continent. There was a cultural

> authenticity among the 500 representatives to the colloquium from sixty-seven nations.

Thus, even though the West attempted to 'erase' Africa from the repertoire of the African descents in the United States and elsewhere, African people retained the most crucial idiosyncrasies of their African homeland in terms of their desires for freedom, to attain a nation they could call their own, a land of their own, leadership, and an unrestricted creativity in the arts. In religion, they named their churches African or Ethiopian Churches into which they transported their African extended family system, the syndrome of caring for the needy, elders, and hospitality to visitors and strangers, the African call-and response tradition, the traditional African emphasis on the 'word', oratory, and orature.

In the minds of the African descents Africa was the center, and must be freed from foreign control and be ruled by African people. Therefore, one of the greatest aims of Toussaint L'Ouverture was to go back to Africa, free it from Western domination, and make out of it a great nation. In the words of C.L.R. James (1963:265):

> ...While (Toussaint L'Ouverture) was loaded with the cares of government he cherished a project of sailing to Africa with arms, ammunition, and a thousand of his best soldiers, and there conquering vast tracks of country, putting an end to the slave trade, and making millions of blacks 'free and French' as his constitution had made the blacks in San Domingo. It was no dream. He had sent millions of Francs to America to wait for the day he would be ready. He was already 55. What spirit was it that moved him?

The spirit that moved Toussaint L'Ouverture was the same spirit that was to later move a host of other African nationalists determined to free Africa from colonialism, neo-colonialism, and Apartheid. It was that spirit that moved Alexander Crumwell (1819-1898) to a advocate, for instance, that "...the enlightened sons of Africa wrest..." the continent from ruin (Crumwell, 1860:70), and David Walker, Henry Sylvester Williams, George Padmore, W.E.B. DuBois, Ras Makonnen, Kwame Nkrumah, and others to demand that Africa and African people be developed in terms of economic, political, technological, and social institutional modernization, so that African people would constitute an ineluctable part of the global system.

In the truest form of Pan-Negroism, David Walker's *Appeal to the Colored Citizens of the World* (1829) examined the historic global conditions of Black people, especially of those in the United States. He observed four major contradictions between the American Declaration of

Independence and the continued enslavement of African people in America. He deplored Thomas Jefferson's support of the enslavement of Africans and saw the American system of slavery as the most abominable in world history. David Walker wished that his appeal would be read by all colored men, women, and children, even though he noted the rampant illiteracy and ignorance among his brethren. Nonetheless, Walker envisioned a world-wide unity of Black people against slavery, ignorance, and the exploitation of Blacks. Though Walker's appeal was not a call for the establishment of a black nation, it addressed some of the fundamental issues that still afflict African people. He stressed the need for the proper education of Blacks, emphasizing the political, academic, and psychological liberation of African people. The impending global, capitalistic, village does not nullify David Walker's expectations for his African brethren. He could not see what Blacks had done to Europeans for Africans to be so horribly treated by Europeans, collectively. He urged his enslaved brothers to fight for their liberation or remain in bondage forever. In the early 1800s, David Walker was seen as a radical, and a price was offered for his head. The mysterious death of David Walker in 1829 illustrated the Euro-American determination to keep Blacks in their assigned place of servitude, but the fact that Walker even spoke at all made all the difference: his appeal intimidated the status-quo and illustrated the continuation of the Black struggle for freedom (Harding, 1983); it brought out a global (common) desire of Blacks for the achievement of universal manhood/peoplehood with particular emphasis on the elimination of the negative effects of Western education, religion, the colonization plan, and compulsory ignorance (Walker, 1829). Unlike some contemporary Black writers intimidated by Blackness (Appiah, 1992), David Walker recognized the universal plight of Black people and therefore their special duty to do for themselves what others should not do for them; cognizant of the threats on his life, he did what he thought he must for his people, come what may; though he was not as much of a religious man as Alexander Crumwell (1819-1898), David Walker was religiously inspired to write on behalf of his brethren in bondage.

The emancipation of African slaves after the American Civil War did not dampen the desire on the part of some African-Americans to advocate for the development of Africa, their ancestral homeland. Moses (1975:229-51) and Uya (1971:63-71) illustrate Crumwell's religious attitudes toward Africa and Africans and his solemn desire to see Africa Christianized, educated, and civilized. To regenerate Africa spiritually and materially, to improve the conditions of African natives in the African interior, to build schools and send missionaries to Africa and to establish trade and commerce between the United States and Africa (not unlike that advocated by Gustavus Vassa earlier), were some of Crumwell's greatest concerns about Africa and African people in the United States. Like Henry McNeal Turner, Crumwell viewed that Black emigration to Africa would be one solution to America's racial problems. In Africa, furthermore, Black people could have their own state, government, and could establish a respectable power to which the younger generations of Blacks would look for inspiration.

While some African descents advocated that Blacks return to evangelize, civilize, and modernize Africa (Blyden, 1888), a good number of African-Americans remained ambivalent toward Africa; they wished to remain in the United States wherein they could cast their own lot, a United States to which they had already contributed by fighting for it in wars against outsiders as well as insiders. The promises of the Reconstruction period had created some aspirations that the United States could be relied upon; the emerging Black middle-class could at least provide a Black leadership that could also speak on behalf of the downtrodden Black masses. For a brief spell between 1865 and 1877, Black schools and churches proliferated and it seemed that Blacks would be accommodated in the higher offices of the United States. By the 1890s, however, the picture had changed; Jim Crowism became the rule rather than the exception; lynchings intimidated Blacks in the North as well as in the South. Partly because of blatant racism in the South and promises of easy employment and a good life in the North, an exodus of Southern Blacks to the U.S. Northern cities and states took place; they came to Northern states and cities enmasse with the hope that the 'promised land' would indeed be kind to them. Thus, by the 1920s, the cities of New York, Chicago, Detroit, and others could boast of dense Black populations. The gestations of Toussaint L'Ouverture, Alexander Crumwell, David Walker, Henry Turner, etc., about the regeneration of Africa began to become more focused and more publicly articulated.

## Black Cultural Nationalism and Pan-African Nationalism:

By the early 1900s, the African continent had already been carved up, as though it were a cake, by a group of West European colonizers. At the 'famous' Berlin Conference of 1884-85, Britain, France, Portugal, Belgium, Germany, and the others decided for themselves which sections of Africa each could have without deliberation or consultation with those whose lands they had decided to claim. As if the enslavement of Africans had not been enough (had not been brutal enough), the Europeans decided to once more 'rape' Africans in Africa by forcing Africans to produce for the world market, so that Africa continued to be a market for European goods and to take out of Africa mineral resources for the industrialized European nations. Where Africans failed to work on roads, grow palm trees, groundnuts, coffee, tea, maize, or cotton and the like, they were forced, taxed, or exiled from their homelands. By the 1890s, the so-called British Protectorates had been incorporated as Crown colonies of the Queen of England. The remaining pockets of African resistance had been co-opted or contained (Esedebe, 1971:19; Adewoye, 1971:28).

While the African protectorates were being 'annexed' a small group of educated Africans was emerging and challenging discrimination against Africans within the colonial infrastructure. Often articulate, this group of educated Africans (the fortunate few) began to intimidate the colonial system by demanding certain rights for themselves in the colonial civil service and the legislative councils. Members of the National Congress of British West Africa (NCBWA), for an instance,

> ...pressed for the Africanization of the government service, the Sierra Leone National Congress...declared that some of its aims were to ensure the formulation of a government of the people by the people for the people and equal opportunity for all; to preserve the lands of the people and to save the people from any kind of exploitation. (Esedebe, 1971:21)

In the Gold Coast, Nigeria, and Sierra Leone, there was already an anti-colonial feeling among the educated Africans who saw themselves as members of two worlds but masters of neither; whites discriminated against them in the colonial administration, but they (the educated Africans) were not totally sympathetic toward traditional African leadership institutions. By the 1920s this small group of educated Africans had established cultural as well as semi-political institutions of their own to perhaps mitigate their state of alienation or anomie. They were at least educated enough to identify with the promises of the French revolution and the American war of independence from Great Britain; they had models to refer to, or even emulate. They were certainly aware, as journalists, educators, businessmen, lawyers, theologians, etc., that they too were entitled to higher paying jobs, equality, one-man, one-vote, liberty, and fraternity. As colonized Africans, they did not often see these 'liberalisms' extended to them; they then therefore began to agitate within the legal frame of the colonial system to obtain jobs without their color being used against them. As early as the late 1800s, there was already a Pan-African spirit in the lectures of Edward Wylmot Blyden, Caseley Hayford, Africanus Horton and some of the objectives of NCBWA tended to link the non-contiguous British West African territories of Gambia, Sierra Leone, the Gold Coast and Nigeria. In South and Eastern Africa, educated Africans formed cultural and political organizations which later became political parties that demanded independence from Britain, France, Portugal, and South African Europeans.

In America, the West Indies, and Europe, African descents also agitated for the better treatment of African people globally.

> The Chicago Congress on Africa of 1893 may be taken as the beginning of Pan-Africanism as a movement.... Among the participants were Africans and persons of African descent in the New World notably Alexander Crumwell; Yokub Pasha, presumably an Egyptian; Bishop Henry Turner, an ardent advocate of the back-to-Africa movement and founder of the African Methodist Episcopal churches in Sierra Leone and Liberia. (Esedebe, 45)

Other efforts of the African diaspora in the West are well illustrated in the words of Marcus Garvey, who saw Africa as his fatherland that he aimed to develop.

> Africa! Nearly twelve million square miles of it! What a wonderful gift from God! If only he could get his people to appreciate it the way he did, and use it as God predestined. He must! He will fulfill God's purpose. (Garvey, 1971:15)

The efforts of Sylvester Williams (1869-1911) from Trinidad have also been well documented (J.R. Hooker, 1975). Born in an environment that was intimately in tune with Africa and African customs, Williams grew up to be one of the founding fathers of the concept and ideology of Pan-Africanism. Williams' concerns for his African people were highly influenced by the zeitgeist of the late 1800s. He was fifteen years of age when the Berlin Conference 'balkanized' Africa; Cecil Rhodes was taking over Zimbabwe, he named Rhodesia; African Kings were being exiled and the British colonialists in Trinidad seemed bent on suppressing African cultural traditions including drumming. Sylvester Williams' background also illustrates that he was not far removed from Africanisms and African affairs of his day; he could sympathize with the British African colonies of Sierra Leone, the Gold Coast, Nigeria, Rhodesia, etc., with respect to the Europeans' treatment of Africans and African people's desire to oppose colonial domination. In Great Britain, Williams associated closely with African students to further acquaint himself with the conditions of African people in several African countries. He had, by this time, already experienced racism in the United States of America where he had planned to continue his education. In 1897, Williams formed the Pan-African Association which aimed to

> secure Africans and their descendants throughout the world their true civil and political rights, to ameliorate

> the condition of our oppressed brethren in the continents of Africa, America, and other parts of the world, by promoting efforts to secure effective legislation, to encourage our people in educational, industrial, and commercial enterprises, to foster friendly relations between the Caucasian and African races, to organize a bureau, a depository, for collections of authorized writings and statistics relating to our people everywhere, and to raise a fund to be used solely for forwarding these purposes. (Hooker, 1975:23)

Sylvester Williams' Pan-African Association (PAA) also wrote several letters to British colonial authorities including one regarding "...the reinstatement of slavery in South Africa under the leadership of Cecil Rhodes,...women slavery - concubinage of the meanest character..."(27). Williams' PAA's conference of 1900 remains as one of the pioneering efforts of the African diaspora to form a united African front against the exploitation of African people by Europeans. The PAA's 1900 conference mildly opposed colonialism, urged that African people have unity of purpose to see to it that they were humanely treated, and urged a closer relationship between the races in business and commercial interactions.

In retrospect, Williams' PAA's platform was not radical in not advocating African unity and in its continued attempts at making mild appeals to the European colonizers to humanely treat African people, which must have later seemed to have been terribly naive; nonetheless, Mr. Williams' life's work showed his unbending dedication to the upliftment of his people on the three continents of America, Europe, and Africa; he showed himself a non-racialist Pan-Africanist in his choice of a European wife and his strong belief in the integration of the races based on equality and fair play. As a lawyer, he was an advocate of the legislative power to solve social and political problems between the races, even between the colonized and their colonizers.

Mr. Williams' endeavors were not all in vain in the sense that his platform was improved upon and empowered by other sons of Africa who also believed that African people must materialize a unity of purpose. Mr. Marcus Garvey and Dr. W.E.B. DuBois are cases in point. Despite the conflicts between these two men, they both illustrate an undaunted interest in the upliftment of African people on the continents of Africa, America, and Europe. In the long run, both men gave African people a sense of awareness, unity and an unparalleled commitment to Africa which later inspired the commitments of George Padmore and Kwame Nkrumah. W.E.B. DuBois called four Pan-African conferences that continued the tradition of Mr. Sylvester Williams, while Mr. Marcus Garvey's Universal Negro Improvement Association (UNIA) advocated the creation of a large African state, industrialized and powerful enough "to protect us wherever we choose to live" (Garvey 1970:29). The redemption of Africa and African nationalism became the goals of Kwame Nkrumah and George Padmore, the next generation of African people that adamantly advocated African unity.

## A New Generation of Pan-African Nationalists

In addition to the pioneering efforts of Toussaint L'Ouverture, David Walker, Alexander Crumwell, Sylvester Williams, Marcus Garvey, and W.E.B. DuBois, etc., to uplift African people globally, European racism, colonialism, imperialism, and the rising consciousness of African people in Africa all went to reinforce Africans' belief that they too must have nations they could call and run as their own. West Indians and Africans in the European metropoles of the 1920s and the 1930s had organizations established that spoke for the better treatment of African people and condemned racism. In the metropoles, African students and professionals were in intimate contact with European radicals and liberals who did not share the ideology of colonialism. Furthermore, colonialism was by the 1930s becoming too blatantly aggressive and racist so much so that only the most illiterate could not have seen European attempts at complete African humiliation and domination.

In 1935 Italy attacked Ethiopia in her second attempt, in the eyes of African people, to subdue and humiliate one of the only two African nations to have resisted white colonialism that far. Some writers state that Liberia could also have been considered an independent African country at that time; in reality, Liberia could also have been considered as much of a colony of Americo-Liberians as any of the British African colonies of Sierra Leone, Gold Coast, Nigeria and Gambia. It should therefore not have qualified as a 'free' African nation. Ironically, the African descents from America who were supposed to take Western civilization to Africa ended up practically enslaving the Liberian natives. The Americo-Liberians transported from America the political ideology, racism, intra-racism, religious, and educational ideas of the United States as the Creoles of Sierra Leone had transported British institutions and ideas and transplanted them into that other African soil.

Nonetheless, the Italian invasion of Ethiopia in 1935 was a global event in the evolution of the ideas, feelings and sentiments of Pan-Africanism. The invasion was seen by African people as a threat to the safety of all Africans wherever they were. The only nation that African people could rightly claim to have been truly beyond Western domination was then being humiliated by Italy which had signed a treaty of friendship with Ethiopia in 1928. The then young emperor, Haile Selassie, gave one of the greatest speeches in history to the

League of Nations in which he challenged the then members of the free world to listen to their consciences; however, it all seemed concluded that the African race was to be dominated by the European; that, where the African was involved, Europeans stuck together as a group to defend their own interests. After all, had they not already divided Africa amongst themselves, dominated South Africa and the black aboriginals of Australia and the Dravidians of India? Thus, in the African mind, the Italian invasion of Ethiopia was a threat to all African people, a telling force to Africans that in European eyes African liberty was not respected. Even though some Europeans denounced Mussolini's fascism, the pro-fascists within the League of Nations were much more powerful than the anti-fascists (Davison, 1989:60).

> The brutal rape of Ethiopia combined with the cynical attitude of the great powers convinced Africans and peoples of African descent everywhere that black men had no rights which white men felt bound to respect.... Not only did the Western powers turn a deaf ear to the Emperor's appeal to the League of Nations for help, but actually connived at Mussolini's gassing of defenseless Ethiopians by selling oil to the dictator. With the realization of their utter defenselessness against the new aggression from Europeans in Africa, the blacks felt it necessary to look to themselves. (Padmore, 1972:123-124)

Educated blacks everywhere were not blinded to the fact that their responsibilities must include fighting for political independence from a Europe that seemed to have the express purpose of dominating non-white peoples in Europe, Asia, Africa, the Americas, and the tropical islands.

The Italian invasion of Ethiopia in 1935 greatly affected Kwame Nkrumah, who was then enroute to Lincoln University, Pennsylvania, U.S.A.; it was then he vowed that he would work for Africa's redemption (Nkrumah, 1957:22). Born in 1909 in Nkroful, Ghana, Nkrumah's resourcefulness had quickly manifested itself. He became a teacher at a relatively young age and began to organize people into study and professional groups. His student days in the United States were financially difficult, but he was able to organize African students, teach, and at the same time read widely and published articles on African culture and education. Some people would probably think of Nkrumah as a natural leader in that whether he was in Ghana, the U.S.A., or Britain, he organized or participated in leading African people to study or examine themselves in their historical and social contexts. From his philosophical readings of Karl Marx, Mazzini, Lenin, Hegal, and Marcus Garvey, he was able to formulate his own ideas relative to the

African revolution. In his *Towards Colonial Freedom* (1962), *Consciencism...* (1970), *Neo-Colonialism: The Last Stage of Imperialism* (1965), *Africa Must Unite* (1963), and other publications, he submitted his views on Pan-Africanism and Africa's relationship to global capitalism.

After ten years of toil, study, teaching and organizing in the United States, Nkrumah went to London in 1945 with the intention to continue his education in law. London was conducive for Nkrumah's academic and organizational temperaments. Rather than pursue his legal studies, however, he became actively involved in meetings, conferences, and organizations relative to the African colonial question. He was particularly active in the West African Student's Union (WASU) of which he became Vice President.

The London of 1945 was vulnerable to political agitations. Radical Europeans were sympathetic to Marxism relative to the colonial question and monopoly capitalism; the radical, articulate and prolific West Indian writer, George Padmore, saw eye to eye with Kwame Nkrumah; East Africa's Jomo Kenyatta, South America's Ras Makonnen, South Africa's Peter Abrahams, and other African political and intellectual aspirants took advantage of the anti-colonial zeitgeist of the 1940s. West European colonial powers had been weakened by World War II and greatly depended on Africa and the United States for agricultural, financial, and technical assistance to rebuild their infrastructure (Feit, 1968:183). Europe's apparent weaknesses gave courage to Asian and African colonials to demand their own liberations; if they could fight to liberate their colonial masters from the threat of German racism (Nazism), they could also demand their own freedoms. Furthermore, the then U.S.S.R. provided an alternative path to national development, other than those of Western Europe and the American models. As India, Ceylon, Burma, and Pakistan agitated for political independence, they also provided a model for other subjugated peoples in Africa and the Caribbean region.

African ex-servicemen had also 'seen' Europe and had had 'intimate' experiences with European soldiers and women and had come to the conclusion that Europeans were at least not too different in terms of bravery and manhood. In Africa, however, European administrators and their wives and children still carried themselves as too far superior to the African natives; they worked in offices and directed a slew of Africans with the snap of their fingers; their wives hired domestic hands to cook, launder, and all Africans were at their beck and call. The mystic that surrounded the white man in Africa was shattered as African soldiers, students, and professionals became 'fully' acquainted with the European in European cities and in the battlefield. Bildad Kaggia (1975:44-45) was one of the Kenyan ex-servicemen who returned to his native land with a new attitude relative to the European; the ex-serviceman relates some of his experiences thus:

> Our stay in the U.K. was enjoyable and peaceful. Although most of us had many other friends, we valued the friendships among ourselves, because we reminded one another of home. Most of the African soldiers were my friends and looked up to me. Besides Aaron and Tipappe, who were especially close friends, my relations with Sgt. Kawesa of Uganda and Sgt. Hayub of Arusha were very friendly.
>
> One night my storeman, Edward, brought a girl into the camp who refused to leave in the morning. When I came into the office I found Edward looking very gloomy. He said there was a girl in his quarters in the adjoining room. After many questions he told me the whole story of what went on the night before. I went with him and begged the girl to leave. She refused to move, claiming that she could not bear to leave Edward. As all our appeals failed, and I did not want Edward to get into trouble, we agreed to move the girl to other quarters where she would not be easily detected.
>
> *During this incident I realized how different the British police were from the colonial police in Kenya. These gentlemen spent hours trying to persuade the girl to come out. The girl only sneered at them. They did not want to force her. They did not succeed, however, until they threatened to call in the military police, who would mis-handle her, they said. She gave herself over to the civil police who led her away without further incident.*
>
> In a village near Newcastle called Silverdale I found a family who were very friendly to me and to the other East Africans. Mr. and Mrs. Evans introduced me to English life. Mr. Evans and his elder son John worked in the mines. *The Evanses were different from all the Englishmen I had met before. I was used to the bossy D.C.'s and settlers at home. I had known mostly arrogant and rude army officers who had no sympathy for African advancement. The Evans family was different. They toiled in the coal-pits during the day, and at home they did not have a single servant. Mrs. Evans did everything at home, just like my mother. As workers, they were very close to Africans. They were friendly and understanding, and I found them willing and sympathetic listeners.* They wanted to know about East Africa, and especially about Kenya.
>
> *They were surprised and indignant to hear about how their own government was oppressing Africans. This was news to them.* At that time the majority of English people believed that their government in the African

> colonies was a benevolent one which 'worked very hard to uplift the African'. *They felt ashamed to hear that the main task of 'their' government was to exploit Africa and to do everything possible to keep Africans poor and backward.*
>
> Mr. Evans belonged to a non-conformist church known as the Assemblies of God. He was touched by the conditions in Kenya and made a habit of praying for Kenya in their gatherings. Soon, the congregation wanted to hear about Kenya, and I was introduced to the church. After my first address I was invited to speak to one after another of their churches in the district.

In Western Africa, Ghanaian ex-servicemen had too had close encounters with the European in Europe. An articulate set of African students and intellectuals had also observed that the European society was not in perfect order; there were various social classes, poverty, manual laborers, homelessness, semi-literate and illiterate Europeans the African colonials were 'unaware' of in the colonies, where the colonial administrators worked in offices, as foremen, and directed scores of African laborers; Europeans were never perceived as cabbage collectors or street sweepers in Europe. In Africa, the European had numerous servants to do the dirty work and he lived on the hill, away from his subjects, in the European quarters. If he wished to visit the hinterlands where roads had not been constructed under his direction, he had 'muscular' African men take him in a hammug to his destination up-country. For African students and others to come to Europe and see some Europeans at the poorest level of society was an eye opener, an 'Aha' experience for colonized Africans. As William Conton (1960:45) notes, in his fiction *The African*,

> The sight of white people enmasse was itself something which required some getting used to; but the thing that took us really aback was our first sight of a white man sweeping a gutter. ...and actually standing right down in the gutter sweeping it, collecting the rubbish.... We stood in utter disbelief.... 'Thank God for bringing me here,' breathed Appiah reverently.... 'I always suspected there was some good reason for my coming to Britain.'

Albert Memmi (1991:11) also observed that the European colonizer was a different creature in his own country and a totally different one in his African colony; in the latter he must exploit, but not transform for he is in Africa to "invest only what will bear fruit in his time" (69). In Nigeria one European could lord it over 54,000 Africans without any fear for his life (Hodder-Williams, 1984:27).

It was into this intellectual and cultural zeitgeist that Nkrumah, George Padmore, and other African nationalists found themselves in England in 1945. In cognizance of the Sylvester Williams' 1900 Pan-African conference and the four W.E.B. DuBois Pan-African conferences, the 1945 Pan-African congress convened by George Padmore, Nkrumah and their African nationalist colleagues was radically different and took advantage of the weakened colonial powers. The fight against Hitler's racism was linked to the fight against West European colonial domination in Africa, Asia, and elsewhere. If Hitler's attempt at world domination was not to be tolerated, European domination of non-Europeans should also not be tolerated. The Atlantic Charter, signed by Churchill and Roosevelt in 1941, though not intended for African nations, inadvertently encouraged African people to declare that they too should rule themselves; if the Atlantic Charter was good for West Europeans, it must also be for Africans who were then being ruled from without, by the same Europeans declaring that all peoples should have the right to choose the form of government under which they wished to live. In signing the Atlantic Charter, Roosevelt and Churchill had 'inadvertently' aided the colonialized peoples of the world. Certainly, the Charter must include all people regardless of race, nationality or colonial status. To interpret the Charter in any other way, such as that it applied only to European persons, was in itself racist, and blatantly vexatious; educated colonials then began to outspokenly question the duration of colonialization. For some colonialists it was not unreasonable that as soon as the war was over, African countries should be given internal self-government, there be a stoppage to forced labor and the implementation of universal suffrage.

The ideas of educated West Africans such as Edward Blyden, James Africanus Horton, Caseley Hayford, and others were in vogue and concerned the unification of British West Africa so that there could be produced an African 'personality' sympathetic to African conditions. Irrespective of their degrees, experiences, and competencies, educated Africans felt the brunt of European racism in the colonies as well as in the metropoles, from having it difficult to getting a lodging in England to the actual refusal of promoting Africans to higher administrative positions in the colonial service. Furthermore, though Europeans somehow knew that they would someday lose their colonies, they were not prepared in the 1940s to be asked to leave Africa for Africans themselves to rule. To the European colonial masters, Africans had not yet been sufficiently prepared for parliamentary democracy and needed to be in the colonial fold until they had matured for leadership. The sentiments of the League of Nations that Africans still needed to be 'tutored' must have still been in vogue to some Europeans (Spiro, 1962:18).

Assembled in Manchester, England, an elite African nationalists formed the Pan-African Federation in 1944; the federation recruited its membership from the various local African organizations then in existence in England. Some of these pro-African organizations such as Harold Moody's League of Colored People (LCP) were conservative and reconciliatory, but most were overtly anti-Western and in a hurry to see to it that Africa was ruled by Africans themselves. The Fifth Pan-African Congress was dominated by the radical group, headed by George Padmore and Kwame Nkrumah and others who later became heads of African states or top civil servants in the independent African states of the 1960s through the late 1970s, and even later.

The resolutions of the Fifth Pan-African Congress of 1945 were anti-imperialist and demanded African independence by force, if necessary. It abandoned the conciliatory strategies of Sylvester William's 1900 platform and those of W.E.B. DuBois' of the early 1900s. Partly because of the weaknesses of Western Europe after World War II, the Fifth Pan-African Congress was bold enough to demand the dismantling of the colonial system, repudiated racism and classism, and urged the unity of especially the colonials to organize against imperialistic domination of the non-Western people and the working classes of all nationalities. To achieve independence, the African elites were urged to organize the masses and employ 'positive action' to gain their independence. Nkrumah defined 'positive action' as the unmitigated surge to gain independence by the use of all the legal means at the disposal of subject people; strikes, the radio, boycotts, mass rallies, and newspapers were to be employed whenever expedient. Nationalistic political parties were to be encouraged in every African country with the ultimate goal of gaining independence within the shortest possible time, from the point of view of the subject people. Unlike the other Pan-African Conferences and Congresses of Mr. Williams and W.E.B. DuBois, the 1945 Pan-African Congress united African intellectuals, labor union leaders, and African workers of varying qualifications and socioeconomic status. Furthermore, the Fifth Pan-African Congress was the springboard that propelled Pan-Africanism into the African continent through George Padmore and Kwame Nkrumah to be later joined by the famed W.E.B. DuBois, who had earlier opposed Marcus Garvey's back-to-Africa movement as bombastic. Ironically, it was he, not Garvey, who finally migrated to Africa and helped in the 'redemption' of his fatherland.

**Pan-Africanism in Africa:**

With Kwame Nkrumah in the then Gold Coast, Pan-Africanism was planted in Africa in earnest. The son of African peasants, Nkrumah, from his childhood to his death was an organizer, social and political activist (Nkrumah, 1957; 1968). Coming directly from the African "bush" (Nkroful), he was more in tune with traditional African values as compared to the coastal, urbanized Africans who had been in contact with the European's educational, legal, trade, and colonial institutions as early as the 1600s. Eight years of Catholic education prepared Nkrumah enough to be a primary school teacher at the age of seventeen. At Achimota College, he founded the Aggrey Student Society as a platform for debates; as a teacher at Elmina after Achimota College, he organized the Teachers' Association, and at Axim the Nzima Literature Society. These early experiences as an organizer became part and parcel of Nkrumah's life story. In the United States, he lectured, preached, and helped to form organizations in the interest of Africa, in addition to his regular studies and other personal interests.

Through Nkrumah's readings of Marx, Lenin, Marcus Garvey and other philosophers, he educated himself broadly and dedicated his life to maximize the realizations of Marcus Garvey's dream for a powerful and industrialized Africa. In England in 1945, Kwame Nkrumah was in the very good company of George Padmore and other African nationalists dedicated to the redemption of Africa. Like others before them, including Edward Blyden, Caseley Hayford, and Africanus Horton, Nkrumah and Padmore envisioned, at the least, a united West Africa.

It was therefore a well-prepared politician who was called upon to join the United Gold Coast Convention (UGCC) party in 1947 as the publicity secretary. Not inadvertently, Pan-Africanism by that very invitation was planted on African soil, taken from the diaspora, the originators of Pan-Negroism, Negritude and Pan-Africanism. Only now, Pan-Africanism in Nkrumah's hands transcended pleading to colonial masters for the better treatment of the African elites and natives to one acknowledging African people, globally, as belonging to the African nation, to mobilizing for African independence, the consolidation of that independence, the achievement of a United States of Africa for the economic, social, cultural, and the industrial transformation of the African continent, and thereby the empowerment of African people whenever they are.

For Nkrumah, there was no turning back or shrinking away from the goal of African unity. When he saw that UGCC was timorous about Gold Coast independence within 'the shortest possible time', he broke away and formed his own Convention People's Party (CPP). Using positive action, he antagonized the colonial administration and members of the UGCC; none, however, was able to interrupt the tide of Nkrumahism. Threatened and imprisoned, Nkrumah was bent on seeing the Gold Coast independent. His election as minister of Government Business in 1951 did not fool him into acquiescence with the colonial administration. In 1957, the Gold Coast became Ghana under Nkrumah's leadership, but the independence of Ghana was meaningless, as Nkrumah himself aptly put it, if it was not at the same time 'linked up with the independence of other African countries'. "Before Nkrumah", writes Thompson (1969:76), "even Ethiopians, Egyptians, and Somalis did not conceive themselves as Africans in the sense in which Ghanaians or Malians are...." Ghana's independence was the Black star that stirred the imaginations of a host of African leaders and statesmen to be combatant about the independence of their respective territories. To some African countries such as Liberia, Nkrumah was a threat to the Americo-Liberians who had ruled the aboriginal Africans, practically, as colonial subjects. To some French African leaders such as Felix Boigny and Blaise Diange, Nkrumahism must have been antagonistic to their pro-French sentiments, as opposed to that of Ahmed Sekou Touré, who opted for immediate independence from France and refused to be integrated fully into France's neo-colonialistic paradigm of 1958. Generally, the 'Frenchified' African elites were more concerned about their cultural, economic, linguistic, and political attachments to metropolitan France than to their English-speaking African counterparts. Most of the 1950s and 1960s French African elites had risen to levels of distinctions in the French government and, as such, saw and felt less need to negate themselves from their cultural 'benefactors.' Blaise Diange, a Senegalese cabinet minister in the French government, is noted to have opposed Marcus Garvey's platform in the former's desires "to remain French" (103).

As Black French men (Mumford, 1970), a good number of colonialized French Africans, such as Leopold Senghor, opted for Negritude, the cultural or artistic arm of Pan-Africanism. But these distractions were not going to prevent Kwame Nkrumah and the other Anglo-Africans from espousing their concept of the African personality and Pan-Africanism. Nkrumah was the first to practice practical Pan-Africanism in 1958 in aiding Ahmed Sekou Touré of Guinea to recover from the desertion of Guinea by French teachers, technicians, and administrators in retaliation to Guinea's refusal to be a satellite of metropolitan France. In the same year (1958) Kwame Nkrumah called two major conferences in Ghana that irrevocably planted Pan-Africanism in African politics and society.

## Pan Africanism at the Tower of Babel in Africa

Who would today refute that a united Africa, with one government, one citizenship, one currency, one foreign policy, a high military command, an integrated economy, a Pan-African educational system, a continental supreme court, a common industrial plan, etc., are not in Africa's interest? In the face of global capitalism, who would today argue that Nkrumahism is too bombastic for Africa? Furthermore, why was Nkrumah's platform for African unity diluted in Addis Ababa to produce the Organization of African Unity (OAU) charter of 1963? To a certain extent, what did the failure of Nkrumahism mean for Africa? It is to these set questions that the rest of this chapter now turns.

As we've already alluded, Nkrumah's two Pan-African conferences in 1958, in Accra, Ghana, were continuations of the Pan-African protest against Western domination of African people in Africa and in the Diaspora. Nkrumah knew that Ghana, the first black African nation south of the Sahara to attain political independence, was a bright star, an example which other African countries could imitate, or even emulate. Therefore, Nkrumah spared no time after Ghana's independence in 1957 to call upon his African brethren assembled in Accra to do all they must for the speedy liberation of their own territories. "Nkrumah described the African revolution as proceeding in four stages: the achievement of independence, its consolidation, the attainment of political union, the economic and social reconstruction of Africa" (Sklar, 1967:3). The first stage in Nkrumah's paradigm might have been attained, but not the last three. Indeed, by the end of the 1960s, most of the African nations were politically free. In Algeria, it took an all-out warfare to get the French to give in; in Kenya, Mau Mau assaults were effective enough for the British to yield; in Nigeria, Sierra Leone, the Gambia, and elsewhere constitutional means were followed to attain independence; for the Portuguese colonies of Guinea-Bissau, Angola and Mozambique, a long drawn guerrilla warfare was necessary to oust the first European colonialists in Africa out of Africa. As more African countries obtained political independence (17 countries in 1960 alone), the ideology of Pan-Africanism became muggy. If Africa was to unite, when should this come about? Was Kwame Nkrumah in a hurry to expect immediate African unity? Should African leaders give up their newly acquired sovereignties for a larger, continental, unitary political system? Who is to lead this new continental government? Are the Arab, North African countries willing to join such a unitary government? Would the Western powers permit such a large group of ex-colonials to have, immediately, the economic and political power that Africa intended? These, and a lot more questions, contributed to the state of confusion over Pan-Africanism in the 1960s.

The question of when 'Africa must unite' was indeed a vexing one; Nkrumah advocated an immediate unity as soon as the other African countries had attained their political independence, before they had entrenched their balkanized, nationalistic identities, such as the sentiment that 'we are Ugandans, and they, over there, are Tanzanians', in the stead of 'we are all Africans', or even 'we are all east Africans.' Furthermore, should the separate, liberated African nations (artificial nations) first attempt to consolidate (nation-build) their new nations before attempting to join a larger group of the other nations in, say, the East African Community, the Organization of African States of Ghana-

Guinea and Mali, or the Franco-phone community? The temperamental unity between Ghana, Guinea, and Mali did not last long, neither did the East African Community; it seemed that each newly independent African nation was bent on propagating its new identity, not giving that up to a larger group of African nations in the name of 'we are all Africans.' Even though 'African unity' was on the lips of most of the Africans and their leaders, no date for a united Africa could be set because the new African leaders (moderates and radicals alike) and the non-African interests of the West would not allow it. Ambitious African leaders did not want to submit their newly acquired powers to another African leader of more ability, charisma, and/or of a different ideological orientation. Thus, as soon as the Pan-African idea moved into Africa in the late 1950s, dissensions from the radical brand of the ideology emerged. The April-May 1958 meeting of the eight independent African nations in Accra, Ghana, emphasized co-operation between African nations, not complete African unity; in December of the same year, Nkrumah convened another meeting of political party leaders from the African countries then still under colonial rule, but there were no representatives from the French African Rassemblement Democratique Africaine (RDA), or the Northern Nigerian People's Party (NNP). At this latter meeting, Nkrumah warned against western interference in African affairs and urged the African leaders present to organize themselves for the speedy liberation of their respective territories and suggested African unity after all the African nations had been freed. In 1959, Nkrumah, Touré, and Keita, leaders of Ghana, Guinea and Mali respectively, formed the nucleus of 'the union of African states'; but by this time, however, other ideas concerning African unity was already on the table. A turn of events came when William Tubman of Liberia invited both Sekou Touré and Kwame Nkrumah to Sanniquellie, Liberia, to propose his own brand of African unity. While Modibo Keita, Sekou Touré, and Kwame Nkrumah proposed a complete African unity with common citizenship, common foreign policy, common defense, a union bank and a union flag, William Tubman, a moderate, submitted that there should instead be (ASA), an 'Associated States of Africa' (Esedebe, 1982:202). In a sense, William Tubman, an Americo-Liberian, might have been expressing North American political and economic interests. After all, Americo-Liberians had functioned "as the local (African) intermediaries of foreign enterprise" (Davidson, 1974:84). In Liberia, they had negated themselves from the African natives, some of whom they had even used practically as slaves. Furthermore, Mr. Tubman must have felt left out in Pan-African politics, having been a leader of a 'free' African nation, second only to Ethiopia, since 1944; why had it not been Mr. Tubman to have championed African liberation until Ghana came to be in 1957, until Nkrumah came to be Minister of Government Business in 1951,

Prime Minister in 1952? What could have Mr. Tubman being waiting for? What could have been going through his mind regarding the other African nations that were colonies of Britain, France, Spain, Germany, and Portugal? Nonetheless, Mr. Tubman seemed to have also being speaking for a host of other moderate African nations in Sanniquellie in 1959. Haile Selassie of Ethiopia, Abubakar Tafawa Balewa of Nigeria, Sir Milton Margai of Sierra Leone, and Julius Nyerere of Tanzania all quickly fell into the moderate camp. Julius Nyerere, son of a tribal African chief, attested that he had "...learned to be 'moderate' through observing...the Europeans" (Italiander, 1961:85). Compared to these men then, the Nkrumahs, the Keitas, and the Lumumbas were radicals, moving too fast in trying to achieve their dreams of a united Africa.

Mr. Tubman must have also felt threatened by Nkrumah's categorization of certain African leaders as puppets of western imperialist countries, who were willing and even content to hold fast to their neo-colonial positions as selected political, not economic, leaders of their artificial states. Kwame Nkrumah's Marxist-Leninist language did not also earn him many friends from the western countries to which he sold Ghana's mono-crop-cocoa; he also needed the west and the U.S. in particular, for financial and technical assistance. In addition, the Osagyefo's vehement denunciations of the then Apartheid South African regime must have been unsettling to a host of western countries and their corporate leaders in that region of the continent; Nkrumah's ideological affinity with Prime Minister Lumumba of the former Belgium Congo must have too been seen as an unholy alliance of two African radicals by western multi-national mineral diggers in that rich, central African nation. Thus, before the 1963 Addis Ababa OAU charter, there was already a deep division between African leaders as to the nature of African unity. Mr. Tubman's concept of the Association of African States seemed to have been the one favored by the majority of African leaders; it was this moderate brand that came to be endorsed in the 'Lagos Charter' of 1962, from which the Ghanaians and the north Africans absented themselves.

The competition for continental African leadership had emerged with the independence of Nigeria in 1960; Ghana's star place in African affairs, as the first black African nation south of the Sahara to attain its independence, under the Pan-Africanist Nkrumah, was irrevocably challenged. Nkrumah might have been dynamic and charismatic, patriotic and adamant about African unity, but Nigeria was larger, wealthier, moderate, and bent on challenging Ghana's dominance in Pan-African affairs. As the then 'China of Africa', Nigeria was not about to sit idle and allow smaller Ghana dictate to bigger and wealthier Nigeria. Furthermore, the French African countries, led by Felix Biogny of the Ivory Coast, also attained their independence and began to have their own conferences regarding the French African Community.

When the French Africans leaned toward the Nigerian-Liberian position of moderation and co-operation, the radical Pan-Africanists were overwhelmingly outnumbered. Some African leaders began to accuse Nkrumah that "Ghana's demand for immediate union, was a device to make Nkrumah leader of the entire continent" (Esedebe, 1982:207). Colonel A.A. Afrifa, one of the men who couped Nkrumah in 1966, asserted that "the real motive...to quickly and artificially bring this union (government) about (was) so as to make himself (Nkrumah) the president of the (Pan-African) union government" (Afrifa, 1966:113). He goes on to ask: "Could not we see it in the gigantic state house he erected, at the cost of over eight-million pounds of Ghana taxpayers' money, for an eight-day conference of the OAU"? (113).

Thus, Nkrumah's radicalism against colonialism, neo-colonialism, imperialism, the commonwealth, and his advocation of a complete united Africa brought him into conflict not only with the pro-French group of Mr. Felix Biogny, but also with the moderate group led by Nigeria, Liberia and Ethiopia, and some Ghanaian military and police forces (Odetola, 1982:90-91). On the debate over the Congo crisis, it seemed that Nkrumah stood on a lonely road against most of the other African leaders; Nkrumah was also accused of subversiveness in the internal affairs of other African states. When President Sylvanus Olympio of Togo was assassinated in January, 1963, many wondered whether it was not Nkrumah who had been subversive in the internal affairs of his neighbor; after all, had Nkrumah not been desirous of uniting Ghana and Togo, so that the Ewe people of Togo would be Ghanaians? Furthermore, because Nkrumah was perceived as a radical, he therefore must have been a scientific socialist; he himself had written that Pan-Africanism and socialism were intimately interconnected and that the economy of his united Africa will be centrally planned (Nkrumah, 1970:170).

Nkrumah's insistence on Pan-Africanism and socialism as pre-conditions for African development did not sit too well with the oil rich Nigeria that was not about to share its wealth with poor African nations such as Chad, or even Ghana, for that matter. Another reason for Nigeria's opposition to Ghana was the former's "wish to become the industrial heart of Africa. The very possibility of Nigerian economic domination...was perceived as at least one reason for Nkrumah's insistence on immediate continental political union" (Oyo, 1980:573).

Thus, when the thirty Heads of Independent African States met in Addis Ababa, Ethiopia, from May 22nd to May 25th in 1963, Kwame Nkrumah's radical position was directly rejected. It seemed that the Addis Ababa conference was most singularly an anti-Nkrumah conference; that the conference was clearly an anti-Nkrumah conference is depicted in the 'purposes' and 'principles' of the final version of the

OAU Charter that the conference resolved to produce (*Africa Report*, June-1963:9-13).

**The 1963 OAU Charter:**

The 1963 OAU Charter was the "greatest" compromise between two ideologically different African groupings:

> On the one side were the African states who thought that the attainment of political independence was just a minor step in a more basic and revolutionary thrust for African liberation. This group of states advocated an organic political unification of African states. It believed that political independence had little meaning unless it was accompanied by 'economic independence'. Therefore, African states should totally reject neo-colonial links with their former colonial masters and the Western European capitalist states. This school of thought was led by Ghana and Guinea....
>
> On the other side were the African states who based their argument on a quite different premise. They held that because many African states were small and weak they needed assistance from the Western world in order to make economic progress. They advocated a pragmatic approach to African unity beginning with the co-ordination of effort in every field, including foreign affairs, economic development, health and education. They thought African political union to be a utopian goal. Instead of breaking economic ties with the West they wished to reinforce and expand them. (Arifalo, 1982:136)

The first group, the radical group, seemed to have leaned towards the then USSR, the other definitely towards the West. The first group, headed by Nkrumah, insisted on the creation of a continental African government to ensure Africa's political stability and development; "it urged unified action in the areas of defense, foreign policy, economic development," the creation of a common currency, common African citizenship with common obligations (Nkrumah, 1973:278). For Nkrumah, "the artificial divisions of African states (were) too numerous and irrational for real permanent and harmonious settlements to be reached, except within the framework of a continental union" (282). The other African leaders were, in contrast, 'content' with the established colonial boundaries and bent on safeguarding their inherited territories without interference from expansion-prone African leaders such as Nkrumah. Therefore, the 1963 OAU Charter was unmistakably an anti-Nkrumah document; it was, realistically, an organization of

African co-operation, as opposed to the organization of African unity. Indeed, it should have been called The Organization of African States (OAS), after the OAS of the Organization of American States that the 1963 OAU 'imitated.'

The 1963 OAU Charter over-emphasized 'co-operation' and de-emphasized 'unity'; in article two of the charter, 'unity' is used only once while co-operation is used eight times (*Africa Report*, June 1963:12). Number five of article three of the said charter unreservedly condemned "...in all its forms...political assassination as well as...subversive activities on the part of neighboring states or any other state" (12).

As if these warnings to Nkrumah were not enough, article six reiterates that "the member states pledge themselves to observe scrupulously the principles enumerated in article three..." (12), which, as we have seen, concerned the fear of subversion, or interference in the internal affairs of the member states to the charter. Nonetheless, by the 1990s one of Nkrumah's prophecies had already materialized:

> ...until we in Africa are able to establish our own independent currency and financial institutions, we shall continue to be at the mercy of financial arrangements imposed by foreign governments in their own and not in our (own) interest...we will be unable to break the economic pattern of exploitation established in the days of outright colonialism. (Nkrumah, 1973:295)

Indeed, Nkrumah's assertion that without African unity Africans will continue to be manipulated was also realized in the cold war competition between the East and the West. The principle of non-interference in the internal affairs of each of the member states of the Organization of African Unity practically gave a license to a good number of African leaders to make havoc on their citizens, in the name of the sovereignty and territorial integrity of each member state. The Obotes, the Amins and others were practically 'permitted' by the 1963 OAU Charter to slaughter thousands of innocent African peasants who would have gladly seen a United States of Africa. Since the 1963 OAU Charter had no place for a high military command, as Nkrumah had suggested, there was no African army large enough to prevent the Amins of Africa from brutalizing their own people and others, or the coups and counter-coups that proliferated in Africa from the 1960s to the 1990s. The 1963 OAU Charter did also not institute a Pan-African court of Justice; thus the Amins, Bokassas, the Siad Barries, Mengistus, and others could send thousands upon thousands of their fellow Africans to their deaths without accounting for their deeds. Boundary problems, Civil Wars, refugee problems, abuse of human rights, assassination of political leaders and political opponents such as

J.M. Kariuki and Tom Mboya of Kenya, Patrice Lumumba of the former Belgium Congo and countless others took place throughout the African continent, without any means of redress. The 1963 OAU Charter was also ineffective in terms of preventing cessionists from rebalkanizing African countries, or political aspirants disrupting civilian governments with imported weapons from the former USSR or the West, and even from South Africa.

Above all, Africa's failure to unite in the 1960s caused numerous hardships to the African masses, all of which had a lot to do with Africa's general underdevelopment in this global village. Even though Nkrumah's platform was defeated in the 1960s, it has become increasingly clear that Africa must indeed unite. Even Mr. Botha and de Klerk of South Africa came to the inevitable conclusion that "if there is something Africa now needs urgently, it is one voice," and that "if we do what is right...Africa could become one of the most lucrative and fastest expanding markets on the globe" (cited in Wren, 1992:A21). What Mr. Botha and de Klerk said in 1992 was what Nkrumah had been saying from the late 1950s to the early 1970s. The micro-nationalisms that were enshrined in the 1963 OAU Charter undoubtedly impeded Africa's development politically, technologically, economically and socially. The African leaders from the 1960s to the 1990s contributed, in no small measure, to the development of under-development in Africa; the African masses did not benefit much from African independence, in large part, because of the failure of the Pan-African movement that should have united Africa as Nkrumah and a few others had wanted.

## Fruits of African Independence or the Burdens of Freedom

When Frederick Douglass (Douglass, 1968:112) escaped from slavery in 1838, he quickly realized that there was much more to freedom than 'freedom' itself. He no longer had the overseer or master expropriating his hard earned wages and labor, but he then had to find shelter, clothing, friends, economic, and psychological security; he could, in freedom, choose his own friends, change his name and assume an identity independent from his former master; he could die poor, but a free man; he could also prosper as a free man or sink low into economic insecurity and obscurity. As a relatively free man, there were several things he could have done, several paths he could have taken; several things could have also happened to him without the 'protection' of his former owner. He could have been recaptured and sent back to the South to join his brethren in bondage, until 1865.

Luckily for Mr. Frederick Douglass, he was not only talented and motivated to prosper in his freedom, but he also ran into a few good white and black friends. Douglass did something good with his freedom; he did not only free himself, but he also continued to work for the freedom of his brethren in bondage. From bondage, he became a bright shining star (as was Ghana from 1951 to 1966) for the liberation of all oppressed persons, including women.

Such a progressive movement from 'bondage' to freedom cannot be said of most African countries from the late 1950s throughout the 1990s. Ayittey (1993) is completely disappointed by African leaders' political and economic performance record from the 1960s to the 1990s; he catalogues the atrocities of African leaders against their own people for the first thirty-odd years of African independence. The 1960s' African leaders who had formed opposition parties to oust or challenge colonial rule, turned around to deny the same from their own people; the leaders instituted black neo-colonialism over the African masses; they imported the alien ideologies of Marxism and Scientific Socialism in 'disguised' forms, to repress the African masses, opposition parties, and other interest groups and thereby impeded African development. They, who had opposed colonial rule, instituted one-party states and 'eliminated' all opposition parties, groups, individuals, journalists, intellectuals, students, writers, and others who showed any signs of discontent or recalcitrance under the Sekou Tourés, the Amins, Mobutus, Kaundas and the Bandas. These and other black African leaders installed themselves as life-Presidents with minimum or zero economic development in their respective countries; some even sank deeper into debt to International Monetary Fund (IMF), World Bank, and other international financial institutions than during colonial times.

For the African masses (those who cannot participate in Swiss-bank socialism), political freedom did not materialize into economic freedom; there was 'political freedom from the West', but not from Western capitalism, which most of the African leaders of the 1960s had bitterly criticized as contributing, in no small measure, to Africa's political and economic wretchedness. Instead of returning to viable traditional African institutions (Ayittey, 1991), the new African leaders became superficially skeptical about western capitalism and traditional African institutions, much of which they viewed as inappropriate for their own schemes of 'capital flight' and kleptocracisms.

Military and civilian dictatorships characterized African regimes from the 1960s to the 1990s (Ayittey, 1993:166). African peasants became victims of machine guns imported from Asia, Eastern and Western Europe and from even South Africa.

While these black African leaders headed 'quasi-apartheid' regimes, they still had the 'right' to denounce, vehemently, the apartheid of white South Africa, even as they also inflicted countless atrocities in Ethiopia, Uganda, former Zaire, the Central African Republic, Equatorial Guinea, Somalia, Rwanda and Burundi, the Sudan, Liberia, Sierra Leone and others. Whether a civilian or military regime, the

African masses did not pick much fruit from the tree of African independence. In fact, military interventions in African governments, which were supposed to retard the rapacities of civilian governments, added more afflictions on the African masses. When African regimes should have been trimming their military budgets, they instead began to spend more on the military in terms of expensive weapons and manpower. Where the military was supposed to protect civilian governments, they took over those very governments; where the military were expected to be disciplined and efficient, they showed they were not much better than the civilians they purported to have been helping out of office for corruption in Sierra Leone, Liberia, and elsewhere (See Table One).

**Table 1**
**POLITICAL CONFIGURATION OF AFRICA BY 1990**

***1.MILITARY DICTATORSHIPS (years of military rule/years of (independence)***

| BRUTALLY REPRESSIVE | VERYREPRESSIVE |
|---|---|
| Benin (27/30) | Burunadi (25/28) |
| Burkina Fasso (20/30) | Congo-Brazzaville (12/30) |
| *Ethiopia (16/--) | Equitorial Guinea (11/22) |
| Ghana (20/33) | Guinea-Bissau (10/16) |
| *Liberia (10/--) | Guinea (7/32) |
| Mauritania (12/30) | Lesotho (7/24) |
| Libya (21/30) | Niger (16/30) |
| *Somalia (21/30) | Rwanda (17/28) |
| Sudan (27/34) | Togoland (27/30) |
| Uganda (15/28) | Zaire (25/30) |

**REPRESSIVE**
Central African Republic (9/30)
*Chad (15/30)
*Mali (22/30)
Nigeria (20/30)
Gabon (23/30)

SUBTOTAL: 25

***2. CIVILIAN DICTATORSHIPS (years of one-party rule/years of independence)***

**BRUTALLY REPRESSIVE**
*Angola (15/15)
Comoros (14/14)
Malawi (26/26)
Mozambique (15/15)
Zimbabwe (10/10)

**VERY REPRESSIVE**
Cameroon (30/30)
*Cape Verde Islands (15/15)
Madagascar (18/30)
Kenya (27/27)
*Sao Tome & Principe (15/15)
Tanzania (29/29)
Tunisia (34/34)
Zambia (26/26)

**REPRESSIVE**
Algeria (28/28)
Coted'Ivoire (30/30)
Djibouti (13/13)
Egypt (20/--)
Seychelles (13/14)
Sierra Leone (29/29)

SUBTOTAL: 19

**MONARCHICAL RULE**
Morocco
Swaziland

**WHITES-ONLY RULE**
*Namibia
South Africa

**INDIGENOUSLY AFRICAN (CONSENSUAL DEMOCRACY)**
Botswana
Senegal
Mauritius
The Gambia

***Notes:***
1. Asterisks indicate countries where changes in government occurred in 1990-1991.
2. Reunion (a French island off Madagascar) and Western Sahara (under Moroccan rule) have been excluded.

*SOURCE OF TABLE I: George B.N. Ayittey. Africa Betrayed. New York: St. Martin's Press, 1993, p. 116.*

Explicitly, African military and civilian regimes further deepened Africa's economic crisis by increasing expenditures on weapons to kill their own people, outdistancing expenditures on education and social services.

> During the 1970s arms importation by African countries grew faster than any other region in the world, doubling between 1970-77. Since the beginning of the 1980s, this trend has trailed off, due as much to the saturation of military inventories as the continent-wide economic crisis. But in most African states, defense still consumed an excessive share of the national budgets, easily outstripping social spending. One million dollars could provide 1,000 classrooms for 30,000 children, and yet it is the cost of a modern tank. The price of a single helicopter is equivalent to the salary of 12,000 schoolteachers. The policy choice of more tanks means less classrooms with inevitable consequences for economic growth and social development....
>
> Theoretically an efficient military institution is an investment. It ensures stability and maintains the stability necessary for economic growth. But all too often in the African setting they are part of the problem. African armies modeled on the Western example, as opposed to Frelimo in Mozambique and the NRA in Uganda, are not productive; they simply consume. There is also a very high probability that the tanks and armored cars bought for the defense of the country's frontiers will be used to surround the radio station for the announcement of a military coup, which is statistically likely to be followed by a countercoup. (Cited in Ayittey, 1993:153-154)

Both military and civilian African regimes (Neo-colonialist regimes) delinked themselves from the African masses, barricading themselves in the ex-residences of their ex-colonial masters, naming streets, bridges, national buildings and other edifices after their leaders of life-presidents. In times of political upheaval, some of these life-presidents 'hopped' the plane to Europe or to a friendly African country, leaving the African masses holding the bag. Setting themselves beyond criticisms, the African leaders from the 1960s to the 1990s repressed 'freedom of speech', journalists, students, academicians, novelists and other cultural agents, some of whom disappeared in dubious car or plane accidents. Thus, the very people that these African leaders were supposed to lead became victims of imported military weapons or reduced to second class citizenship, fit to be segregated in the shanty towns of Nairobi, Abidjan, Freetown, Kampala, Lagos and other African cities and villages across the continent. As Ayittey (117) explains,

> After independence two classes emerged from African society: the elites and the peasants. There were five subgroups within the elite or educated class. The first included professional politicians, represented by head of state, cabinet ministers, party functionaries, and leaders of the opposition parties, if any. The second was the intelligentsia, members of professional bodies, vice-chancellors of universities, university professors, and lawyers. The third was the military. The fourth included bureaucrats-civil servants, and chairmen of public corporations. The final subgroup, the lowest level of elites, included urban workers and secondary school and university students.
>
> Although the peasant class constituted over 95 percent of the population, they exercised no political power. Of the 45 black African countries, only four-Botswana, Mauritius, The Gambia, and Senegal-gave their people the right to choose their leaders, twenty-three were military dictatorships. The rest were 'democracies' where only one candidate ran for president under a one-party system, always won the election, and declared himself president-for-life.

In the bureaucracies of these African leaders, capital flight, ghost workers, fake salaries, payroll fraud, incompetence and kleptomania reigned supreme. Kleptomania might have been officially sanctioned when Mobuto Sese Seko of former Zaire is reported to have 'officially' stated that "if you steal, do not steal too much at a time. You may be arrested. Steal cleverly,...little by little" (cited in Ayittey, 233). Capital flight might have also been sanctioned when the late President, Felix Houphouet-Boigny of the Ivory Coast, is reported to have said: "What sensible man does not keep his assets in Switzerland, the whole world's bank? I would be crazy to sacrifice my children's future in this crazy country without thinking of their future" (Cited in Ayittey, 342). This Switzerland bank euphoria affected the heads of African states, their ministers and top civil servants, including some academicians and intellectuals in haste to be appointed by such African regimes. The "Rapaciousness of the (African) ruling elite" (251) and their 'hideous display of affluence' amidst appalling poverty" (250) make these African leaders not much different from their ex-colonial masters, perhaps even worse.

In actuality, it is not the African masses that are indebted to the IMF, the World Bank and other multinational financiers, but the African leaders whose monies, stashed away abroad, that could radically reduce Africa's external debts; for an instance, Ayittey (243) states that "Kenya would have no foreign debt problem if its citizens returned the capital that they have accumulated abroad." For another example, "The Morgan Guaranty Trust Company estimated that Nigeria's Foreign debt of $32 billion (in the late 1970s) would have been only $7 billion had there been no capital flight" (252).

Africa's economic, political, and even leadership problems, however, are not totally indigenous. Western and Eastern (the then U.S.S.R.'s) input are not infinitesimal. The Cold War between the West and the East, Chinese Communism and Russian Revisionism all had impacts on African disorientation from the mid-1940s up to the end of the 1990s. But, the "externally generated solutions" (208) to Africa's problems did not abate Africa's economic and political "downward spiral" (Sandbrook, 1985:112-144). "Unfortunately," writes Ayittey (117), "there are many difficulties associated with foreign experts who devise these solutions may be sincere to help Africa overcome its problems, but lack an understanding of the complexity of those problems and their interplay with cultural, historical, and political factors" (208).

To make matters worse for Africa, a good number of the educated African leaders of the 1960s could be classified as 'cultural foreigners' in the African context. Educated in Europe, America or in westernized schools in Africa to be mostly teachers, civil servants, theologians, military and policemen (not economists), these leaders were socialized out of the African cultural context, and were no longer "rooted in the traditional culture" (326), nor were they fully accepted in the metropolitan cultures of France, Britain and the United States. Indeed, what would have one expected from Kamuzu Banda who says that "if my people don't want me, I'll go back to London"? (Ayittey, 326). What really would one expect from black Africans educated to be French in all but the color of their skin? (Mumford, 1970). If these African leaders were negated from their traditional African cultures through the process of western education, they were not totally integrated into the metropolitan cultures on account of their 'Africanness.' As such, they were 'simply' intermediaries, marginal men, between their ex-colonial masters and the African masses, those who had not been opportuned to 'evolve' into French, Portuguese, or English men and women. These partially westernized and *dis-Africanized* African leaders opted to enrich themselves at the expense of both the west and the African masses, who do not have the choice or means of whether to go back to London or remain in Blantyre, Malawi.

To try to be fair to the African leaders from the 1960s to the 1990s, it is not unreasonable to note that it is as easy today to criticize these African leaders as it was easy to criticize colonialists from the late 1800s to even the 1970s. It certainly is easy to criticize a government or a leader from afar, outside of the crucible of government in power, a mile or thousands of miles away from the literal competition for scarce resources. One does not know what one might have actually done under Nkrumah or Sekou Touré, inside the government, as a minister of transportation, or of the interior of Ghana, or Guinea. African leaders were certainly confronted with a multitude of problems and pressures that could have gravely challenged any national leader from any region of the globe. African leaders who had been educated in western schools or 'westernization schools' in Africa, with insufficient experience in the administration of complex, global institutions, were suddenly, as it were, propelled, or called upon to lead artificially created Nigeria, Ghana, the former Zaire, Kenya and others with multiple ethnic groups, nations, and cultural orientations. How was the new Nigeria of up to two-hundred ethnic groups to be governed peacefully? How was the Ivory Coast, a new nation of sixty ethnic groups, to be governed as a multiparty state? Indeed, of the two major developmental models 'provided' by the West and the East, which one was more workable in Africa, wholesale, or modified? Was it to be African socialism, Marxism, Capitalism, Humanism, Negritudism, Authenticitism, or some other-isms? With inadequate physical infrastructure, how were African leaders to get their messages across the nation and in what language? Now that they were politically free, how could they have been also economically free from the already developed economies? How were they to improve the intangible resources of their new nations economically and technically tied up to western financial institutions and expertise? For all the African leaders, these problems were real and constituted the burdens of freedom, responsibilities they had to deal with as 'free' men and women.

If these problems confronted the African leaders from the late 1950s to the 1990s, the impending global village of the 21st century, with its enlarged political and economic units of Western Europe, U.S.A.-Canada-Mexico, a strengthened OAS (Organization of American States) and an Asia Pacific Economic Co-operation pose a new set of problems for the present and forthcoming African leaders, the African masses and African-Americans, for sure. It is to these set of issues that we now turn to in the next chapter.

## References: Chapter IV

Adewoye, O. 1971. "Nationalism in Kenya, 1920-1963." *Tarikh*, 4/1:28-40.

*Africa Report*. 1963. 6/9-13.

*African Research Bulletin*. 1994. "Economic Groupings: Casablanca Economic Summit." 31/10(Oct. 16-Nov. 15) pp. 11889-11890.

Afrifa, A.A. 1966. *The Ghana Coup, 24th February 1966*. New York: Humanities Press.

Arifalo, S.A. 1982. "Pan-Africanism and the Organization of African Unity," pp. 127-149, in Richard Olaniyan (ed.). *African History and Culture*. Nigeria: Longman.

Asante, Molefi K. and Kariamu Welsh Molefi Asante. 1993. *African Culture: The Rhythms of Unity*. Trenton, N.J.. Africa World Press, Inc.

Ashby, Eric. 1964. *African Universities and Western Tradition*. Cambridge, Mass: Harvard University Press.

Ayittey, George B.N. 1991. *Indigenous African Institutions*. New York: Transnational Publishers, Inc.

______. 1993. *Africa Betrayed*. New York: St. Martin's Press.

Blyden, Edward. 1994. *Islam, Christianity and the Negro*. Baltimore, Maryland. Black Academic Press.

Bonner, Raymond. 1997. "The Foreign Aid Gamble in Africa." *New York Times*, 6/28: E5.

Conton, William. 1960. *The African*. London: Heinemann.

Crumwell, Alexander. 1962. *The Future of Africa*. New York: Charles C. Ribner.

______. 1860. "The Relations and Duties of Free Colored Men in America to Africa," pp. 63-71, in Okon Edet Uya (ed.). *Black Brotherhood: Afro-Americans and Africa*. Lexington, Mass: D.C. Heath and Company.

Davidson, Basil. 1974. *Can Africa Survive? Arguments Against Growth Without Development*. London: Heinemann.

______. 1989. *Modern Africa: A Social and Political History*. London and New York: Longman.

deGraft-Johnson, J.C. 1986. *African Glory: The Study of Vanished Negro Civilizations*. Baltimore, Maryland: Black Classic Press.

Douglass, Frederick. 1968. *Narrative of the Life of Frederick Douglass*: New York, New York: National American Library.

Esedebe, P. Olisanwuche. 1971. "The Independence Movement in Sierra Leone." *Tarikh*.
Vol. 4, No. 1, pp. 15-27.

______. 1968. *Pan-Africanism: The Idea and Movement 1776-1963*. Washington, D.C.: Harvard University Press.

Feit, Edward. 1968. "Military Coups and Political Development: Some Lessons from Ghana and Nigeria." *World Politics*. XX/2:179-193.

Garvey, Amy Jacques. 1971. *Garvey and Garveyism*. New York, New York: Collier Books.

Gates, Henry Louis, Jr. (ed.). 1987. *The Classic Slave Narratives*. New York, New York: Penguin Books, Inc.

Haley, Alex. 1976. *Roots: The Saga of an American Family*. New York: Dell Publishing Co., Inc.

Harding, Vincent. 1981. *There is a River: The Black Struggle for Freedom in America*. New York: Vintage Books.

Harris, Joseph E. 1987. *Africans and Their History*. New York: New American Library.

______. 1971. *The African Presence in Asia*. Evanston, Illinois: Northwestern University Press.

Hooker, J.R. 1975. *Henry Sylvester Williams: Imperial Pan-Africanist.* London: Rex Collins.

Italiander, Rolf. 1961. *The New Leaders of Africa.* Englewood Cliffs, N.J.: Prentice-Hall.

James, C.L.R. 1963. *Black Jacobins.* New York: Vintage Books.

Jennings, James. 1973. "Pan-Africanism Reconsidered." *Pan-African Journal.* VI/3:321-340.

Kaggia, Bildad. 1975. *Roots of African Freedom 1921-1962.* Nairobi, Kenya: East African Publishing House.

Kenyatta, Jomo. 1965. *Facing Mount Kenya.* New York: Vintage Books.

Mazrui, Ali A. 1971. "On the Concept of 'We Are All Africans,'" pp. 42-58, *Pax-Africana: A Study of Ideology and Ambition.* The University of Chicago Press.

Mbiti, John S. 1970. *African Religions and Philosophy.* New York: Anchor Books.

Memmi, Albert. 1991. *The Colonizer and the Colonized.* Boston, Mass: Beacon Press.

Moses, Wilson J. 1975. "Civilizing Missionary...." *The Journal of Negro History.* 15 12:229-51.

Mumford, W. Bryant. 1970. *Africans Learn to be French.* New York: Negro Universities Press.

Nkrumah, Kwame. 1950. *What I Mean by "Positive Action."* Accra, Ghana: Ministry of Information and Broadcasting.

______. 1957. *Ghana: The Autobiography of Kwame Nkrumah.* Edinburgh: Thomas Nelson and Sons, Ltd.

______. 1962. *Towards Colonial Freedom: Africa in the Struggle Against World Imperialism.* London: Panaf Books, Ltd.

______. 1963. *Africa Must Unite.* London: Heinemann.

______. 1965. *Neo-Colonialism: The Last Stage of Imperialism.* London and Edinburgh: Thomas Nelson and Sons, Ltd.

______. 1970. *Consciencism: Philosophy and Ideology for Decolonization.* New York: Monthly Review Press.

______. 1973. *Revolutionary Path.* New York: International Publishers.

Odetola, T.O. 1982. *Military Regimes and Development: A Comparative Analysis of African States.* London: George Allen and Unwin.

Oyo, Olatunde J.B. 1980. "Nigeria and the Formation of ECOWAS." *International Organization.* 34/4:571-604.

Padmore, George. 1972. *Pan-Africanism or Communism.* New York: Doubleday and Co., Inc.

Sandbrook, Richard. 1985. *The Politics of Africa's Economic Stagnation.* Cambridge University Press.

Sklar, Richard L. 1967. "Political Science and National Integration." *The Journal of Modern Africa Studies.* 5/1:1-11.

Spiro, Herbert J. 1962. *Politics in Africa: Prospects South of the Sahara.* Englewood Cliffs, N.J. Prentice-Hall, Inc.

Thompson, Vincent Bakpetu. 1969. *Africa and Unity: The Evolution of Pan-Africanism.* London and Harlow: Longman.

Uya, Okon Edet (ed.). 1971. *Black Brotherhood: Afro-Americans and Africa.* Lexington, Mass: D.C. Heath and Co.

Van Sertima, Ivan. 1976. *They Came Before Columbus*. New York: Random House.

Wiltse, Charles M. 1915. *David Walker's Appeal*. New York: Hill and Wang.

Wren, Christophers. 1992. "Pretoria Sees a New Unity with Africans." *New York Times*, 4/12:A21.

# Chapter V:

## The Political Economy of African People in the Modern Global Zeitgeist

United (Western) Europe (Hallstein, 1962), 'Greater' China, the emergence of new democracies in the various parts of the world, the demise of authoritarian-centralized form of communism, Japan's global economic and technological advancements, 'the mass enlightenment of people globally' (Heyneman, 1990:29) and their examination of their place within their respective social and the larger global system, etc. constitute the modern global zeitgeist (24). The downfall of Apartheid, the political independence of Namibia, Africa's continued overwhelming poverty and its seeming inability to lift itself up are also some of the major characteristics of the contemporary period. In no small measure, what affects Africa has its ripple effects on African-Americans in the United States of America. As a matter of fact, in the modern global system, whatever affects one constituency of the globe affects all others. As the Atlantic Charter affected the ruled and rulers, so also did the 1955 Bandung Conference, the 1947 Indian and the 1957 Chanaian independence and, to no less degree, even Rosa Park's seeming recalcitrance to give up a front bus seat to a white passenger affected major institutions of the American status-quo and contributed to far fledging changes within the immediate nation as well as without.

African people, more now than ever before, should not only be cognizant of the modern global zeitgeist in Eastern, Central and Western Europe, the United States and Japan, South and Southwest Africa, Iraq and Kuwait, China and Hong Kong, Cuba and Nicaragua, etc., but must also be more than prepared to fit into this ever changing and constricting global system. The 'Asia Pacific Group' (Friedman, 1994), NAFTA (North Atlantic Free Trade Area), and a strengthened

OAS (Organization of American States) must not leave African people in a miasma or inertia.

This chapter examines Africans on the African continent and African-Americans with particular emphasis on Pan-Africanism and Pan-African education. It isolates and examines the four major variables of economics, politics, culture and education, and how these have impacted African people in the global system. Pan-Africanism, and its Pan-African education component, forever insist that even though African-Americans have been in the United States for more than three-hundred years, they remain an African people, and the fact that they remain so illustrates that the American 'melting pot' has refused them essentially because they are Africans and Black (See Chapter Six). That this is so has been shown by African people's experiences in America, including their efforts to migrate to Africa, or change American institutions in their own image. The endeavors of Toussaint L'Overture, Marcus Garvey, Dr. W.E.B. DuBois, Malcolm X, and others too far numerous to enumerate, aimed to see to it that African people are made part of the American and the global system as full members of the human society.

The Black Nationalist movements of the 1960s and 1970s were varied but all attempted to address the old issue of racism and the lack in the decent treatment of African people in Africa as well as in the United States. Essentially, African people demanded that they must be included into this global system not any longer as subjects, but as equal participants. African-Americans demanded more voice and representation in the American political process, schools, workplaces, residential areas and participation in the other American opportunity structures in words and in deeds. However, as pressures from African-Americans went on seemingly unabated in the 1960s, the American system accommodated the most articulate, skilled and the fairly well-educated segment of the Black American society; the 1980s and the 1990s emerged with a large segment of African-Americans as prisoners of the American economy (Wilson, 1987). Crackdowns on drug abusers continue to land a host of African-American men into prisons, depriving their women of potential husbands, a situation which culminates into Black female poverty and further Black family disorganization and other social anomalies associated with poverty in a wealthy social system that benefits in sustaining a pocket of poverty (Rodgers, 1987; Gans, 1977).

Certainly, the mass improvement of the lives of the African-American masses does not really seem to be on the high priority list of the rulers of America. Witness, for instance, the accusations of 'reverse discrimination' on the part of white America as soon as a few African-Americans were opportuned to climb the ladders of the economic and political institutions in the 1970s. Liberals and conservatives were quick to point out the great gains African-Americans had made since the 1960s. There certainly have been Black presidential and vice-presidential candidates, Black senators, mayors and executives in the federal, state, municipal and county governments. But as Walton (1985:264) has shown, "The white man doesn't want to become tainted with something wholly black." And even though African- Americans have been elected and appointed to numerous local, state and federal positions in the United States, the higher up one goes to the seat of power, the fewer Blacks are found. Blacks closer to the presidency are relegated to the "... outer cabinet departments rather than serving in positions as counselors to the president" (264) where political power really lies. Furthermore, Blacks in high positions are often not only 'powerless', but also tend to abstain themselves from issues deemed 'too black.' "In the Reagan Administration" for instance, "black appointees decided that they would not get together and to stay away from working on racial issues. In point of fact they decided to specialize in non-racial matters" (264). Thus, appointed Black American politicians often become part and parcel of the status quo for fear, perhaps, of losing their jobs and other rewards associated with working with the ruling race and class; Black politicians in this category often become apologists or spokespersons for the American system. "Basically, they advance economics and the free-market system as the solution to black problems. Big government and social programs are castigated as twin evils that are destroying the black community, black initiatives and individualism" (266).

In addition to this 'natural' desire on the part of some African-American leaders to advance themselves within the American system, as they should, they are also often co-opted into agreeing with the system as-it-is, irrespective of the system's unpreparedness to address the fundamental economic issues of the African-American masses. Walton (247) further records that "the white man is looking for someone who agrees with him, in part or in whole and that if he can get this, he need not change any of his thinking, he was right all the time, in what he was doing, in what he was thinking, and in what he was preparing to do." And if this process does not work as 'planned', the system then begins "'to give awards, ...promote or ...look out for the children when they finish school,... they have money and positions to use at will'" (248). In this way, the Euro-American selects *his* Black leaders from the African-American group who 'naturally' become spokespersons for the system, and thus "...a splitting (up) of the black leadership" (Berry and Blassingame, 1983:354). The Euro-American power structure then elevates its own type of Black leadership. African-American leaders not so molded are discredited in the public media as well as covertly. Berry and Blassingame write, for instance, that "In 1967, J. Edgar Hoover... ordered his agents 'to expose, disrupt, misdirect, discredit, or otherwise neutralize the activities of Black nationalist, hate type organizations and groupings, their leadership, spokesman, membership, and supporters'" (354).

African-American nationalist movements in the 1960s and the 1970s failed partly due to the fact that the larger system could tolerate only so much change and partly because Africa remained disunited, and could therefore not function as a powerful lever for the Euro-American system to reckon with; the African diaspora could therefore not promote the interests of African-American masses who still remain prisoners of the American economy (Wilson, 1987). Nonetheless, the failure of Black leadership cannot all be blamed on European-Americans bent on protecting their privileged positions. To radically rectify the positions of African-Americans in the macro-American system would involve destabilizing a powerful status-quo which has a vested interest and has the tangible as well as the intangible means to maintain the system as-is. To attempt to change that system from a position of disunity, from a frog perspective (Wright, 1967:5-7), would be folly and inexpedient. Furthermore, Poussaint (1972:64-66) submits ten major factors as obstacles to African-American unity and victory within the macro-American system:

A. The tendency of Black organizations to be preoccupied with form and rules than with functions and programs;
B. Black community's lack of confidence in Black leaders;
C. Deficiencies in Black organizational and leadership skills
D. The projection of self-hatred and feelings of inferiority on the part of the Black masses onto their Black leaders;
E. Legacy of distrust, e.g. who does he think he is?;
F. Black organizations being led by whites, but conversely, who would think of a Black person being chosen/accepted as leader of the American Jewish Federation, for an instance?;
G. Black leaders toeing the militant rhetorical line, but found wanting in practice;
H. Focus on divisions between Blacks rather than on similarities and group needs;
I. Focus on building personality cults rather than focusing on building strong organizations;
J. And African-Americans not realizing that their survival depends upon group strength and not individual strength.

But how could African-Americans be united when Africa remains disunited, when African-Americans are taught to be ashamed of their Africanness, their color, the shape of their noses and the thickness of their lips, and are constantly reminded of Africa's backwardness, fragmentation and inability to develop? (Mazrui, 1986:99-113).

Conversely, how can Africa develop so as to have a positive image in the global context, and so that African-Americans can utilize Africa as a positive reflection of African people? How can Africa modernize so that her sons and daughters in the diaspora do not have to hide their faces to avoid seeing starving Africans on their nation's televisions? To a large measure then, Africa's failure to develop is African-America's failure; Africa's failures to unite, build institutions of its own, in its own image, are also the failures of African-Americans and African people globally.

When in the 1960s several African countries attained political independence, African-Americans correspondingly began to assert and identify themselves with Africa, formed nationalist organizations of their own and demanded that they too be recognized and treated as human beings whose African brothers were members of the United Nations, were presidents, ambassadors and diplomats. Upon Malcolm X's return from Africa, for instance, he formed the Organization of Afro-American Unity (OAAU), patterned after the 1963 Organization of African Unity (OAU). As African nations advocated African unity, so also did African-Americans opted for Afro-American unity. But of singular importance was that Euro-Americans and west Europeans were against the unity of purpose of African people on the continent as well as in the United States (Stockwell, 1978:160; 201). In Africa, those African leaders who were adamant that *Africa Must Unite* (Nkrumah, 1970) were branded unrealistic. Western propaganda against Nkrumah, for instance, was so effective that he was overthrown in 1966, a clear signal for the demise of the radical movement for an African continental union government (Rooney, 1988:169; 210-211). The African leaders could not agree on the radical approach to pan-African unity due to the varying ideological positions, tribalism, micro-nationalism, classism and petty jealousies within the African leadership. Nigeria and Ghana, the then two key players in African affairs, were ideologically antagonistic to each other. Was Ghana to be the star of Africa or was it to be Nigeria? While Nigeria boasted of its size and might, Ghana boasted of its pioneering insights into African liberation; within Nigeria, tribal antagonisms were mounting and culminating into regionalism. "To tell you the truth" writes Aluko (1976:98), "the common people of the north put more confidence in the white man than... in their black southern brothers." Jaja Wachuku and Kojo Botsio, foreign ministers of Nigeria and Ghana respectively, had ideological confrontations in May, 1963, in Addis Ababa, at the founding of OAU, with each arguing for the sort of African unity his respective country wanted; these antagonisms over the nature of African unity were later transferred to the U.N. debates over the Congo crisis and sovereignty (163). The split between Ghana and Nigeria manifested itself in the emergence of two major schools of thought concerning the timing and type of African unity that was to be. In addition to the conservative and radical split, the linguistic, regional and other variables obfuscating complete unity between the African nations surfaced. As we've already seen, the charter of the OAU formed in 1963 clearly favored the conservative African leaders and western powers that disparaged the formation of a powerful African nation. Essentially, the 1963 OAU charter was an anti-Nkrumah document, arising from such myopic allegations as that Nkrumah wanted to be the first president of his proposed African union government. In Kenya, Uganda and Tanzania, the issue over who was to be leader of the promising East African community was one sublime reason for the break-up of the East African Federation. Was the federation to be led by Dr. Nyerere, the proclaimed African socialist, charismatic Mr. Mboya, or Jomo Kenyatta? Where would have this leadership left the Kabaka? Indeed, "The Baganda (were) opposed to federation because they (felt) that it (was) impossible for the Kabaka to defeat such people like Dr. Nyerere ... or Mr. Kenyatta" (*East African Institute of Social Research,* 1963:3). Uganda felt too small and was suspicious of the overwhelming sizes of Kenya and Tanzania in a unified East Africa. The failure of the East African community was not unique in Africa. The Mali and Senegal Federation of June 1960 to August 1960 failed mostly because Modibo Keita of Mali and Senghor of Senegal, both French-Africans, were ideologically suspicious of each other; Keita the Marxist was not a bedfellow of Senghor the pro-French, Negritudist. The Ghana-Guinea-Mali Union; the Greater Maghreb; the United Arab Republic of Egypt and Syria; Ethiopia and Eritrea; the French African Federation; Senegal and Gambia; Sierra Leone, Liberia and Guinea; etc. have all been attempts to integrate various African countries that have not amounted to unions of which one could boast. The 1957 successful case of Ghana and British Togoland, Italian and British Somaliland in 1960, the Cameroons Federation in 1961 and Zanzibar and Tanganyika in 1964 have not culminated into larger regional unions, nor has the Organization of African Unity (OAU) matured into a 'powerful' African organization, or institution. The Economic Community of West African States (ECOWAS) that promised various integrative strategies for the sixteen West African states in 1975, to be achieved in 1990, has not integrated West Africa. In 1983, Nigeria expelled up to two million African aliens, and there have developed within ECOWAS minor groupings aiming at specific forms of unity. Even though monetary union is the long term goal of ECOWAS, there has been the proliferation of different, powerless, currencies. Furthermore, the French African countries within ECOWAS are more linked to each other and to France than they are to English-speaking African countries.

The South African Development Coordination Conference of the nine Black African states of Zambia, Tanzania, Angola, Mozambique, Swaziland, Lesotho, Botswana, Malawi and Zimbabwe has no substantial strategy of its own for economic, social and political integration; in fact, the organization "...relies heavily on the West for underwriting its various projects, including those designed to set up agricultural production" (Tordoff, 1984:238). Certainly, the interference of non-Africans into internal African affairs obfuscate African integration, but to this must be added ideological differences among the African leadership, suspicions between African leaders, different stages of development of the various African countries attempting unity, etc....

Numerous examples of discord between African people and within their organizations could be enumerated, but it could hardly be disputed that Africa should unite in order to provide a power base for Africans globally; Africa's unity and progress will also be the progress of African-Americans. "In a real way," states Randall Robinson for African-Americans (Brit, 1990:46),

> Africa's success will be ours, the Caribbeans will be ours as well. We can't be permanent supplicants, asking people to be fair to us... We have to ensure against their failure to be so with a power base of our own. The fledging connection between black Africans and black Americans is the beginning of a larger unity....

But, impressionistically, for Africa to unite most of the following loyalties must first of all be transcended, partially or wholly:

1. Myopic loyalties to the immediate and the extended family;
2. Clannish interests; for an example, the promotion of tribal alliances and supremacy as well as nepotism over efficacy.
3. Province, district, or state within a given nation;
4. Myopic class interest across tribal and national boundaries;
5. Micro-nationalism and regionalism within the continent;
6. Political ideologies - Marxist vs. others;
7. Anglophone, francophone, or lusophone, etc.;
8. The major religious and racial loyalties within the continent.

Specifically, without African unity, how are Africans and African-Americans to face the future of powerful nations that are regrouping themselves into larger economic and political units? Wayas

(1979:15) was also concerned with African unity and economic development when he asked:

> ... in the absence of ... a continental economic union,... how can Africa best confront the present global economic situation? Can African countries, as individual entities seeking individual interests and advantages, be expected to bargain effectively with the rest of the world in the ensuing struggle for a new economic order? Obviously, the answer is no. African countries must unite more strongly and speak more forcefully with one voice.

In addition to the call for African countries to integrate their economic and political diversities, so as to have greater African voice in the current global zeitgeist, African people in Africa and America must also necessarily synthesize the various cultural influences to which they have been subjected, and must do so Afro-centrically.

Continental Africa's experiences with the Arabs and West Europeans include humiliation, exploitation, dehumanization, hatred and other abominations. The destruction of African civilizations in Egypt and the empires of Ghana, Mali, Songhai, etc. records a history of trials and tribulations, successes and defeats, colonialism, neo-colonialism, and the resurgence of African nationalism of the 1960s. Fundamental to the European and Arabic influences remain traditional Africa, resilient, pervasive and perennial. Mazrui (1986) has termed these major influences on Africa as Africa's triple heritage while Nkrumah (1970:78-79) has called the three broad influences as constituting the African personality, or philosophical consciencism.

The necessity to synthesize these three broad influences in Africa is undoubtedly exigent. North African Arabs and the penetration of their Islamic religion into sub-Saharan Africa can no longer be expected to be subdued, nor can the Arabs subdue non-believers through a jihad. Christianity can no longer be used to denounce non-Christian religious followers as pagans or degenerate animists, for the practitioners of Christianity have long alienated a good number of Africans, in the ways they've acted toward their Black brothers and sisters in Christ. Was it not Christian Portuguese who commenced the Atlantic slave trade and the Islamic Arabs the Trans-Saharan Slave Trade? Furthermore, have not these two people, Europeans and Arabs, denounced Africans as incapably inferior compared to themselves? (Lewis, 1971). Do not the Sudanese Arabs even up-to-date feel superior to the Black African Sudanese? (Wai, 1982:20-26).

The 1960s African 'revolution' changed a lot of negative attitudes toward Black Africa, but the essential history of discord between Africans and Arabs, Africans and Europeans remain intellectually, historically and culturally antagonistic. Until African people fully integrate their economies, politics, cultures and currencies, they will hardly be able to dynamically synthesize the various antagonistic forces that impinge on Africa. Certainly, west Europeans and Arabs imported into Africa some positive aspects of their cultures, religions and institutions, but these have not integrated or developed Africa to any significant degree. Some African scholars would even argue that the European and Arab advent into Africa contributed to Africa's depopulation, the exportation of Africa's natural and human resources for the development of non-African people (Mazrui, 1986:101-105). Whatever the major positive contributions of western Europe and Islamic Asia have been, the masses of African people still remain the most poor, illiterate and underdeveloped globally and suffer the concomitant powerlessness and a depreciated self-image, which are manifested in the sublime attempts of African people globally to negate themselves from some of the major images, symbols, and characteristics of traditional African cultures and contemporary African poverty (110-111).

Various writers on traditional Africa have attempted to glorify the African past. Focusing their examination on rural Africa, these writers have often emphasized the 'classlessness' of traditional Africa, de-emphasizing the exploitative role of Africa's ruling classes of the African masses. Julius Nyerere (1968:338), for instance, argues that:

> Some individuals within the family, and some families within the clan or tribe, could own more than others, but... the social system was such that in time of need it was available to all. Inequalities existed, but they were tempered by comparable family or social responsibilities, and they could never become gross and offensive to the social equality which was at the base of the communal life.

Other African leaders have re-echoed Nyerere's stance on traditional African communitarian nature, and posit that traditional Africa experienced neither class conflict nor the existence of class consciousness. Africa's traditional extended family system, the general closeness of man to man and the expectation of care for all family members, respect for elders, and the care syndrome that pervaded rural Africa (Essan, 1973:205-211), have been examined, hoped for, and exalted as indigenous African values that must remain perennial in African societies. Nonetheless, such desires, hopes and wishes are no durable materials in a dynamic, materialistic human history. With the penetration of Africa by the west and the concomitant development of large urban centers and industries, African societies began to develop stringent stratification of roles. The educated elite, African chiefs, coastal merchants and civil servants in the colonial African bureaucracies emerged as formidable classes to reckon with; thus by the 1950s a small, but powerful, articulate segment of highly, and not-so-highly, educated Africans were in existence in most African countries. Corresponding to the emergence of classes in Africa, other obfuscating factors to African social integration and development became apparent in contemporary African social values and practices. Nkrumah (1972:100), for instance, states that

> our family system actually discourages family heads from saving, for the system, in effect, penalizes the man with initiative in favour of the lazy and weak. The indigent members of the family live upon the more fortunate ones. A praiseworthy and useful practice in our past, more or less stagnant society based on subsistence farming, it acts today as a break upon ambition and drive. At the present time, the man who makes a reasonable living finds his money eaten up by his relatives (and this includes the most extended members reaching to the -nth degree of relationship)....

The Arab/European presence in Africa alongside traditional African values and practices, the emergence of classes, class consciousness and analysis among the African masses constitute the modern zeitgeist in African societies. Kofi Buenor Hadjor (1987) has been so aware of the pervasiveness of African classes that he sees, in contemporary Africa, a class of rulers and a class of the ruled; he explicates in his own words (Hadjor, 1987:65):

> In Africa there are two tribes - the exploiters and the exploited, the rulers and the ruled. The real tribalists of course are the ruling classes, everyone else the victims. In reality, ruling class tribalists are not preoccupied with their ethnic identity. They mix with each other at Western embassy parties. Despite their fervent advocacy of ethnic traditions, they are not in the least inhibited about sending their children to Western schools abroad. In the cities they lead a comfortable Western style life. Ruling class tribalists are drawn from across ethnic lines....

To a certain extent then, class analysis of society has found its way into Africa and has contributed another variable to the perception of the African personality, or the discourse of philosophical consciencism.

In the troubled East as well as in Western capitalist countries, the masses of people are becoming increasingly conscious of their places in society and are willing to challenge systems that were, until a few years ago, thought of as solidly intact. The changes in the former apartheid South Africa, the former U.S.S.R., China and elsewhere are not simply temperamental eruptions, but responses of a mass of people against well-established norms, values and institutions. Traditional African cultures, European and Arabic institutions in Africa cannot remain intact in the face of this global zeitgeist, nor can African-Americans; for as one changes, so must the other. Even Arabic institutions, in Arab countries, must today confront the West for good or ill.

As African culture must synthesize the various major elements that affect and influence it, so also must African-Americans in the United States synthesize *their* cultural components eclectically; to mitigate the cultural inertia of African people globally, to project the African personality and Afrocentricity, African people must be more than clear that the synthesis of the various global cultural elements that impinge upon them as a people is exigent and must be synthesized in their own dear image of themselves first and foremost; for far too long African people have been defined by others not particularly interested in their well-being. African- Americans, for instance, have been referred to as being "...thoroughly Americanized" and "...do not want either a cultural or biological connection to Africa" (Thorp, 1977:19). To the extent to which the African-American has been Americanized is often left out of the paradigm that advocates his 'thorough' Americanization.

In accordance to the African proverb that 'the snail does not leave its shell behind, even in a foreign environment', some scholars have noted 'African Survivals' in the cultural fabric of African-Americans (Herskovitz, 1967; Hale-Benson, 1982). But it was W.E.B. DuBois (1935:5) who first unmistakably unearthed the cultural limbo of the African-American; DuBois states at length that

> After the Egyptian and the Indian, the Greek and the Roman, the Teuton and Mongolian, the Negro is a sort of seventh son, born with a veil, and gifted with second-sight in the American world, - a world which yields him no true self-consciousness, but only sees himself through the revelation of the other world. It is a peculiar consciousness, this double-consciousness, this sense of always looking at one's self through the eyes of others, of measuring one's soul by the tape of a world that looks on in amused contempt and pity. One ever feels his two-ness, - an American, a Negro; two souls, two thoughts, two unreconciled strivings; two warring ideals in one dark body, whose dogged strength alone keeps it from being torn asunder. ...seeking to satisfy two unreconciled ideals... has sent them often wooing

> false gods and invoking false means of salvation, and at times has even seemed about to make them ashamed of themselves. ...the contradiction of two double aim... could only result in making him a poor craftsman, for he had but half a heart in either cause.

The African-American's Negroness, or African-ness, is the one devalued in 'this double-consciousness,' in which Africa is ridiculed, rejected, suppressed and perennially regarded as a badge of inferiority; and as long as Africa remains politically, culturally, economically and technologically backward, the 'African' in the African-American will continue to be ridiculed, rejected, oppressed, perennially regarded as a badge of inferiority and partially integrated into the American 'melting pot' at convenient times and rejected whenever deemed pertinent by the Anglo-Saxon rulers of America.

Following DuBois' lead, more recent scholars have attempted to re-emphasize the bi-cultural nature of African-American culture (Valentine, 1972; Chimezie, 1983, 1984; de Anda, 1984). The major arguments have centered around the extent to which African-American culture is bicultural, different from and or similar to Euro-American culture. In other words, to what extent have African-Americans been able to adapt to Western culture? Those who are highly educated are said to have been thoroughly Americanized in the middle-class sense of the word, even though they often experience status-discrepancy in their professional lives because of their blackness and are forever associated with Africa in the European mind (Cose, 1994; Page, 1986:12-15).

Lower class African-Americans have had it the worst in terms of discrimination, minimal life chances and opportunities to be American in the sense of being able to realize portions of the American dream of 'unmitigated' opportunities for social mobility (Wilson, 1996). In the battlefield as well as in civil life, African-Americans have had to prove their citizenship, manhood, and their loyalty to America more so than any other ethnic group in the United States, simply because they are African descents, Black, and because of Africa's powerlessness in the global context. Recent immigrants to the United States from Western and Eastern Europe, and even from Asia, have been more easily integrated into the American melting pot because they approximate the Anglo-Saxon in culture and skin-color. Furthermore, Japan's current economic and technological triumphs are positively reflected on Japanese-Americans. But even when the African-American is inducted into Euro-American culture in terms of language, conceptual style and problem-solving approach, etc. he/she still must be concerned with his/her physical appearance and characteristics. de Anda (1984:106) details that

> The dissimilarity of physical appearance between individuals in the minority and majority cultures is a self-evident obstacle to the process of bicultural socialization. It appears obvious that pronounced differences, such as those of skin color and distinguishing facial features, are not likely to be easily 'melted' into the mainstream....
>
> Similarities in physical appearance made it easier for the European immigrant to blend into the American populace and, thereby, by privy to an 'insiders' socialization experiences. By contrast, ethnic minorities whose physical appearance is dissimilar, are more likely to experience socialization as pressure exerted upon 'outsiders.' Messages offered to outsiders ('them') in contrast to ('us') are likely to be less complete and initiated less frequently, thereby limiting socialization opportunities....
>
> Because there is generally substantial variation in physical appearance within ethnic groups, a portion of each minority population will be closer in appearance to individuals of the majority culture. These individuals have more mobility within the mainstream culture....

Thus, African-Americans who are dissimilar to Euro-Americans in their standard of beauty, physical characteristics, culture and problem-solving approach, just to take a few examples, have had less mobility into the American mainstream. Blacker African-Americans do not only have racial problems with white America, but also experience intra-racism based on the degree of their skin-color. As de Anda has noted, lighter African-Americans, all things being equal, would have more mobility within the mainstream culture. Despite the 1960s rhetoric that 'Black is beautiful', the truism remains that it is even more 'beautiful' to be Anglo-Saxon in America. It is not surprising therefore that a good number of African-Americans undergo cosmetic surgery on their noses, for example, to approximate one of the major physical characteristics of the Anglo-Saxon ruling race.

To be Black in America has its own unique set of trials and tribulations; to be Black, poor and minimally educated has additional negative badges or syndrome of disadvantages; to be all these and be 'culturally' and racially associated with a disunited, underdeveloped, famine, Aids prone and powerless Africa is to be, in the words of DuBois, "...a sort of seventh son" (DuBois, 1935:5).

> He would not Africanize America, for America has too much to teach the world and Africa. He would not bleach his Negro soul in a flood of white Americanism, for he knows that Negro blood has a message for the world. He simply wishes to make it possible for a man to be both a

> Negro and an American, without being cursed and spit upon by his fellows, without having the doors of opportunity closed roughly on his face. (4)

In addition to the psychological and cultural problems of African Americans in the United States, the entrenchment of classes within the Black race is a further obfuscating factor to African-American racial integration into the American mainstream, especially for those from the lower classes. The concept of the "New Mainstream" (Bennet, 1990:28), which would recruit the most articulate, capable, educated, and 'palatable' members of the African-American ethnic group would undoubtedly leave out the most articulate, capable, educated and uneducated African-American masses and their 'non-palatable' spokespersons. Thus, while the David Dinkins and the Douglas Wilders, etc. might be palatable and are of the reasonable sort, from the point of view of the ruling race, the Farakans and their religious followers are outsiders to the mainstream culture.

In the cultural lives of Africans and African-Americans, then, the need to synthesize the various cultural, religious and ideological influences is not only exigent but also ineluctable, if they are ever to be considered full members of the modern global village. As Africans and African people in the diaspora, they must be tolerant of all sorts of people, for among them are present the major cultural, religious and ideological spectrums in addition to the various shades of color that are included in the African race, not to mention the presence of various races on the African continent. African people, wherever they are, must be imbued with what Asante (1981:78) has termed a "collective cognitive imperative."

For African people to attain a "collective cognitive imperative", however, African continental unity, as espoused by Kwame Nkrumah (1970), is fundamental. Essentially, Nkrumahism advocates an African continental union government with one currency, one foreign policy, a high military command, a continental economic plan and industrialization, and one citizenship. C.L.R. James (1977:104) has also summarized Nkrumahism to include:

> A) The position that every vestige of colonialism be wiped off from every corner of Africa;
> B) The belief in the emancipation of all oppressed peoples and classes in every sector of the globe;
> C) *A union government for all African states*;
> D) *The surrendering of Ghana's sovereignty in the interest of African unity*;
> E) Non-alignment of either to the East or West;
> F) Repudiation of Nuclear Warfare as a modern form of barbarism;
> G) Opposition to the establishment of basis of any kind

of military organization on the continent of Africa;

H) Formation of a non-nuclear club of governments that oppose nuclear warfare and the destruction of humanity;

I) And aid to all freedom fighters in Africa and abroad.

Even some of those who bitterly opposed Nkrumah during the euphoria of the 1960s must now admit that Africa's powerlessness derives from its lack of unity, and that lack in unity has had detrimental effects on African people's image globally. Should Africans remain balkanized into small, widely differently endowed entities, how are they to politically, psychologically, culturally, economically and even scientifically face formidable economic and political blocks such as a united Western Europe, greater Europe and greater North America, a greater South-East Asia, and a greater China?

Undoubtedly, the economic, cultural, political and psychological benefits of African unity are far too numerous to be adequately dealt with here with justice, but it must suffice to reiterate that a balkanized Africa is an Africa of poverty, of international beggars, and an Africa that will continue to be viewed and treated as an unequal member in the global arena and drama of politics, the kind of Africa currently urged to institute western style democracies or receive no aid (Perpes, 1991:10; Bonner, 1997:E5).

It must also suffice to state that the movement for African unity is as old as soon as African nationalists realized in the early 1900s that they too needed powerful political, economic, military and educational institutions to fend for themselves, as other nations and peoples had done, were doing and are still doing.

For example, the spirit that moved Toussaint L'Overture was (as we've seen in the previous chapter) the same spirit that was to later move David Walker, Marcus Garvey, Sylvester Williams, George Padmore, Dr. W.E.B. DuBois, Malcolm X, Kwame Nkrumah and countless others who saw, and others who still see that in African unity lies the salvation of African people, their economic, political and institutional development globally. Though Pan-Africanism developed different tangents and brands, it still represents the highest stage of African nationalism, and Nkrumah's school of thought on African unity remains the most challenging and advanced. Those who viewed his ideas as premature, unrealistic, bombastic, untimely, etc. have now had their own brands since 1963 which have neither developed Africa nor *ameliorated* the conditions of the African masses, but to a large degree, have contributed to their miseries under some of the worst authoritarian African leaders, including Amin, Mobutu, Bokassa, Samuel Doe, etc.

Nonetheless, contemporary boswells of Nkrumah insist on African unity, that is, the economic, political, industrial, monetary and educational unity and development of Africa; they're aware that the enemies of African nationalism, illustrated in their historic oppositions to African people's self-determination from the killing of Toussaint all the way down to the usurpation of Nkrumah himself (Stockwell, 1978:200), would perennially create obstacles to deter African development. If need be, they would even recruit certain African nationals and install them as prime ministers and presidents of balkanized African nations. But a united Europe, Africa's biggest trading and cultural partner, dropping all restrictions on movements of goods and people across their national boundaries and instituting a common European currency, should now demonstrate to Africa's regional groupings that *they* have been postponing the ultimate: complete African political, economic, monetary and other institutional unities, that Africa's very survival lies in complete African integration and unity.

The increase in the number of independent African states in the 1960s and 1970s encouraged African-Americans in the United States to also demand their own human rights at home and were proud to point to the gains Africans on the continent were making, but those gains stopped short in the defeat of Nkrumah's brand of Pan-Africanism which led to stagnation in Africa and its concomitant effects on African-Americans in the diaspora including their psychological dis-association with Africa, depreciated self-image and powerlessness.

Africa's current reliance on international aid is more or less similar to the predicament of welfare recipients in the United States: they get their welfare checks and food stamps, pay their landlords, purchase food from the grocery-store man (who, often, doesn't live in their neighborhood), pay their gas, water and electricity bills, etc., and at the end of the month, they are right back in line to get the next month's check and food stamps and continue their monthly and yearly circle of poverty, inability to invest or buy new technology, house, or educative resources for their offsprings, to whom the culture of disadvantage is handed down. In the meanwhile, however, professionals and semi-professionals in the welfare offices hand down to *their* offsprings syndrome of advantage in terms of saleable skills and therefore their ability to earn middle-class salaries and the concomitant resources that go with the possession of technical and approved social and cultural skills. In this context, one actually wonders about who is helping whom. Nonetheless, despite the 'massive' aids 'given' to Africa from the mid-1950s to the 1980s, the 1990 Worldwatch Institute Report states that about 62% of Africans south of the Sahara lived "... in absolute poverty" in 1989 (Durning, 1990:40). The report goes on to assert that

> The poor are overwhelmingly illiterate. ...The group most plagued by poverty is children. Many of those who survive are physically stunted and mentally impaired as a

> result of chronic hunger during the critical age of six months to two years.(39, 40)

African people should be concerned not only with the present global problems, but also with the future human potential of the next generations of Africans who must produce for Africa's development in the years to come; if these are mostly 'stunted' and 'mentally impaired,' it is behooving that all concerned about African development closely examine Nkrumah's platform for African unity, and to do so with African people's developmental interests at heart.

Despite Western humanitarian contributions to aid African countries from the late 1950s to the 1990s, Africa's economic picture did not improve for the African masses. In addition to Africa's Mobutus, Bokassas and Amins, Western aid to Africa did not stimulate that "...self-sufficiency in food production that (Africa) enjoyed before development assistance was invented and, during the past few decades, has become instead a continent-sized beggar hopelessly dependent on the largesse of outsiders - per-capita food production has fallen in every single year since 1962" (Hancock, 1989:44). Not meaning to sound as an alarmist or pessimist, but to further detail Africa's current economic futility, Hancock (192), goes on to state that the African continent "...has the highest infant mortality rates in the world, the lowest average life-expectancies in the world, the lowest literacy rates, the fewest doctors per head of population, and the fewest children in school" (192). There are even jokes about African poverty:

> ...for example, (there is) the story of the fat man and the thin man that does the rounds during every crisis of hunger: 'you should be ashamed of yourself,' said the fat man to the thin man. 'If a foreigner saw you before he saw anyone else he would think there was a famine here.' 'And if he saw you next,' replied the thin man, 'he would know the reason for the famine.' (177)

In this global village there should really be no need for the fat man to attempt hiding the thin man for their lives are intricately connected. The well-fed African-American and the few fortunate Africans on the continent can't successfully employ fantasy of denial in pretending that all is not so bad with African people, for the statistics on the lives of African people globally illustrate powerlessness and socio-economic underdevelopment, irrespective of the fact that the African continent is far from being poor in terms of mineral wealth, which could be collectively exploited for the development of African people.

Even though Africa's economic development is exigent, Africa should not expect massive technological transfer from the West, at least not in the scale of a Marshall Plan; after all, Africa has been intimately involved with the West for more than four hundred years and there has been no technological transfer for the sole purpose of African development. The technology that Africa needs for rapid economic development will either have to be created by Africans or bought from Western or Eastern Europe, Japan, China, or elsewhere. Africans can create or buy this technology in concert, not as individual entities as they today stand confronting Western Europe and other formidable economic and political units. Kwame Nkrumah's call then for an African common market, a common currency, a continentally planned economy, and the rapid industrialization of Africa is no longer unrealistic, nor was his stance that an injury to one African nation is an injury to all, for in the final analysis, about the only people African people have for their own salvation is themselves; their long history of contact with the West must testify to that impressionism.

That the salvation and development of African people lie in African unity, or in Nkrumah's brand of Pan-Africanism is now abundantly clear. However, this African-continental unity, where the Sahara is no longer a dividing, but a connecting line, where Egypt is no longer in the Middle-East, but in Africa, where Afrikaners will not be driven into the sea, where traditional, European and Islamic Africa are harmonized into a renaissant Africa, etc., must have Pan-African education as an ineluctable constituent of Pan-Africanism. It is not hyperbolic that West European educational systems 'denationalized' the African and attempted, though not totally unsuccessfully, to make him into a European, to make him detest his past and was even taught that he had no past at all (Nkrumah, 1970:49). Christianity and Islam educated Africans to consider those who do not ascribe to these two religions as pagans or kaffirs, and the associated connotations were, and are still not complimentary to animists, agnostics and other African skeptics. Furthermore, the failures of traditional African educational systems illustrate their inadequacies for the contemporary social, political, scientific and economic zeitgeist. In no small measure, traditional African systems of education were tribal systems mostly adequate for tribal stages of development; although some aspects of tribal educational systems remain challenging to the modern zeitgeist (Boateng, 1983: 321-336), they are wholly unable to stop the tide of the need for broader systems of education that call for the transcendence of certain primary alliances. As Pan-Africanism is at present the highest stage of intellectual debate for African development, so also is Pan-African education the system of education that enhances that process of African development. But what is this Pan-African education?

> Pan-African education is the education of Africans for larger, continental African citizenship; this education goes beyond 'education for nation-building' that was so

> adamantly espoused in the 1960s and has led to the intellectual, geographical and psychological balkanization of the African continent. Pan-African education should mitigate racial, tribal, ethnic, religious and geographical boundaries currently entrenching themselves between the peoples of Africa. Pan-African education goes beyond the mere exchange of 'privileged' students between two or more African countries or universities; it calls for the integration of African schools, colleges and universities without regards to race, color, religion or nation in which one happened to be born. (Marah, 1989:255)

Pan-African education calls for the total integration of Africa's educational institutions by Africans from various African countries, where they will be melted into the essence of Pan-Africanism. As "...the purpose of European education is to Europeanize..." (Watson and Farley, 1966:471), and the purpose of American multicultural education is to produce Americans in that multicultural American context, so also must Pan African education Pan-Africanize its students, staff and other workers in Africa's educational institutions. As Nkrumah's Pan-Africanism calls for the total integration of Africa at the macro level, Pan-African education calls for the total integration of Africa's educational institutions at the micro-levels. Furthermore, we have also submitted that Pan-African education advocates:

> (1) the establishment of a Pan-African university as suggested by Haile Seleasie in 1963; (2) that the Pan-African university be established ... in the Central African Republic, where it symbolizes a centripetal force; (3) French and English be the language of instruction in the Pan-African university; (4) that the Pan-African University be a model for other African national universities in terms of the recruitment of staff, student body and other school personnel; (5) that African educational institutions build intensive language institutes where French speakers can learn English within a short period of time and English speakers French; (6) that Africans be trained and educated to be citizens of Africa; (7) that Africans be trained and educated to the economic, social, political, cultural and international realities of Africans and the African continent; (8) that African schools, especially at the levels of higher learning, establish departments of Black American Studies, Caribbean Studies, Latin American Studies, West European Studies, North American Studies, Asian Studies, East European Studies, and (9) that these various departments be conducted with a Pan-African perspective. The curriculum in Pan-African education

> should be Pan-African centered, not European or narrowly nationalistic-centered. (Marah, 1989:259)

Pan-African education is a secular system that will respond to and perpetuate the concept of African unity, implement the ideology of Pan-Africanism practically and could become the nucleus for the establishment of other fundamental institutions for larger African unity and the achievement of complete African integration. Until Pan-African educational institutions are built specifically for the achievement of African unity, the Organization of African Unity will waste millions of its various (internationally impotent) African currencies in vain and continue to ineffectively compete in the world market where individual African currencies are practically worthless, and would continue to be so in the face of integrated Europe, a greater North America, and a greater Asia pacific, not to mention a greater China and Hong Kong!

Pan-African educational institutions would be authentic and are development oriented institutions. They would conduct valuable researches that are currently 'unheard of' and also create political, social, economic, and psychological attitudes that will 'revolutionize' African economics, culture, politics, and social psychology. Pan-African education will abate the psycho-social gaps between the diaspora in the West and those in Africa.

Since schools are the main institutions where boys and girls, whites and blacks, Jews and Gentiles, the beautiful and ugly ones meet, Africa's schools are the starting points for African integration, and with the help of effective and dedicated teachers, administrators, and other school personnel, a Pan-African character can be formed and the balkanized African continent can become a united Africa.

Education only in one African country narrows one's intellectual, cultural, and psychological dimensions. Above all, it confirms the political balkanization of African states and substantiates the entrenchment of nationalistic and provincial sentiments; it confirms the notion that these are Nigerians and those are Ghanaians; these are East and those are West Africans; these are North and those over there are South Africans.

The balkanization of African states promotes the entrenchment of small African communities which feel that they are different, and therefore their problems are different from other African communities, and they begin to see themselves and act in those lights. The people become (are made to become) intimately familiar with mostly their own national heroes of politics, literature, sports and other cultural agents at the expense of other heroes and figures in the other African countries or regions.

It was easy in the 1960s, and it still is not difficult, to blame Europeans for balkanizing Africa. While this remains true, it is even truer that the current African states were thoroughly balkanized by the very African leaders who were outspoken in support of African unity in the 1960s. They further divided Africa into 'self-contained' nations economically, politically, and 'solidified' the boundaries that were set up by Europeans during the scramble for Africa in the late 1800s and the early 1900s.

The balkanization of Africa by Africans themselves is excruciating. In a sense, the Europeans did not balkanize Africa to the extent that Africans themselves have done. For instance, the European settlers in East Africa 'integrated' Kenya, Uganda, and Tanganyika with respect to transportation, communication, educational systems, and the administrative infrastructure. Makerere University College, the then 'Harvard of Africa', produced some of the African nationalists of Kenya, Uganda, and the present-day Tanzania. Makerere served as a regional college in a similar way Fourah Bay College had served as a West African university. William Ponty in Senegal recruited students from most of the other French West African countries. During colonial times, Cameroonians worked in the Ivory Coast and didn't need work permits. The common colonial power could move workers from one African country into another without fear of crossing boundaries. There were many Nigerian traders in Ghana during colonial times, but it was Nkrumah's regime that implemented the Alien Registration Law. Even though Nkrumah himself supported the free movement of African people between African countries, Ghanaians, in general, came to view themselves as Ghanaians first and 'Africans' second, especially during the Cocoa crises when the Ghanaian economy was at one of its more trying stages. The Yorubas in Ghana were viewed as strangers now that Ghana had its own national identity and hero. In times of economic crises, strangers are usually viewed, in part, as responsible for the economic chaos, especially when the strangers are traders and/or occupy high positions in the administration. The belief is that when the strangers are gone, the national economy will improve and at least the citizens will get the jobs. In the cases of Ghana, Uganda, and even Nigeria, this belief has not been substantiated. What has been accomplished is that each African nation has defined itself as an entity on to itself and the process of the entrenchment of each African country's identity is almost complete.

This entrenchment has happened in many ways. As African leaders were talking of African unity in the 1960s, they were also pre-occupied with building national universities in their respective African states. Indeed, it became fashionable for each African leader to build a national university; this subsequently reduced the presence of various African nationalities in one regionally located university. In 1963, Seleasie recommended the establishment of an all-African university, but this didn't and has not materialized.

Regardless of leadership and political ideology, African countries continue to compete with each other in the world market instead of putting up a united front. As they disagree on economic issues, so also do they on political issues, for the two go hand in hand; but the longer Africa remains disunited, the more the poverty of African people globally.

In summary, the masses of Africans and African descents all over the world face similar economic, cultural, political and social conditions. The majority of Africans and African descents are illiterate, inhabit poor housing with backward sanitary conditions; their human resources are not being fully utilized; their natural resources have been and are being exploited for the benefits of the highly developed technological societies and their African agents put in positions of leadership as educators, journalists, social science researchers, military men, and professors in particular African training institutes.

African political and intellectual leaders who have stood for Pan-Africanism and the total upliftment of the black masses have been systematically deposed, discredited, or eliminated by the 'enemies' of African people in collaboration with their African supporters, military and police agents. The names of such positive leaders are far too numerous but a few can be named here: Patrice Lumumba, Malcolm X, Walter Rodney, Amilcar Cabral, J. M. Kariuki, Steve Biko, Dedan Kimathi, Toussant L'Overture, Kwame Nkrumah, etc. Those African political and intellectual leaders who have collaborated with the distracters of African people have been systematically promoted and upheld as the epitome of African leadership.

In the final analysis, Pan-African education is that ineluctable aspect of Pan-Africanism that teaches the African that he must learn to do for himself, not to rely on others, or "...look to some force from without to do for him what he must learn to do for himself" (Woodson, 1972:187). Furthermore, Pan-African education, like Pan-Africanism, advocates the theory that African people in Africa and in the diaspora share a common destiny, a common experience in the global context, and holds that Africa's development and unity would have direct positive ripple effects in the lives of African- Americans. Pan-African education will not only provide more opportunities in Africa to study Africa, but it will also help to mitigate global racialism against Africans and African people wherever they are. In addition, Pan- African education would provide an intellectual, cultural, psychological understanding, stimulate cooperation and integration between Africans, Africans and African-Americans and project the African personality onto the global stage where Africans must speak out from a position of strength, power and authority. As nations gather in groups for a larger stake in the global economy, so also must African people, if they are ever to discontinue being drawers of water and hewers of wood for everyone else. They have to have their own institutions that will integrate the various cultural, technical, economic, educational, and political forces that impinge on them and prepare them to be equal participants in the impending global village.

The twenty-first century should be the "defining moment" (Safire, 1990:20) for Africa and African people; it should be the period in which Africans had better synthesize the various global cultures in Africa and proceed to Africanize the globe as Europe and Japan have Europeanized and Japanized the globe; but for Africa to Africanize the globe, that is, to infuse its own into the stream of world opinion, technology, economy, social and political ideas, with a force commensurate with its potential, it must do so with a united front monetarily, militarily, educationally, economically, etc. Finally, the choice for Africa is hardly between unity or no unity; it is more a question of 'survival' and the propagation of the 'African tribe' as an irrefutable constituent in this impending global village of powerful and technically advanced and consolidated national groupings.

A united Africa does not mean all of Africa's problems will evaporate, but a united Africa could certainly abate the continued significance of racism against African people; it is this theme, then, that we now turn to in chapter six.

## References: Chapter V


Aluko, Olajide. 1976. *Ghana and Nigeria: A Study in Inter-African Discord.* New York: Harper and Row.

Asante, Molefi. 1981. "Black Male and Female Relationships: An Afrocentric Context," pp. 75-82, in Lawrence E. Gary (ed.) *Black Men.* Beverly Hills, CA: Sage Publications.

Bennett, Lerone. 1990. "Inaugurating the Future." *Ebony.* Vol. XLV, No. 6 April: 28.

Berry, Mary Francis and John Blassingame. 1983. *Long Memory: The Black Experience in America.* New York, New York: Oxford University Press.

Boateng, Felix. 1983. "African Traditional Education: A Method of Disseminating Cultural Values." *Journal of Black Studies.* Vol. 3:321-336.

Britt, Donna. 1990. "Randall Robinson Continues to Fight for Africa's Freedom." *Democrat and Chronicle.* Rochester, New York. 20 March: 46.

Chimezie, Amusie. 1984. *Black Culture: Theory and Practice.* Shaker Heights, Ohio: The Keeble Press.

______. 1983. "Afro-centricity and Ethnicity: Definitive Concepts of Culture." *Western Journal of Black Studies.* Vol. 7, No. 4: 216-228.

de Anda, Diane. 1984. "Bicultural Socialization: Factors Affecting the Minority Experience." *Social Work.* March-April: 101-107.

DuBois, W.E.B. 1935. *The Souls of Black Folk.* New York, New York: A.C. McClurg and Co.

Durning, Alan B. 1990. "Ending Poverty," pp. 135-153, in Brown, Lesser R., et. al. *State of the World 1990.* New York: W.W. Norton & Co.

*East African Institute of Social Research.* 1963. "Attitudes of Makerere Students Toward East African Federation." Uganda: EAISR (East African Institute of Social Research).

Esen, Akpan. 1973. "The Care Syndrome: A Resource for Counseling in Africa." *Journal of Negro Education.* 2:205-211.

Farley, D.W. and Watson, T. 1966. "Education in Tanganyika Between the Wars: Attempts to Blend Two Cultures." *The South Atlantic Journal.* Vol. XLV, No. 4: 471-490.

Friedman, Thomas L. 1994. "Asia Pacific Group Has Upbeat Start," *New York Times*, March 21:A10.

Gans, Herbert J. 1977. "The Positive Functions of Poverty," pp. 69-75 in Peter Wickman (ed.) *Readings in Social Problems: Contemporary Perspectives (1977-1978 edition).* New York: Harper & Row, Publishers.

Hadjor, Kofi Buenor. 1987. *On Transforming Africa: Discourse with African Leaders.* Trenton, NJ: Africa World Press, Inc.

Hallstein, Walter. 1962. *United Europe: Challenge and Opportunity.* Cambridge, Mass: Harvard University Press.

Hancock, Graham. 1989. *Lords of Poverty: The Power, Prestige and Corruption of International Aid Business.* New York: The Atlantic Monthly Press.

Herskovitz, Melville J. 1967. *The Myth of the Negro Past.* Boston, MA: Beacon Press.

Heyneman, Stephen H. 1990. "Education in the World Market." *The American School Board Journal.* Vol. 177, No. 3: 28-30.

James, C.L.R. 1977. *Nkrumah and the Ghana Revolution.* Westport, CT: Lawrence Hill and Co.

______. 1963. *The Black Jacobins.* New York: Vintage Books.

Lewis, Bernard. 1971. *Race and Color in Islam.* New York: Harper and Row.

Marah, John, K. 1989. *Pan-African Education: The Last Stage of Educational Developments in Africa.* Lewiston, NY: Edwin Mellen Press.

Mazrui, Ali. 1986. *The Africans: A Triple Heritage.* Boston, MA: Little Brown and Co.

Nkrumah, Kwame. 1970. *Consciencism: Philosophy and Ideology for Decolonization and Development with Particular Reference to the African Revolution.* New York: Monthly Review Press.

______. 1970. *Africa Must Unite.* New York: International Publishers.

Nyerere, Julius. 1968. *Ujamaa: Essays on Socialism.* New York: Oxford University Press.

Perlez, Jane. 1991. "U.S.Reveals Sum of Aid it Withheld from Kenya." *New York Times,* 1/12: 10.

Poussaint, Alvin. 1972. *Why Blacks Kill Blacks.* New York: Emerson Hall.

Rodgers, Harrell R. 1987. "Black Americans and the Feminization of Poverty: The Intervening Effects of Unemployment." *Journal of Black Studies*. Vol. 17, No. 4: 402-417.

Safire, William. 1990. "Those Defining Moments." *New York Times Magazine*. September 23: 20.

Stockwell, John. 1978. *In Search of Enemies*. New York: Norton.

Thorpe, Earl E. 1977. *The Mind of the Negro: An Intellectual History of Afro-Americans*. Westport, CT: Greenwood Press.

Tordoff, William. 1984. *Government and Politics in Africa*. Bloomington, IN: Indiana University Press.

Valentine, Charles A. 1971. "Deficit, Difference, and Bi-cultural Models of Afro-American Behavior." *Harvard Educational Review*. Vol. 41, No. 2: 137-157.

Wai, Dustan M. 1982. "Crisis in North-South Relations." *Africa Report*. March-April: 20-26.

Walton, Hanes Jr. 1985. *Invisible Politics: Black Political Behavior*. Albany, NY: State University of New York Press.

Wayas, Joseph. 1979. *Nigeria's Leadership Role*. London: The MacMillan Press.

Wilson, William Julius. 1987. *The Truly Disadvantaged*. Chicago, IL: University of Chicago Press.

Woodson, Carter Goodwin. 1972. *The Mis-Education of the Negro*. New York: AMS Press.

Wright, Richard. 1967. *White Man, Listen!*. Garden City, NY: Doubleday and Company, Inc.

# Chapter VI:

## The Continued Significance of Race and African People in the Global Village

> The Horrors of Racism are on the rise once again. Almost daily, the newspapers tell of new viciousness abroad or in the streets of our cities by people who have conceived and acted upon a deep distrust and dislike of those who are different from themselves. We did not defend racism with the victory over Hitler and Nazism, nor have we banished it with equal-opportunity laws. Racism is a plague that continues to flourish, poisoning too many interactions and shredding too many communities to be ignored. (Pat Shipman, 1994)

The elite manipulation of the issue of race and crime was illustrated in dramatic fashion by the case of Susan Smith. In October 1994 this 23 year-old White woman from the small town of Union, South Carolina reported that a young Black man had ordered her out of her Mazda at gun point, then drove it away with her two baby sons - 3 year old Michael and 14 month old Alexander - still strapped in the back seat. The community was horrified, and desperate searches for the children were launched. Then, nine days later, Susan Smith admitted that she had, in fact, got out of her car and rolled it into the local lake, deliberately drowning her own children. The young Black man with the gun did not exist.

The Smith case evoked memories not only of old-time racist lynchings but of a 1989 incident in Boston. In that incident, a White man, Charles Stuart, had shot and killed his pregnant wife, Carol, in their car, and blamed

> the murder on a Black carjacker. And again, he was immediately believed; police launched stop and search sweeps through Black housing projects, and even charged a Black man with the murder, before Stuart's story was exposed and he killed himself. (Hadjor, 1995)

Both African and non-African writers have, within the last five decades, amply documented the continued significance of race in the United States in particular and in the global village in general (Gordon Allport 1954; John Howard Griffin, 1976; Ronald Takaki, 1987; Ellis Cose, 1993; Bruce Wright, 1993; David Allen, 1993; Toni Morrison, 1991; Derrick Bell, 1992; Cornell West, 1992; and even the U.S. President, Bill Clinton (*U.S.A. Today,* 1997: 18A). Furthermore, numerous national and international newspapers and magazines have continued the debate about racism against Africans and other non-European peoples. Even though Europeans have made great strides in medicine, science, literature, technocracy, and even technopoly (Postman, 1993), the West has continued to 'disgracefully' keep African people at the periphery of the global village, at a time when "the world is becoming a smaller place. The interactions between peoples of different civilizations are increasing" (Huntington, 1993:23). Would this increasing contact between European and non-European people excercebate ethnic antagonisms, or would greater contact abate antagonistic contradictions between African and non-African people in particular? Is racism against African people a 'temporary' phenomenon, reflecting a stage in the development of a world community or is it perennial?

Since we're not 'prophets' or forecasters, we must rely on what we already know and attempt to see through that veneer and hope for the best; in this chapter we intend merely to 'learn' from some of the authorities who have 'penned' about the issues of race, racism and the continuation of prejudice against African people in the West and elsewhere.

In his seminal essay, "The Clash of Civilizations?", Samuel Huntington (1993:22-49) states that "civilization identity will be(come) increasingly important in the future, and the world will be shaped in large measure by the interactions among seven or eight major civilizations. These include Western, Confucian, Japanese, Islamic, Hindu, Slavic-Orthodox, Latin American and *possibly* African civilization" (25). Modernization and technology are ever increasingly moving people about, 'dislocating' them, as it were, outside their 'tribal' domains into 'outlandish' civilizations, among strangers. And because "...cultural characteristics and differences are less mutable and hence less easily compromised and resolved than political and economic ones" (27), we should expect no easy solutions to the problems of racial and ethnic-cultural conflicts around the globe. In Eastern Europe, Burundi and Rwanda, Mauritania, Canada and the United States, cultural and ethnic antagonisms simmer, and have often erupted at exigent points in time. In Huntington's mind, differences in cultures are going to be the basis for conflict between the various civilization groups.

Conflicts between Africa and the West are not new, at least not to the Africans who have had their cultures and persons denigrated, bastardized, vulgarized and continue to be discriminated against. Gordon W. Allport (1954:107-141), in his classic, *The Nature of Prejudice,* submits several reasons as to the persistence of racism; "there are several reasons," he states, "why-especially in the past 100 years 'race' has become the core for the categorization of ideas about human differences" (107). Mr. Allport goes on to submit that Darwinism, family inheritance, appearance, physical characteristics, the concept of 'blood', and the impact of propaganda about human differences (Herrnstein and Murray, 1994, for example) have kept the argument about racial differences alive in the West and elsewhere (Allport, 107-100). Again, African people have not been unfamiliar with the propaganda about race, or the ideological and 'scientific' arguments against the African race; African people have, for a long time, known that on the scale of Western racial categorization, theirs was put at the bottom with 'brilliant' explanations as to why this should be so. In the United States, some whites have been fascinated about how it actually feels to be black; are black people complaining too much about their treatment in the United States? Are blacks really what the white society thinks of them? Indeed, how does it actually feel to be black in a white dominated society, especially in that of the United States?

John Howard Griffin (1976), a white American journalist, set out to find out in 1959, in Mississippi, Georgia, Alabama, and Louisiana, how he would be treated if he 'disguised' himself as a black man. Even though he received warning that "they are not going to ask you any question. As soon as they see you, you'll be a Negro and that's all they'll ever want to know about you" (10), the 'recalcitrant' Griffin was bent on performing his 'little experiment' about a white man 'passing' for a Black man, incognito. We could certainly critically examine Mr. Griffin's 'scientific' procedure, timing, and method to determine if his experiment was actually useful; couldn't he have learned the lessons he wanted to learn from the 'horse's mouth', from black people themselves? Didn't he already know the things he found out ?

Nonetheless, Mr. Griffin got himself medications to darken his skin to become a "Puerto-Rican or something,... a fierce, bald, very dark Negro" (15), "...a newly created Negro,... the Griffin that was had become invisible," and he "did not like the way (he) looked" (16). He quickly observed that "the lighter the skin the more trustworthy the Negro" (14). He was to observe and experiment more about how blacks were treated in the South in 1959. From early November, 1959 to

December 14th of the same year Mr. Griffin traveled through four Southern States to document his experiences as a 'new' black man. But Mr. Griffin could not have actually felt black as black people feel black, to be born, live, experience, and die black. Mr. Griffin could not actually get rid of his Anglo-American accent, memories about his white wife, white children, and white society; and, he had the full knowledge that he will again emerge as a white man.

Furthermore, a white man living as a black man for about four to six weeks is hardly enough time to feel, think, and see from black African people's point of view, from a life's time of daily experiences of discrimination in schooling, housing, workplace, shopping centers, infinitum. We also note that Mr. Griffin's experiment took place in the winter of 1959 and he could therefore afford the luxury of covering up his arms, legs and other parts normally exposed in the other seasons of the year, when skimpy attires might be in vogue. Could have Mr. Griffin accomplished the same, in, say, the Spring, or Summer? In addition, Mr. Griffin's four to six weeks of experience in four Southern States in the winter of 1959 is hardly representative of the United States at that time or any other; from black people's point of view, Mr. Griffin did not "discover if America was involved in the practice of racism against black Americans" (161); black people have known that since the day they were dispossessed of their homeland. As Mr. Griffin himself disclosed, his experiment did not 'qualify' him to discuss racism in the North (145), or any other place beyond the places he visited at that time of the year, in those four Southern States. In addition to his extensive learning and knowledge about black people as an interested American in black people's predicament, his four to six weeks of experience as a black man made Mr. Griffin into a celebrity (174); but after he was exposed, albeit a target of scorn and hate mails, he became an authority on black people and a whole host of cities called upon him to discuss the American race problem, at the expense of equally knowledgeable black men and women, who could have done the same thing he was called upon to do for city governments desirous of peaceful co-existence between the races.

Mr. Griffin did not attempt, in his disguise, to rent an apartment or buy a house in a white neighborhood, nor did he even think of sending his 'black' children to a 'white' school; he did not also attempt to date a white woman (of some substance) or propose to one. Had he done so, what would have been some of the intricacies that would have confronted him? He did not try to get a bank loan, nor did he attempt an opinion on Africa to his friends, white or black. The people he encountered during his 'experiment' hardly represented a cross-section of the black population of the South in 1959. Had he spoken to some of the faculty members at Tuskegee Institute in the winter of 1959, he might have been told about Kwame Nkrumah of Ghana, West Africa, or Sekou Touré of Guinea of the same region.

What all of these might have done to Mr. Griffin's 'little' experiment could be rightly speculated. Should Mr. Griffin have taken longer to conduct his experiment, say for a full year, so as to attempt to get a fuller grasp of the black condition in 1959-1960? Shouldn't have Mr. Griffin's experiment included many more representatives of the black and white populations, again, to gain a fully insight into American Black-White race problems? Certainly, there are various other questions that any reader of *Black Like Me* would want to ask him or herself relative to the shortcomings of Mr. Griffin's so-called experiment. However, it seems clear that Mr. Griffin did his utmost under the circumstances; he had to keep his hairy hand and his head shaved clean because he could not grow dark curly hair; he had his white wife and white children to return to, and he hated being 'black like me'.

Nonetheless, Mr. Griffin's 'little experiment' provides a unique opportunity (a window) from which to view the pervasiveness of racism, American style, from a disguised white man's point of view. Even though being a prisoner for four to six weeks, all things being equal, would certainly not be as excruciating as a life sentence without parole, Mr. Griffin contributes to the theme of the continuing significance of race in American society. Mr. Griffin 'discovered' for himself that socially, culturally, politically and even sexually, the way things are viewed in the United States is racially tainted. Crime, criminology, the police, sexual potency, intelligence, etc., are all viewed from a racial point of view (Daniels, 1995). Where Mr. Griffin had been solicited to engage white girls when he was a white man (before the 'experiment' started), he was no longer solicited, when they saw his blackness (after the experiment had started); the most important difference was the darkness of his skin-color, not his height, weight, accent, or behavior; Mr. Griffin himself explains:

> I got off and began walking along Canal Street in the heart of town, carrying one small duffel bag in each hand. I passed the same taverns and amuse-ment places where the hawkers had solicited me on previous evenings. They were busy, urging white men to come in and see the girls. The same smells of smoke and liquor and dampness poured out through half-open doors. Tonight they did not solicit me. Tonight they looked at me but did not see me (as in Ralph Ellison's *Invisible Man*).
>
> I went into a drugstore that I had patronized every day since my arrival. I walked to the cigarette counter where the same girl I had talked with every day waited on me.
>
> 'Package of Picayunes, please,' I said in response to her blank look.

> She handed them to me, took my bill and gave me change with no sign of recognition, none of the banter of previous days. (17-18)

As an articulate 'black man' looking for jobs that might not have been problematic for a white man, Mr. Griffin saw, first hand, a few of the rejections black people deal with on a daily basis; he "wanted to discover what sort of work an educated Negro, nicely dressed, would find. I met no rebuffs, why gentleness when they informed me that they could not use my services as a typist, bookkeeper, etc." (41). He came into intimate contact with the stereotype of black people's sexual potency and white fears about that supposedly black capacity and the propaganda about black intellectual inferiority (85-94). Thus, if black people were feared sexually, they were not intellectually; Mr. Griffin opined that "the two great arguments-the Negro's lack of sexual morality and his intellectual inferiority are smoke screens to justify prejudice and unethical behavior" (111).

Mr. Griffin seems to ascribe to the notion that blacks' "economic emancipation" would be "the key to the (American) race solution" (135). For an example, if the African continent were economically developed, this would most likely put a great dent in white people's prejudice against blacks, for as "so long as the (black) race had to depend on a basically hostile source of financing, ...it would simply refuse loans for any project that did not meet with its approval" (135). Black education, political power, literature, etc. could all go to mitigate racism against blacks in America, but as it will be soon evident, American education of black people has not radically reduced racism and most of its nuances that daily afflict African-Americans. Thus, with all the shortcomings of Mr. Griffin's little experiment, he was able to illustrate the continuing existence of racism in the American South in the last two months of 1959.

If Mr. Griffin did not like his big, black, and bald self during the four to six weeks of his experiment, a self-proclaimed white racist writes why he hates the Negro (Hill, 1975:15-16). Even though this 'Euro-American' claims to be a friend of the African race, he goes on to illuminate the reasons for his hatred of black people; from his own pen, he states:

> In addition to being lazy, the Negro is positively indifferent and oblivious to all those fundamentals that must be considered and seriously negotiated by the thoughtful and cultivated individual. It is surprising that up to this late period of our civilization the Negro has not evolved an independent system of nationalism or materialism. Quite the opposite, he is found a squatter among all peoples, willing and satisfied to be only used

> by such peoples as slaves and serfs, peons and cheap laborers (sic). (15)

Apart from this white racist's ignorance of great black civilizations and contributions to western Christianity and science, it must be sincerely taken that, even today, he speaks for a silent group of Euro-Americans, who are not bold enough to actually pen down their own real feelings toward African descents in the United States of America (Dyson, 1996: 2-9). Actually, black people hardly need white people to explain to them why they (African people) are despised by Euro-Americans and other non-African peoples. In Columbia, where blacks are 15% of the 35 million of the nation, African people are effectively neglected by the national government, dominated by European descents (Brooke, 1994:A3). Among African people in the black Choko State of Columbia

> infant mortality rate is 155 per 1000 live births - five times Columbia's national rate. Life expectancy is 52 years, 25% below the national level. Illiteracy is twice the national rate. The spine-wrenching 150 - mile dirt track to Medellin, takes 15 hours on a good day.

Mr. Brooke goes on to state that the Colombian government is a pigmentocracy, in which whites have more schools and hospitals as compared to blacks and Indians. It hardly is therefore not surprising that "Blacks are avoiding being black. They are trying to be as white as possible" (A3), knowing that whiteness in Columbia has its own syndromes of advantages. In India as well as in England, African descents are not highly valued. Even though Africans and West Indian blacks have been in England since the 1700s, after the American war of Independence, blacks who no longer even speak their traditional languages are still not fully integrated into that European society. In India, dark-skinned Indians (Dravidians, an African people), are still not greatly valued; they find it difficult to marry outside of their own dark-skinned group. The Australian aborigines (black people), like the American Indians, too have their color used against them; attempts have been made "to wipe (them) out...," especially the dark skinned ones (Farnsworthy, 1997:18). Until perhaps most recently, South African blacks from 1652-1994 were the hewers of wood and drawers of water for their European masters, aside from those Africans 'lucky' enough not to have been eliminated during the Great Trek, or by the Apartheid regime from 1948 to 1994. In the Sudan, Saudi Arabia, and Mauritania black African people continue to occupy the lower levels of these societies. It is needless to re-iterate that a few African people have always made it to the top of any society in which they have found themselves, but the African masses, globally, remain hewers of wood and drawers of water in their respective societies.

Even though there seems to be more racial toleration in Latin America, it is still the case that the darker one is, the more one is socially (and economically) negatively categorized. Ellis Cose (1995:72-73) writes that

> The Latin American experience doesn't exactly offer reassurance that more third racial categories are better. Latino cultures aren't characterized by racial bickering, but they are far from colorblind. An array of Latin American terms have arisen to describe various racial compositions, with the most pejorative ones reserved for people of dark hue and *pelo malo*–or bad (meaning kinky) hair. Status in some Latin societies is so linked to color that *mejorando la raza*–bettering the race–is taken to mean marrying someone lighter in order to have whiter children. Uruguayan writer Eduardo Galeano observes: 'In the Dominican Republic there are a lot of black people, but you never see 'black' listed as skin color on their identity card...It would damage the possibilities for work, for a social life'.

In much of Latin America, ingrained racism and self-hatred have taught many black citizens to ignore their African ancestry (Robinson, 1996:20). In Cuba

> ...While there are far more expressions of solidarity, community, and general interest in intermingling (in the neighborhoods, at work, dating and marriages, at schools, etc.) among whites, mulattos, blacks, Chinese, and other groups...than one currently sees or could imagine in the United States, it appears that an inferior status is still unofficially assigned to blacks (notwithstanding, as in the United States, their being "recognized" as gifted or potentially gifted entertainers and athletes). For example, there are stereotypes about black sexuality, the inevitable "nigger" jokes that are popular among ordinary Cubans, and a continuing preference for self-defining racially/ethnically as anything but black (consequently desiring to distance oneself, and presumably one's country, from Africa).

In multicultural United States (an epitome of the global village), African-Americans are collectively above only the Native Americans in terms of family income; Sowell (1981:5) explicates graphically:

**Family Income Index**
**(U.S. Average = 100)**

| | |
|---|---|
| Jewish | 172 |
| Japanese | 132 |
| Polish | 115 |
| Chinese | 112 |
| Italian | 112 |
| German | 107 |
| Anglo-Saxon | 107 |
| Irish | 103 |
| TOTAL U.S. | 100 |
| Filipino | 99 |
| West Indian | 94 |
| Mexican | 76 |
| Puerto Rican | 63 |
| Black | 62 |
| Indian | 60 |

Of all the African diaspora across the globe, African-Americans alone have been the most prolific and outspoken about their economic, political, psychological and cultural oppression; they have been able to 'triumph' over the plantation tradition of multiple exploitation (where 'African' women were used as wenches and breeders), sharecropping, disappointments of the Reconstruction period, Jim Crowism, the KKK, school segregation, the ghettoes of Harlem, South Side Chicago, and other U.S. urban centers, and are still struggling against contemporary, covert barriers put in their path to full social integration (Massey and Denton, 1993).

In his seminal work (Hacker, 1992), the Euro-American Andrew Hacker documents the continuing disparities between blacks and whites in terms of income, employment, educational achievement, crime statistics, and other fundamental indicators. Since the inception of the American republic, blacks and whites have not had a continuously harmonious relationship, the fundamental reasons being color and cultural differences between the two groups of citizens (Reeves, 1994). While the Irish, Italians, Jews, Japanese and even the Chinese have been relatively accepted (the European ethnic groups more so than the non-European groups), African people collectively, even African Americans who have educationally and meritoriously made it into the macro-America society, experience being looked at askance, with suspicion.

We think Ellis Cose (1993), an African-American journalist, has made an important contribution in illustrating the psychologically painful experiences of the academically and occupationally successful African American 'elites'. He asserts that "for most blacks in America, regardless of status, political persuasion, or accomplishments, the moment never arouses when race can be treated as a total irrelevancy. Instead, too often it is the only relevant factor defining our existence" (28), and that "...many successful blacks know that if it were not for discrimination, they would have done much better" (33).

This does not say that other ethnic groups, the Irish, Italians, Jews, Chinese and the Japanese have not also experienced negative stigmatization, inferiorization, segregation, and stranger-fear, but African people are one of the most saliently dispossessed, next to the Native Americans. The Irish, for an instance, have so completely assimilated that they now fear losing their salient cultural idiosyncrasies (Sowell, 1981:42); African people, compared to the Irish, Italians, Jews, Chinese and Puerto-Ricans, to take a few examples from the American cultural 'Mosaic', were brought to the United States not only against their will, but also the only ones who could not write back to their relatives, or bring their family members to the United States to keep their lineage continuous; they needed no visas, passports, and had no religious-political leader, or a powerful African state to talk on their behalf. The Japanese "immigrants were required to apply to the (Japanese) government for permission to leave for the United States and were screened by review boards to certify that they were healthy and literate and would creditably maintain Japanese national honor" (Takaki, 1993:248). If the Irish experience under the English in Ireland helped them in the United States (Sowell, 1981: 15-42), traditional African cultural idiosyncrasies from West Africa were 'bastardized' or outrightly rejected in the American wilderness. The racial and cultural divide between African-Americans and European Americans continue to be insurmountable (Herrnstein and Murray, 1994; Massaquoi, 1996:56-58, 60).

Toni Morrison (1993:57) observes that when new immigrants arrive in the United States, they go through a rite of passage that includes the denigration of African-Americans, a 'passport' to being accepted as Americans. "It doesn't matter anymore what the newcomer's skin is. A hostile posture toward the resident blacks must be stuck at the Americanizing door before it will open. ...race talk...is the real stuff, the organizing principle of becoming an American." Thus, Asian Americans have been labeled the model minority, not the second oldest minority (blacks) who have experienced untold brutalities, but are expected not to be angry, and are urged to emulate Japanese- Americans, who enthusiastically came to the United States because of their infatuation with American culture (Williams, 1968:31) and Takaki (1993:248).

Morrison (1992:63), in her *Playing in the Dark*, goes on to note the continuing significance of race in multicultural and multiracial United States; in white American literature, for instance, race has had a fundamental place, and "Racism is as healthy today (in the 21st century) as it was during the Enlightenment. It seems that it has a utility far beyond economy, beyond the sequestering of classes from one another, and has assumed a metaphorical life so completely in daily discourse that it is perhaps more necessary and more on display than ever before."

Even though there have been 'some improvements' in American race relations, especially from the point of view of Euro-Americans and some privileged African-Americans (note Wilson's *Declining Significance of Race* and even his *When Work Disappears...)*, for the disadvantaged African-American masses, and a host of privileged black Americans, however, race (still) matters (West, 1993). In fact, it matters so much so that Lawrence Thomas (1990:84) hyperbolically writes that in (his) next life, (he'll) be white. He states that "Black men rarely enjoy what is properly called the public trust of whites, no matter if their deportment or attire conform to the traditional *standards* of well-off whites. To enjoy the public trust is to have strangers regard one as a morally decent person in a variety of contexts." But *in* 'a variety of contexts', Dr. Lawrence Thomas, a black Syracuse University professor, found himself reacted to by whites as though he were a purse-snatcher, irrespective of his attire, and perhaps scholarly presence. To illustrate, Dr. Lawrence Thomas (1990:84) explicates:

> I was recently walking down a supermarket aisle with handbaskets full of groceries, one in each hand. A White woman saw me and rushed for her pocketbook, which she had left in her cart. I would have had to put my own groceries down in order to take her pocketbook. No doubt she thought to herself: 'he won't fool me with that old basket-in-each-hand trick.'
>
> Similarly, it would not occur to anyone to think that a 6-foot-tall, 150-pound well-groomed White male in traditional academic attire-tweed jacket and tie-with briefcase in hand was actually seeking to break into a university office simply because he was reading a bulletin board outside of the conference hall. Yet not long ago, when I was in just such a situation at a Midwestern university, four campus police officers were summoned to investigate. What on earth was I reported as, a -10-feet tall in military garb? Or, did someone say, 'There's a Black man...'? Now when was the last time that a headline read 'A group of roving Black males in tweed jackets and ties attacked a White person'?
>
> Even abroad, White American women have responded to my presence by leaping for their pocketbooks. In the Middle East

> recently, I simply had to say to one woman who did such a thing, 'Do you really think that I traveled nearly 6,000 miles in order to steal your purse when it is obvious that you are not much better off than I am, since we're staying in the same hotel?'
>
> Many of my well-placed Black friends report similar mind-boggling stories. Now if we, well-groomed and mannered Blacks, do not enjoy the public trust, it is discomforting to think how less well-off Blacks fare.

As pointed out in Ellis Cose's *The Rage of a Privileged Class* (1993), African-American professionals are not immune to being feared as strangers in white society, and to be so treated, overtly or covertly. We might as well here refer to David Dinkin's epigram that "a white man with a million dollars is a millionaire, and a black man with a million dollars is a nigger with a million dollars" (cited in Cose, 184). Ellis Cose goes on to state that Euro-Americans have a difficult time separating the well-off black middle class from the downtrodden black masses, because race alone seems to be the primary preoccupation in American cultural life. "A black skin, in and of itself, can arouse a dangerous degree of suspicion" (184). Thus, American real estate agencies, for another instance, continue to track African-Americans to certain areas of American cities, giving rise to black 'oppositional culture' (187). A neighborhood without blacks is referred to as a good one (42).

"According to the 1990 census figures, between 1970 and 1990, the number of black families with incomes under $15,000 rose from 34.6 percent of the black population to 37 percent, while the number of black families with incomes of $35,000 to $50,000 rose from 13.9 percent to 15 percent of the population, and those with incomes of more than $50,000 rose from 9.9 percent to 14.5 percent of the black population" (Gaiter, 1994:43). But in the social-psychology of white America, a black earning $50,000 a year and a white earning the same are not the same; whiteness overshadows achievement; the 50,000 dollar white man knows he belongs to the ruling race and views the African-American 50,000 dollar man as a descendant of ex-slaves, whose 'original' land is still the poorest of the poor. All things being equal, the most ignorant European feels a taint of superiority to the most accomplished African and African-American male or female. In his exquisite essay "stranger in the village" (1957:159-175), Baldwin tells us that there is a great difference between being a descendant of a conquered race and that of a conquering race; there is indeed a great difference between the first white man in Africa and the first black man in colonial America. In Baldwin's explicit experience in a Swiss village, he observed that he was a curiosity case; people came to verify whether his black skin would rob off and whether he was from Africa; since all blacks to them, in their unsophistication, came from Africa, they marveled at his 'African' hair texture. Mr. Baldwin was perceptive in his analysis of his Swiss experience; he explicates:

> For this village, even if it were incomparably more remote and incredibly more primitive, is the West, the West onto which I have been so strangely grafted. These people cannot be, from the point of view of power, strangers anywhere in the world; they have made the modern world, in effect, even if they do not know it. The most illiterate among them is related in a way that I am not, to Dante, Shakespeare, Michelangelo, Aeschylus, DaVinci, Rembrandt, and Racine: the cathedral at Chartres says something to them which it cannot say to me, as indeed would New York's Empire State Building, should anyone here ever see it. Out of their hymns and dances come Beethoven and Bach. Go back a few centuries and they are in their full glory - but I am in Africa, watching the conquerors arrive.
>
> ... He is inescapably aware, nevertheless, that he is in a better position in the world than black men are, nor can he quite put to death the suspicion that he is hated by black men therefore. He does not wish to be hated, neither does he wish to change places, and at this point in his uneasiness he can scarcely avoid having recourse to those legends which white men have created about black men, the most usual effect of which is that the white man finds himself enmeshed, so to speak, in his own language which describes hell, as well as the attributes which lead one to hell, as being as black as night. (165, 166)

Even though Mr. Baldwin should have taken refuge in that Africans had also built monuments, conquered extensive land areas, and colonized other people centuries before Europe emerged out of 'darkness', as it were, and that different ethnic groups have had civilizations at different historical points in term, he nonetheless felt powerless and inferior for not having been a descendant of, say, Rembrandt; the unsophisticated Swiss villagers were able to make a metropolitan, Black New Yorker, feel less than adequate; they called him "Negger, Negger" (161). In the West and in Africa, Black people are 'Niggers' and all the mental images that that appellation may conjure; irrespective of the individual black man/woman's sophistication and accomplishments, he/she is simply the black major of New York, the black governor of Virginia, the black Presidential candidate, infinitum; a white governor of New York is simply the governor of New York, and there should be nothing unique about that, even though he might be an Italian or Jewish American.

African-Americans then in the United States experience status-discrepancy; they are Americans, but black Americans; they maybe doctors, but black doctors, engineers, mayors, governors, senators, ambassadors (mostly sent to Africa), black lecturers or professors, infinitum. In this status-discrepancy, the black person's ascribed status (being born black) becomes the major basis of judgement before any 'objective' evaluation takes place. If she/he becomes a good journalist, he must have scored lower than his white counterparts and aided by affirmative action or he/she must have been a 'first' because of 'reversed discrimination'; in this paradigm, discrimination against blacks seems 'accepted' but not one against whites.

Leanita McClain (Campbell, 1984:67-70; 73-74; Page, 1986) suffered from status-discrepancy; her professional accomplishments (achieved status), conflicted not only with her low class background, but also with her sex and race (her ascribed status). She experienced "stress from the oppressive combination of racism, sexism, and professional competition that separates black women not only from their white colleagues, but also insidiously pits them against their black male professional counterparts (Campbell, 1984:68). Granted that McClain came from an improvised background (lower class culture/neighborhood and predominately black), which posed cultural problems in a white middle-middle class environment, she also had to deal with the ramifications of her sex and race; professional blacks are expected (required) to "make whites around them feel comfortable..." (69). These Black professionals must 'learn' to speak standard American English; "Black women consciously choose their speech, their laughter, their walk, their mode of dress and car" (60). All these extra-efforts they must make in order to function in the white professional world. Even though McClain was fair skinned (69), approximating the epidermis of the ruling race, she was still 'black' and female and was "prejudged by (her) color" (69). White women too experience sexism in the workplace, but not racism or the effects of cultural differences from their white male bosses or employers.

Though McClain's suicide was an extreme way of dealing with the cultural, racial, and sexual conflicts inflicted on her by her middle-class workplace and her improvished background, she strongly illustrates the types of cultural, social, and psychological pressures African-American professional black women encounter in the workplace within the majority culture. In the words of Maya Angelou, in her well-known *I Know Why the Caged Bird Sings* (1970:231),

> The Black female is assaulted in her tender years by all those common forces of nature at the same time that she is caught in the tripartite crossfire of masculine prejudice, white illogical hate and Black lack of power.
>
> The fact that the adult American Negro female emerges a formidable character is often met with amazement, distaste and even belligerence. It is seldom accepted as an inevitable outcome of the struggle won by survivors and deserves respect if not enthusiastic acceptance.

Maya Angelou's grandmother (Momma) was a strong black woman who had weathered three calamitous marriages, but remained focused, religious, hardworking, and imparted these values to her grandchildren; she expected cleanliness from her grandson Baily and granddaughter Maya, whom she urged to "...'wash as far as possible, then wash possible'" (21); for all practical purposes, Momma was an accomplished 'matriarch'; she owned her own store and some other properties. Her achievements, however, were not as important as her sex and race, from the point of view of even the white children of Stamps, Arkansas. A white dentist's refusal to treat Maya Angelou's toothache provides a good example of Momma's experience of status-discrepancy; a dentist she had loaned money to start his dental practice refused to treat Angelou's toothache because he would rather stick his hands into 'a dog's mouth':

> Momma said, "I wouldn't press on you like this for myself but I can't take No. Not for my grandbaby. When you come to borrow my money you didn't have to beg. You asked me, and I lent it. Now, it wasn't my policy. I ain't no money lender, but you stood to lose this building and I tried to help you out."
>
> "It's been paid, and raising your voice won't make me change my mind. My policy..." He let go of the door and stepped nearer Momma. The three of us were crowded on the small landing. "Annie, my policy is I'd rather stick my hand in a dog's mouth than in a nigger's." (160)

Thus, despite grandma's accomplishments, she was rejected by the dentist, not respected by young whites and was not expected to be called Mrs. Henderson among adults, in public (29).

Accomplished African-American men also experience status-discrepancy. Bruce Wright (1993) states that he was rejected by Princeton University with this simple explanation: "We did not know you were colored when the scholarship was arranged" (37). Mr. Wright, who could be considered by most whites as 'too' sensitive about racial issues, goes on to tell us in his *Black Robes, White Justice* that America's Justice system, as is perhaps well-known, is not shielded from the macro-society which it mirrors (24); the courts purport to defend the interest of the status-quo and disproportionately trash black criminals more severely than white criminals of similar offenses. Black criminals know very well that their fate in the society at large and in the justice system in particular is similar to that of Bigger Thomas's in Richard Wright's popular fiction, *Native Son.*

In *Black Robes, White Justice,* the black, New York State Supreme Court Judge, Mr. Bruce Wright, goes on to document, from personal and professional experiences, the continuing significance of race in American society in general and in the Justice system in particular.

Wright opines that "white people are conditioned from the time of their birth to the preferred status of their skin color. Their views of the world at large and their own environment become solidified by circumstances, pre-suppositions, myths, clichés, and traditional folklore" (19); let's face it:

> ...In America, there has never been an example of the oppressed when liberated, becoming the oppressor. It is rare and unusual white person who will revolt, even within the limits of Constitutional speech and public declarations, against this country's way of life. It is an even more unusual white who can consider his fellow man just another person, as opposed to a 'colored' person, a 'Negro friend' or 'black' one. The use of such terms to refer to another human being imposes an immediate classification. It is an indication that a colored person is not simply another citizen, but something less. The description is an instruction to the listener of how such a person of color must be regarded, not only as different, but as diminished in status as well. It is a debased and debasing classification.
>
> There have been genuine relationships of affection and mutual esteem between whites and blacks, and I am willing to believe that each could regard the other simply as a human being and not as 'my black friend' or my white friend. All too often, white humanitarians decline in their zeal for equality, move to the white suburbs, and become occasional liberals with black visitors now and then. ( 23-24)

As already alluded to, other ethnic groups in America have also faced their own 'unique' problems in the process of 'assimilation' into the macro-American society. The Irish, Jews, Italians, Mexicans, Puerto-Ricans and the Japanese have all had their rebuffs at particular points in time, in their efforts to be 'nothing' but 'Americans', but none have had it so hard and fought for so long to join their American brethren (Sowell, 1981:224), and still continue to face rejection by their American homeland, than African-Americans. Racism may not be as overt today as it was in the days of lynchings, blatant segregation and Jim Crowism, but it is nonetheless present and potent; Blacks "are still regarded with suspicion as though they do not meet white standards. There are implicit insults even in remarks meant as compliments" (Wright, 1993:186).

Mr. Bruce Wright, a product of a 'white mother and a black father' (29; 33; 93), was not treated as a bicultural or a biracial child, but as a black man, and all the connotations that go with that categorization in the United States (25). In terms of Mr. Wright's experience of status discrepancy, he once fell ill while performing his duties as a Judge in a New York court, and required medical attention. When the medical doctor arrived, despite Mr. Wright's well-attiredness and professional demeanor in comparison to a 'wretched' white patient in the same hallway with Mr. Wright, the white doctor quickly, as it were, approached the filthy white man and called him Judge instead of Mr. Wright, who was indeed the Judge. Judge Wright himself explains:

> One afternoon, during a trial, I felt so faint and weak I could not carry on. The clerks, with affectionate concern, feared that I was having a heart attack. I was taken out of the courthouse lashed to a stretcher. It was an embarrassment to be so helpless and publicly exhibited.
>
> In the emergency room of the hospital, I was placed in a curtained-off area where there were two beds some distance apart. On one was a white man, obviously one of the poor derelicts now and then brought in from the Bowery. He appeared to be in a state of joyous alcoholic bewilderment. He needed a shave; neither his soiled sneakers nor his socks matched; he drooled a bit and sang softly in garbled syllables.
>
> As I watched him from my bed, I felt pangs of pity. He seemed much worse off than I. I felt guilty for being dressed in a three-piece suit and clean shirt.
>
> I heard a nurse outside the curtained area say, "Hurry, doctor, we have a judge who is ill." A white doctor parted the curtains, paused at the entrance, looked at me and then at the white derelict. He hurried to the side of the white man, lifted his wrist, as though to test his pulse, and said, 'Judge, what seems to be the matter?'
>
> It was a bracing experience, wholly therapeutic, and I began to recover without delay. (24-25)

Outside of Court and apart from Mr. Wright's hospital experience, African people continue to be discriminated against not only in the New York City police force (Kilborn, 1994: PAI, 26), but also in one of the most popular American restaurants (Labation, 1994:46). Even though New York City could be 'correctly' termed a 'global village' in terms of its diverse ethnic and racial composition, it is reported, as late as the early 1990s, that the New York City police remained definitely 'segregated' in terms of the number of black policemen in the higher ranks of the police force. In July 1994, there were no black captains; there were only 12.5% black detectives, 7.3% sergeants, and 5.9% lieutenants, in a city that was 29% black (AI 26); most of the New York City black policemen lived in Brooklyn (28.6%), Queens (27.3%), while most of the white New York City policemen (38.1%) lived in the Long Island suburbs (26). Thus, they, black and white policemen, could work for the same city government but at different levels of the police hierarchy and mostly live apart (segregated) from each other in terms of residential 'preference'. Clearly, the New York City police department needs to do a thing about "the most entrenched old boy network" that favors white male dominance in sheer numbers and in the higher ranks of the police force (AI). The number of black policemen (and black women, who were even the least represented) should ideally approximate their proportion in all the ranks within the police force; it is certain that the New Police Department (NYPD) will find enough qualified black men and women willing to be 'coppers' in New York City. One would have thought that New York City, one of the most diverse and enlightened cities in the world, would have been ahead of all the other major cities in the United States in affirmative action in the city's police force.

The cases of Denny's Restaurant and Texaco Corporation explicitly discriminating against Africa-Americans in 1994 and 1996 also illustrate the continuing significance of race in America society. Labation (1994:4E) reports that managers of Denny's Restaurants were unmistakably instructed to 'discriminate' against black customers. Though blacks could not be turned away or refused service blatantly, they could be made to pay a 'little more' for the services rendered to them; they could be inconvenienced, told to sit away from public view, and could even be told that the restaurant was closed should they 'inundate' the place at particular times of the day. A manager at one of Denny's restaurants confesses:

> I am a white male formerly employed as a manager with Denny's restaurants in San Jose, California...After approximately eight months as assistant manager at the Capitol Expressway Denny's, I was promoted to general manager of the Tully Road Denny's in San Jose. I remained in that capacity for approximately one year until I was placed on disability in May 1991.
>
> While employed with Denny's I was instructed by my district manager to implement policies designed to limit or discourage black patronage.
>
> Instructions on policies applied to black customers were given at district meetings and, to a greater degree, individually at the restaurants by district managers. District meetings occurred weekly, usually at the Denny's. During these meetings the term "blackout" was used on many occasions in the presence of district and regional managers.
>
> I first heard the term "blackout" when I was assistant manager at Blossom Hill. The Blossom Hill general manager commented to me that we were better off than the Tully Road Denny's because they have a lot of blackouts. At the time, I didn't know what the term meant. In time, I heard the term with enough frequency to learn that "blackout" was used by Denny's managers to refer to a situation where too many black customers were in the restaurant.

> At district meetings, managers would comment that they had a blackout the previous weekend and the district managers would acknowledge the problem and just ask how it was dealt with. We were taught to avoid blackouts by requiring black customers to pay for their meals in advance and simply close the restaurant for a few hours when we started getting too many black customers. Both prepayment and closing policies were discussed at district meetings. At district meetings, the upper-level managers were careful not to say too much about the discriminatory policies, but they would pull you aside later at your restaurant and tell you face to face. I took comments regarding prepayment lightly when I heard them at district meetings until my district manager spoke to me personally about the policy when I was general manager at Tully Road... .(4E)

Even though the U.S. society is now a technopoly (Postman, 1993), 'civilized', and an epitome of the global village, and intimately informed by the African presence, it continues to discriminate against black people in many areas of American social life. Most blacks are at the bottom of the society because that is where the white society seems to want them, feels comfortable with them that way, and appear more secure that African-Americans are segregated into the black ghettos; blacks are overwhelmingly represented in the prison population because the U.S. legal system views most blacks as criminals or potential ones, some of whom would continue be caught and sent to serve some long prison terms. At Attica in upstate New York, for instance, there are mostly Black and Hispanic inmates, but mostly white male guards and administrators. It should not take a genius to quickly determine that there might be something amiss here. As we've seen in the case of *Black Robes, White Justice,* under white justice blacks have rarely won; in white society blacks are not highly valued. If these were not so, popular U.S. Restaurants, the police, real estates agents, educational and economic institutions, and the macro-American society at large would have 'totally' accepted African-Americans, one of the earliest 'citizens' of the United States, as they have the Japanese, Italians, Germans, the Irish, and even the Chinese.

But why is this continuous racism against African-American? Is it because of African people's extreme differences in color and culture? We are not unaware that whites in Kenya, Zimbabwe, and Southern Africa are indeed extremely different in epidermis, but they are not so vehemently hated as blacks are in white societies. Is racism in the West a black or a white problem? Can racism be exterminated or abated? Would we achieve a color-blind society? These, indeed, are not unimportant questions, and there seem to be no clear-cut answers. Even though racism has been continuously challenged by both blacks and whites, we do not seem to see an end to it. Derrick Bell (1992) seems to be highly convinced that racism is a perennial phenomenon in

American society. He states that "Blacks will never gain full equality in the United States", and that blacks will remain in a "permanent subordinate status" (12), "remaining (as) this country's designated scapegoats" (13, 198).

Using "the dramatic perspective of fiction" (XI), Derrick Bell goes on to illustrate, socratically, the permanence of racism in American society, affecting even the so-called affluent blacks, the talented tenth, in DeBoisian terms. The members of the talented black tenth are in the same racial boat with the down trodden black masses; and for both the black masses and black professionals, there are no 'Afrolanticas' to which to escape from racism; in the United States, African Americans must remain to face the experiences of racism, hate stirs, limited job opportunities, residential segregation, dead-end jobs and must engage in the struggle to fight against racism (98); blacks, according to Ellis Cose (1993:53-72), experience coping fatigue, guilt of association, and other pressures 'simply' because they are in a racist, white society that devalues their accomplishments and their very persons.

The Blacks who make it into the system most often "minimize their blackness" (Bell, 1992:140) in other to fit in, even if partially, at that. Dyson (1996:21-22), states that "once (O.J.) Simpson put away his youthful law-breaking in San Francisco's Potrero Hill projects, he adopted a winning formula: he would play by the rules within the limits of the Givens. The Givens amounts to whites being on top. To win you must act and talk white." On white University campuses black professors are hardly tenured, the frequent explanation being that these "faculty openings require qualifications that few, if any, blacks hold" (Bell, 1992:131); "Hire one if you must, but only one" (130), goes the directive from college deans and presidents. After more than 370 years of blacks and whites 'living together', blacks are still not fully accepted as full members of the American society by their American white brothers and sisters; to Derrick Bell, it seems highly dubious that blacks will ever be fully accepted as full fledged American citizens.

In the United States there is "a strong preference for" (143) the white race and white culture; this strong preference for Europeanisms color all types of interactions between African-Americans and European-Americans, the 'real' Americans, whose standards of beauty, civilization, education, curriculum and legal systems (just to mention a few) are the guiding posts. Those who fail to assimilate (such as most blacks and Chinese) are relegated to the black ghettos and Chinatowns; African-Americans whose appearance (skin color) does not approximate the European race stand out, negatively, in American society; those with dark skin are not infrequently wished away back into the African jungles, to be separated from this Anglo-American society, since the days of George Washington, Thomas Jefferson, Benjamin Rush, and the other founding fathers who felt that blackness must have been a curse.

Each society seems to need its own scapegoat, and the American society seems to have been provided one by the almighty himself–African-Americans, especially the dark-skinned ones and members of the lower classes in American cities and rural areas. But does this mean racism is permanent, as Derrick Bell has intimidated, or would have us convinced? The answer seems to be a qualified 'no'.

Robert Park (1972:27-28), and John Howard Griffin (1976) both suggest that racism *cannot* be permanent. Furthermore, impressionistic historical lessons seem to suggest that racism will eventually 'die'; the timing, however, of its death seems to be beyond the scope of this text. Nonetheless, it is necessary to illustrate that historically, races have progressively intermingled. In Egypt, black Africans, Arabs, Persians, Romans, and others have been intermingling from ancient times; in Haiti, Brazil, Guinea-Bissau, Angola, Mozambique, South Africa, Kenya, and in the U.S.A., blacks and whites have continued to mix biologically. Even though inter-racial dating, sex, and marriages were formally and informally forbidden (which caused the lives of a few whites and many blacks), those dejure and defacto laws did not prevent race mixing. Slave masters (including Thomas Jefferson) and their sons indulged in sex with black women in their homes and outlying plantations. In fact, on the plantations, the white man was the 'king', 'having' at his disposal both black and white women whenever he so desired.

The stigmas attached to inter-racial children have not prevented inter-racial sex, marriage, and bi-racial children. The Portuguese have been said to 'boast' that 'as God created blacks and whites,' *they* would produce the mulatto! In the United States in particular, one never can be too sure whether an African, Indian, or Jewish 'blood' is not running through one's veins (Williams, 1995). And when societies become more and more cosmopolitan, and schools and workplaces become more and more integrated, one must then acquiesce that inter-racial mixing will tend to increase. From this empiricism, it seems clear that people are progressively going to be more alike than different in the global village. Like all progressive movements, there will always be nay-sayers and anachronistic sentimentalists who will attempt to obfuscate the movement toward an ineluctable goal; there were the luddites against the factory system, techophobes against technopoly, and traditionalists who attack new systems of thought, government, values, and norms; advocates of inter-racial mixing continue to challenge racist thoughts, values, and norms and render advocates of pure races anachronistic.

According to Robert E. Park (1972:27-28), race relations proceed through four, ineluctable stages:

> The race-relations cycle proceeds in four stages-contact, conflict, accommodation, and assimilation-in the course of which there

> unfolds a great cultural and social drama. Each act of this drama is dictated by laws of history and culture, Park writes, and the sequence cannot be halted or diverted. The first stage, contact, occurs when two races meet on a 'racial frontier' and are obligated to interact. Conflict arises when the races compete for valuable resources. The conflict is resolved by accommodation, in which a stable but asymmetrical and unequal social order is established. Finally, accommodation gives way to assimilation, when the two races merge culturally and, ultimately, physically. In the end, society becomes homogenous. ...Park regarded his race-relations cycle as a law of historical development, to be treated as virtually ineluctable: 'The race relations cycle ...is apparently progressive and irreversible. Customs, regulations, immigration restriction, and racial barriers may slacken the tempo of the movement; may perhaps halt it altogether for a time; but cannot change its direction; cannot at any rate reverse it.'

Again, occasional interruptions-lynchings, defacto and dejure laws, negative stigmas attached to inter-racial children, racial riots in Los Angeles, pogroms, ethnic cleansings, Apartheid South Africa, texts about racial-superiority-inferiority, etc. have delayed, but have not prevented biological integration. Even though each race is said to have its own unique temperament (49), this too has not prevented race mixing; even though there has been a lot of hatred between blacks and whites, this too has not prevented love across the great gulf. There have been marriages between whites and Native Americans, Jews and gentiles, 'primitive' Africans and 'civilized' Europeans, sons of masters and daughters of slaves, and any other polar opposite one cares to include.

Even in the crucible of racial hatred of the south of *Black Like Me* in 1959, Mr. Griffin observed that some members of the younger generation of whites were sympathetic, if not empathetic, to the plight of Blacks in the United States. After all, in American history, there have been a John Brown, the Quakers, an anti-slavery society, white civil rights lawyers and other white 'Nigger Lovers' who have been compelled by compassion, religious belief and humanitarian sentiments to go against the zeitgeist of racial intolerance. A Roman Catholic bookstore keeper was able and willing, without any qualms, to cash Mr. Griffin's travelers' check, "a Negro's check" (51-52); the Monks in Georgia welcomed Mr. Griffin with no feelings of racial superiority (130-131); a college professor of English who could no longer get along with his parents because of their negative views about the black race, entertained Mr. Griffin (131); the Massachusetts European-American who gave him a lift to Mobile, Alabama, was not a 'racist' even though he was unwilling to challenge Southern racism (83); some of the younger whites Mr. Griffin 'ran' into during his sojourn were 'kinder (to him) than their older ones" (113).

Furthermore, the urbanization of Atlanta and other Southern cities, Mr. Griffin observed, tended to question blatant racism (134). A determined black leadership in Montgomery, Alabama (116), that took a stand against racism and for responsible journalism (134) have all made a dent in American racism. Liberation Theology, preached and practiced by both blacks and whites, could also abate racism. Finally, education, literature (such as *Black Like Me*) and African-American political and economic development could also go to make a great dent into the custom of discrimination, racism, and segregation between the races and ethnic groups.

Even though David Allen (1993) has taken the position that *strangerfear* is a primordial defense mechanism, an innate fear of strangers observed even among ants and animals, including man, it seems reasonable to suggest that humans are not only superior, but have also been able to attain a higher level of sophistication and civilization that should aid them to make social policies conducive to the stage of technopoly and the global village. While Mr. Allen is persuasive about strangerfear globally, it might be equally persuasive to state that the lower animal kingdom has not greatly evolved; human beings have had the foresight to have established the League of Nations, the United Nations, the Arab League, the Organization of African Unity, the Organization of American States, NAFTA, etc. to contain not only ethnic and racial strife, but also promote political and economic development. Laws have been promulgated in human society to 'prevent' discrimination against minority groups, women, and the disabled; human rights organizations monitor violations across the globe and, with the aid of technopoly, political extremists, apartheid leaders, anti-Semites and man's inhumanity to man have all been brought to a 'global court of Justice.' Man may not still be totally 'civilized', but he has been deliberate enough to learn from history and has created 'complex' bureaucracies to stem some of the barbaric practices of his 'primitive' days. Man's language has evolved to a high level of sophistication to name and be imaginatively responsive to the concept of the global village and most of the nuances associated with that concept; man has created machines that make machines, has made advances in science and engineering that could startle the ancients of Egypt and Mesopotamia.

Even though "it is extraordinarily difficult to change habits, personality traits, culture, and social institutions" (Etzioni, 1994:14), it is also of import to note that human beings have constantly challenged barriers placed in their path toward progress. They have even created literature and the other art forms to depict their dreams, fantasies, desires, hopes, and their other sensibilities that cannot be abolished by the waving of a magic wand by hate mongers, geneticists, eugenicists, homophobics, or misanthropes (Wills, 1994:76-81). African people, as members of the global community, have too 'penned' about their dreams, hopes, desires, and about their other sensibilities relative to their positions in their respective societies and cultural experiences in this impending global village; it is to this set of issues that we now turn in chapter seven to examine some of the novels and biographies that African people themselves have penned down (for themselves and the global village at large).

**References: Chapter VI**

Angelou, Maya. 1969. *I Know Why The Caged Bird Sings*. New York: Bantam Books.

Anonymous Author. 1975. "Why I hate the Negro," (By a White Man), pp. 15-16 in Robert A. Hill (compiler), *Marcus Garvey: The Black Man, A Monthly Magazine of Negro Thought and Opinion*. Millwood, New York:Kraus-Thomson Organization Limited.

Baldwin, James. 1984. *Notes of a Native Son*. Boston, Massachusetts: Beacon Press.

Bell, Derrick. 1992. *Faces at the Bottom of the Well*. New York, Basic Books.

Brooke, James. 1994. "Long Neglected, Columbia's Blacks Win Changes," *New York Times*, March 29:A3; See also Charles Whitaker, "Blacks in Brazil: The Myth and the Reality," *Ebony*, February 1991, pp. 59-60, 62,64.

______. 1994. "U.S. Blacks Find Study in Brazil Bittersweet Experience," *New York Times*. January 12:A17.

Cose, Ellis. 1993. *The Rage of a Privileged Class*. New York: Harper Collins Publishers.

______. 1995. "One Drop of Bloody History: Americans Have Always Defined Themselves on the Basis of Race." *Newsweek* 2/13:70-71.

Dyson, Michael Eric. 1996. *Race Rules: Navigating the Color Line*. Reading, MA: Addison-Wesley Publishing Company, Inc.

Etzioni, Amitai. 1994. "Incorrigible," *The Atlantic Monthly*, Vol. 274, No. 1 (July), p. 14, 16.

Farnsworth, Clyde H. "Australians Resist Facing up to Legacy of Parting Aborigines from Families," *New York Times*, 6/8:18.

Gaiter, Leonce. 1994. "The Revolt of the Black Bourgeoisie" *New York Times Magazine*, June 26:42-43.

Griffin, John Howard. 1976. *Black Like Me*, New York, New York: Penguin Books.

Hacker, Andrew. 1992. *Two Nations: Black and White, Separate, Hostile, Unequal*: New York: Ballantine Books.

Hadjor, Kofi Buenor. 1997. *Another America: The Politics of Race and Blame*. Boston, Mass.: South End Press, p. 98.

Herrnstein and Murray. 1994. *The Bell Curve: Intelligence and Class Structure in American Life*. New York, New York: The Free Press.

Huntington, Samuel, P. 1993. "The Clash of Civilizations," *Foreign Affairs*. Summer, pp. 22-49.

Kilborn, Peter T. 1994. "New York Police Force in Recruitment of Black Officers," *New York Times*, July 17:A1, 26.

Labation, Stephen. 1994. "Denny's gets a Bill for the side orders of Bigotry," *The New York Times*, May 29:4E; see also Howard Kohn, 1994; "Service With a Sneer," *New York Times Magazine*, Nov. 6, Section 6, pp. 43-47; 58, 78, 81.

Lyman, Stanford, M. 1972. *The Black American in Sociological Thought: New Perspectives on Black America*. New York Times: G.P. Putnan's and Sons.

Massay and Denton. 1994. *American Apartheid: Segregation and the Making of the Underclass*. Cambridge, Mass: Harvard University Press.

Morrison, Toni. 1993. "On the Backs of Blacks," *Time*. Fall, p. 57.

______. 1993. *Playing in the Dark: Whiteness and the Literacy Imagination*. New York: Vintage Books.

Postman, Neil. 1993. *Technopoly: The Surrender of Culture to Technology*. New York: Alfred A. Knopf, 1993.

Sowell, Thomas. 1981. *Ethnic America: A History*. New York: Basic Books.

Shipman, Pat. 1994. "Facing Racial Differences Together". *The Chronicle of Higher Education*, August 3, pp. B1-B2; see also Ref (1994) *The Evolution of Racism: Human Differences and the Use and Abuse of Science*. New York, NY: Simon and Schuster.

Takaki, Ronald. 1993. *A Different Mirror: A History of Multicultural America*. Little, Brown, and Company.

Thomas, Laurence. 1990. "In My Next Life, I'll be White". *Ebony* (December), p. 84.

*U.S.A. Today,* 1997. "Inclusion, Not Rejection, Will Spur Racial Harmony." 6/30:18A.

West, Cornel. 1993. *Race Matters*. Boston, Massachusetts: Beacon Press.

Williams, Barry. 1968. *Emerging Japan*. New York, McGraw-Hill Book Company, p. 31.

Williams, George Howard. 1995. *Life on the Color Line*. New York, New York: Dutton.

Willis, Christopher. 1994. "The skin we are in." *Discover: The World of Science*. 15/11:76-81.

Wilson, William, Julius. 1980. *The Declining Significance of Race*. The University of Chicago Press.

Wright, Bruce. 1993. *White Robes, Black Justice*. New York, New York, Carol Publishing Group.

Wright, Richard. 1987. *Native Son*. New York: Harper and Row Publishers.

# Chapter VII:

## And Now African People Write About Themselves: African and African-American Male Writers

What is art? Is art an imitation of nature or is it an emulation, distortion, description, representation, criticism, exaltation, etc. of nature? Bohannan and Curtin (1988:87) state that "All art can be said to have two sweeping characteristics: it embodies a message within an idiom of communication, and it arouses a sense of mystery – a feeling that it is more than it appears to the intellect to be." Accordingly, what does contemporary African people's literature embody? Does contemporary African people's literature contain messages about the past and present, or does it 'simply' react to contemporaneous events affecting individual African artists, tribes, nations, and therefore, to some extent, African people in general?

These and other pertinent questions are undoubtedly difficult to adequately describe, or answer to everyone's satisfaction, across cultures, tribes and classes. The interest in this chapter is simply an attempt at a descriptive sketch of a representative African and African-American writers with particular emphasis on the impact of the western world on the selected African and African-American writers' world view. Are the protagonists, themes, and major characters of the selected 'Pan-African' writers a way of understanding African people? What messages do African people's novels, protagonists and themes embody?

If art embodies a message, it can be said that "African art speaks both for the (African) culture and for itself. Like all art, speaking for one culture allows it, in some degree, to speak for all" (110). After all, "...cultures must have narratives and will find them where they will, even if they lead to catastrophe (Postman, 1993:173).

Irrespective of the various shades of negative attitudes towards African people globally, African artists have produced works of literature that 'speak' profitably, to all humanity, including the enslavers and colonizers of African people. In no small measure, contemporary African people's literature can be said to be greatly informed by the impact of external, European influences on Africa and Africans. As Africans were 'fully' defeated militarily, technologically, culturally and otherwise, their languages, religions, and cultural idiosyncrasies were profoundly challenged. African people, under western influence, were not only linguistically and physically challenged, but also in terms of dress, accent, manners, standards of beauty, concept of time, law, leadership, education and politics.

It is this enormous challenge to African people's humanity that has informed their literature, which must be read, understood and critically evaluated by all who wish *to at least understand the black man, woman, and child in Africa and elsewhere*; for it certainly cannot be refuted that to 'know' a people one must 'appreciate' their literature as an expression of their desires, wishes, feelings, and their reactions as a given tribe, sex, age group, or a people and their cultural particularities, sensibilities, perceptions, and adaptations to their environs.

The reactions of the Ibo of Nigeria to their contacting the white man in Chinua Achebe's classic, *Things Fall Apart*, exemplifies the European's general contact with African people (Achebe, 1990:128):

> He was not an albino. He was quite different...he was riding an iron horse. The first people who saw him ran away, but he stood beckoning to them. In the end the fearless ones went near and even touched him. The elders consulted their Oracle and it told them that the strange man would break their clan and spread destruction among them. It said that other white men were on their way. They were locust, it said, and that first man was their harbinger sent to explore the terrain.

A similar case is recounted in Jomo Kenyatta's *Facing Mount Kenya* (1965:41-51). Thus, once the white man entered Africa, Africa was to no longer be the same. The white man had not come to merely visit for a short while; he had come to live, dominate and change African people irrevocably. The whites built their churches, schools, courts, roads, and chose the types of African leaders they wanted; they humiliated and imprisoned those who didn't fall in line; they educated, christianized and favored those who accepted their rule. They recruited Africans and trained them to be messengers, catechists, teachers, clerks, translators, and village leaders, based on the European's paradigm; traditional African ways, and in North Africa, the Islamic ways, were subjected to untold brutalization (Memmi, 1991). Since 'they spoke through their noses' (Acbebe, 129), they taught the Africans to do likewise - to pray, marry, dress, dance, and 'perceive' like the European, who had not just come to stay, but to live by force. Thus in *Things Fall Apart,* Achebe skillfully depicts the moral, religious, political, educational, and legal conflicts that ensued from the contract between Europeans and Africans.

The Africans did not simply just roll over to let the European in; they challenged his authority, audacity, and his religion; they at first kept him at an arm's length in the Evil Forest, but as time progressed, the Europeans entrenched themselves in the midst of the Africans. Again, in Achebe's *Things Fall Apart* (162), the Africans recognized that the white man was

> ....very clever. He came quietly and peacefully with his religion. We were amused at his foolishness and allowed him to stay. Now he has won our brothers, and our clan can no longer act like one. He has put a knife on the things that hold us together and we have fallen apart.

The European did not stop in West Africa, or Iboland, but went further into Zululand (Abrahams, 1989), Kikuyuland (Ngugi, 1987), Acholiland (P'Bitek, 1984), and Malinkeland (Camara, 1990). In all of these cases, he reigned supreme and entrenched his religion, language, schools, laws, political, and other cultural institutions at the expense of African traditional languages and institutions. In Iboland, Yorubaland, Kikuyu and Acholiland, Africans resisted covertly as well as overtly, but their weapons were no match for the French, the Portuguese, the Dutch, the German, Spaniards, or the Anglo-Saxons. Okonkwo, the protagonist, agriculturalist-warrior-patriot in Achebe's *Things Fall Apart*, attempted to challenge the Europeans, who had undermined his culture while he was in exile to his mother's people; he was eventually driven to hang himself in despondency and impotency to successfully deter the white man from further destroying his sacred beliefs, standards of excellence, leadership and family. Okonkwo's own son, Nwoye, had already been converted to Christianity and Chuku, the Ibo's supreme God, had been disinstituted at the expense of Western Christianity. "From the very beginning religion and education went hand in hand. Mr. Brown's mission grew from strength to strength and because of his link with the new administration, it earned a new social prestige" (166-167). Graduates of these two famous western institutions, the priesthood and secular western classrooms, would accumulate "forests of books" (P'Bitek, 1984:113), to be the new Ocols of Africa, quiet disrespectful of Negritude and traditional African institutions.

Okonkwo, he who could not 'live on the bank of a river and wash his hands with spittle' (Achebe, 154), was driven by the white man... "to kill himself"; and (was to) "be buried like a dog" (191). This African hero's 'abominable death' symbolizes the death of that which was the pumpkin and the 'homestead' in P'Bitek (1984), the 'North' in Abrahams (1989), the 'Kouroussou' in Laye (1990), the 'Ancestors' in Toni Morrison (1970), and the pulsations in Negritude. The dangling Okonkwo from a tree represented a threat to the Africa the Europeans encountered, the trial of the spirits of Africa's rebelliousness against European invaders. The picture of that dangling African hero evokes shame, a sense of defeatism and signals change, but a change for the worst for African traditions and traditionalists. It is no wonder that "Okonkwo (had) deeply grieved. And it (had) not just (been) a personal grieve" (Achebe, 168); he had grieved for the whole of Africa.

Okonkwo's village may not have been 'perfect,' from the point of view of many moral standpoints, even that of Okonkwo himself, but Achebe "...shows Rev. Smith to be far more vicious, brutal, and violent man than Okonkwo" (Iyasere, 1978:109). To Mr. Smith, '"Black was evil. He saw the world as a battlefield in which the children of light (whites) were locked in mortal combat with the sons of darkness" '(109). Okonkwo may have overemphasized his manliness, but where does one's manliness stop, especially in defense of one's country, culture, belief systems and other sacred values and institutions? On the other hand, Okonkwo should not have been so inflexible, so confocal, so ambitious, and so driven to be the exact opposite of his lazy father who was always in debt; but cowards and the lazy are not the one's who make history, who become heroes of fiction and the past. And finally, Okonkwo should have been more accommodating; but to what extent were the Europeans willing to accommodate on Okonkwo's own terrain?

In Mr. Smith and Mr. Okonkwo are established two opposing perspectives, two themes, two, perhaps, irreconcilable points of view; in Memmi (1991), the perspectives of the colonizer and the colonized; in Dubois (1982), the Euro-American and the American 'Negro'; in Baldwin (1984:165) the Lambrandts and the African, in P'Bitek (1984:150), the Negritudists, the advocates of the gloriana school of African studies versus the Lawinos who could not write 'proud poems for their vanquished African ancestors' (151). To C. Eric Lincoln (1984:130), it (in Okonkwo's case) could have been a question of truth:

> Truth is the one and final expression of reality. Truth cannot be divided. It must be one. If A is true, and B is different from A, then B cannot be true. And by extension, if B is not true, then B is false and ought to be suppressed at the very least; what is false (and not true) should not be permitted to enjoy the prerogative of truth. Similarly, if truth is consistency, then truth is whole and cannot be divided against itself. Perfection is oneness, wholeness, uniformity. Whatever divides the oneness of an entity destroys the perfection that made it what it was

> and what it was meant to be. 'A house divided against itself cannot stand' because a divided house has lost its integrity–that quality of wholeness essential to its being rather than something different. To divide is not merely to weaken. To divide is to change the nature of a thing, to compromise its identity to perjure its perfection: To make it something other than what it was or what it was intended to be.

To the Europeans, and to some 'Europeanized' Africans, Okonkwo was too recalcitrant, too confocal, inflexible, too backward, and a cultural throwback in his strong desires to maintain his anachronistic culture and standards of living; too Mau-Mau-ish. Like the homeguards of Kenya, East Africa, some of Okonkwo's own people refused to fight against the European; they aided him instead. "The white man whose power (they knew) too well..." (Achebe, 188), was all too pervasive for Okonkwo to endure. The Europeans would have to rule his village without him; he chose death over 'slavery,' colonization, dehumanization, humiliation and the 'total' destruction of his 'negritude'. He believed too much in his own ways to be forced into another person's institutions, including schools, churches, and the concept of law and order; to Okonkwo, his Ibo culture was the truth and the only truth, without which he was no longer what he must be.

Had the Europeans not been unbending themselves, in their determinations, with their military weapons, to subdue the Africans by force (177-178), perhaps, Okonkwo might not have been not unchangeable; Okonkwo might have changed, had the change come from within the tribe; had Mr. Smith not seen blacks as evils and whites as the epitome of purity, Okonkwo might have accommodated the Europeans. To Okonkwo, the Europeans' presence in his village meant unwelcomed, uncalled-for destruction of the homestead; it was indeed to "live on the bank of a river and wash (his) hands with spittle" (154). In Okonkwo's African village, he epitomized success; in the hands of Europeans, a humburg, a liability to their schemes. As such, he had no place in the white man's paradigm; but before the Europeans could lay hands on him, he took his own life; nonetheless, the white man was already all over Africa.

In Kenya, East Africa, Ngugi's *Weep Not Child* (1987) deftly reveals the complexities involved in the Europeans' claims made on the lands of the Kikuyu. Interestingly, the original owners of the land, the Africans, came into conflict with Europeans' forceful occupation of the land given to the Kikuyu by the Almighty himself. The Europeans saw themselves as the protectors of Kenya and the protectorates of Sierra Leone, Ghana, Gambia, Nigeria and others under the British government; the Africans were the protected, the dependent. As if Africans had asked to be protected or be dependent, the Europeans, like

Lord Delamere, carved out large chunks of African land for themselves to 'protect' and develop in their own image, using Africans as squatters and homeguards. Like some of the Ibos in West Africa, some of the East Africans were used to support European domination in the form of teachers, evangelists, minor bureaucrats and soldiers in both World War I and II, and even during the Mau Mau emergency of the 1950s.

What we have in Ngugi's *Weep Not Child* then is a depiction of European settlement and colonization of another part of Africa; only this time, it is a deeper penetration of east Africa than that of Iboland. The Kikuyuland of *Weep Not Child* is fully settled by Europeans in terms of roads, schools, agriculture and western Christian churches and the 'full' acceptance of western education by some Africans as a means of liberation. Unlike Okonkwo's village, where Okonkwo was reluctant to have his son Nwoye in western schools, in Kikuyuland, western education had already been accepted as a tool to liberate one's family, family land and the nation as a whole. Njoroge's village is not isolated or insolated from European influences, for there was already "... the big tarmac road that was long and broad and had no beginning and no end except that it went into the city" of Nairobi (*Weep Not Child,* 28), where there were already shoe factories, industrial laborers, highly educated Africans, World War I and II veterans. Christian education had so entrenched itself that the protagonist, Njoroge, "...thought that schooling was the very best that a boy should have. It was the end of all living" (38). Kamau, his brother, too believed in the strength of western education as a means to upgrade their own family and free the land (38). Like Okonkwo in West Africa, Njoroge does not want to be like his father (44); he wants, however, to be 'westernized' and Christianized. Njoroge believed in the literal translation of the bible, the righteousness of God, and sees similarities between his people and the Exodus story of the bible (49).

At the outset then, Ngugi depicts the theme of oppression and freedom. The Kikuyu's land had been taken by the westerners, but this land must be reclaimed; however, there is the 'war' between the land owners and those who worked the land, traditional ownership of the land and the current ownership, traditional and the modern Africa, the educated and the trained, European and African history with respect to the land. The question about the land of the Africans is all too pervasive. (I feel like asking the European, Mr. Howlands, how is the Kikuyuland, and the black sons of the land, and bombs that destroy the land, and are you content with owning the land that you live on? (5-6)).

In this 'war' over the land, another element, the Indians, are introduced as intermediaries between the Europeans and the Africans with Africans at the bottom of the totem pole in their own country. "The Indians feared Europeans and if you went to buy in a shop and a white man found you, the Indian would stop selling to you and, trembling all over, would begin to serve *him*" (7); the Indian shop was the stage for the contest over land ownership and even citizenship. Even though the Indians were colonized by the British, they too looked down on the Africans, the natives. The real contest, however, is between the Europeans and the Africans, Africans who had fought for the Europeans for their own liberation from another group of Europeans, not once, but twice. These Black ex-service men had learnt a lot in their sojourns abroad; they had had white prostitutes, of all places, in Jerusalem (10). Bildad Kaggia (1975) had already, in reality, experienced such an encounter as an ex-service man (see Chapter 4).

In Kenya, however, the all-encompassing land was indeed the umbrella. The question was who was going to own the land? Mr. Ngotho, Njoroge's father, loves the land historically, traditionally and even religiously. He feels ashamed of himself to even suspect that he had mistreated the land or fruits of this ancestral gift on which he now works as a shambaboy. On the other end of this is Mr. Howlands, who feels that his soul and life are also in this land which produces for him so bountifully because he had tamed it so well. It is the case of the black man and the white man on the black man's land and the black man is working for the white man, and both are looking at each other suspiciously in regards to the "ownership" of the land.

> Both men admired (the) shamba for Ngotho felt responsible for whatever happened to this land. He owed it to the dead, the living and the unborn of his line, to keep guard over this shamba. Mr. Howlands always felt a certain victory whenever he walked through it all. He alone was responsible for taming this unoccupied wilderness. (31)

As it was in South Africa, Mr. Howlands in Kenya felt that he was conquering an unoccupied land, yet using native black labor to develop that wilderness. Mr. Howlands would like his son, Stephen, to inherit the land; "Mr. Ngotho...too was thinking of his children" (32). In this way, the land question assumes another level of importance, going beyond the two adults to include the fates of their children in the contest over the territory the two adults were claiming to own, from the point of view of their own individual perceptions; Mr. Ngotho thinks of England as Mr. Howlands' home, who sees England as only his *old* home. Both adults are embarking on their children to take over where they would leave off.

The African child, Njoroge, has been sent to school expressly to aid in regaining the land. "Njoroge did not want to be like his father working for a white man, or worse, for an Indian. He would be different" (44). He therefore took his Christian education seriously, paying particular attention to the Christian emphasis on love, equality, righteousness of God, justice, and mercy. His people were the chosen people, and his people's Moses, Jomo Kenyatta, would one day come to liberate them from the European pharoahs; why, he, Njoroge, might even be that Moses!

In the meanwhile, however, Mr. Jacobo, an African 'homeguard,' has been recruited by Mr. Howlands to defend European dominance against the Mau-Mau-ish Africans who had gone into the forests to take back their homeland. Wealthy Jacobo and poor Ngotho represent two classes of Africans in relation to land ownership and the Europeans' presence in Kenya; they confront each other during a strike by the African peasantry. Like Okonkwo, Ngotho could not abandon his cause, the cause of the African masses, betrayed by the Jacobos, a segment of Africans recruited by the European settlers to defend European privileges.

It is into this drama of events that the young Njoroge is caught, to find his western Christian education practically useless. His education could not reconcile the conflict of interests over the land in which his father loses his life, and his brothers Boro, Kamau, and Kori are in the hands of the white man's law, just like the elders of Okonkwo's village in West Africa were subjected to the white man's law and justice. "God meant little to him now. For Njoroge had now lost faith in all things he had earlier believed in, like wealth, power, education, and religion" (134). Like Okonkwo in West Africa, Njoroge in East Africa saw his failure, and walked away to commit suicide. Njoroge felt guilty for his impotence to stop the tide of European dominance, and was driven to end his own life. It was "...the guilt of a man who had avoided his responsibility for which he had prepared himself since childhood" (136). Had his mother not saved him, he would have ended like Okonkwo, dangling from a tree, the African who had failed to challenge the tide of European hegemony. Njoroge finally accepted himself as a coward, as a no-match for the tide of European power. "Ngugi does offer some hope, however, by leaving Njoroge alive at the end" (Dathorne, 1975:127).

Thus far, two African protagonists have lost the battle to mitigate European presence in Africa; western schools, churches, factories, roads, prisons, courts, and laws have been introduced into the African cultural landscape, and there seems to be no other choice but for Africans to painfully accept their colonial predicament. Both Achebe (1959) and Ngugi (1982) would later acquaint us with what became of the 'Njoroges' and the 'Nwoyes' of Africa; in addition to other African writers such as Okot P'Bitek (1984) and Camara Laye (1990), the colonized African protagonists are going to demand some changes in the colonial relationship because "the colonized does not exist in accordance with the colonial myth, but he is nevertheless recognizable. Being a creature of oppression, he is bound to be a creature of want" (Memmi, 1991:119).

One of the things the colonized wants to master is the colonizer's language and the corresponding European culture (Douglass, 1968:50); Conton (1969:49); and even Mathabane (1986:207). This was evident in the cases of Njoroge's naive desire for more western education and Christianity and Okonkwo's son's recruitment into the Christian church, thus putting a knife on the very things that had held the Ibo tribe together, resulting in cultural disengagement for both African characters. "Okonkwo's son, Nwoye, who was now called Isaac..." (Achebe, 167), was as disengaged from his father's culture and society as Njoroge was from the tribal history of his Kikuyu people; by forgetting the history of his Kikuyuland (Ngugi, 1964:17), Njoroge appeared weaker and weaker, especially in terms of his ability to be the Moses of his people. How could he have forgotten his people's folklore and still be the Moses of his people?

A similar cultural disengagement could also be observed in the case of Camara in French Guinea, West Africa (Laye, 1954). By this time, European presence in Guinea had been 'fully accepted.' Unlike Njoroge's failure in western education due to the Mau-Mau emergency, Camara in Guinea progressively succeeds in the French schools of Guinea to the extent of obtaining a scholarship to study in France, the 'mother' country. The more Camara succeeds in school, however, the more he is removed from his people linguistically, culturally and physically. His mother in Kouroussa, for an instance, made changes in his abode commensurate, in her own way, to her son's progress in European culture (169-170). Physically, Camara 'progresses' out of Kouroussa to attend a school in Conakry, the capital city of Guinea, that epitomized European standards of living and culture in that French west African country.

Unlike the bi-cultural foundations of Nwoye and Njoroge, Camara could be said to have been impacted by three major cultures: the traditional African, the Islamic and the European, but it was the European culture that appeared the most forceful; the first two he held in high esteem, but the European culture was the most profoundly decisive. Dedicating the book to his "Dark woman, African woman, O - Mother, I thank you for all you have done for me...," Camara Laye begins to reveal the significance of the African mother, the traditional transmitter of sound moral norms and values, the umbilical cord to the outside world. The autobiographies of Kwame Nkrumah (1957), Mark Mathabane (1986), Frederick Douglass (1968), and Kaunda (1965) all reflect these 'African' children's closeness to their mothers. Camara's excellent autobiography has been called a testimonial (8) about the love he had for his family, culture, society, the African people and the Negritudistic appreciation he had for the mysteries that surrounded the relationship between African people and nature itself. Indeed, Camara's simplicity, his insistence on the closeness of man to man and his trust in his people brings him into the forefront of the negritude school of thought (Laye, 1984:13). Nostalgically, Camara Laye recounts his childhood experiences and the mysteries that abound his African and Islamic heritages. The incident with the snake, his father's Muslim prayer rugs, workshop and hospitality in his sharing of meals with non-biological members of the household (19-20) reminds one of Kenneth Kaunda's household in *Zambia shall be free* in terms of his extended family and the closeness of man to man. Camara's trip to Tindican to visit with his maternal grandmother and uncles provide a delight in humanism and hospitality; they pampered him and made a festive occasion of his visits. The people examined his western clothes and the whole village of Tindican seemed to rejoice each time he visited. As a city-boy, Camara was admired and treated like a little aristocrat in his "precious clothes" (53).

The harvest seasons always found him in Tindican and he seemed to have greatly appreciated the festivities that went with the harvesting of the first fruits. But already, Camara was a 'new' African, for he could stay in Tindican for only so long before he had to return to school to continue his western education (a promising scholar, already taken away from the way things were in the tribe); he was being pulled from communalism to individualism, from the rhythms of the planting, growing, and harvesting seasons, to the culture of western schooling that emphasized individual progress. "...I was not entirely one of them. I was a schoolboy on a visit; how gladly I would have forgotten that fact" (61). But he certainly could not have forgotten that fact, for that fact made all the difference between him and his family, Tindican and the form of livelihood that his people continued to practice. He could sing "...the song of the rice" (64) with them, but he was no longer part of the rice fields as the villagers were. The world was certainly changing rapidly for Camara in spite of his seeming appreciation and even fidelity to the ways of his people. He confesses to his inability to adequately understand the "strange powers his mother possessed" (69). He states:

> I hesitate to say what these powers were, and I do not wish to describe them all. I know that what I say will be greeted with skeptical smiles. And today, now that I come to remember them, even I hardly know how I should regard them. They seem to be unbelievable; they *are* unbelievable. Nevertheless, I can only tell you what I saw with my own eyes. How can I disown the testimony of my own eyes? (69-70)

The eyes with which he saw his mother convince a recalcitrant horse to rise up after all other efforts had failed (70-71) were tainted eyes, no longer of totally the traditional African eyes, because European 'school work' had become to Camara "a deadly serious matter" (79). Was he then a man of two worlds? Had he a choice between the African and the European? Was it a case of approach-avoidance? It seems to be all of these and more, but the colonial system seemed a lot more persuasive, because in the western school system (Camara and his schoolmates had to undergo that colonial education), the African students had to undergo punishments from the older students, work for the school, receive beatings, etc. which were tolerated only if "one's love of knowledge was very strong to survive these ordeals" (80). To avoid punishments, one had to bribe the older scholars with food or money. This scheme of the older boys was not tolerated for long, but it depicted a common practice in the western school system, transplanted into their African colonies (See *Tom Brown's School Days*, for an example).

In contrast to the western school system, Camara gives a passionate description of the traditional circumcision ceremony he underwent. Here, older boys served as helpers to the initiates, not tormentors. An age group between twelve and fifteen years of age is gathered and led away to be educated in traditional Malinke cultural values and norms that had been handed down from one generation to the next. Separated from the general population, the youngsters are taught lessons in bravery, honesty, social and cultural responsibilities; the elders advise them thus:

> This has happened to all men. Has it done them any harm? It won't do you any harm either. Now that you are going to become men, conduct yourselves like men; drive away your fears. A man is afraid of nothing. (119-120)

In fact, the whole circumcision process represented a stage in traditional African education through which these young men had to pass in order to be considered adults, adults who would have already been socialized to price group cohesion, exhibit good manners and honesty, and take family responsibilities into their own hands as adults; it separated children from their mothers, for they would no longer be children but men. But Camara's progress in western education was to progressively take him away from his roots. After being a man in the African tradition, he still remained a schoolboy in the western system that kept taking him away from home. He travels from Kouroussa through Dabola, Mamu and Kindia to arrive in Conakry for additional western education. Physically, linguistically and culturally, he was undergoing the process of disengagement from his traditional African cultural norms and values. His first night in Conakry "...was the first night (he) had passed in a European styled house" (147). In spite of the comfortable European bed and European styled house, Camara felt lonely and ambivalent, torn between his Kouroussa and Conakry, between the European and the African (150-151). His progress in French schools in Conakry was to further take him away from his Kouroussa to France. His mother's recalcitrance about his departure would not prevent Camara's going further in western education and farther from the village; his destiny was to go away from home to France, not to retreat to the songs of the rice harvest.

> And so one day I took a plane to France, Oh! it was a terrible parting...I can still hear my mother wailing. I can still see my father, unable to hide his tears. I can still see my sisters, my brothers...No, I do not like to remember that parting. It was as if I were being torn apart. (186-187)

From Okonkwo and Nwoye, Njoroge and Ngotho, to Camara and his parents, an interesting phenomenon could be observed. Nwoye, Njoroge and Camara, members of the modern African generation, have been irrevocably dislodged from the traditional Africa, not mainly because of any internal African dynamism, but because of the European presence in the explicit form of western education, Christianity and colonization, which Okonkwo outrightedly rejected, but which Njoroge and Camara's parents accepted, somewhat reluctantly by Camara's mother. Regardless of the older African generations' traditions, the pull of the west with regards to the younger generations was overwhelming. Camara nostalgically leaves the rice farms and the traditional African forms of ritualism only to be correspondingly pulled to western culture, society and metropol; Njoroge hears of the great city of Nairobi and Nwoye is enrolled in the mission school. The three African youths, Nwoye, Njoroge, and Camara, were products of traditional African societies, but found themselves in a process of modernization to which they must adjust, however painfully; a change had come to Africa that was to challenge the very fabric of African society and culture. The European cultural presence in Africa was going to be the most forceful, decisive and compelling in comparison to the traditional and Islamic cultures, in the case of Camara, at least. The west irrevocably disrupted Okonkwo's society as he knew and wanted it; it monopolized Njoroge's people's land and radically changed his ideas about life, and the west cut Camara off from his African roots, most of which he will never again understand fully, despite his nostalgia; he certainly will never again fully understand the depths of some of the mysteries surrounding African animism, about which he could only speculate. Of the three African youths, Camara was the most opportuned with the luxury of nostalgia. The European presence in Guinea was not as forcefully drastic as in the case of Nigeria and Kenya; furthermore, Camara, in *The Dark Child*, had had a long and proud tradition to draw upon, having been grounded in the traditional African and Arabic cultures; the same cannot be said of Nwoye and Njoroge. Finally, Camara's father most realistically accepted the fact that times were indeed changing in Africa, and that Camara could participate in that change, armed with western education and exposure; Njoroge had taken western education and Christianity too literally, at the expense of his tribal lore, which he forgot to recite in front of this class. In all these cases, however, western education was overwhelmingly powerful; it dislodged Okonkwo's son, gave an unrealistic hope to Njoroge and took Camara away from a recalcitrant and loving mother and a foresighted father. In these contemporary African stories, there is a 'progressive' movement from traditional African society to the European metropol. Thus, Camara ended his narrative with a metropolitan subway map of Paris, to be enmeshed in French culture much more than Nwoye and Njoroge were to into British culture in, say, England.

Kamara, in William Conton's *The African,* takes us further into European culture. Like Nwoye, Njoroge and Camara, the Kamara in William Conton's art is compelled by European education to leave his village to advance himself in European culture despite his Negritudist fascination with traditional African humanism, childhood experiences, and his "...early and natural behavior (that he) was used to among (his) own people" (6), among whom his "...world was...a supremely secure one" (2). His love for the African past, the west African empire of Songhai, the simplicity of rural Africa, the rhythmic sound and movement in his village, etc. had all provided "love and security" (14) to the young Kamara.

All this love and security, however, were no match for the western culture that Kamara was pulled into via the European school. Like Njoroge and Camara, Kisimi Kamara considered himself extremely fortunate to have been chosen to be sent to school through which he could enter western culture and learn the master race's language. He describes one of his white female teachers with fascination: "her skin was white and red, and looked so soft and smooth that I longed to touch it" (4). Being so close to a member of the ruling race, he hoped to learn, go with her to Segrese (Freetown), the capital city of Songhai (Sierra Leone), and perhaps finally to England, the metropol, or the mother country, as we saw in the case of Camara Laye with his map of the subways of Paris.

As Camara Laye left Kourousssa in French Guinea to come to Conakry and France for further education, so also did Kisimi Kamara left Lokko, in British Sierra Leone, to come to Freetown and finally to England to further his education in western culture; they were both accompanied by their relatives before their departures and special rituals had to be conducted before their sendoffs. For both Camara and Kamara, leaving their places of birth for alien lands, including the capitals of Conakry and Segresa to further their educations, represented not only a physical break from their roots, but also a cultural and psychological break from the Africa that they knew. It is significant to further note that the two Kamaras, as in Njoroge's case, were 'expected' to use their learning for the benefit of their people; in the case of Kisimi Kamara, his educational attainment was likened to a palm-tree climber, who must be reminded of his duties to the tribe:

> ...My father went on to remind me that I had now started to climb a palm tree which was high and difficult to climb; that many were watching my progress, and much ripe fruit was awaiting me on the successful conclusion of my climb. He ended with the meaning that if I failed to reach the top, those watching me, both living and dead, would curse me for failing them. On the other hand, if I reached the top in order simply to gorge myself with fruit, I would surely become sick and fall to the ground and die. But if I returned to my people to share with them the fruit of my labours, then all would sing to my praise and thank me and honor those who had brought me to life. (21-22)

Like Njoroge and Laye, Kamara does extremely well in the European school system and eventually goes to the metropol, to be 'baptized' in European culture. To leave Africa was to leave behind his 'negritude,' his tropicality, naiveté, his tribe, and his fantastic admiration for the European in Africa. Liverpool introduced him to one of the many contradictions he had never thought would happen; he saw, for the very first time, a dirty white man sweeping gutters in heavy work boots (45). To the western reader, this might appear trivial, but to the colonialized African, a dirty white man, street sweeper, would come as a shock, an eye opener. Until African 'independence,' the colonizer made sure that he was the boss everywhere; he was the D.O., the D.C., the foreman, director, etc. commanding Africans in all works of life. To go to his country and find some of them not even highly educated was an 'Aha' experience for Kamara and countless colonial Africans.

Kisimi Kamara did not deal only with lower class Englishmen; he also was able to befriend Greta, a white South African girl from Pretoria, who had "...the complexion of great delicacy and smoothness" (62), thereby coming face to face with certain elements of the then Apartheid system. Kamara's trials and tribulations, including loneliness, acquainted him with some of the hard realities of life away from one's home. Nonetheless, Kamara was fortunate enough to meet kind Europeans who helped him in times of financial need. He managed to complete his studies with emphasis on the English language, his colonizer's language, and returns to Africa determined to help himself and his people; among his people, however, he observed a lust for quick money and power, materialism, individualism, and corruption (101); "birthrights were being sold for a mess of pottage" (103), and there was a total breakdown in the social and moral values among his people. The society he had left behind was no longer the same; Kamara himself began to feel that he should be interested only in himself, but fate was to push him into national and Pan-African politics (109). As prime minister of Songhai, he was opportuned to meet other New African heads of state, such as Mr. Owoo-Jones (Kwame Nkrumah) who was determined to have a United States of Africa (177). Kamara "sensed all at once the meaninglessness of all colonial boundaries in Africa" (109).

In his native Songhai, however, he deliberately exploited his traditional culture, so as not to appear too Europeanized. To succeed in Songhai politics he adopted some traditional African cultures and customs: he practiced polygamy, let his parents chose for him a wife, traveled through the country entreating chiefs and elders, wore African attire and spoke English only when it was required. He was satisfied with his parents' choice for a wife; "Fatmata was as black as satin, and as soft. She had the teeth and smile of a goddess"; Kamara's "anti-western revolt was gaining momentum" with his nationalistic spirit (121).

After much real 'politiking', Kamara was eventually elected Prime Minister of Songhai, a long distance away from Nwoye, Njoroge and Guinea's Camara. But like most African Nationalists of the 1960s, being the first African Prime Minister or President was one thing; it was quite another to use that power with positive action. "The next few years (after Kamara's election) saw no dramatic developments in Songhai. It (was) much more difficult to work miracles in office than to demand them out of it" (172). Kamara's ministers looked wise but were totally ignorant about the workings of government, most especially the technical, or scientific aspects of government (173). Again, it was one thing to learn the colonizer's language, but quite another to run the institutions he left behind in Africa.

Even though Kamara was interested in African unity, he was more of the gradual school of thought, unlike Owoo-Jones (Nkrumah), who was adamant about immediate continental African unity. To Owoo-Jones, Pan-Africanism was an imminent consideration; Kamara was skeptical and "wondered whether (Owoo-Jones) cherished a secret ambition to become the first Prime Minister of a United State of Africa" (18). Mr. Owoo-Jones of Kanem undoubtedly resembles Kwame Nkrumah of Ghana who, in 1958 called two Pan-African conferences to effect the speedy liberation of African states still then under colonialism, and urged the unity of African states after all had attained their independence; the then Apartheid South Africa was popularly the common enemy, easily attackable with eloquent speeches.

Prime Minister Kamara would not mind going to South Africa himself to help organize the people against apartheid, even though the African National Congress (ANC) did not need an organizer but financial assistance from other African nations. Kamara's decision then to go to South Africa was, subjectively, to 'avenge Greta', his white South African girlfriend who had been killed in England by the jealous Afrikaaner, Friedrik.

In South Africa Kamara "followed (Friedrik) to the door of his club, and next day secured a job in the club's kitchen" (212). The African Prime Minister from Songhai then worked for an Afrikaaner who had killed Greta in England for befriending a black African; the white south African who abused blacks and who was to later ask that Kamara be fired from his kitchen duties, was the same man Kamara found helplessly drunk and took him home to safety; he could not feel hate for Friedrik, despite all he had done, but pity.

In Kamara's negritude and humanism, he could not see himself hurting a drunken man, not even a drunken racist; as such, despite his failures in Songhai (no dramatic developments occurred under his government), he showed himself a Christ-like figure in helping and loving his enemy, Friedrik, instead of exacting a retribution; another black character with a more violent humor would have smitten Friedrik for his killing of Greta, for his hatred of blacks and for his stance as a clear symbol of apartheid; in Kamara's pity, and perhaps his weakness, lay his moral strength over a wicked, albeit a helpless man, who, in his drunken stupor, would not have presented any physical challenge to Kamara.

## Post-Colonial African Literature

William Conton's *The African* is both a colonial and a post-colonial African literature; in fact, it includes parts of traditional African literature as well; these three sources (the pre, the colonial, and the post-colonial) of African literature are not disengaged from one and the other; for our purposes here, we can make this schematic presentation:

A Paradigm of African Literature

| TRADITIONAL | COLONIAL | POST-COLONIAL |
|---|---|---|
| Achebe | Achebe | Achebe |
| Conton | Conton | Conton |
| Camara | Camara | Camara |
| Armah | Armah | Armah |
| P'Bitek | P'Bitek | P'Bitek |

While traditional African literature (orature) uses fables, songs, legends, proverbs, praise songs, and provide moral directives on the local and the universal scales, contemporary African literature about Africa's colonial experience depicts Africans in conflict with their traditional culture and the conquering forces; the protagonists are marginal men and women in search of an African personality which has not yet entrenched itself. Colonial African literature, as can be seen in the cases of Okonkwo and Nwoye, Ngotho and Njoroge, Camara and his family, Kamara and his nationalism, etc. depict the alienation of Africans from their authenticities, their negritude, and portray their "exploitation, inferiorization..., condescension" and in a process of transformation (Jeyifo, 1993:226).

Post colonial African literature is a continuation of the colonial and the traditional in a never-ending transformation of the African; it "involves the exploration of Africa's place in the world...the relationship of Africa to itself, the encounter of African nations, societies, and the peoples with one another" (226), and these concerns are not radically negated from the colonial and the precolonial; "complex and ambiguous historical dynamics link" them together in many subtle ways (226).

In post-colonial African literature African writers find themselves and their characters in European-created African nations and institutions to which the educated and the illiterate, the powerful and the powerless Africans alike must adjust. In post-colonial African literature, the European created nations of Kenya, Ghana, Nigeria, Sierra Leone, etc. are in the hands of the Kenyattas, the Nkrumahs, Azikiwes, the Stevens, or the Ocols. The literature of post-colonial Africa "is...profoundly pessimistic, even melancholic..." (224). Characters are often alienated from the new state and the new leadership in the 'neo-colonial' state; they often face moral paradoxes, ambiguities, corruption, kleptocracy, classism, conspicuous consumption, scatology and a general physical, political, institutional and moral decadence. Most of these themes alluded to above are readily apparent in Ayi Kwei Armah's *The Beautyful* (sic)*Ones Are Not Yet Born* (1968),P'Bitek's *Song of Lawino and Ocol* (1984) and James Ngugi's *Devil on the Cross* (1982).

Armah's *The Beautyful* (sic)*Ones Are Not yet Born* depicts the plight of an African state under African leadership; perhaps Okonkwo's grandchildren are now in power; it exposes the filth and the putridity of an African nation in the hands of the sons of Africa. As a scatological novel, it is filled with maggots, chichiddos, public thieves, bribers and sleepwalkers in filth.

The protagonist, The Man, is torn between his sense of decency, morality and poverty and the public's (including his mother-in-law's desire for material possessions), sense of what is moral, decent and the 'gleam'. In this post-colonial African state, the man who takes bribes and steals from the government gets to enjoy the gleam of life.

The Man, however, is a decent man in the putrid African state of Ghana; in the bus, he is mistaken for a watchman who 'sees' the bus conductor pocketing government money, the Cedi, that stank rotten. Thus, at the outset, the Ghana of West Africa, under Kwame Nkrumah, or Owoo-Jones in William Conton's *The African*, the mood of the country is devastatingly signified in The Man, "the watcher (who) was no watcher after all, (but) only a sleeper" (5).

The capital city, despite campaigns to clean up the place, is filthy with overflowing dust bins:

> People did not have to go to the dust bin anymore. From a distance they aimed their rubbish at the growing heap and a good amount of juicy offal hit the face and slides off the box before finding a final resting place upon the heap. (8)

The city has a gloomy looking post office building; other government buildings are in need of badly needed repairs; "The sons of the nation (who) were now in charge" (10), do not seem to be in charge at all. Like Kamara's Songhai, things have not changed for the better for the African masses. The highly educated few are now the ministers and top civil servants, but do not seem able to make any progressive change in the lives of their own people; the European colonialists had been replaced by African Neo-colonialists – the sons and daughters of Africa.

The banister in the building where The Man works as a clerk in a traffic control office, also signifies the condition of this West African nation; the banister had been painted over and over again, but people keep soiling the painted banister with their soiled, filthy hands on their way back from the lavatory. In the offices, there are no functioning telephone lines (10); the fan in the traffic control office moved slowly, and everyone sweated profusely, creating a "stewy" atmosphere (20).

As if these physical putrefactions were not enough, there is also moral putridity. The 'dash' that was once used prevalently in West Africa has now been elevated to bribery, and those who took bribes and enjoyed the 'gleam' of conspicuous consumption and shiny long cars, imported spirits and flamboyant homes, fine clothes and jewelry are now the new rulers. Those who do not, such as The Man, remained poor because of their honesty and dedication to fairplay.

If The Man remained poor because of his honesty, by not taking bribes, or stealing from the government, Minister Koomson represented the gleam, the epitome of the new African elite for his epicureanism and unaccountability to humility. Koomson, The Man's classmate, had not been a bright student but had learned to play the new game of get-rich-quick; "money was life" (77) in the eyes of the new African elite, as well as the African masses, but not The Man and his teacher, who remained aloof, bamboozled by the physical and moral putridity around them; they are analytic but powerless to affect any moral or political change; they see the African leaders as aping their former colonial masters. "There is something so terrible in watching a black man trying at all points to be the dark ghost of a European..." (80).

Koomson exemplifies that aping black man. He had come into the new government "...believing nothing, but saying (he believed) everything that needs to be believed, so long as the big jobs and the big money follow(ed). Men who knew nothing about politics have grown hot with ideology, thinking of the money that will come" (89).

How can The Man live in poverty and see his stupid classmate, Koomson, enjoy the material things that came with his new power? How could he close his eyes to the fact that Koomson and his wife lived luxuriantly and he, barely? What could he do about his wife, children and his mother-in-law, who make him feel less of a man, because he refused to grab the high-life of life, even if kleptocratically? The Man himself reflected:

> How can I look at Oyo (The Man's wife) and say I hate long shiny cars? How can I come back to the children and despise international schools? And then Koomson comes, and the family sees Jesus Christ in him. How can I feel like a human being? (91-92)

Genuine hard work in his office was certainly not going to give him the gleam, the long shiny cars, the white bungalow, or pay for his children to attend international schools in the capital city. To get the gleam, the young man must take bribes, cut corners, and be obnoxiously fraudulent; others were doing it in the lumber business, selling government scholarships and purchasing aristocratic foreign cars and drinks; they did not like the 'made-in-Ghana spirits' (116).

The Man was put in a moral dilemma; he dearly wanted to provide for his family, like Koomson was doing for himself and his wife, Estella, but he also could not deviate from his moral rectitude. His wife, children, and mother-in-law all make him feel less of a man because he lacked material things. The maternal grandmother lambasted The Man through the children:

> 'My poor husband!' said the old woman, over and over again. 'You have no shoes to wear, so your poor little feet get torn to pieces. Ei, my husband, you have nobody, nobody to buy you shoes, so your little toes will all be destroyed.' She went close to the boy and

> peered down at his feet, looking for the one with the cut on it.
>
> 'Where is the wound, my husband? Where is it? You must know you have nobody, you are an orphan, a complete orphan. You mustn't run around, like people who have men behind them, to buy them shoes. My poor husband!'
>
> The Man stood quietly, watching and listening, wondering whether he would have any moisture left in his mouth for framing words. This was done so very often, the tender heads of children serving as things on which adults could bounce their bullet words into the hearts of their enemies. He had come to expect it, yet everytime it happened it made him angry. (123)

When the Koomsons came to visit The Man's home, the minister could not use the poor man's lavatory; it was too low-class, putrid, and below his dignity; his wife, Estella, does not like locally made beer; it did not "agree with (her) constitution" (131).

Koomson and Estella live in the exclusive, upper class residential area named the Esikafo Aba Estates; Koomson's house is furnished by "The State Furniture Corporation" (148). Estella's sister is in London on a government scholarship, arranged by Koomson, and she is specializing in dressmaking. In London, she has fallen in love with a Jaguar; Koomson's daughter is named Princess, to top his gleam off. To the Koomsons, one must have material things at all cost, if not for oneself, then for one's children; those who did not join 'the new wave' were left out of the material world of shiny cars and the Esikafo Aba Estates and other privileges enjoyed by members of the new African elite.

Ironically, when the Osagyefo's socialist government was overthrown by a group of army and police officers, it was The Man who helped Koomson escape through the poor man's lavatory, which he had felt too dignified to use during his previous visit to the man's poor house; this time, he had to escape to the Ivory Coast. Koomson, the party man, became the smelly man, the hungry and the frightened man at the mercy of the poor, honest man; he even had to beg his servant for safety and to escape in a boat he had fraudulently bought.

Armah did not leave us there; even though the coup replaced the corrupt government of the Osagyefo, bribery still went on as before; there had simply been a new coating added onto the putrid banister! Indeed, the beautiful ones were not yet born in Ghana, Kenya (Ngugi, 1982), or Uganda (P'Bitek, 1984).

If Armah's *The Beautyful Ones Are Not yet Born* is a scatological 'study' of socialist Ghana in West Africa, James Ngugi's *Devil on the Cross* is a sociological 'study' of capitalist Kenya, East Africa, with a Marxist taint. In this post Njoroge, post Mau-Mau, Jacobo, Ngotho and post-Howlands novel, Ngugi depicts the Koomsons of Kenya boasting about their exploitation of the masses and publicly advocating capitalism. Ngotho, in *Weep Not, Child,* would have probably advocated a communualistic Kenya after the Howlands had been usurped by the Mau-Mau, but in Ngugi's *Devil on the Cross*, the 'fight' now was for dollarism and materialism.

The writer, Ngugi, is simply the medium through whom the exploitative conditions in Kenya are transmitted (8); the writer himself is not to be blamed for depicting the scenarios portrayed. If Wariinga, a secretary at the Champion Construction Company, on Tom Mboya Street, near the National Archives building, is dismissed for insubordination to sexual advances from her boss, Boss Kihara, that was so because it was so expected. That evening, Wariinga was abandoned by her boyfriend, Kimwana, who thought she was her boss's mistress. To add more to Wariinga's plight, she was kicked out of her apartment by her wealthy landlord, who climbed in his Mercedez Benz to bring back thugs to evict her. Thinking of herself as ugly, Wariinga hated her blackness and tried to imitate concepts of white beauty; in her delerium to be white, she is totally disoriented in a 'westernized' Nairobi, pervaded by an alien lifestyle.

In this 'westernized' Nairobi, young girls are exploited by their male bosses who tell them to meet them at five p.m., after office hours (19). These sugar daddies are well educated, wealthy, have power and use these to get to the thighs of good looking young girls, leaving their wives at home (23).

Wariinga must leave this wicked city for Illmorong, and she does so in a Model T. Ford, a Matatu, whose driver could do anything for money. "Nothing is free in Kenya. Kenya is not Tanzania or China" (37). The new Haraambe is the Haraambe of money (39). The advocates of the new nationalism are the capitalists, imperialists and other exploiters whose love of money is immeasurable. The African peasants are at the mercy of not only the peripheral African capitalists, but also the international capitalists who employ their African collaborators to exploit their African subjects.

At a conference of capitalists (thieves), the Hell's Angels band entertain, while each capitalist confesses his dedication to exploitation; one capitalist confessed that his father had advised him to learn well from the white man; to be wealthy, one had to be cunning; like Jacobo in *Weep Not, Child*, his father was an anti-Mau-Mau gang member. Another confesses that he exploited people's thirst for western education by putting white dolls in his school windows to show that white children were attending the school, and therefore charged parents exorbitant sums of money for school fees. Should these domestic capitalists talk otherwise, their American benefactors would withdraw all the aid necessary for their survival in this dependent capitalism. The

American representatives to the conference (173) would withdraw all western factories from Kenya, should the Africans fail to exploit Africa; "everyone should (even) go home and rob his own mother" (170).

At the other end of this extreme exploitation, in Marxist terms, is of course the laboring classes, the peasants who are in naked contrast to these neo-African bourgeoisies now ruling the post-colonial, post Mau-Mau state of Kenya. Acting as intermediaries between western and Japanese capitalists, they are superficially western, and are quite satisfied with the crumbs of international dollarism. What could be the fate of these gang of robbers of the African masses?

Karl Marx (1818-1883) had observed in Western Europe that such a state of affairs would denote antagonistic contradictions that must be resolved in favor of the laboring classes. Marx, not from the laboring classes, had intellectually identified with the industrial working classes and saw that history was informed by the struggle between the oppressed and their oppressors, who were in constant opposition to each other; their opposition to each other would eventually culminate into a reconstituted society.

In Ancient Rome it was the Patricians and the Knights versus the Plebians and the slaves; in the European Middle Ages, it was the feudal lords and their vassals versus serfs, apprentices and journeymen.

Marx was undoubtedly concerned about the European working classes who were then subjected to extreme exploitation (the expropriation of the surplus value from their labor), including child labor, long working hours, poor and dangerous working conditions, the alienation of the workers from the products of their efforts, etc. With the European industrial revolution came urbanization and the concomitant housing, sewage and antisocial problems in the impersonal European centers. Marx's observations of Western Europe convinced him that the historical conflict between the oppressed and their oppressors would culminate into a revolution that would lead to a proletarian victory, thereby abolishing bourgeois property relations.

Theoretically, a thesis and an antithesis would 'collide' to create a synthesis, which in turn would create its own dynamism and this dynamics is the stuff of the historical process. Even though there have been instituted intervening variables in the capitalist world in the form of laws against child labor, poor wages and the abuse of workers, the 'skeleton' of Marx's thesis informs James Ngugi's *Devil on the Cross* about peripheral capitalism and the post-Mau-Mau society of Kenya.

Wariinga, the African female peasant, reflects on the troubles she's encountered with the class of the African exploiters, petit capitalists, in collaboration with their western and Japanese bosses. Her parents' land had been taken; her pregnancy from one of the sugar daddies, the attempts of her boss Kihara to get between her thighs, the landlord who evicted her and the conference of thieves and robbers extolling the exploitation of their own people were all antagonistic contradictions to Wariinga. Wariinga then, and the army of workers, students, and the petty traders, "led by a small group that seem(ed) well dressed" (203) provided the antithesis to the gang of robbers and thieves. "The workers (were) at the forefront of the fight against neo-colonialism" (209). Wariinga, the African woman, the most exploited and conscious of that exploitation, is certainly the most antithetical to the peripheral male capitalists of this post Mau-Mau Kenya; the workers attack the conference of the gang of thieves in which many lives are lost; the workers proclaim their solidarity: "...we, the workers, are of one clan, and hence we should not allow ourselves to be divided by religion, color or tribe" (210); Mr. Ngugi might as well have added 'sex', which is often used to oppress African women in particular, in traditional as well as in modern Africa, where they are still second class citizens.

Two years after the devil's feast, the conflict between the 'Wariingas' and the gang of thieves, Wariinga is in Nairobi, in a studio apartment of a seven story building. As a transformed Wariinga, she no longer burns her hair or lightens her skin; she wears jeans and khaki shirts, keeps a gun, learns Judo and becomes an accomplished mechanic. But the conflict between Wariinga and the African bourgeoisies is not yet over, or reached a denouement. Even though her position in Kenyan society had been, to a large extent, clarified, there was one little more melodrama to unfold in her life: Where was the sugar daddy-father of her daughter, Wambui? Where are the sugar daddies of Africa who, because of their wealth and power, take advantage of vulnerable, young African girls in the cities and even in the countrysides; where were the top African civil servants who lure their secretaries to hotel rooms after office hours in order to sexually exploit them and then go home to their Estellas, as in *The Beautyful Ones Are Not Yet Born* about Ghana?

These top African civil servants, as we saw in the case of the Koomsons in West Africa, seemed to be unaccountable for the putridity in the society in which they lived, for the feelings of the Wariingas, the peasants of the African society. This peasant, Wariinga, fell in love with Gatuiria, an American educated Kenyan of a wealthy father; it was Gatuiria's father, however, who was also Wambui's biological father (249). "The rich old man stood up...and said to Wariinga: Let's kneel down and pray together" (249). Wariinga was of course not in the mood or in need of prayer. This rich old man had impregnated her, contributing to her dropping out of school; now *his* son wants to marry her... "Wariinga shrugged her shoulders. She remained on her feet" (249). The rich old man continued to beg Jacinta Wariinga for forgiveness and even attempted to bribe her:

> Please my little lady, my fruit, listen to my words. Release me from this shame today. Be my woman, and I will rent a house for you in Nairobi, Mombasa or

> wherever you choose. I will furnish the house with furniture and carpets you see in this house, and with mattresses and curtains and other things imported from abroad–from Hong Kong, Tokyo, Paris, London, Rome, New York. Name it, and it's yours....I will also buy you a shopping basket, a basket to take to market, like a Toyota Corona, a Datsun 16B, an Alfasud or any other car of your choice. (251)

All these material things could not buy Wariinga's forgiveness, shame, and the history of exploitation by the sugar daddies of modern Africa, and

> The people outside heard the shots. When they entered the room, they found Gatuiria's father kneeling, still clinging to Wariinga by the knees. But three bullets were lodged in his body. (253)

Therefore, in Ngugi's *Devil on the Cross* we see a progression in terms of the exploitation and the oppression of the African masses by African native leaders who now ruled and exploited their own people economically and sexually. But the Wariingas of Africa, conscious of the new class structure and armed with Marxist analysis of society, are no longer going to stand idle and allow rich old men feast on their "thighs and breasts" (143). These educated, modern African women are not going to be bought with materialism that men have always used to 'buy', dominate, and exploit womenfolk globally. In this universal contest of man's exploitation of man and women, Mr. Ngugi has eloquently added the other African voice, the voice of African women, the Wariingas of Africa, of the Third World, and of the global village in general. In making Wariinga radically conscious of her society, neo-colonialism, imperialism and her place in that society Ngugi makes her the new African woman, who will contribute to the new African society from an empowered position, never to be again sexually exploited by the modern-day African sugar daddies.

If James Ngugi could be said to have utilized the Marxist analysis of Kenyan society, Okot P'Bitek should be said to have depicted the conflict between cultural nationalism (Negritude) and the process of the westernization of Africa in his *Song of Lawino and Song of Ocol* (1984). In his *Africa's Cultural Revolution* (1975), P'Bitek dealt with the social and cultural ills in African societies; he criticized African Socialism as a socialism for the New African elites and called for the unity of the African working masses, the illiterates. He further criticized the African elite for aping European mannerisms, behaviors, attire and other 'mentalities'. In his *Song of Lawino and Song of Ocol* the traditional, 'illiterate' Africa and the modern are exquisitely dramatized. In the introduction to the *Song Lawino...*, G.A. Heron observes that "...the 'Ocols' and the 'Lawinos' of Africa...have become prototypes of two opposing approaches to the cultural future of Africa" (2). The Lawinos are African traditionalists; the Ocols are anti-African traditionalists; this intellectual/cultural 'battle' continues and will continue to be of concern for quite sometime, for political economists as well as literary artists.

What foundations should African nations utilize in their moves for development? Should they rely solely on their traditional foundations or solely on western foundations imposed on them from above and without? Of course, like the Japanese, they could be eclectic and consciously select from both the West and Africa; but which aspects of the West should Africa adopt? Which aspects of traditional African culture should Africans retain? These are some of the crucial questions debated by Lawino and Ocol, wife and husband, the illiterate and the literate, the traditional African and the westernized, (post-colonial) African, the Negritudists and the anti-Negritudist, the call from Lawino and the response from Ocol, etc.

Lawino invites Ocol to a cultural debate; she castigates Ocol for most of the things P'Bitek had written against in his *Africa's Cultural Revolution*; Lawino, for an instance, lashes out at Ocol for his choice of attire, European dances, religion, games, aesthetics, foods, concept of time, medicine and contemporary (westernized) African politics. To Lawino, Ocol had become the white man's good dog and "a good dog pleases its master" (115).

Listen, my husband,
Hear my cry!
You may not know this
You may not feel so,
But you behave like
A dog of the white man!
A good dog pleases its master,
It barks at night
And hunts in the salt lick
It chases away wild cats
That comes to steal the chicken!
And when the master calls
It folds its tail between the legs.

The dogs of white men
Are well trained
And they understand English!

Lawino did not simply criticize Ocol; she made specific recommendations for him to reclaim his rightful place as a husband, a man with a working spear. Ocol is exhorted to clear his throat so that he talks like an Akoli; Ocol should go to the shrine of his ancestors, make sacrifices and ask for blessings through his father. He should ask his ancestors for a new spear that will trust and not bend easily like the earthworm; Ocol should not uproot the pumpkin (120).

Lawino does not understand why Ocol and his politician brother do not join forces for the development of the Uganda nation. According to Lawino, Ocol should first of all try to get his own house in order before he begins to think of solving the nation's problems at large.

Actually, "...Lawino manages remarkably well. Because she is not intellectual, it does not mean she is not intelligent" (14). She is quite able to perceive the cultural dilemma of contemporary Africa, the subtle desire to maintain traditional Africa juxtaposed with western materialism, science and ideas about what should constitute development.

Ocol, on the other hand, responds by lashing out against traditional Africa as a tourist attraction (136), and against failed African warriors and leaders.

> Blackness
> Deep, deep fathomless
> Darkness
> Idle giant
> Basking in the sun
> Sleeping, snoring
> Twitching in dreams;
> Diseased with a chronic illness
> Choking with black ignorance
> Chained to the rock of poverty. (125)

Ocol's views of Africa are pessimistic and they reiterate Africa's backwardness in technology, the persistence of tribalism and the anachronistic clinging to outmoded forms of government, medicine, and the past. Ocol will not go back to repent to his ancestors; he would rather destroy the homestead, 'uproot the pumpkin' and traditional African cultures that have held Africa down, including Negritudists and Pan-Africanists. African socialists, historians and artists that remind him of the past must be gone.

When Ocol looks into the contemporary and the African past, he does not see what Lawino sees; he sees the oppression of African women, whom he exhorts to rebel against their subjugation. He tells them to

> shatter that pot,
> shatter taboos, customs, traditions,...
> You are no mere
> Donkey cart;
> Burn the Kyondo sacks
> That bow you down.... (131)

To the African male warriors, and cattle rearers and others, he lashes at them for their now "... barren empire" that has remained "closed to progress" (136). To Ocol, the African past is in the past and need not be recalled in the name of Negritude or cultural nationalism; either the villagers join the modernization process or kill themselves, and "what proud poem/can we write/for the vanquished?" (151)

Thus, Ocol's response attempts to demolish Lawino's criticism and the lashings at her husband who once proclaimed his 'love' for her, but is now in love with Tina, the westernized African woman, who paints her lips and burns her hair.

Can Lawino and Ocol be synthesized to create a renaissant African? Theoretically, and for the good of Africa, a way must be found to integrate the two opposing paradigms or points of views. Despite the hyperbole, P'Bitek has dealt with a key African problem that cannot be brushed aside artistically, psychologically, politically, or even economically. Lawino cannot get all she wants, and Ocol must be tempered.

As we've seen, the European presence in Africa has profoundly affected African culture, literature and in other ways as well. This has been reflected in the negation of Nwoye from his culture in *Things Fall Apart*, Okonkwo's death, Njoroge's blind ambition, Camara's alienation, Kamara's impotency, Koomson's kleptocracy, the Marxist analysis of Kenyan society and the profound conflict between Lawino and Ocol. A similar conflict, or contradiction in contemporary African society could also be observed in the case of the literature of black South Africa.

## The Special Case of South Africa

Much has been written about Apartheid South Africa since, say, 1960, the year of the Sharpville Massacre of "sixty-seven men, women, and children...(several of whom were) found to have been shot in the back while running to escape," in which "186 others were wounded" (Davidson, 1989:173); this epitomized white South Africa's determination to continue the separation of the races. From 1652 to 1994 white South Africa maintained many lines of demarcation between Africans and Europeans, even though they were never completely successful, due to the presence of coloreds and the demand for black labor in South African industries.

The 1960 Sharpville Massacre, as though it were an omen, greeted the birth of Mark Mathabane, a 'Kaffir' boy, who was able to eloquently record his childhood experiences and observations about that part of the Pan-African experience.

In Mathabane's *Kaffir Boy* (1986), the South African drama/stage is brought so close to the reader/audience that those familiar with the works of the late James Baldwin would readily recall the concept of 'nightmare.' In *Kaffir Boy,* the then notorious pass-laws become living organisms tormenting Black Africans in their houses, work places, shebeens, schools and dreams. Black families are stripped of their familihood; individual blacks are stripped of their dignity, sense of decency, manhood/womanhood, childhood/adulthood; some are driven to alcoholism, gambling, homosexualism, fear, nightmare, mesmery, myopia, inertia, etc. In their native land of birth, blacks are seen constantly under the threat of deportation to barren Bantustans; grown women, black mothers and grandmothers, are kitchen girls or domestic servants; black schools are torture chambers, transmitting inferior, anachronistic education; in the black child's repertoire, the white man becomes a bogeyman; black policemen are not protectors, but agents of terror, collectors of bribes and arresters of Bantus without valid papers. Often, blacks willing to work for penal wages can't get valid papers to apply for jobs, and can't hunt for jobs without valid papers, and remain there in limbo.

In this drama of pain, humiliation and alienation from both the traditional and the 'Europeanized' Africa, blacks are exhorted by Christian Evangelists to accept their sinfulness/evilness, denounce their tribal religions for christianity so that '"when the day of judgment comes"' they '"will board that glory train to heaven"'(59). On the other hand, however, African traditional religion, so-called Animism, remains a spiritual and psychological bedrock, to the older black generations at least, and provides a sense of worth and resistance against the nightmarish white domination to which the black masses are subjected.

As though providing a catharsis from this nightmare of white oppression, Mathabane includes a sensitive look at a few white South Africans who were willing to dilute his hellish experiences in South Africa, even though, "there (weren't) many like them around" (171) to offset the nightmare, hunger, poverty and the dehumanization of the black African masses. Underlying Mathabane's childhood experiences and resolve to succeed out of the pit of hunger, illiteracy and hopelessness, include his unique personal characteristics and the unflinching stamina, determination and energy of two black women: his mother and grandmother. In addition to these two was also a non-familial support system of people, Europeans and Coloreds, who recognized Mathabane's abilities and desires and helped him attain his 'passport to freedom' to the world of ideas and individual liberty. Mathabane explicates:

> To learn to express my thoughts and feelings effectively in English became my main goal in life. I saw command of the English language as the crucial key with which to

> unlock the doors leading into the wonderful world of books. (193)

Mathabane's strong desire for an education is not unique in black autobiographies. For instance, like Frederick Douglass, the more Mathabane read, the more he was aware of the contradictions between white people's religious doctrines and their religious practices relative to black people. Furthermore, the conflict between Douglass and Master Auld, and that between Mathabane and his father with respect to education, are not only similar, but the language and reactions of Douglass and Mathabane are almost identical. For an example, Douglass' reactions to Mr. Auld's attempts to keep him compulsorily ignorant went thus:

> What he most dreaded, that I most desired. What he most loved, that I most hated. That which to him was great evil, to be carefully shunned, was to me a great good, to be diligently sought; and the argument which he so warmly urged, against my learning to read, only served to inspire me with a desire and determination to learn. In learning to read, I owe almost as much to the bitter opposition of my master, as to the kindly aid of my mistress. I acknowledge the benefit of both. (Douglass, 1968:50)

Mathabane similarly reacted to his father's determination to keep him out of books and from the white man's education:

> I was set in my ways, he in his. He disparaged education, I extolled it; he burned my books at every opportunity, I bought more; he believed all that the white man said about him, I did not; he lived for the moment, I for the future.... (Mathabane, 207)

In this connection, we find Mathabane rebelling against his father's world view as much as Okonkwo did his father's in Achebe's renown , *Things Fall Apart* (Achebe, 1958:16-17).

Though thousands of miles apart, the African people's reactions to Arthur Ashe's triumphs on the tennis courts in South Africa were aptly similar to the reactions of blacks in Maya Angelou's Stamps, Arkansas, to Joe Louis's winning in a boxing match over a white opponent. For the black South Africans, "Arthur Ashe's triumphs on the court were...triumphs for the black race. His name was everywhere: in stores, in schools, in churches, in shebeens, in the Madam's kitchen and garden" (Mathabane, 253).

For the Blacks of Stamps in Maya Angelou's *I Know Why the Caged Bird Sings,* Joe's losing would have meant that the whole black race had lost. Angelou writes for the Blacks of Stamps about their reactions to Joe Louis' fighting with a white man:

> My race groaned. It was our people falling. It was another lynching, yet another black man hanging on a tree. One more woman ambushed and raped. A black boy whipped and maimed. It was hounds on the trail of a man running through swamps. It was a white woman slapping her maid for being forgetful.... If Joe lost we were back in slavery and beyond help. It would be true, the accusations that we were lower types of human beings. (Angelou, 1969:113)

At one level then, Mathabane's *Kaffir Boy* depicts a Pan-African predicament of African people in their confrontations with the white man. In addition to Maya Angelou's *I Know Why the Caged Bird Sings,* where a white dentist refused to treat 'blacks" dental problems (159-162), and Frederick Douglass' *Narrative...*, where Douglass was aided by some sympathetic whites (112-119), *Kaffir Boy* could be more fruitfully read with much more appreciation for the experiences of African people wherever they've come in contact with the white man, alongside Alex Haley's *Autobiography of Malcolm X*, Richard Wright's *Black Boy*, Kenneth Kaunda's *Zambia Shall Be Free*, and even that of Nkrumah's *Ghana: The Autobiography of Kwame Nkrumah.*

As in much of black people's autobiographies and biographies, *Kaffir Boy* is a tribute to the human spirit of triumph against 'all' odds, and then be able to maintain an integrity and freedom from hatred. Mathabane's autobiography is also a tribute to black mothers who have been able, by doing slave jobs, to see to it that their sons and daughters, husbands and grandchildren succeed in the face of adversity, minimal educative resources and dismal life chances.

At another level, the handful of whites who were able to assist Mathabane are appreciated by the reader/audience for their 'uniqueness' to cross accustomed barriers in words and in deeds; if only there were more of this group of whites!

Of no less importance, however, is that *Kaffir Boy* belongs to that group of world literature that celebrates man's triumphs over man-made obstacles, against man's inhumanity to man, and depicts the yearnings of the human spirit to search for its own place in the sun, irrespective of some seemingly insurmountable obstacles placed in the way.

Finally, *Kaffir Boy* devastatingly exposes the 'irrationality' of the then Apartheid system that, for instance, created two different gates to a zoo, one gate for blacks, the other for whites, "but once inside, whites and blacks walked along the same paths to see the same animals" (Mathabane, 203).

## A Selection of African American Writers

As African writers have protested against colonialism, neo-colonialism and apartheid in Africa, so also have African-Americans against slavery, Jim Crowism, and all the other forms of inferiorization; African-Americans have done so covertly and overtly (subversively as well as boldly). The purpose of this section is to, in broad strokes, illustrate how some of the significant African-American male writers have depicted African people in the diaspora in the modern American 'wilderness' from slavery to the 1990s.

"Writers," writes Toni Morrison (1993:15), "are among the most sensitive, the most intellectually anarchic, most representative, most probing of artists." They are the listening posts to their societies and have the ability "to familiarize the strange and mystify the familiar" (15). She goes on to observe that white American literature has not been oblivious to the presence of Africanisms in the United States, and that those "Africanisms are the vehicles by which the (white) American self knows itself as not enslaved, but free; not repulsive but desirable; not helpless, but licensed and powerful; not history-less, but historical; not damned but innocent; not a blind accident of evolution, but a progressive fulfillment of destiny" (52). She cites several famous white American writers, including Faulkner, Hemingway, Poe, etc. to illustrate her point that these Euro-American writers utilized the presence of Africanisms to depict blackness as "evil and protective, rebellious and forgiving, fearful and desirable-all of the self-contradictory features of the self" (59). Whiteness is used as the yardstick by which African people are measured in terms of personality, sense of self and of power, and to portray Africans in American culture as sensuous, nationless, deficient in morality and nameless; to deny African people's historicality; from a European-American vantage point of view, whiteness has been the preferred case, since they must feel superior to someone else unlike, definitely, themselves.

However, is Euro-American literature the only American literature? Is there an African-American literature that 'counters' Euro-American literature? If there is an African-American literature, what are its peculiarities, sensibilities, pre-occupations and themes that set it apart, but at the same time be considered a part of the Macro-American literary canon? "National literatures, like writers," writes Morrison again, "get along the best way they can, and with what they can. Yet they do seem to end up describing and inscribing what is really on the national mind" (14).

What have been some of the things on the African-American 'national mind' or psychic since his 'arrival' in the United States? What does it mean to be an African-American? These are some of the questions that African-Americans have been preoccupied with and are still overwhelmed by the two-ness of being an American of an African decent (DuBois, 1982:45-46). In her most popular poem "On Being Brought from Africa to America" (Miller, 1971:34), Phillis Wheatley depicts the two-ness of the African-American psychic that DuBois was to later elaborate upon. Even though Wheatley utilized stereotypes about her African 'pagan land' where she had not sought any redemption from God, she was still able to assert the humanism of her people in

> some view our sable race
> with scornful eye
> 'Their color is a diabolic die.'
> Remember, Christians, Negroes,
> Black as Cain,
> maybe refin'd, and join th'
> Angelic train. (Miller, 34)

Thus, Africans might be many things Euro-Americans are not, but African people's humanity could not be denied; they are also human beings and, as such, could 'be refin'd and join th' angelic train,' whatever that 'angelic train' might be. In her short life span (1753-1784), Phillis Wheatley wrote as an African-American whose people were not only human beings, but also ones who insisted on their freedom. Indeed, how could Euro-Americans demand freedom for themselves and maintain slavery in that freedom? How could one look at a man and say he is not a man? (Baldwin, 1985:31). How could Americans be Christians and deny blacks to read the bible? How could blacks be citizens and not be treated as native sons? Should blacks rejoice on America's 4th of July? (Douglass: 1987:284-288). Where do mulattos fit into the two-ness that some African-Americans find themselves in, in the United States? These have been some of the 'things' on the African-American national mind, and will form the foci of the foregoing presentation.

Jupiter Hammon (1720 (?) - 1800 (?)), in his poem "A Dialogue entitled The Kind Master and the Dutiful Servant" (Miller, 1971:31-33), the African slave theologically challenges his master's overlordship; to the slave, the master was only an earthly master, not the ultimate; both the earthly slave and the earthly master are subject to the one Almighty God who will be the final arbiter and judge of what is sinful or righteous. The 'servant' (not a 'slave' in Hammon's poem) subversively accepts his master's overlordship only on earth, not in the hereafter; in the other world, the servant and the earthly master are both equally subject to the mightiest authority, that of the Almighty God, to whom even the slave master must kneel down for judgment. If the 'slave' and the master are equal before their maker, how then should the master claim superiority or a guaranteed dominance over all of God's children?

Didn't the Lord work in mysterious ways? Couldn't the last one one day be the first? Hammon ends his religious subversive dialogue this way:

> Thus the Dialogue shall end,-
> Strive to obey the word;
> When ev'ry Nation acts like friends,
> Shall be the sons of God.
>
> Believe me now, my Christian friends,
> Believe your friend call'd Hammon;
> You cannot to your God attend,
> And serve the God of Mammon.
>
> If God is pleased by his own hand
> To realize distresses here;
> And grant a peace throughout the land,
> "Twill be a happy year.
>
> *'Tis God alone can give us peace;*
> It's not the pow'r of man,
> When virtuous pow'r shall increase,
> "Twill beautify the land.
>
> Then shall we rejoice and sing
> By pow'r of virtue's word,
> Come, sweet Jesus, heav'nly King,
> Thou art the Son of God.
>
> When virtue comes in bright array,
> Discovers ev'ry sin;
> We see the dangers of the day,
> And fly unto *our* King.
>
> Now glory be unto our God,
> All praise be justly given;
> Let *ev'ry* soul obey his word,
> And seek the joy of heav'n. Finis.

In this context, the servant cannot be viewed as a pagan, or an animist African; he has accepted Western Christianity from his own point of view, independent of his earthly master, and finds his master not more or less of a human being, and as such the master is also subject to a mightier master in 'Tis God alone who can give us peace / It's not the power of man," not even his earthly master. Africans may have come from a 'pagan land,' as in Phillis Wheatley's poem, but they brought with them their sense of humanity and ideas about right and wrong; this was what could not be taken from them; they may have hidden their true feelings, or wore the mask, but they were nonetheless a thinking and a feeling people.

Paul Laurence Dunbar (1984:167), in his classic "We wear the mask" reveals African people's determination to survive in the hostile environment of the American plantation:

We wear the mask that grins and lies,
It hides our cheeks and shades our eyes,–

This debt we pay to human guile;
With torn and bleeding hearts we smile,
And mouth with myraid subtleties.

Why should the world be over-wise
In counting all our tears and sighs?
Nay, let them only see us, while
We wear the mask.

We smile, but O great Christ, our cries
To thee from tortured soul arise.
We sing, but oh the clay is vile
Beneath our feet, and long the mile;
But let the world dream otherwise,
We wear the mask!

To wear the mask, a defense mechanism, is to protect oneself psychologically; to project the opposite of how one exactly feels, a reaction formation, in psychological lingo. Blacks in the plantation tradition had numerous reasons to wear the mask: to prevent beatings, lynchings, deter being sold away from one's friends and family, to obtain a favorable ear from one's master or mistress, and to receive lenient treatment and other favorable opportunities within the plantation setting.

While some slaves wore the mask to abate the harshness of chatteledom, others were too frank and recalcitrant to hide their true feelings; they ran away, burnt their masters' barns, and instigated insurrections; others employed covert means to register their disdain for slavery. Frederick Douglass employed both covert and overt means to protest against the enslavement of himself and his brethren. In his *Narrative of the Life of Frederick Douglass* he eloquently depicts the life of the African slave on the American plantation and in the city of Baltimore and elsewhere. In his own way, he uses pathos, soliloquy, wit, persuasion, oration, and parallelism to expose the American slave system.

The big house and the slave quarters were not only physically close but also psychologically dependent on each other. To the slave, the big house was not only impressive but also the seat of power, source of information and directives; it employed house servants and stable boys, the Big Mammy, field hands, overseers, artisans, and chambermaids. The slave community had its own life but not exclusively negated from the Big House; in fact, Douglass was the product of the master of the Big House and Douglass' black mother of the slave quarters. Though he was his master's son, he could not as such be a free man; he inherited his mother's status, not that of his father-owner.

At an early age, Douglass observed severe beatings of slaves, whom he compared to horses for their not knowing their ages or why they had to endure brutish hardships. Captain Anthony, his first master, had an overseer named Mr. Plummer, who "...was a miserable drunkard, a profane swearer, and a savage monster. He always went armed with a heavy cowskin and a cudgel. I have known him to cut and slash women's heads so horribly, that even master would be enraged at his cruelty" (24).

But Captain Anthony was no angel either:

> I have often been awakened at the dawn of day by the most heart rending shrieks of an Aunt of mine, whom he (Captain Anthony) used to tie up to a joist, and whip upon her naked back till she was literally covered with blood. No words, no tears, no prayers, from his gory victim seemed to move his iron heart from its bloody purpose. The louder she screamed, the louder he whipped; and where the blood ran fastest that's where he whipped the longest . (24-25)

If Captain Anthony's treatment of Douglass's Aunt does not inspire pathos, overseer Austin Gore's handling of the slaves could easily achieve that effect; using parallelisms, Mr. Douglass describes overseer Gore as "arftul, cruel, and obdurate" (38). To Mr. Austin Gore, for a slave to be accused of anything meant that that slave was already "convicted, and to be convicted was to be punished. The one always followed the other with immutable certainty. To escape punishment was to escape accusation; and few slaves had the fortune to do either, under the overseership of Mr. Gore" (39).

> Mr. Gore once undertook to whip one of Colonel Lloyd's slaves by the name of Demby. He had given Demby but few stripes, when to get rid of the scourging, he ran and plunged himself into a creek, and stood there at the depth of his shoulders, refusing to come out. Mr. Gore told him that he would give him three calls, and if he didn't come out at the third call, he would shoot him. The first call was given. Demby made no response, but stood his ground. The second and third calls were given with the

> same result. Mr. Gore then, without consultation or deliberation with anyone, not even giving an additional call, raised his musket to his face, taking deadly aim at his standing victim, and in an instant poor Demby was no more. His mangled body sank out of sight, and blood and brains marked the water where he had stood. (39-40)

Douglass gives other examples of the conditions of slaves, but none seem to be as heartless as that of Demby's case. Mr. Gore, not to be fastidious, was not even punished for the killing of Demby; after all, slaves were chattels and property, counted as cows and horses were counted, bought and sold with little or no compunction.

Even though it took sometime for Douglass himself to be inducted into the 'pure' slavocracy, he was eventually subjected to the treatment of adults slaves. After he 'graduated' from simply running errands to working like any other slave on the plantation, he found out he could not bear the institution of slavery. His own experiences with the contradictions inherent in the 'peculiar institution' came about when he was prevented from learning how to read and write by Mr. Auld while in Baltimore, Maryland, where he observed differences between urban slaves and those on the plantations. The city slaves were not only better fed, but were also better clothed and had some privileges (51).

Mr. Auld preventing Douglass from learning how to read and write, thereby imposing compulsory ignorance, inspired Mr. Douglass to rebel, to subvert the whole slave system. Because the master was determined to keep Douglass illiterate, Douglass aimed to learn all the more how to read and write. As we've already noted, Douglass was adamant about learning how to read and write:

> What he most dreaded that I most desired. What he most loved, that I most hated. That which to him was a great evil, to be carefully shunned, was to me a great good, to be diligently sought; and the argument which he so warmly urged, against my learning to read, only served to inspire me with a desire and determination to learn. In learning to read, I owe almost as much to the bitter opposition of my master, as to the kindly aid of my mistress (who had commenced teaching him to read and write.) I acknowledge the benefit of both. (50)

But learning to read and write compounded Mr. Douglass' problems; literacy certainly sharpened his mind, but did not necessarily abate or soften his feelings about his condition. In fact, the more aware he became, the more he wished he were as ignorant as his illiterate brethren; because literacy expanded his repertoire, Douglass could find a myriad of contradictions in human bondage. With literacy he could see that not all whites agreed with slavery, that there were other personalities who vehemently opposed slavery; this knowledge brought him to a larger universe of ideas, personalities and convictions; he began to dream of other places and possibilities. Because he could reflect about his condition much more eclectically than his ignorant brethren, he later articulated their sentiments in his oratories, writings in *The North Star* and other publications.

In the meantime, however, he was still a slave fit to be treated as a beast of burden; but Douglass was not just any piece of property. His literacy and observations in Baltimore City irrevocably changed Mr. Douglass, making him unfit to be perennially exploited and manhandled, physically or intellectually. Like contemporary black professionals (Cose, 1993), Mr. Douglass became extremely sensitive to the injustices of slavery, the exploitation of man by man and the paradoxes in western Christianity. With his ability to read and write, achieved by employing various unconventional means, Mr. Douglass resolved to fight the peculiar institution; he was no longer satisfied with his status as a slave; despite Mr. Freeland's 'gentility' and kindness to Mr. Douglass, Douglass wanted to be on free land (91).

His resolution to fight against slavery compelled him to resist Mr. Covey, a well-known slave-breaker, who had been charged with the responsibility to subdue Mr. Douglass into being a good slave. For the first time Mr. Douglass became a field hand on Mr. Covey's 'farm'. Here, he experienced Mr. Covey's breeding of Caroline, so as to acquire more slaves; here Douglass said he was transformed into a brute and a rebel. After being terribly beaten, Mr. Douglass resolved not to ever again be brutalized by Mr. Covey. "You have seen how a man (who) was a slave; you shall see how a slave was made a man" (77). By boldly resisting Mr. Covey's attempt to subdue him the second time and in actually defeating Mr. Covey, Douglass had already triumphed over slavery; he had, in reference to Ken Kesey's novel's title, flown over the 'Cuckoo's nest' (Kesey, 1962).

Mr. Douglass' defeat of slave-breaker Covey became a crucial event in his challenge to slavery. At least Mr. Douglass became fully aware that Mr. Covey was not the bogeyman he had reputed himself to be; that to change one's relationship with an authority, one must challenge it; it is the oppressed who must do something to elevate themselves; those who do not fight for their freedoms were doomed to be perennially exploited; an 'educated' man will not make a good, submissive slave; 'education' should set one free to be the best one could be; Master Auld was right: give the black man an inch, he will take a mile; Mr. Douglass resolved to take more than a 'mile' from the bosom of slavery:

> ...from whence came the spirit I don't know – I resolved to fight: and, suiting my action to the resolution, I seized Covey hard by the throat; and as I did so I rose. He

> held on to me, and I to him. My resistance was so entirely unexpected, that Covey seemed taken all aback. *He trembled like a leaf. This gave me assurance*, and I held him uneasy, causing the blood to run where I touched him with the ends of my fingers. Mr. Covey soon called out to Hughes for help. Hughes came, and while Covey held me, attempted to tie my right hand. While he was in the act of doing so, I watched my chance, and gave him a heavy kick close under the ribs. This kick fairly sickened Hughes, so that he left me in the hands of Covey. This kick had the effect of not only weakening Hughes, but Covey also. When he saw Hughes bending over with pain, his courage quailed. *He asked me if I meant to persist in my resistance. I told him I did come what might; that he had used me like a brute for six months, and that I was determined to be used so no longer.* With that, he strove to drag me to a stick that was lying just outside of the stable door. He meant to knock me down. But just as he was leaning over to get the stick, I seized him with both hands by his collar, and brought him by a sudden snatch to the ground. By this time, Bill came. Covey called upon him for assistance. Bill wanted to know what he could do. Covey said, "Take hold of him, take hold of him!" Bill said his master hired him out to work and not to help to whip me; so he left Covey and myself to fight our own battle out. *We were at it for nearly two hours. Covey at length let me go, puffing and blowing at a great rate, saying that if I had not resisted, he would not have whipped me half so much. The truth was, that he had not whipped me at all. I considered him as getting entirely the worst end of the bargain; for he had drawn no blood from me, but I had from him.* The whole six months afterwards, that I spent with Mr. Covey, he never laid the weight of his finger upon me in anger. He would occasionally say, he didn't want to get hold of me again. "No," thought I, "you need not; for you will come off worse than you did before."
>
> *This battle with Mr. Covey was the turning-point in my career as a slave. It rekindled the few expiring embers of freedom and revived within me a sense of my own manhood.* (81-82)

While this encounter obviously strengthened Douglass, it weakened Mr. Covey, destroyed his reputation and ashamed him in front of the other slaves. It gave Mr. Douglass more confidence and an enhanced standing in the eyes of his brethren in bondage.

Mr. Douglass did not only physically fight against slavery, but he also did mentally. He could see that the holidays given to slaves was in fact a mechanism to enhance the continued subjugation of the 'African' slaves on the plantations. During these holidays, the slaves were encouraged to indulge in alcohol for recreation and to occupy their time with festivities rather than reflecting on their depraved conditions in bondage. "These holidays served as conductors, or safety-values, to carry off the rebellious spirit of enslaved humanity... to disgust the slaves with freedom, by plunging them into the lowest depths of dissipation. ...in getting whole multitudes to drink to excess" (84, 85), the slave masters expected to have a more 'complete' control over their slaves; drunken men (Africans or not) would certainly not have much time to reflect or plan for the future.

In this connection, one is tempted to make a comparison between the southern plantations and the modern day urban black ghettos. As alcohol was available to the plantation slaves, so also today is alcohol readily available to African Americans in the inner cities, where churches are finding it difficult to compete with prisons and the streets (Lincoln and Mamiya, 1990:322-323), ghettoes where certain types of beers are sold that are not generally available to the general population. It is dubious that a drunk and a 'high' person would have time for reflection or for a critical analysis about his/her place in a system that keeps him/her 'sedated.'

Douglass was one of many 'African' slaves who 'flew over the Cuckoo's nest;' he was able to do so in part due to his literacy. With literacy, he was not only able to sharply see the antagonistic contradictions within the system of slavery, but he could also subvert that system by using the master's language, writing style and education to help educate his brethren in bondage (89-94).

Mr. Douglass was soon to learn, however, that freedom had its own responsibilities. As a slave he could at least depend on his master to provide him food and shelter, however meager and crude those were. Immediately after his escape to the north, the burdens of freedom raised their ugly heads:

> ...I say let him place himself in my situation–without home or friends–without money or credit–wanting shelter and no one to give it–wanting bread and no money to buy it–and at the same time let him feel that he is pursued by merciless men-hunters, and in total darkness as to what to do, where to go, or where to stay,–perfectly helpless, both as to the means of defense and means of escape,–in the midst of plenty, yet suffering the terrible gnawings of hunger,–in the midst of houses, yet having no home,–among fellowmen, yet feeling as if in the midst of wild beasts, whose greediness to swallow up the trembling and half-famished fugitive is only equaled by that with which the monsters of the deep swallow up the helpless fish upon which they subsist,–

> I say, let him be placed in this most trying situation in which I was placed,–then, and not till then, will he fully appreciate the hardships of, and know how to sympathize with, the toil-worn and whipped-scarred fugitive slave. (Douglass, 112)

But again, with Douglass' literacy and determination to be free at all cost, he was able to succeed and agitate for the freedom of his brethren and all women. Until his death, he never relented an inch in his attempts to gain full citizenship for African-Americans. His numerous speeches, lectures, travels and publications are legacies to Africans and all oppressed people. Nonetheless, Frederick Douglass was not uncontroversial.

One of the greatest controversies over Mr. Douglass concerns his choice of a white woman for his second wife. How could Douglass, after so eloquently denouncing white slave masters and religious slave holders (120-124), have justified marrying a member of a race that had owned and brutalized him and members of *his* race? Indeed, how could one love one's 'enemy' to that extent? Some contemporary college students find Mr. Douglass a 'sell-out', a disappointment after his oratory about whites' inhumanity to African people

Perhaps, in Mr. Douglass' defense, we must note that after his escape, and even during his 'trek' to the north, he was aided by some whites who were anxious to see him on free land, away from Mr. Freeland (91). Like Mr. Ex-Colored Man, whom we will meet later, Mr. Douglass was a product of an 'unsanctioned love' between a black slave woman and her white master, a product of two-worlds, and therefore, a marginal man, who could decide to go either way? Furthermore, though white men have lynched and tortured black men for sometimes simply looking at white women the wrong way, in South Africa and the United States, these have hardly prevented interracial sex, love, or marriage; for when two people 'love' each other, defacto and dejure laws cannot prevent their knowing each other as Adam knew Eve, as Romeo knew Juliet, and as Thomas Jefferson allegedly knew Sally Hemings, etc.... After all, opposites do attract each other. Furthermore, Mr. Douglass' interest in women was not just sexual, but also ideological, and there seems to be a thin line between the two; other great men have been known to blur the two including Elijah Muhammad, Martin Luther King, Jr., Richard Wright, Jomo Kenyatta, and Sedar Leopold Senghor, Henry Louis Gates, Shelby Steele, William Julius Wilson, Ali Mazrui, Kofi Annan, just to name a few prominent African people who have loved and married outside of their race, including the Pan-Africanist, Sylvester Williams in Chapter Four.

Perhaps, we should consult a psychologist! Joseph L. White (1972), a black psychologist, states that African Americans go through four levels of awareness in their relations with the white world: 1) The Negromacy stage; 2) The Encounter stage; 3) Immersion, and 4) The Universal stage. At the first stage, blacks generally have negative perceptions about themselves, relative to whites. They see the European-American as more culturally sophisticated; they (African Americans) rebuke each other for not working hard enough, for not being like them (the European Americans). At the Encounter stage, African Americans find it not only difficult to enter Euro-American culture fully, but also discover, as it were, positive aspects of their own black culture that they wish to retain. The more difficult they find it to enter the Euro-American culture, the more they will embrace their own black culture. At the Immersion stage then, blacks could become obsessed with their own blackness and exhibit this by (elaborately) embracing their African heritage, wearing African hair-dos and African attire; some change their names to African ones and see white folks as evil. Some, in their disgust with the American system, have migrated to Africa or elsewhere, or have joined religious organizations that shield them from mainstream America. Some become African cultural nationalists in an effort to abate the harshness of American racism. The opposite of this, of course, could be a total separation from anything that has to do with blackness or black issues; and some "... black executives (have been known to) cut themselves off from other blacks in their quest to be more acceptable to (white) management" (Cose, 1993:82).

The universal stage, the fourth in Joseph L. White's paradigm, is one in which self-actualization has been reached. By this stage, black individuals would have transcended the first three stages to identify with the liberation struggles of all oppressed peoples: women, Indians, Vietnamese, U.S. blacks, black South Africans, etc. This stage is similar to the self-actualization stage in Abraham Maslow's hierarchy of needs. Perhaps by the time Mr. Douglass' first wife, Ann Murray Douglass, died, he had already become a universal man interested in all oppressed people regardless of race, nationality or sex. Certainly, those who have not yet intellectually and culturally reached the universal stage in White's paradigm would find objections to Mr. Douglass marrying a white woman.

Nonetheless, some African-American females feel 'duped' by Douglass' choice of a white woman for a second wife, and not a few feminists would take objections to Mr. Douglass' treatment of Ann Murray Douglass, his first, black, wife who "...even made the sailor suit that Douglass wore during his escape" (DeCosta-Willis, 1991:131).

> There were many differences between the newlyweds: she was born free, while he was an escaped slave; she was twenty-five, and he was twenty; she was illiterate, but he had learned to read and write; she had money...but he was

> penniless; she had personal possessions...while he had nothing but the clothes on his back. (132)

Ann Murray Douglass' contributions to Mr. Frederick Douglass' fame are not acknowledged in Douglass' *Narrative of the Life of Frederick Douglass* (132); "father was mother's honored guest" (133), writes their daughter Rosetta Douglass Sprague; Douglass was openly friendly to white women, even when married to Ann Murray Douglass. Was this the case of educational incompatibility, or the 'failures' of a great man?

Despite the controversies over Douglass' marriage to a white woman and his lowly treatment of Ann Murray Douglass, the ex-slave contributed immensely to American society politically, historically and literally. As an American hero who emerged from the depths of society, he functions today as a model of resistance, determination and perseverance. Douglass's story is indeed an American story in which effort, talent, skill and educational attainment are rewarded, all things being equal. In Douglass' advocation of women's rights, he showed himself a man of foresight; however, his adamant stance that the African American be accepted as a full member of the American society still has not been fulfilled (Cose, 1993). Of no less importance, nonetheless, Mr. Douglass' various speeches, publications and oratory can only humanize the reader and contribute to making a better world in which descendants of slaves and slave owners can live more humanely.

Another African American who emerged or 'upped from slavery' to become a spokesman for his people was Booker T. Washington (*Up From Slavery*, 1963). Immediately, a few similarities and differences are discernible between these two great African Americans; both Douglass and Mr. B.T. Washington were products of 'unsanctioned love' affairs between their white 'masters' and 'African' female slave mothers; they both valued western education and the upliftment of their people politically, economically and socially. They both knew that their African race was at the bottom of the global capitalistic structure, the United States epitomizing that global structure. Both in the North as well as in the Southern States of the U.S., Euro-Americans saw to it that African people remained in their place relatively lower than that of the Anglo-American. In education and politics, particularly, African people were expected and, to a large extent, are still expected, to be hewers of wood and drawers of water for the Anglo-Saxon race.

To bring the plight of their people to a larger (global) audience, both Washington and Douglass made numerous speeches in the United States and Europe and left us published materials (classics) upon which to reflect. Both men, however, have not been without controversies. As we've seen, Douglass's choice of a white woman for his second wife was, and is up to date eminently scorned upon, especially by black female students; how could have Douglass written so eloquently against

Euro-Americans' treatment of African people and still had the gall to marry into the white race? The fact that Mr. Douglass was bi-racial is often not a potent argument for his choice of a white woman as his second wife. Others have submitted that Mr. Douglass should have been much nicer to his first wife, (a free black woman) who helped him out of bondage (DeCosta-Willis, 1991:131-138).

Mr. Booker T. Washington is also not without controversy. After describing in his *Up From Slavery* (1963) the hardships he endured to educate himself at Hampton Institute in Virginia, under General Armstrong, who advocated educational adaptation, Mr. Washington goes on to exhort his brethren to start building themselves up gradually in agriculture (143) and to abstain from political agitation. Despite the perennial discord between white and black America, Mr. Washington urged that blacks 'cast down' their buckets where they were, and that "no race can prosper till it learns that there is dignity in tilling the field as in writing a poem. It is at the bottom of life we must begin, and not at the top" (155). In his famous Atlanta exposition speech, he assured whites that "in all things that are purely social we can be as separate as the fingers, yet one as the hand in all things essential to mutual progress" (156). Mr. Washington believed that "when a Negro girl learns to cook, to wash dishes, to sew, to write a book, or a Negro boy learns to groom horses, or grow sweet potatoes, or to produce butter, or to build a house, or to be able to practice medicine, as well as or better than someone else, they will be rewarded regardless of race or color" (198-199).

Mr. Washington died in 1915, and African-American doctors, lawyers and other black American professionals are still not highly rewarded or regarded as equals to their white American counterparts (see Chapter Six).

Furthermore, Mr. Washington's emphasis on "educational adaptation" (Marah, 1987:460-481) for African Americans did not sit too well with W.E.B. DuBois (1982:79-95). A poet has attempted to 'explicate' the differences between the two men (Randall, 1968: 470-471):

***(Booker T. Washington and W.E.B. DuBois)***

*"It seems to me," said Booker T.,*
*"It shows a mighty lot of cheek*
*To study chemistry and Greek*
*When Mister Charlie needs a hand*
*To hoe the cotton on his land,*
*And when Miss Ann looks for a cook,*
*Why stick your nose inside a book?"*

*"I don't agree," said W.E.B.*
*"If I should have the drive to seek*
*Knowledge of chemistry or Greek,*
*I'll do it. Charles and Miss can look*
*Another place for hand or cook.*
*Some men rejoice in skill of hand,*
*And some in cultivating land,*
*But there are others who maintain*
*The right to cultivate the brain."*

*"It seems to me," said Booker T.*
*"That all you folks have missed the boat*
*Who shout about the right to vote,*
*And spend vain days and sleepless nights*
*In uproar over civil rights.*
*Just keep your mouths shut, do not grouse,*
*But work, and save, and buy a house."*

*"I don't agree," said W.E.B.*
*"For what can property avail*
*If dignity and justice fail?*
*Unless you help to make the laws,*
*They'll steal your house with trumped-up clause.*
*A rope's as tight, a fire as hot,*
*No matter how much cash you've got.*
*Speak soft, and try your little plan,*
*But as for me, I'll be a man."*

*"It seems to me," said Booker T.-*
*"I don't agree,"*
*Said W.E.B.*

Nonetheless, both Dr. W.E.B. DuBois and Mr. B.T. Washington left African people in the United States and elsewhere models to be emulated. Mr. Washington, with the help of northern whites, the Alabama legislature, and other contributors, left behind a school that has and continue to employ and graduate African and non-African people to help themselves and their brethren. Dr. W.E.B. DuBois left us an eclectic intellectual tradition and the ideology of practical Pan-Africanism, all of which continue to aid African people to do for themselves, as they must continue to do, in order for them to be ineluctable constituents in this global village.

## The Harlem Renaissance: 1900-1935

By the time of Mr. Washington's death in 1915, a new intellectual and cultural movement was already in the making in Harlem, New York City. Progressively moving away from the plantation tradition, the failures of the Reconstruction Period (1865-1877), Jim Crowism, sharecropping, and other hardships in the south, African-Americans, in increasingly large numbers, began to 'up' from the south to inundate, as it were, northern states and cities of New York, Pennsylvania, Illinois, Harlem, Philadelphia, and Chicago. Of all these states and cities, Harlem, New York became the black metropole from the early 1900s to the mid 1930s.

The Harlem Renaissance period has received a lot of attention as the period of the great migration when large numbers of African-Americans moved to northern and western states in search of better living conditions. The push factors from the south included blatant racism, lack in opportunities for employment, education and other socio-economic amenities. In 1865, Nathan Forrest formed the infamous KKK which 'terrorized' African-American people with abandon. To the blacks, the north symbolized the promised land, while the south the Pharoah's Egypt . The pull factors to the north included the belief that employment opportunities existed in Northern States and cities; personal freedom, the excitement of the city, the glamour of urban life as compared to the drudgery of the rural south, all 'pulled' African Americans in large numbers to the Northern states and cities. More than sixteen southern states contributed to the New York City population, with Virginia, South and North Carolina and Georgia topping the list of the contributors (Osofsky, 1966: 17-24). By the 1930s Harlem was truly a black metropole; included were West Indian immigrants and a few Africans.

Harlem became, so to speak, not only a Pan-African city, but also one bursting with artistic, political, and intellectual activities. Two major schools of black writers emerged between the early 1900s and the mid 1930s. These writers differed from the previous generation of African-American writers in that they seemed more assertive than the Booker T. Washingtons in their intellectual, cultural and political outlook. The radical school of literary thought was represented by men such as Langston Hughes, Claude McKay, and Marcus Garvey. Marcus Garvey's Back-to-Africa movement, McKay's *Home to Harlem* (1928) and his famous poem, "If We Must Die" epitomize that radicalism. Even though Harlem was home to blacks, most blacks did not own their homes; as more blacks moved into Harlem, white flight correspondingly began to occur. Black employment and ownership of property, as B.T. Washington had urged African-Americans to do, had not materialized for the black masses; the radical school of the Harlem

Renaissance writers such as Langston Hughes and Claude McKay wrote on behalf of those simple people in Hughes's *Simple Speaks His Mind* (1951) and in McKay's "If We Must Die" (Bontemps, 1974:31):

> If we must die–let it not be like hogs
> Hunted and penned in an inglorious spot,
> While round us bark the mad and hungry dogs,
> Making their mock at our accursed lot.
> If we must die–oh, let us nobly die,
> So that our precious blood may not be shed
> In vain; then even the monsters we defy
> Shall be constrained to honor us though dead! Oh,
> Kinsmen! We must meet the common foe;
> Though far outnumbered, let us show us brave,
> And for their thousand blows deal one deathblow!
> What though before us lies the open grave?
> Like men we'll face the murderous, cowardly pack,
> Pressed to the wall, dying, but fighting back!

The genteel school of literary thought of the Harlem Renaissance period emphasized the characteristic outlook of the members of the 'talented tenth', in DuBoisian terms. W.E.B. DuBois and James Weldon Johnson represent this school of thought. Jean Toomer (1894-1967) opted out of being considered a black writer. Andrews (1994:15) writes that

> Toomer never lived in Harlem, and Harlem receives merely a passing reference in *Cane.* Most significant, the introduction to *Cane,* by a white writer and close friend of Toomer's named Waldo Frank, avers that the greatness of *Cane* lies in Toomer's artistic transcendence of race, not in his expression of his own racial identity or a black perspective. According to Toomer's biographer, Nellie McKay, the author of *Cane* was grateful to Frank for recognizing him as an American artist to whom racial designation was secondary to an expression of personal vision. As if to underline a sense of himself as an individual whose art must be understood and judged first on that basis, Toomer refused to allow publicity for *Cane* to mention his African American heritage. Yet in response to an inquiry from the Associated Negro Press just before *Cane* appeared, Toomer stated, 'In so far as the old folk-songs, syncopated rhythms, the rich sweet taste of dark-skinned life, in so far as these are Negro, I am body and soul, Negroid."Toomer's ambivalence about both his identity and the degree to which his writing should be identified as peculiarly African American has been seen as both a

> help and a hindrance to his psychological and artistic development'.

"Toomer's ambivalence about... his identity..." (15) is reflected in James Weldon Johnson's fictional protagonist in *The Autobiography of an Ex-Colored Man* (1960). Writing from the point of view of the genteel school of literary thought of the Harlem Renaissance period, Mr. Ex-Colored Man exhibits his disdain for the lower class blacks; they repulsed him (55-56).

In Mr. Ex-Colored Man we are confronted with the theme of "passing" and intra-racism, as in William Wells Brown's *Clotel, or The President's Daughter* (1854), Nella Larsen's *Passing* (1929), Zora Neale Hurston's Mrs. Turner, in *Their Eyes Were Watching God* (1927), Maureen Pearl in Toni Morrison's *The Bluest Eye* (1970) and even in Howard Griffin's *Black Like Me* (1960). In Mr. Ex-Colored Man, we are also confronted with the theme of flight, dual culture, dual identity, marginalism, conflict between Africanness and Europeanness, and the fate of the tragic mulatto, as in Langston Hughes' poem "Cross" (Bontemps, 1974:62):

> My old man's a white old man
> And my old mother's black.
> If ever I cursed my white old man
> I take my curses back.
>
> If ever I cursed my black old mother
> And wished she were in hell,
> I'm sorry for that evil wish.
> And now I wish her well.
>
> My old man died in a fine big house.
> My ma died in a shack.
> I wonder where I', gonna die,
> Being neither white nor black?

Mr. Ex-Colored Man's dualism, rooted in an unsanctioned love affair between his white father and his mulatto mother, was unmercifully brought to him, in no other place than in a classroom (a place of learning) and by an educator, a significant cultural agent, and at an impressionable young age (Johnson, 1960:16):

> One day near the end of my second term at school the principal came into our room and, after talking to the teacher, for some reason said: "I wish all of the white scholars to stand for a moment." I rose with the others. The teacher looked at me and, calling my name, said: "You sit down for the present, and rise with the others." I did not quite understand her, and questioned: "Ma'am?"

> She repeated, with a softer tone in her voice: "You sit down now, and rise with the others." I sat down dazed. I saw and heard nothing. When the others were asked to rise, I did not know it. When school was dismissed, I went out in a kind of stupor.
>
> A few of the white boys jeered me, saying: "Oh, you're a nigger too." I heard some black children say: "We knew he was coloured." "Shiny" said to them: "Come along,don't tease him," and thereby won my undying gratitude.

From this point on, Mr. Ex-Colored man went on numerous flights in search of his authentic-self. Who was he in American society, being 'neither white nor black', in a culture that 'required' that one must either be black or white? In all, Mr. Ex-Colored Man had to go through more than ten flights, some physical, others psychological, in search of his roots and, therefore, himself. His flights from the north, where he was raised, into the south, back to the north and Europe, again into the south, and finally to the north, where he finally abandoned his mother's (black) people epitomize his marginalism. The final push to abandon his mother's people came about after he witnessed the lynching of a black man while he was in the 'deep' south, in search of uncontaminated black folklore and songs that he intended to compose into classics, to make himself great as well as to upgrade his people's culture. But before he could accomplish his mission,

> ...they brought him in. Two horsemen rode abreast; between them, half dragged, the poor wretch made his way through the dust. His hands were tied behind him, and ropes round his body were fastened to the saddle horns of his double guard. The men who at midnight had been stern and silent were now emitting that terror-instilling sound known as the "rebel yell." A space was quickly cleared in the crowd, and a rope placed about his neck, when from somewhere came the suggestion, "Burn him!" It ran like an electric current. Have you ever witnessed the transformation of human beings into savage beasts? Nothing can be more terrible. A railroad tie was sunk into the ground, the rope was removed and a chain brought and securely coiled round the victim and the stake. There he stood, a man only in form and stature, every sign of degeneracy stamped upon his countenance. His eyes were dull and vacant, indicating not a single ray of thought.
>
> It was over before I realized that time had elapsed. Before I could make myself believe that what I saw was really happening, I was looking at a scorched post, a smouldering fire, blackened bones, charred fragments

> sifting down through coils of chain; and the smell of burnt flesh - human flesh - was in my nostrils. (186-187)

The lynching of this 'simple' black man, whose mind had not been quickened by western civilization (170), compelled 'bi-racial', sophisticated, highly talented Mr. Ex-Colored Man to pass into the white race, which he confirmed by marrying a white woman. Instead of fighting for his mother's people to make sure that such a deed did not happen again, as Walter White did in *A Man Called White* (1948), as James Weldon Johnson himself did for the NAACP, Ex-Colored Man took his final flight into the white world, stating

> My love for my children makes me glad that I am what I am and keeps me from desiring to be otherwise; and yet, when I sometimes open a little box in which I still keep my fast yellowing manuscripts, the only tangible remnants of a vanished dream, a dead ambition, a sacrificed talent, I cannot repress the thought that, after all, I have chosen the lesser part, that I have sold my birthright for a mess of pottage. (Johnson, 1960:211)

Maybe Mr. Ex-Colored Man's mother should have, perhaps, read him this poem by Langston Hughes (Bontemps, 1974:67), especially after his classroom experience:

**Mother to Son**

Well, son, I'll tell you:
Life for me ain't been no crystal stair.
It's had tacks in it,
And splinters,
And boards torn up,
And places with no carpet on the floor–
Bare.
But all the time
I'se been a-climbin' on,
And reachin' landin's,
And turnin' corners,
And sometimes goin' in the dark
Where there ain't been no light.
So boy, don't you turn back.
Don't you set down on the steps
'Cause you finds it's kinder hard.
Don't you fall now–
For I'se still goin', honey,
I'se still climbin',
And life for me ain't been no crystal stair.

But brought up "as a little aristocrat..." (Johnson, 1960:3), Mr. Ex-Colored Man grew up shielded from some of the harsh realities of black life in the global village, the United States epitomizing that global village.

In addition to being ashamed of his mother's people's powerlessness, who could be so treated with impunity, and of his native land that could so treat them (his mother's people), he gave up his race "for a mess of pottage." Rather than defend the weak, he joined the strong, white race, not only because he was light-skinned enough to pass, but also because he was a coward or, as his millionaire white friend said, he was really not a black man (144). Of no less importance, however, is the argument that Mr. Ex-Colored Man succumbed to some of the pressures on black people in the United States to abandon most of their Africanisms, as it were. Some African-Americans are pressured to the extreme to lighten their skin color, conk their hair, 'straighten' their flat noses and reduce their bulging hips; they must approximate the white race or suffer the consequences of their recalcitrance. In the conking of his hair to approximate whiteness, and in his choice of a white woman over black Laura, Malcolm X remarks that "the only excuse I can offer is that like so many of my black brothers today, I was just deaf, dumb, and blind" (Haley, 1990:68). As late as the 1990s Nathan McCall (1995:13-14) could explicate why he was fascinated with 'white beauty.'

But Mr. Ex-Colored Man cannot be said to have been 'deaf, dumb, and blind' for he knew that whiteness in America (and in Africa), carried with it syndromes of advantages. All things being equal, it might still be easier to get a job as a white man than a black man in America, as Mr. John Howard Griffin quickly learned in his *Black Like Me* (1960); Mr. Griffin found that it was convenient to be white in America; Mr. Ellis Cose, in his *Rage of a Privileged Class* (1993), asserts that being black in America has its own peculiar prize, the x-factor. Mr. Bruce Wright (1993), in his *Black Robes, White Justice,* also records some of the inconveniences black professionals in the United States encounter. From Mr. Ex-Colored Man's point of view then, he would rather be white than black in the United States; and since he could, he did, unlike the dark skinned Emma Lou in Wallace Thurman's *The Blacker the Berry* (1929).

To a certain extent, in Mr. Ex-Colored Man taking his father's people's side, he illustrates the power of patriarchy, the ruling class and race. Through his education, travels, acquaintances, enculturation and habits, he had been socialized to be a Bohemian, an epicurean, a European-American. To be a full member of the European race, he had to marry a white woman and like Solomon's lover in "Song of Solomon," he had to apologize for having a drop of African blood in his veins. In rejecting the African blood in him, Mr. Ex-Colored Man 'abandoned' that part of himself to which he could psychologically not remain true. In his marginalism, Mr. Ex-Colored Man leaves us with a classic theme that African-Americans will continue to confront in a non-color blind society, in fiction as well as in non-fiction.

## The Chicago Renaissance (1935-1950)

If Mr. Ex-Colored Man abandoned his mother's people because they were powerless and could be lynched with abandon, ritualistically, and with impunity, in Richard Wright's "Between the World and Me," we are confronted with a different black man, one that empathized with the victim of a lynching, similar to the one witnessed by the 'opportunistic' Mr. Ex-Colored Man.

> And one morning while in the woods I stumbled suddenly upon the thing, (*The remains of a lynched black man.)* Stumbled upon it in a grassy clearing guarded by scaly oaks and elms. And the sooty details of the scene rose, thrusting themselves between the world and me.
>
> ...And while I stood my mind was frozen with a cold pity for the life that was gone.
>
> The ground gripped my feet and my heart was circled by icy walls of fear – The dry bones stirred, rattled, lifted, melting themselves into my bones.
>
> The grey ashes formed flesh firm and black, entering into my flesh. Panting, begging I clutched childlike, clutched to the hot sides of death.
>
> Now I am dry bones and my face a stony skull staring in yellow surprise at the sun.... (Bontemps, 1990:103-104)

After viewing the remains of a lynched black man, the protagonist 'I' *empathized* with the unknown black victim. The lynching had been done ritualistically, in the presence of a diverse group of people including cigar and cigarette smokers, gin drinkers, and even a whore (103); the protagonist puts himself in the lynched man's shoes and becomes the victim of the lynching, unlike Mr. Ex-Colored Man who, true to himself, runs away into the arms of the very white race that had lynched one of his mother's people.

Richard Wright (1908-1960) is the most outstanding figure of the Chicago Renaissance. Born in Natchez, Mississippi, Mr. Wright experienced blatant racism, poverty, hunger, and was moved around constantly. In his *Black Boy* (1945) and *American Hunger* (1944), he explicates the complex socio-economic forces that impinged on him, that were to later inform his political and artistic outlook. A high school drop-out, Mr. Wright grew up feeling alienated from his family, black and white society; sensitive about the issues of race in the United States, Mr. Wright ventured into existentialism, France, Spain, Asia, and Africa in his later years.

At a very early age, the sensitive Richard Wright observed his utter powerlessness to affect changes around him, and because he was so powerless in the white, "... objective world, (he) made things happen within" himself (Wright, 1945:83). He created an inverse relationship between himself and his environment. "Because my environment was bare and bleak, I endowed it with unlimited potentialities, redeemed it for the sake of my own hungry and cloudy yearning" (83). Whites were a constant threat to him, near and afar. "I had never in my life been abused by whites, but I had already become conditioned to their existence as though I had been the victim of a thousand lynchings" (84); McCall (1994:62) could still say the same fifty-nine years later, regarding his fear and hatred for whites in his *Makes Me Wanna Holler.*

As an adolescent, Wright began to hang around other black boys 'at the crossroads.' Though they appeared independent, they frantically concealed how dependent "...they (in fact) were on each other" (88). Among themselves, they constantly talked about whites, and about how mean whites were to black people, etc. (91); again, similar to that of McCall's 1994 *Makes Me Want to Holler* (12-17).

Wright , like Ngugi of Kenya, was also to be later influenced by Marxist philosophy of society; as depicted in his *Native Son* (1945), the protagonist, Bigger Thomas, was anti-religious, anti-capitalist and anti-black bourgeoisie. In his travels to Africa (*Black Power: Reactions in a Land Pathos*, 1974), Mr. Wright observed that the educated Africans were more 'bourgeois' than the Europeans themselves, whom they tried to imitate; in the United States, he felt excluded culturally from Euro-American life. "Culturally," he states, "the Negro represents a paradox: Though he is an organic part of the nation, he is excluded by the entire tide and direction of American culture. Frankly, it is felt to be right to exclude him, and it is felt to be wrong to admit him freely" (Wright, 1944:13). In his *White Man, Listen!,* he confessed that he had "never been allowed to blend" (47). Thus alienated from Africa and the United States, Mr. Wright became an outsider, as it were, looking in. Perhaps to compensate for his alienation, he embraced Marxism and existentialism and felt more comfortable in metropolitan France than in Africa or the United States.

In addition to existentialism, Richard Wright was also influenced by Parkian sociology (Bone, 1986:446-468). Robert Park, the European-American, who had assisted Booker T. Washington from 1906-1913, had also toured the southern states of the United States extensively, observing Negro life. As a journalist and keen observer of black life in the south and in the north, Professor Park developed some ideas concerning the American Negro in the American zeitgeist, and about human history in general. Generally, he believed that societies progressively moved from simple to complex, from rural to urban, from the sacred to the secular and profane; human societies are progressively going to be more and more complex, cosmopolitan and sophisticated, than the other way around. This movement is beneficial to civilizations and people, for it frees individuals from traditional bondage, parochialisms, and naiveté; urbanism releases one's creativity, enhances one's individuality and gives the largest room to individuals to be themselves. It is in urban centers that the greatest civilizations emerged, where sophisticated ideas and edifices are assembled. The city, in Parkian terms, is a liberating phenomenon.

While the city has the above positive qualities, it is also the place with slums, ghettos, prostitutes, alcoholics, hoboes, youth gangs, high crime rates and the other pathological and scatological aspects of urban life. As rural persons move into urban centers, it takes time for them to be urbanites; to be an urbanite, one must be both physically and mentally mobile; one must also shed one's confocalisms, naiveté, primitivity, and embrace complexity, alienation, and impersonality. As rural people move into urban centers, they often face conflicts in the process of urbanization.

Mr. Richard Wright, moving from rural Mississippi to south-side Chicago in 1927, must have gone through cultural, intellectual, and psychological conflicts. In that great, stimulating, mechanical city of Chicago, Richard Wright became intimately aware of black, urban, ghetto life. He worked at various odd jobs that brought him closer and closer to poor black urban life; the great depression of the late 1920s had a stupendous impact on black people in these urban ghettos. "No jobs for niggers until every white man has a job," white men shouted (Takaki, 1993:366-367). If the depression was hard on everyone 'globally,' it must have been more so on the African American masses in the United States ghettos.

In this atmosphere of poverty, unemployment, and discrimination against blacks, Marxism became attractive to Mr. Richard Wright, an ideological organization he joined in 1933. Even though American Marxists disappointed him on the issues of race and color later on, Mr. Wright imbibed much of Marxist analysis of society. Unlike the Harlem Renaissance, the Chicago Renaissance, in the hands of Richard Wright, insisted on the class and racial analysis of society: How are the black native sons of the United States treated by the status quo? What would be the fate of the young black men from the south-side of Chicago, in this mechanical and impersonal urban center? What impact does sex play in black-white relations? These are some of the issues Richard Wright deals with in his most popular novel, *Native Son.*

"Charles I. Glicksberg is speaking hyperbolically when he asserts that 'Richard Wright is Bigger Thomas–one part of him anyway. Bigger Thomas is what Richard Wright, had circumstances worked out differently, might have become'" (Kinnamon, 1969:66). There are certainly many similarities between protagonist Bigger Thomas in *Native Son* and Richard Wright, the author. *Native Son* reflects Richard Wright's diverse readings in sociology, psychology, history, Marxist ideology and literature. At the outset, we see that both Bigger Thomas and Richard Wright are both from Mississippi, school drop-outs, Marxist influenced, 'fatherless' at home, alienated from both blacks and whites, sensitive about racial issues and racial segregation (they live there (whites) and we (blacks) live here), existentialists, and protest against both capitalism and organized religion.

Beyond these similarities between the author and his protagonist, we could also look at Bigger Thomas as a metaphor, a native son who should, as such, benefit from the macro system, but who, in fact, does not because of his Africanness in a society that rejects African blood, color and features. His rejection by his native land sets Bigger Thomas against the values of the status quo, which views him as an alien, a jungle man, a criminal, an intruder, and even a big black rat, at that.

Growing up black, poor, not highly educated, and living in the black belt of Chicago, Bigger Thomas becomes intimately familiar with the harsh realities of black American urban ghetto life. To be black in the United States could in itself be an awful thing; but to be also poor, 'uneducated,' recalcitrant, and take the life of a white girl from a wealthy family (the Daltons), is to get into a fight with a system bigger than Bigger Thomas. With such a resume, Bigger Thomas' life was shielded and predetermined at the very beginning of *Native Son* (1993: 1-13).

From the point of view of environmental determinists, Bigger Thomas' one room, rat invested, and crowded environment spelled disaster for a rebellious young black man, wishing he could fly a plane, a dream deferred. "An alarm clock clanged in the dark and silent room. A bed spring creaked. A woman's voice sang out impatiently: 'Bigger, shut that thing off'"(7). And thus began Bigger Thomas' drama of fear, flight and fate. In the very beginning, there are conflicts between Bigger Thomas and his mother who denounces him in the place of 'good morning, son', and between Bigger Thomas and the big black rat whose "belly pulsed with fear"(9); Bigger's sister, Vera, is frightened by the dead rat in her big brother's hands, dangling in front of her face. Bigger's mother, full of fear, resorts to praying to the Lord, and says: "'Bigger sometimes I wonder why I birthed you'"(11). Thus, very early in the morning, Bigger Thomas' 'breakfast' included a fight, chaos, and a challenge to Bigger Thomas' self-esteem, identity, and manhood. His mother continued to 'pounce' on him with awful predictions:

> ... I am telling you again and mark my word. Some of these days you going set down and cry. Some of these days you going wish you had made something out of yourself, instead of just a tramp. But it will be too late then. (13)

And when Bigger Thomas leaves the house that morning to join a group of his friends, a poster of a representative of the status quo, Mr. Buckley, had his finger pointing at him, saying "if you break the law you can't win" (16), at the very time that Bigger was going to join his friends to rob a white man's store. Afraid to rob a white man's store, unlike that of a black man's, Bigger Thomas projects his fear onto Gus, a member of the gang of four.

Bigger Thomas fears the white man's wealth, political, economic and psychological power over him and his black race. Whites lived over there, and his people lived on the other side of town, in the black belt of the city of Chicago, renting from the Daltons of the macro-American society. Bigger Thomas hates the black society for its inability to unite against the mighty white force that kept them down; the few prominent black politicians are mostly interested in themselves, not caring for the likes of Bigger Thomas, except during elections. His mother and other black people are too religious for him, too inactive, too beaten down by the white man's religion.

We therefore see Bigger Thomas as an alienated individual, who dearly wants to be nothing but a native son, but who is rejected by his 'American' father; Mr. Dalton, the symbolic father and a wealthy white man, is many times removed from the black Bigger Thomases, including culturally, racially, psychologically, politically and economically. Mr. Dalton is blind to the likes of Bigger Thomas, whom he 'dearly' wants to uplift. Daltonism, a kind of red/green color blindness, describes the extent to which the Dalton family is actually unaware of black culture. Mrs. Dalton is literally blind, and Mr. and Mary Dalton are culturally blind to the feelings of the black Bigger Thomases. To the Daltons, Bigger Thomas is 'new' (53). Mary Dalton confesses:

> 'You know, Bigger, I've long wanted to go into those houses', she said, pointing to the tall, dark apartment buildings looming to either side of them, and just *see* how *your* people live. You know what I mean? I've been to England, France and Mexico, but I don't know how people live ten blocks from me. We know so *little* about each other. I just want to *see*. I want to *know* these people. Never in my life have I been inside a Negro home. Yet they *must* live like we live. They're *human*. . . . There are twelve million of them. . . . They live in *our*

country. . . . In the same city with us...", her voice trailed off wistfully. (70)

The radical, communist, Mr. Jan Erlone, is also blind to Bigger Thomas' culture, racial attributes and sensibilities; he groups blacks generally and refers to them as 'you people,' 'your people' as the Ex-Colored Man had distinguished himself from his 'mother's people'.

In Mr. Jan Erlone, we see a representative of the Communist Party doing his utmost to talk on behalf of the dispossessed in the U.S. capitalist system, ideologically trying to narrow the great gulf between race and class; but the more he tried, the more his ignorance about black culture and aspirations is confirmed.

In the U.S. capitalist system, Bigger Thomas is a black rat, similar to the black rat Bigger himself had killed at the opening of *Native Son*. Interestingly, the language Bigger Thomas uses while he pursues the rat in that one bedroom apartment is similar to the language used by the police while they chased *him* on the roof tops of Chicago, for the murder of Mary Dalton, the daughter of an outstanding member of the status-quo:

| **Bigger Thomas on the Black Rat** | **The Status-Quo on Bigger Thomas** |
|---|---|
| "There he is" (p. 4). | "There he is" (p. 248).<br>"There it is" (p. 252). |
| "Kill him" (p. 9). | "Kill him" (p. 253).<br>"Kill that Black Ape" (p. 253). |
| "I got him" (p. 10).<br>"By God, I got him" (p. 10). | "It's no use fighting, boy, you're caught" (p. 250). |
| "You sonofabitch" p. 10). | "That Black sonofabitch" (p. 253). |

Furthermore, the rat and Bigger Thomas were both black and were on all fours while being chased. They were both running away from forces bigger than themselves; the rat tried to hide in corners of the one bedroom apartment, similar to Bigger Thomas' attempts to hide from the law on the rooftops of the Black Belt of Chicago. They were both caught and killed; they had both been "trapped" (230).

Before Bigger Thomas' death, the fate of many more black criminals than white ones in the United States, the newspapers describe him as though he was an animal from the jungles of Africa:

> "He looks exactly like an ape!" exclaimed a terrified young white girl who watched the black slayer being loaded onto a stretcher after he had fainted. Though the Negro killer's body does not seem compactly built, he gives the impression of possessing abnormal physical strength. He is about five feet, nine inches tall and his skin is exceedingly black. His lower jaw protrudes obnoxiously, reminding one of a jungle beast.
>
> His arms are long, hanging in a dangling fashion to his knees. It is easy to imagine how this man, in the grip of a brain-numbing sex passion, overpowered little Mary Dalton, raped her, murdered her, beheaded her, then stuffed her body into a roaring furnace to destroy the evidence of his crime.
>
> His shoulders are huge, muscular, and he keeps them hunched, as if about to spring upon you at any moment. He looks at the world with a strange, sullen, fixed-from-under stare, as though defying all efforts of compassion.
>
> All in all, he seems a beast utterly untouched by the softening influences of modern civilization. In speech and manner he lacks the charm of the average, harmless, genial, grinning southern darky so beloved by the American people.

The fate of this 'jungle' man had already been predicted by his mother at the outset of the novel (p. 13) and the '"tall red letters"' that stated: '"If you break the law, you can't win!"' (p. 16). Bigger's poverty, blackness, racial sensitivity, powerlessness, alienation, rejection of organized Christianity and the American capitalist system all converge on him at his trial for the killing of Mary Dalton, but not that of Bessie, his black girlfriend, whom he had also brutally killed.

Because of Bigger Thomas' anti-Christianity, Reverend Hammond could not help him in jail; he was not going to repent for the murder of Mary Dalton, an excellent representative of the American status-quo. The State, represented by Mr. Buckley, wants him dead; black politicians are not in the position to help him out; there is no African nation powerful enough to intervene on his behalf. In this American 'wilderness' Bigger Thomas' fate was self-evident; Mr. Max's Marxist defense was eloquent, but the die had already been cast. As a true existentialist, Bigger Thomas had to take responsibility for his own actions without repentance, and with "a faint, wry, bitter smile," he "heard the ring of steel against steel as a far door clanged shut" (392).

In summary, *Native Son* reflects Mr. Richard Wright's diverse readings in psychology, sociology, Marxism, politics, literature, black urban life, class, and cultural conflict. His consciousness of the environmental impact on the dispossessed urban black masses in the United States remains realistic to the present day. His concerns regarding the Black American male youth's attempts to grapple with racism, classism, and cultural imperialism are re-echoed in the works of James Baldwin, Nathan McCall, and Malcolm X, the next generation of black writers that took off where Mr. Richard Wright left off (280). Black writers continue to 'debate' and signify the place of the black man in this global village of technopoly, racism, and capitalism.

## Malcolm X, Africa and African Americans

The popularization of Malcolm X by Spike Lee's movie catapulted one of the late aggressive Civil Rights leaders of the 1960s into international fame. Academicians and laymen have all had much to say about Malcolm X, the black nationalist, racist, spokesperson for the downtrodden black masses, or the trickster who challenged the American status-quo. Interpreters of Malcolm X's life have come in many shades of ideological persuasion. Some feminists were perturbed by Mr. Lee's movie fashion that portrays Malcolm X as a symbol of the black warrior, of black masculinity. Black Muslims are perhaps still worried that blaming some of their followers for assassinating Malcolm might still turn away many Black youths from the nation of Islam. Others might judge that Malcolm X did not really contribute much in terms of helping African Americans gain certain civil rights to aid them in entering fully into the American opportunity structure. Others still might argue that Mr. Lee's movie overemphasized Malcolm Little's Boston-Harlem days of hustling and female exploitation, paying less attention, therefore, to some of his positive contributions to the American macro society.

Certainly, therefore, there are many Malcolm Xs, with each Malcolm satisfying the fancy of various groups of people on the political, cultural, ideological and psychological spectrum. Pan-Africanists would perhaps 'blame' Mr. Spike Lee for not including Malcolm's sojourn to Africa where he was received as a brother, Omowale - who had returned whether as a Muslim, Christian, or what not; where he was accepted in the spirit of Pan-Africanism, met Nkrumah, the champion of continental Pan-Africanism, and upon his return to the United States organized his own brand of the African OAU, OAAU (Organization of Afro-American Unity), and urged African leaders to be aware of global capitalism. Some Africanists would even criticize Malcolm X for taking too readily to the Arabs, whom he categorized as whites without the sort of racism he had observed and experienced in the United States; but the Arabs, in regards to Black Africa, have not been color blind. Had Malcolm not been fooled by the euphoria of his pilgrimage to Mecca, and had he taken time to look beyond the hospitality of his august Arab hosts, he would have realized that the white Arabs who received him so unconcerned about his epidermis, were not without their hatred for Blackness, even Black Muslims. One only needs to read Bernard Lewis' *Race and Color in Islam* to know that thousands of African slaves were exterminated in Iraq in the 800's for rebelling against their servitude. In the present day Sudan and Mauritania, many Black Africans are 'slaves' to white Arab rulers. Prophet Mohammad certainly might have preached brotherhood amongst Muslims, but in practice Black African Muslims have been treated as the younger brothers, fit to be exploited, enslaved and looked down upon in the Middle East and in Africa.

Nonetheless, Mr. Spike Lee's movie on Malcolm X showed Malcolm urging African Americans to be proud of their Blackness, their Africanness and to be 'schooled' enough in the ways of the white man so as to develop their own economies and communities. With some eclecticism, Malcolm X is shown convincing African Americans that their Blackness must not deter them from taking responsibilities into their own hands, to do what they must for themselves and to identify with Africa.

Ironically, the Africa that Malcolm X urged African Americans to identify with was a nightmare in the 1990s; obviously, Somalia, Rwanda, Burundi, and the former Zaire are cases that epitomized growth without development, of lawlessness, banditry, man's inhumanity to man, and Black on Black crime. One is even tantalized by the often racist dictum that maybe Black people need their white brothers and sisters to settle their disputes, protect and guide them to maturity in countries like former Zaire, Burundi, Liberia, Rwanda, Sierra Leone, the Central African Republic and others.

Ironically, also, the white 'devil' that Malcolm X so vehemently denounced before his transformation into orthodox Islam was the same that flew thousands of miles to save some of his African brethren in Somalia and the other places on the continent. Finally, African people must always be grateful for the humanitarian help their brothers received in Somalia, former Zaire, Burundi, and Rwanda, etc., but ultimately they must do for themselves what other races have done and are doing for themselves. They must heed the lessons of Marcus Garvey and Kwame Nkrumah who urged that Africa must be united and industrialized, so that that united African nation will reckon with other nations, not from a frog perspective or as a supplicant, but with strength and renaissant personality. Maybe Spike Lee's Malcolm X movie and the awful drama in Somalia and other African countries provide an opportunity for a renewed faith in Pan-Africanists such as Kwame Nkrumah, Marcus Garvey and George Padmore, and W.E.B. DuBois, from Africa, the West Indies, and the United States respectively.

If these African and African American male writers have emphasized the public sphere, African American women writers have the domestic sphere. In this global village they, like their African sisters, are also concerned about their race and sex in this capitalist, patriarchal global village. In the next chapter, we provide a general examination of a number of popular African American female writers.

## References: Chapter VII

Abrahams, Peter. 1989. *Mine Boy*. Heinemann Educational Books.

Achebe, Chinua. 1990. *Things Fall Apart*. New York: Ballantine Books.

Andrews, William L. (ed). 1994. *Classic Fiction of the Harlem Renaissance*. New York: Oxford University Press.

______ . (ed). 1987. *Frederick Douglass: My Bondage and My Freedom*. Urbana and Chicago : University of Illinois Press.

Armah, Ayi Kwei. 1968. *The Beautyful (sic) Ones Are Not Yet Born*. Heinemann Educational Books.

Baldwin, James. 1955. *Notes of A Native Son*. Boston : Beacon

Bohannan, Paul and Phillip Curtain. 1988. *Africa and Africans*. Prospect Heights, Illinois: Waveland Press, Inc.

Bone, Robert. 1986. "Richard Wright and the Chicago Renaissance." *Callahoo* . Vol.9. No. 3: 446-468.

Bontemps, Arna. (ed).1974. *American Negro Poetry*. New York: Farrar, Straws and Siroux.

Brown, William Wells. 1989. *Clotel or the President's Daughter*. New York: Carol publishing group.

Conton, William. 1960. *The African* . Heinemann Educational Books

Dathorne, O.R. 1975. *African Literature in the Twentieth Century*. Minneapolis, Minnesota: University of Minnesota Press.

Davidson, Basil. 1989. *Modern Africa: A Social and Political History*. London and new York : Longman.

Decosta-Willis, Mariann. 1991. (Co-editor) *Double Stitch: Black Women Write About Mothers and Daughters*. New York: Harper Perennial. pp. 131-138.

Douglass, Frederick. 1968. *Narrative of the Life of Frederick Douglass*.New York: Penguin Books, Inc.

DuBois, W.E.B. 1989. *Souls of Black Folk*. New York: Penguin Books, Inc.

Dunbar, Paul Laurence. 1984. *Lyrics of Lowly Life: The Poetry of Paul Lawrence Dunbar*. New York : Citadel Press.

Emecheta, Buchi. 1974. *Second Class Citizens*. New York: Braziler

Glicksberg, Charles I. 1972. Quoted in Kenneth Kinnamon. *The Emergence of Richard Wright; A Study in Literature and Society*. The University of Chicago Press. p. 119.

Griffin, John Howard. 1960. *Black Like Me*. New York: Penguin Books.

Haley, Alex. 1992. *The Autobiography of Malcolm X*. New York: Ballantine Books.

______. 1976. *Roots*. New York: Dell Publishing Co. Inc.

Hammond, Jupiter. 1971. "A Dialogue Entitled The Kind master and Dutiful Servant." pp. 31-33, In Ruth Miller (ed.) *Black American Literature*. Encino, California: Glencoe Publishing company, Inc.

Heron, G.A. 1976. *The Poetry of Okot p'Bitek*. Heinemann Educational Books.

Hughes, Langston. 1963. *The Best of Simple. New* York: Hill and Wang.

______.1965. *Simple's Uncle Sam*. New York: Hill and Wang.

Hughes, Thomas. 1963. *Tom Brown's School Days*. London and Glasgow: Collins.

Iyasere, Solomon D. 1978. "Narrative Techniques in 'Things Fall Apart.'" pp. 92-110, in C.L. Innes and Berntt Lindfors (eds.); *Critical Perspectives on Chinua Achebe*. Washington, D.C.: Three Continent Press.

Kaunda, Kenneth. 1963. *Zambia Shall Be Free: An Autobiography of Kenneth Kaunda*. New York : Praeger.

Kenyatta, Jomo. 1965. *Facing Mt. Kenya*. New York: Vintage Books.

Kesey, Ken. 1962. *One Flew Over The Cuckoo's Nest*. New York: The Viking Press.

Kinnamon, Kenneth. 1990. "Native Son." pp. 60-72, in *Major Literary Characters: Bigger Thomas*, Harold Bloom (ed.) . New York and Philadelphia: Chelsea House Publishers.

Larsen, Nella. 1971. *Passing*. New York: Collier Books.

Laye, Camara. 1954. *The Dark Child: The Autobiography of an African Boy*. New York: Hill and Wang.

Lewis, Bernard. 1971. *Race and Color in Islam*. New York: Harper and Row, Publishers.

Lincoln, Eric E. 1984. *Race, Religion, and the Continuing American Dilemma*. New York: Hill and Wang.

Marah, John K. 1987. "Educational Adaptation and Pan-Africanism: Developmental Trends in Africa." *Journal of Black Studies*. Vol. 17, No. 4: 460-481.

Mathabane, Mark. 1987. *Kaffir Boy: The true story of a Black Youth's Coming of Age in Apartheid South Africa*. New York: New America Library.

McKay, Claude. 1990. "If We Must Die." p.31 in Arna Bontemps, *American Negro Poetry*. New York: Farrar, Strays and Giroux.

Memmi, Albert. 1991. *The Colonizer and The Colonized.* Boston: Beacon Press.

Morrison, Toni. 1970. *The Bluest Eye.* New York: Washington Square Press.

_______. 1990. *Playing in the Dark: Whiteness and the Literary Imagination.* New York: Vintage Books.

_______. 1981. *Tar Baby*. New York: New American Library.

Ngugi, Wa Thiong'o. 1982. *Devil On The Cross*. Heinemann

_______. 1964. *Weep Not, Child.* Heinemann

Nkrumah, Kwame. 1957. *Ghana: Autobiography of Kwame Nkrumah.* New York: Thomas Nelson and Sons.

Osofsky, Gilbert. 1966. *Harlem; The Making of a Ghetto.* New York, New York: Harper & Row.

P'Bitek, Okot. 1984. *Song of Lawino and Song of Ocol. Heinemann.*

Postman, Neil. 1993. *Technology: The Surrender of Culture to Technology*. New York: Alfred A. Knopf.

Randall, Dudley. 1968. "Booker T. and W.E.B." pp. 470-471, in Abraham Chapman (ed.) *Black Voices: An Anthology of Afro-American Literature. New* York: New American Library.

Takaki, Ronald. 1993. *A Different Mirror: A History of Multicultural America.* Little, Brown and Company (Canada) Limited.

Thurman, Wallace. 1996. *The Blacker The Berry*. New York : Simon And Schuster.

Washington, Booker T. 1963. *Up From Slavery. New* York: Bantam Books.

Wheatley, Phillis. 1971. "On Being Brought From Africa to America." p.34, in Ruth Miller (ed.) *Black American Literature*. Encino, California: Glencoe Publishing Company, Inc.

White, Joseph L. 1984. *The Psychology of Blacks: An African-American Perspective*. Englewood Cliffs, N.J. : Prentice Hall.

White, Walter. 1948. *A Man Called White: The Autobiography of Walter White.* New York: Viking Press.

Wright, Richard. 1968. *Native Son.* New York: Harper and Row Brothers.

_______.1963. *Black Boy*. Harper and Row Publishers

_______.1964. *White Man, Listen*! New York: Anchor Books.

_______. 1974. *Black Power: A Record of Reactions in a Land of Pathos. Westport*, Conn.: Greenwood Press, Publishers.

# Chapter VIII:

## Three African-American Female Writers

### There was a Zora Neale Hurston Before Alice Walker: A Discourse in Black Women's Literature*

The publication of Alice Walker's *The Color Purple* (1982), made popular by the movie fashion, brought considerable attention to Black women writers with respect to how Black men treat their women folk, and to a certain extent, how men treat women in general. A good number of middle-class Black men were offended and complained that Black men were negatively portrayed, and that not all Black men, definitely including themselves, treat their women the way the Black men did in *The Color Purple*. On the other hand, a good number of Black women saw Alice Walker's characterization of Black men as an accurate portrayal of the way Black men treat their women folk. Furthermore, Alice Walker seems to have satisfied the notions of a multitude of white people who privately think, but not publicly admit their view that Blacks are an "oversexed" ethnic group.

One of the purposes of this section is not to duplicate, or reiterate the various interpretations that people have of *The Color Purple*, but instead to: (1) show that the sexual and economic exploitation of Black women by men is a preoccupation of Black women writers--one of the first being Zora Neale Hurston, who influenced Alice Walker greatly (Walker, 1977, p. XIII), and (2) in the process of doing so, isolate and discuss three major themes in Black women's fiction which are abundantly found in Alice Walker's *The Color Purple* (1982) and Zora Neale Hurston's *Their Eyes Were Watching God* (1978). Both of these Black women writers focus on: (1) women as mules of the world; (2) the intellectual movement of black women from innocence to conscious-ness; and (3) the liberated Black woman, who is self-actualized and has come to fully accept herself after numerous trials and tribulations with menfolks, such as found in the work of Ntozake Shange (Shange, 1975).

The theme of Black women as the mules of the world is specifically stated in *Their Eyes Were Watching God* (29), a non-racial novel that explores the lives of common Black folks in the all Black town of Eatonville, Florida, Hurston's birthplace (Hemenway, 1977). The fact that Eatonville was an all Black community had significant linguistic and other cultural impacts on Zora Neale Huston's artistic career. Unlike the young Richard Wright, who experienced extreme racism in the South, where his Uncle Hoskins was murdered by envious whites (Wright, 1945, p.26), Hurston' s Eatonville was run by Blacks with freedom to practice their cultural idiosyncrasies without the interference of others. Hurston's early intimacies with "authentic" Black culture and her later study of anthropology and phrenology under the famed Papa Boas, as Hurston affectionately called him, convinced her that blacks had something to offer. Black linguistic expressions, including orature, hyperbole, playing the dozens, "lying sessions", voodooism, and other nuances of African origin impressed Hurston so much that she was among the first few to oppose the social integration of the races. In her view racial integration would be detrimental to Blacks, because they would be the ones who, in the process of integration, would eventually lose their cultural identities and folklore. She remained adamantly opposed to school integration:

> ...I was not going to part my lips concerning the United States Supreme Court decision on ending segregation in the public schools of the South...I break my silence just this once...whole matter revolves around the self-respect of my people. How much satisfaction can I get from a court order for somebody to associate with me who does not wish me near them?...I regard the ruling of the United States Supreme Court as insulting rather than honoring my race. (Hurston,1985, pp. XI-XII)

As an anthropologist, folklorist and artist, Hurston observed the Eatonville society succinctly, and she recorded what she saw with the eyes of an artist, folklorist and anthropologist in *Their Eyes Were Watching God*. That is to say, it is in *Their Eyes Were Watching God* where the three personalities of Hurston converge.

At one level, the novel can be viewed as a love story, but at another as the protagonist's search for self actualization. However, first and foremost, *Their Eyes Were Watching God*, Hurston's first novel, is about a Black woman in a society dominated by men, intellectually, economically, politically, and psychologically as well as sexually, which all go hand in hand. Hurston narrates about a society where women are not only like mules and sex objects without rewards and appreciation, but also where they are viewed and treated as intellectual inferiors; it was a society where women do not marry for love, but for economic security. With respect to the political domination of Black women by their men folks, Janie Crawford, the protagonist in *Their Eyes Were Watching God*, received exhortation from her grandma in a Hurstonian style:

> Honey, de white man is the ruler of everything as fur as Ah been able to find out. Maybe it's some place way off in de ocean where the black man is in power, but we don't know nuthin' but what we see. So de white man throw down de load and tell the nigger man tuh pick it up. He pick it up because he have to, but he don't tote it. He hand it to his women folks. De nigger woman is de mule uh de world so fur as Ah can see. Ah been prayin' fuh it tuh be different wid you. Lawd, Lawd, Lawd! (29)

Grandma didn't want her granddaughter to be left without a husband as had been the case in her family which had a history of rape and illegitimacies. Janie Crawford was 'pushed' into marrying Mr. Logan Killicks, who offered economic security. To please Grandma, whose "head is ole and tilted towards de grave" (31), our protagonist had to settle for Logan Killicks, not for Johnny Taylor, whom Crawford loves, but who had no property. To a large extent therefore, Janie Crawford was given away to a man of property primarily for security reasons, because Mr. Killicks, the chosen husband, phrenologically speaking, was not "meant to be loved... cause his head is so long one way and so flat on the sides and dat bone uh fat back up his neck" (48), were all repulsive to our protagonist.

The first two months of Janie Crawford's 'marriage' to Logan Killicks were not romantic. Mr. Killicks was not only ugly in terms of his head, but he also had a bulging belly and his "toe-nails look lak mule foots" and "he don't even never mention nothin' pretty" (43). But as long as grandma was alive, Janie Crawford will have to bear it out. As soon as grandma died, however, Crawford began to hope for "...a bloomtime, and a green time and an orange time" (52), but none would come as long as she was with Mr. Killicks. Even when grandma was gone, Mr. Killicks did not relax his treatment of Janie Crawford; he even began to treat our protagonist as though she was a mule. He went as far as buying a mule so Janie could help on the sixty-acre farm. As the mule arrived, Janie's role on the farm doubled; she didn't only have to be a housewife, and all that that entailed, but she was to also help Mr. Killicks shovel manure. According to Logan Killicks, he was doing Janie Crawford a big favor; she should be grateful to be in a big house on sixty-acres of land, and must not fret whether she was being treated as a mule, or even worse.

But Janie Crawford was becoming conscious and changing in accordance to the degree of her oppression. She testified that she didn't worship the sixty-acres of land that Mr. Killicks was using as an instrument of oppression. Furthermore, at Mr. Killicks gate, Janie had met a Mr. Joe Starks, citified and well-dressed, an ambitious Black man on his way to Eatonville, (an all Black town where Blacks could do things for themselves without interference from white folks). In his cruelty to Janie Crawford, Mr. Killicks would bring up her past, and for this Janie changed irreversibly. She began to liken Mr. Logan Killicks to "...a black bear doing some clumsy dance on his hind legs" (52). She was no longer afraid of Mr. Killicks and told him so outright: "you ain't done me no favor by marryin' me. And if dat's what you call yo'self doin', Ah don't thank yuh for it" (53). Janie Crawford seemed to have learned her lessons from Mr. Logan Killicks, and was now in search of her bloomtime and greentime with Mr. Joe Starks.

By marrying Mr. Joe Starks, Janie Crawford 'thought' she could achieve her horizon, but did not know what was really in store for her. With Mr. Killicks, she had worn an apron which symbolized her oppression as a domestic servant, and when she was called upon to shovel manure, she was herself to work like a mule whose labor was not valued, and whose place was dictated by only the owner. Even though her marriage to Joe Starks was her choice, it turned out to be just as oppressive, if not more so, as the first one, into which she was pushed by her grandma. For Mr. Joe Starks, Janie Crawford was a tool to be used to enhance his image in the Eatonville community. She certainly was pretty enough to be a mayor's wife, and she did compliment the charismatic Joe Starks favorably in the eyes of the people of Eatonville.

Joe Starks became an agent of change in Eatonville, building the biggest store in town, a post office, a sawmill and other modern facilities. The porch of his store became the 'nucleus' of the town as well as a school for Janie Crawford to learn her lessons about love and men. In the lying sessions, our protagonist was educated about lovers and how they should behave towards each other. The lying sessions functioned to exhort, ridicule, and enlighten Janie Crawford in terms of how she should be treated by Joe Starks. As Mr. Starks became more and more powerful, he began to be more and more oppressive towards Janie Crawford by restricting her behind the counter, demanding that she use headgear to keep her long beautiful hair covered, and by preventing her from speaking in the public sphere; he even began to call her stupid. Joe Starks' society was one in which women were seen and not heard; it was a society where men had to "...think for women and chillun and chickens and cows. I god, they sho' don't think none theirselves" (110). Men saw one thing and understood ten; women saw ten things, but understood none at all (111).

To a certain extent, and at various levels, Janie Crawford literally began to approximate Matt Bonner's mule in the town of Eatonville. Joe Starks did not only buy the mule from Matt Bonner to free the beast from mistreatment, but also because he wanted the Eatonville community to look upon him favorably. Janie Crawford explicates:

> Jody, dat wuz uh mighty fine thing fuh you tuh do. 'Tain't everybody would have thought of it, 'cause it ain't no everyday thought. Freein' dat mule makes uh mighty big man outa you. Something like George Washington and Lincoln. Abraham Lincoln, he had de whole United States tuh rule so he freed de Negroes. You got uh town so you freed uh mule. You have power tuh free things and dat makes you lak uh King uh something. (91-92)

Similarly, Joe Starks had literally freed Janie Crawford from the hard work on Mr. Logan's sixty-acres. Furthermore, the mule was being mistreated by Matt Bonner as Janie Crawford was by Mr. Joe Starks. Connecting the mistreatment of the mule to her own condition, Janie Crawford not only empathized with the mule, but also began to rebel against her own condition as the mule was doing. Joe Starks had done the mule a favor by buying it, as he had done Janie Crawford a favor by marrying her out of the hard work on Mr. Killick's farm. In these respects, the mule and Janie Crawford are alike; they don't think for themselves, but they both enhance Mr. Starks' image in the community.

The lying sessions that took place on Joe Starks' porch were also helping Janie Crawford to attain a certain level of consciousness. These lying sessions did not only entertain, ridicule, insult, and exhort in a general way, but also taught our protagonist that the mayor of Eatonville did not love her; at least not in the way the storytellers told of their love for mythical Daisy. The male storytellers indirectly told Mr. Starks that had he loved Janie Crawford, he would have been nicer to her, such as allowing her to let her long hair down. At least, other men would have loved beautiful Janie Crawford as they expressed their love for Daisy who in fact resembled our protagonist in beauty and in the length of her hair. The lying sessions gave many more examples of different types of non-exploitative love between men and women totally unlike that between the mayor and Janie Crawford. As these lying sessions became more intense, Joe Starks dismissed Janie Crawford from the porch, and therefore, hopefully from the ideas that were being alluded to by the male storytellers.

By this time, however, it was already too late for Mr. Starks to make a comeback, or gain ground; Janie Crawford had already seen and heard enough to be enlightened and conscious of her relationship with the town's mayor, and by now she could challenge him in public (110).

Janie Crawford was no longer petal-open to her husband. "The spirit of the marriage left the bedroom and took to living in the parlor," and "she was saving up her feelings for some man she had never seen" (111-112).

That man was Mr. Tea Cake. Tea Cake was unlike Mr. Logan Killicks and Joe Starks, who were much older and propertied and who had economically, sexually, and politically exploited Janie Crawford. Tea Cake loved our protagonist for her beauty and made her feel like a woman who was wanted. He did not treat her as a sex object or a political tool. He took her fishing and dancing, and allowed her to be proud of her long beautiful hair. The headtie that symbolized her oppression under Mr. Starks was put away when she married Tea Cake shortly following Joe Starks' death.

The townspeople gossiped about the two 'love-birds' such as they never could have about Crawford and Killicks, or Crawford and Starks:

> Tea Cake and Janie gone hunting.
> Tea Cake and Janie gone fishing.
> Tea Cake and Janie gone to Orlando to the movies.
> Tea Cake and Janie gone to dance.
> Tea Cake making flower beds in Janie's yard and seeding the garden for her.
> Chopping down the tree she never did like by the dining room window...
> Tea Cake in a borrowed car teaching Janie to drive.
> Tea Cake and Janie playing checkers; playing coon-can; playing Florida flip on the store porch all afternoon as if nothing else was there.
> Day after day and week after week. (166-167)

Against the wishes of most of the townspeople, Janie Crawford married Tea Cake, though he was much younger than she and was without property.

After Tea Cake' s death from a dog bite during a hurricane, Janie Crawford returned to her home in overalls, a symbol of her liberation, and related her life experiences to Phoeby, her hometown girl friend. "Ah done been tuh de horizon and back and now kin set heah in my house and live by comparisons" (284).

Janie Crawford was at last fully liberated and self-actualized after reaching her horizon of experiences, maturity and consciousness. It was as though she had been to the mountain top and seen all the contours of the community, in the valley of human beings who had not traveled with her to that mountain top. Now a different and enlightened woman, she would wear her overalls whether the people liked it or not, and she was no longer going to be burdened by petty jealousies and stupidities of those who had remained all their lives in the valley of ignorance and inexperience. After relating her story to her friend Phoeby, the latter remarked:

> Ah done growed ten feet higher from jus' listenin' tuh you, Janie. Ah ain't satisfied wit mahself no mo'. Ah means tuh make Sam take me fishin' wid him after this. Nobody better not criticize yuh in mah hearin'. (284)

These three major themes (experience, maturity, and consciousness) in Hurston's *Their Eyes Were Watching God* are reiterated in Alice Walker's *The Color Purple*. Like Hurston's Janie Crawford, Celie in Alice Walker's *The Color Purple* was pushed into marriage after a series of illegitimacies. Celie was given away into marriage to Mr. Albert, to be worked and used. Like Janie Crawford, Celie had no say concerning her marriage; Celie was inspected like chattel as though Mr. Albert was purchasing a mule from on an auction block, and was described as ugly and like a mule who was not a stranger to hard work (Walker, 1982, 17-18).

In Mr. Albert's house, Celie was not only a housewife and all that that entailed, but also she was a sex object: "I lay there thinking about Nettie while he on top of me" (Walker, 1982, 34). At this point, all Celie knew was how to survive, even though her sister Nettie, and even Kate and Carrie, Mr. Albert's sisters, all advised Celie to rebel against Mr. Albert's domination. But for Mr. Albert and his son, Harpo, women were simply there to be taken, beaten and worked as seen fit by men. Experience had taught Mr. Albert that women were to obey their husbands or be beaten, and Mr. Albert transmitted to his son the mentality that he too should beat his wife to prove his manhood (Walker, 1982, p. 65).

Like Janie Crawford, Celie was not fit to accompany her husband to public places, but must stay at home and in the fields "chopping cotton and plowing" (Walker, 1982, p. 65).

Even Harpo's lover, Sofia Butler, had to be looked up and down like a piece of property one was about to purchase (Walker, 1982, pp. 37-38), rather than like a member of a family, as in traditional Africa. However, Sofia was to prove herself too tough for Harpo to handle. But, even though she proved herself too tough to handle by giving Harpo a black eye, she was no match for white people who would put her 'in her place' in prison where she would do domestic work, general cleaning and laundry, and was hired to work as a domestic servant for Miss Millie, the white mayor's wife whom she had assaulted. To a certain extent, therefore, Celie was being 'schooled', to use Malcolm X's concept, to the facts of a male dominated society; that is to say, women can be tough, but they can do only so much. These were all lessons for Celie to learn from.

Celie was also to learn from Shug Avery who discovered that Mr. Albert had been hiding Nettie's letters to Celie, so as to prevent the latter from learning about her sister who was with missionaries in Africa. Shug Avery educated Celie by telling her the life history of Mr. Albert years ago. Celie was no longer as innocent as she had been before this intimacy between the two women; it was Shug Avery who taught Celie to appreciate her body, to love and to appreciate herself.

In addition to the intimacy between Shug Avery and Celie, Nettie's twenty letters from Africa to her sister in America, continued the education and enlightenment of Celie. The letters filled the void between the two sisters, describing Africa and African people in terms of their traditions and belief systems, the Black missionaries, Celie's Adam and Olivia, the change the Olinka people were undergoing due to the coming of the white man, who their biological father was, and how their so-called Pa was not their real father at all, but one who had swindled their parents' properties.

As Celie gained more knowledge about herself in relation to Mr. Albert and the world around her, she became irrevocably confident and then challenged Mr. Albert's authority over her, in public:

> You a low down dog is what's wrong, I say. It's time to leave you and enter into creation. And your dead body just the welcome mat I need. (Walker, 1982, p. 81)

Like Mr. Killicks and Joe Starks, Mr. Albert had by this time lost control of his machismo when he was publicly challenged by the woman he had dominated for so long. Celie had by this time accepted herself fully and could say: "I'm pore, I'm black, I may be ugly and can't cook,...But I'm here. Amen,...Amen, Amen" (Walker, 1982, p. 187). The rest of the story continued this celebration of life and self to culminate into "Dear God. Dear Stars, dear trees, dear sky, dear people. Dear everything. Dear God" (Walker, 1982, p. 247), at the reception of the other family members from Africa. Like Janie Crawford, Celie, at the end of *The Color Purple*, was fully self-actualized and if she was to remarry it would have to be "...in spirit as well as in the flesh..." (Walker, 1982, p. 247). Mr. Albert and his son Harpo had changed progressively; but Celie had also changed to the point where she would never again be dominated by any man. Like Janie Crawford, Celie had reached her horizon by realizing that she was a member of the big association of life.

In the works of both Zora Neale Hurston and Alice Walker, the women protagonists, including some secondary characters, were treated as 'mules of the world' in the first stages of their encounters with men. At these first stages, they were economically and sexually exploited by the men in their lives.

For instance, it was after two disastrous marriages before Janie Crawford realized that she was really not reaching her horizon. With Mr. Killicks, she was enclosed within the gate of the sixty-acres, worked as a 'domestic servant' and did not really love Killicks, who was not meant to be loved and had 'mule foots'; she was even called upon to shovel mule manure. The apron she had to wear when within Mr. Killicks' folds symbolized her oppression as a domestic servant, rather than a wife. Why, she was even pushed into it by Grandma who was more concerned with the past legacies of rape and illegitimacies in her family than with Crawford's authentic happiness in marriage. Indeed, when was one supposed to love? Before, or after marriage?

The oppression of Janie Crawford continued on the porch of the mayor's store in Eatonville. Here, Crawford's symbol of oppression was the headtie she had to wear to cover her naturally beautiful long hair. She was prevented from speaking in public, participating in the hyperbolic lying sessions on the porch, and from accompanying her husband during public occasions. She also was commanded to keep her place in the background, behind the store counter. She was told what to do as children are told and directed, for they, like Janie Crawford, had to be controlled; children and women have to be directed; they cannot think none themselves.

These cases of oppression and non-personhood are also repeated in Celie's story, who was sexually exploited by her so-called Pa at a very early age. Mr. Albert continued this exploitation in that she simply laid there while he satisfied himself sexually; a joyless sexual experience for Celie. She was pushed into marriage to Mr. Albert as Janie Crawford was to Mr. Killicks. Sofia was also put in her place by the machismo society for failing to accept being a maid. To a certain extent, also, Shug Avery was economically exploited by her man Grady; but the innocence of the female characters could not go on forever, especially when they were continuously being 'schooled' in the ways of Judeo-Christian patriarchy. In essence, these Black men who treated their womenfolk as subhumans can be said to have learned from the Judeo-Christian tradition that assigns inferior positions to women. Tea Cake, who was proud of his blackness treated Crawford as an equal, rather than as subject.

For Janie Crawford, the porch of Mr. Joe Starks functioned like a classroom where men told stories of how a love affair should be. For Celie, it took Shug Avery and twenty letters from her sister Nettie to know where her children were, who her real parents were and about her inheritance. After becoming conscious about the system of patriarchy, the two protagonists rebelled against their men, who by then had lost control over their former subjects. For Janie Crawford, the spirit of the marriage left the bedroom and took to living in the parlor, and she was no longer petal-open to Mr. Joe Starks. For Celie, it was time to leave Mr. Albert in order to begin her rebirth.

Thus, the two liberated, self-actualized Black women would never again be dominated by their menfolks. Janie Crawford reached her horizon by realizing that she was a member of the big association of life. Celie also reached her horizon through trials and tribulations. She learned about her roots, African culture and people, and after such knowledge, she fully accepted herself and rejected the Judeo-Christian tradition that women are to be educated to be submissive (Mill, 1978, p.16). If ever she is to remarry, it would have to be in the flesh as well as in the spirit, but not through 'flesh, cash, or power connection' alone (Braithwaite, 1981, pp. 91-92).

Celie and Janie Crawford have attained a high level of consciousness that makes them accept themselves for who they are, and they will meet men and other women on equal terms, no less. They are not only economically independent, but they are also spiritually, culturally, and intellectually mature enough to differentiate between pure and exploitative relationships between men and women in a materialistic society controlled by the white man. Celie is perhaps the most profoundly enriched by her knowledge of Africa, African religion, people and their traditions, her daughter's knowledge and acceptance of Tashi, the African, and the uniting of the family on the Fourth of July, when they celebrated themselves as a collective and had more than substantial reason for participating, in their own way, in the Fourth of July celebration that now had specific meaning for them as a Black family.

## Terry McMillan's Black Women of the 1960s, 1980s and the 1990s: An Eclectic Approach

Terry McMillan's *Mama* (1987), *Disappearing Acts* (1990) and *Waiting to Exhale* (1992) present groups as well as individual black women of the 1960's, 1980's and the 1990's respectively. Within this thirty-odd year span, McMillan portrays the single black woman with several children, who is intermittently unemployed and on welfare (Mildred in *Mama*); the college educated, songwriter and music teacher (Zora Banks in *Disappearing Acts*); the house-wife with a wealthy husband, the heavy-set black woman with her own business and other professionally successful black women who do not depend on men for economic support (Bernadine, Gloria, Robin and Savannah in *Waiting to Exhale*). Whether these black women are economically independent or not, they are portrayed and come across as womanists, in Alice Walker's conception of the audaciousness of black women with willful behavior, who enjoy being with other women (Walker, 1983: XI-XII). These women are characterized as pragmatic; though not deeply religious, they are not necessarily disrespectful; they have inner strengths, conscious of their immediate social and psychological environments, and are also aware of their place in their macro-universe.

Following the traditions of Zora Neale Hurston (*Their Eyes Were Watching God*), Alice Walker (*The Color Purple*), and Gloria Naylor (*Women of Brewster Place*), McMillan's three novels are peopled with black men and women in love and in conflict, in marriages and separations, with their parents, children and friends and without, in their youths, middle ages as well as with their grandparents in a society not of their making. McMillan's characters are realistically portrayed in a micro-society within a larger society that sends black men into prisons, to wars, the unemployment line, the labor pool and to Jack Daniels (as in Franklin's case in *Disappearing Acts*).

This segment eclectically examines McMillan's 'Mama', Zora Banks and Franklin Swift in *Disappearing Acts*, and the four professional black women: Robin, Gloria, Bernadine and Savannah in *Waiting to Exhale* in their relationships with black men, with each other as sisters, and evaluates the love affair between Zora and Franklin; a particular focus is to try to ascertain the possibilities for Franklin and Zora to have a lasting relationship after they obtain certain knowledge and changes about themselves, each other and the love for their son, Jeremiah. Furthermore, we examine the metaphor of 'disappearing' and the place of Africa in McMillan.

If black men writers have usually portrayed their black female characters as too often religious (Baldwin's saints in *Go Tell It on the Mountain*, Bigger's mother in Wright's *Native Son*) and economically dependent on men (Elizabeth in Baldwin's *Go Tell It on the Mountain*, Ex-colored man's mother in *The Autobiography of an Ex-Colored Man*), black women writers, and especially Terry McMillan, portray black female characters as much more assertive, realistic, womanistic and independent. A good number of black men would probably view the treatment of black male characters in the works of black women writers as male-bashing; these men are entitled to their own interpretations and points of view, but so also is Terry McMillan in her own point of view and sensibilities. Nonetheless, there is hardly any question that McMillan is immensely familiar with the language of black men and women, the culture of sisterhood between black women friends, mothers and daughters, fathers and sons, etc. In *Mama* (1987) for an example, Terry McMillan brings to African-American female fiction a black female character (Mildred), reminiscent of Janie Crawford in Zora Neale Hurston's *Their Eves were Watching God;* McMillan's Mildred 'literally' and figuratively digs herself out of any hole in which she finds herself. At twenty-seven years of age, Mildred already has had five children from three husbands, Crook, Rufus and Billy Callahan, and has had Percy Russell, Sonny Tylor, Spooky Cooper and Big Jim, in addition to her husbands. Mildred falls in and out of love as circumstances change; she also goes on and off welfare as her fortunes change; in between, she pops pills to keep her nerves calm. After all, "...helping out a woman with five kids was not...having a good time, no matter how good she makes them feel in bed" (*Mama* 42). Mama married Rufus who was financially helpful even though he smelled 'funky', did not know how to dress, and she was embarrassed to be seen with him; Rufus was to even later rape Freida, one of her daughters; he was to later get fifteen stitches in the hospital after Mildred shot him for raping her daughter.

When hard times came down, Mildred briefly engaged in prostitution, ran a gambling joint, went into and out of prison without any qualms about what others said about her. Under the pressures of constant unemployment, bad housing, fruitless engagements with men, and even temporary insanity (pp. 102-105), Mildred is not the black woman to throw in the towel. Her son, Money, a school dropout, on drugs, in and out of jail, provides another source of challenge to Mildred's strength to survive in the midst of adversity. Her daughter, Doll, is married to Richard, a dark black man, but gets impregnated by Bryan, a high yellow black man, and their child comes out yellow (p. 104); Angel, Mildred's other daughter, marries a white man, and 'guess who is coming to dinner,' but Mildred was realistic; Mildred herself was even supposed to marry a white man, Big Jim, but times were not conducive for her to finally go through with the marriage. She did not care about his color, as long as she loved him, and as long as Ethan and Angel loved each other. Mildred was imprisoned for writing bad checks, her house caught on fire and her father had a heart attack, all in one day, but she remained intact. With all these trials and tribulations, Mildred goes to church where her brother Jasper was preaching, but came out without feeling "...an inch closer to God" (p. 179). Mildred's strength and determination to survive was tested when she went off the road in snow, had a flat tire at the same time but was able to change the tire and emerge out of the ditch intact, symbolizing her triumph over adversity.

In the end, Freida, her eldest daughter, after her own trials with alcohol, finally becomes a journalist, publishes her articles, and gives her 'Mama' five hundred dollars; Mildred inherits some money after *her* father's death and decided to go back to school to improve herself; mother and daughter celebrate their lives as two matured, strong black women who had been to the 'big association of life', - in the sense of Janie Crawford's triumphant return to Eatonville in *Their Eyes were Watching God.* With five children by the age of twenty-seven, Mildred goes through mountains of trials and tribulations under which a weak character would have succumbed. As a novel of realism, Terry McMillan would probably not have been plausible had Mildred thrown in the towel of defeat in the face of adversity, because realistically, black women have been 'out there' longer than most Americans, raising families and educating themselves, with or without the black man. Mildred in *Mama* exemplifies that black women on the plantations, in the urban south and the urban north and elsewhere have refused to be defeated in a society in which they have had to be mothers and 'fathers' because of the economic marginalism of most black men.

While Terry McMillan emphasized Mildred's strength and determination to survive and triumph in the face of adversities, including economic marginalism and several failed marriages in *Mama* (1987), in *Waiting to Exhale*, we are confronted with professional black women who are comparatively more economically secure, educationally successful and on the move to help the black community with their organizational skills and vast experiences. In *Waiting to Exhale* then, the professional black women of the 1990's are more profoundly aware that they are aware of their abilities and potentialities. They are beautiful, smart, articulate, ambitious, and outwardly and materially independent from men. They can do 'bad' by themselves without unemployed, minimally skilled and lowly educated black men, irrespective of their amorous capabilities in the bedroom. Unlike Mildred in *Mama*, Robin, Savannah, Gloria, Bernadine and their group in Black Women On The Move in *Waiting to Exhale*, are academically accomplished and highly selective with regards to the black men they would care to settle down with; each is in search of a Mr. Right, a "Black Marlboro Man without a hat and horse" (*Disappearing Acts*, 29), whose physical characteristics must not compensate for his grammar (33). The black women in *Waiting to Exhale* have come a long way, in thirty years, from the survival methods employed by Mildred in *Mama* of the 1960's. They have had several sexual relationships during their college days, and are now in their thirties and in search of a Mr. Right, preferably a black Mr. Right, a marriageable black man, with whom they would not have to submerge their personalities, or perform 'disappearing acts'. They are in search of 'professional' black men who do not intermittently disappear or psychologically lose their own identities in love and marriage.

In *Waiting to Exhale* then, McMillan extends the traditions of Zora Neale Hurston, Alice Walker, Maya Angelou (1970) and Gloria Naylor in depicting black women as womanists, dedicated to their communities, their race, Africa and sisterhood. In Zora Neale Hurston, Janie Crawford challenged her two domineering husbands, Mr. Killicks and the Eatonville mayor, Mr. Joe Starks, when she discovered that these men constricted her horizon. Mr. Killicks was not doing her any favors by keeping her confined within the gate of his 60 acre farm and buying her "uh mule all gentled up so even uh woman kin handle 'im" (p. 26). Mr. Joe Starks put Janie Crawford on the pedestal on the store's porch in Eatonville, but constricted her space by 'classing her off' from public debates and the lying sessions on the stage in the store. Janie Crawford had to publicly dethrone Mr. Joe Starks, cut him down to size, in front of the menfolks. In the contest in hyperbole between Crawford and Starks, Mr. Starks' '"big voice" became a mere '"brag" (p. 75). After both husbands had been reduced to size, Janie Crawford claimed her identity by getting rid of the apron and the headtie which had symbolized her subjugation. Janie Crawford had to challenge her husbands' vision of themselves, the political, economic and psychological holds these men had over her.

The black women in *Waiting to Exhale* have gone beyond being intimidated, or restricted, by the economic, political, and psychological domination of patriarchy. They are not the young Janie Crawfords who could be persuaded by their grandmas to marry for economic security to long-headed Logan Killicks. McMillan's women in *Waiting to Exhale*, and even in *Disappearing Acts,* have gone beyond the limitations put on Mildred in *Mama*, whose energies were mostly expended in the efforts to survive, stay out of prison, pay her light bills, see to it that her children succeeded in school and in their professions. She willfully did what must be done to keep afloat and to dig herself out of any hole in which she found herself, without bitterness.

The professional black women in *Waiting to Exhale* are civic minded, as exhibited in BWOTM (*Black Women on the Move* (pp. 243-251)). "...there were twenty-two black women, " dressed in tailored business suits, sitting in the conference room of First Interstate Bank, where Etta Mae (as Etta Mae Johnson in Gloria Naylor's *Women of Brewster Place*), was a vice-president" (pp. 243-244). Of these twenty-two black women, Robin, Bernadine, Gloria and Savannah are singled out for detailed characterization. Generally, these women are all college graduates, in their mid-to-late thirties and on the move to help their black community in education and serve as positive role models. They are also on the move to meet that black man with whom they would not have to be defensive and pensive, who they wouldn't intimidate, so they can exhale at ease. They are ambitious and want promotions in their various endeavors and professions; they are, however, having a hard time finding that accomplished black man, such as those on the front covers of popular magazines. They have their reputations to maintain and are quickly passing the bar-hopping stage in their lives. They've all had several men in their lives, including during their college days, but most of those relationships had not amounted to the ideal-normal-western-middle, or upper class, intact families. The men they now meet all seem to have some intractable problems with their wives or are not willing to commit themselves to any of these smart, good looking, professional black women. These women live in white neighborhoods, in 95,000 dollar homes (Gloria, who owns her own business), but all seem to be sexually deprived or frustrated, except, perhaps Robin, who is portrayed as adventurous and promiscuous.

Specifically, Robin is the youngest and blatantly refuses to settle down with one man; she 'loves' Russell because he has charisma, can have fun, is handsome and he is a "super-deluxe lover" (p. 168). Robin ends up having Russell's child, but would not marry him, choosing to be an unwed mother. She likes Michael but does not want him as a bed partner; she thought she would have liked Troy, but he turned out to have pot-smoking friends, and moved 80 miles an hour and did not "stop too long for nothing'" (p. 239). It was with Russell she was fascinated, but had to finally accept the futility of her infatuation with him, the 'playworld', who has to have as many women as he possibly can. Even though Robin finally matures, she could not be oblivious to the fact that there is indeed a shortage of 'marriageable' black men (p. 332) with whom she did not have to be pensive, with whom she could exhale at ease.

Gloria, like the rest of the four professional black women, is pretty, successful, has her own business, but she is concerned about her weight and her son, Tarik, whose father David, has turned out to be gay. She is a good looking black woman, but 'fat' and unwed, with high blood pressure. The oldest of the four black women, Gloria, settles for Marvin, an older black man, newly arrived to her neighborhood. It was Marvin who gave Gloria mouth-to-mouth resuscitation, and with Marvin around for companionship, there was "nothing in (the) house broke anymore" (p. 407). Gloria definitely had to modify her standards to include men such as Marvin who was helpful, if not a Black Marlboro Man, without the horse and hat.

Of a little more complex character is Savannah, who leaves a 50,000 dollar job for a 38,000 dollar one with the hopes of meeting a descent man in Phoenix, Arizona. Savannah has been with several men during and after her college days but none had appealed to her for marriage. Her college mate, Kenneth, is now a successful doctor, with a staff of ten, and a three year old daughter; he is not forthcoming about making a commitment to Savannah. She meets other successful black men such as Charles and James, but they all seem to only want to have good time with her without nuptial commitment, and she is approaching her late thirties. Lionell, who was a good love-maker (Lionell's bestiality was too much for Savannah, on Interstate 25) (p. 119), was not economically secure. At the end, Savannah 'matured' enough to make it plain to Dr. Kenneth of Boston that she was no longer willing to man-share him with his wife. She was promoted to making 50,000 dollars a year, gave up smoking and bought herself a new car. She may never get married, but she was going to accept life as it was.

The most complicated relationship with a black man was that between Bernadine and John. Robin, Gloria and Savannah were never married even though each of the former had a child from Russell and David respectively. In contrast, Bernadine was married with two children and a complex husband, whose American dream of unmitigated material success had come true. Definitely of the upper-upper class, John has been able to accumulate land, money and investments; he can be likened to Joe Starks in Zora Neale Hurston's *Their Eyes Were Watching God* in his ambitions to dominate by material means. He has been able to economically and politically dominate Bernadine in preventing her from running her own business in a manner similar to Janie Crawford's position in *Their Eyes Were Watching God.* But John goes beyond Joe Starks in abandoning his black family for a white woman, Kathleen. Robin, Gloria and Savannah all sympathize with Bernadine for John's choice of another woman, and a white woman at that. In the end, John and Bernadine are divorced with 964,000 dollars as a settlement and the four sisters celebrate as though they had "...all won the lottery"' (p. 408).

**What choices do these women have?**

Black male/female relationships (Lyons, 1993, 30, 32, 34) depict the shortage of marriageable black men. McMillan's women in *Waiting to Exhale*, should they desire marriage, would have to modify their standards by marrying down, share men (as all of them did several times), have children out of wedlock, as Robin and Gloria did, remain single, as Savannah accepted finally, marry inter-racially, which none of these women wanted to do, unlike Mildred in *Mama* , who was willing to do so. They could also marry inter-culturally, to foreign black men, who were not represented as possible choices in *Waiting to Exhale*, even though Africa was alluded to on several occasions (p. 255, 302, 408, etc.), and Bernadine's Onika and Gloria's Tarik are African names, depicting the persistence of Africa in African-American Literature. A choice that is also available to these black women in *Waiting to Exhale* is lesbianism, which could free them from men sexually, as Gloria's son's father, David, 'elected' to be gay. By modifying their standards, they could also settle down for the Marvin type (p. 407), as Gloria finally elected to do. Whether they modify their standards about black men or not, what is profoundly clear to these professional black women against inter-racial marriages, is the acute shortage of The Black Marlboro Men type, such as an educated Franklin in *Disappearing Acts.* In their own words in *Waiting....* "What happened to all the aggressive men? The ones that aren't scared to talk to you? Where the (hell) are they hiding?" (332):

> "They're not hiding. They're just scared to make a damn commitment," Robin said.
>
> "They're with white women," Bernadine said.

> "Or gay," Gloria said.
> "Or married," Savannah said. "But you know what? They're not all with white girls, they're not all homosexuals, they're not all married, either. When you get right down to it, we're talking five, maybe ten percent. What about the rest?"
> "They're ugly."
> "Stupid."
> "In prison."
> "Unemployed."
> 'Crackheads."
> "Short ."
> "Liars."
> 'Unreliable."
> "Irresponsible."
> "Too possessive."
> "Dogs."
> "Shallow."
> "Boring."
> "Stuck in the sixties."
> "Arrogant . "
> "Childish."
> "Wimps."
> "Too goddamn old and set in their ways."
> "Can't (eff)."
> "Stop!" Savannah said.
> "Well, (eff), you asked," Robin said.
>
> Savannah reached inside her purse in slow motion. She was trying to find some Kleenex, because something was in her eye. She wasn't successful. Robin handed her a handkerchief. "Here, girl," she said. (p. 332)

## A classic love story.

In both *Mama* and *Waiting to Exhale* McMillan emphasizes the contemporary black woman's attempts to grapple with the black family, black men, daughters and sons and to approximate the middle class, white American family standards, values and norms. Mildred in *Mama* was comparatively less successful in these attempts than Gloria, Robin, Bernadine and Savannah in terms of educational attainment, occupational and income levels, and even the standards they expect of men.

McMillan's second novel (chronologically) does not have to be encapsulated into the 1980's as *Mama* and *Waiting to Exhale* are placed into the 1960's and the 1990's respectively, because *Disappearing Acts* is not only a contemporary urban love story between two attractive black people, male and female, but also a classic love story between two educationally and occupationally unequal persons, where the female (Zora) is of the higher status, paid the rent most of the time, while Franklin's economic marginalism, intermittent unemployment, lack of college education, poor syntax etc. become sources of conflict, displaced aggression, misguided masculinity, and humiliation for Zora, especially when her friends expected Franklin to have at least his B.A. degree. Because of its major theme of love between two 'unequal' persons, *Disappearing Acts* is a classic novel transcending race, culture, geographical boundaries and historical times. Because of the pervasiveness of patriarchy in most cultures, men of higher status are the ones often in 'love' with women of equal or lower status in terms of socio-economic class and political power; McMillan reverses that tradition but not the conflicts that arise between two people of different educations, incomes, and occupations. In McMillan's *Disappearing Acts,* it is the female who is put into the position of the bread winner. In that respect, McMillan inadvertently explores to what extent higher income women can tolerate intermittently employed men in an urban center of expensive apartments, where physical labor is less rewarded than professional skills and high level occupations, where anyone hardly grows his/her own tomatoes, collared greens or green peppers. It also explores the frustrations engendered when the man cannot bring home the bacon; from the point of view of both Franklin Swift and Zora Banks, including Banks' friends, Franklin should have been a man not only in physique, but also in the wallet, but 'racism' in the construction business kept him intermittently unemployed, and thus unable to be a desirable man, or the "Mr. Right" (McMillan, 1993: 558).

## Two Ways of Disappearing

'Disappearing' in McMillan's second novel can be taken on two levels: physical and metaphorical disappearances; physical disappearance mostly in the case of Franklin and the metaphorical in the case of both Franklin and Zora, but mostly in Zora's case. With respect to the physical, Franklin Swift's disappearances were times when Zora Banks and Terri (an old friend of Franklin) did not know Franklin's whereabouts. When Franklin could not bring himself to tell Zora that he had been laid-off, and therefore ashamed and stayed out of sight for a while; Zora "...wondered where Franklin was, and where he had disappeared to all last week. Why he acted like he was on his way to work"' (p. 127). When Franklin was involved in an accident at a construction site and went to the emergency to get some stitches, Zora saw that he "...disappeared through a white door" (pp. 1-6). And when Franklin began to live with Zora Banks, one of Franklin's former girl friends, Terri, questioned him when they finally met again: "Where did you run off to? I mean, damn, you just upped and disappeared off the face of the earth" (p. 204).

These various examples of physical disappearances prepare the way for the metaphorical disappearances that go beyond the physical. This second level of disappearance depicts 'psychologically disappearing', losing one's individuality because of one's intimate concern for another's well-being; both Zora Banks and Franklin Swift are so much in love with each other that they submerge their individual personalities to try to please each other. Franklin is ecstatic to be able to work, whenever he could, so he could please his Zora, who had put a hold on her singing career to have their child, Jeremiah. Indeed, the two love birds do not only love each other but are also being 'consumed' by that love, and their individualities are disappearing in the process. As Portia, one of Zora's friends warned her, "you better be careful, or you gon' start disappearing a little bit at a time...won't even remember who Zora Banks is" (p. 217). Even though Zora retorts that she was "...not disappearing, as you put it; I am just giving what I have to offer" (p. 219), the distinction between physical and metaphoric disappearance is manifest. Zora had already 'disappeared' by the time she finally realized that Franklin "was not serving any purpose anymore. He seemed useless and was draining (her) dry.... We haven't gotten anywhere together. He hasn't kept his promises. Jeremiah and I deserve better" (pp. 348-349); her individuality and personal plans for herself had already been 'retarded'. Franklin confirms that he too had 'disappeared': "I just done disappeared. I don't know who...I am no more" (p. 352). He too finally realized that he did not have anything to offer a "...woman of (Zora's) caliber" (p. 352); each had 'disappeared' into the other's dreams of love, and had, in the process, abandoned their individualities. Zora's individualism began to emerge when she frankly tells Franklin, "Franklin, you've scared me so bad that I can't stay in the same house with you another day" (p. 358); she obtains a restraining order, reflected on her past involvement with men: David, Dillon, Perry, Champagne, and now Franklin (p. 355), and questioned herself: "How many times have I (Zora) disappeared into the seams of their worlds and ended up mourning...?" (p. 366). At last, they accept that they "both kind of disappeared somewhere along the way and just stopped moving altogether" (p. 382). Frankly, it was not as though they were disappearing; they had 'actually' disappeared from themselves and from each other in their commitment to each other's welfare.

**Could those two lovebirds redeem themselves and resolve their differences?**

Although literary artists are not expected to solve social, tribal or familial problems in their texts, they do raise fundamental questions relative to their group's experiences and sensibilities that continue to affect them. Literary artists do not only write 'about' their tribe(s), but also their tribal experiences with outsiders, strangers, or their oppressors, as the case may be; they also write from a literary or group perspective. In this regard, one major theme relative to the love between Zora and Franklin presents itself. Would these two lovebirds be able to reconcile and come back together for the sake of their 'family' or Afro-centricity? It is of further interest to examine the presence of Africa in the works of some previous African-American female writers, and those of Terry McMillan in particular. It is these two themes then that the rest of this chapter addresses.

After an intimate acquaintance with the love between Mr. Franklin Swift and Zora Banks in *Disappearing Acts*, one could be 'affected' as Zora was "affected" (p. 33) when she first met the handsome Franklin. Even though Franklin's grammar was terrible (p. 32), his physique, good looks and "even his funk (that) smelled good"(p. 32) compensated for his syntax; with Zora, Franklin felt "like a man who (had) just hit a lottery" (p. 67). Despite Franklin's disappearing acts (p. 127, 156, 204), frequent unemployment, his mother's treatment of Zora at the Thanksgiving dinner table (pp. 170-171), and other pensive moments, such as when Zora aborted, when her epilepsy struck and her girl friends' negative attitudes toward Franklin, McMillan was successful in depicting a classic love story between two people, each willing to give up much for the other, to metaphorically disappear for the other's happiness and well-being.

Nonetheless, Franklin's inability to obtain long term employment, "bring home the bacon" (p. 369), sense of low esteem, displaced aggression, 'alcoholism', etc. all go to put strains on the lovebirds' love for each other. At the end, it was all too much for Zora to handle; "Franklin's been laid off on and on...I've tried to be understanding and patient, but after a while it got to the point where I couldn't handle it all - I just couldn't" (p. 374). Though they had a beautiful son, Jeremiah, mother and son deserved "better" (p. 349) than to be with a 'disappeared' man, who is even jealous of his own son (p. 352). Zora decides to go back to Toledo, her roots, attend and sing in church (p. 381).

One would think that Zora and Franklin are 'through' with each other, but Terry McMillan provides an array of hope for this beautiful love affair gone 'over the cuckoo's nest' to resolve itself. For one thing, Franklin 're-appeared' by going back to school, taking a psychology class that enlightened him about his repressed hatred for his mother, who had not loved him, but had behaved as a matriarch in dominating his father, whom Franklin saw as a 'chump' for reluctantly tolerating his wife's matriarchy; Franklin had used women to do for him what his mother had not done for him: love him, instill high self-esteem in him, and accept him as a valuable person.

Franklin had not only gone back to school to advance himself, because as it were, he did not possess anything to offer a "woman of (Zora's) caliber" (p. 352), but had also discovered that he could, indeed do college-level work; he got his divorce (p. 382), started his woodworking and pumping iron again, and apologized to Zora; furthermore, he seemed matured enough to know that he was incapable of loving another woman as much as he did Zora; Franklin was no longer mostly physical but also cerebral; he had 'dis-disappeared'. He no longer thinks of his father as a chump; he seemed self-actualized.

To be aware of one's dis-disappearance is to be aware that one is aware, which is a higher level of self-knowledge. Zora too had come to a higher self-knowledge of herself: she was not going to be the 'greatest' singer-song-writer she had dreamt of; she had planned to go to Toledo and there sing in church and raise Jeremiah in open space. Nonetheless, she is willing to compromise should Franklin want a family: "We are not leaving you; we're relocating...if you ever get your divorce and you feel like you are ready, come get us" (p. 382).

The self-knowledge that both Zora and Franklin attained in their disappearances and dis-disappearances prepared them for each other; their love for their son, Jeremiah, Franklin's intellectual advancement, his discovery of some of the sources of his attitudes toward women, etc. should in no small measure make him more compatible with Zora. One thing is clear to both of them: when a black man is constantly unemployed, self-hatred, family dissolution, displaced aggression, 'alcoholism' etc. quickly come into vogue. It is some of these social ills that Terry McMillan was able to eloquently depict in *Disappearing Acts.*

## The Presence of Africa in Terry McMillan

In continuing the traditions of her elders in depicting Africa in their literary works (Dixon, 1979: 25-43), McMillan, even in the 1990's, could not be oblivious to Africa, which she depicts in all of her three novels. In these depictions, McMillan has continued the traditions of a host of other black writers in Haiti, Cuba, and the United States (Dixon, pp. 25-43). Phyllis Wheatley, Langston Hughes, Countee Cullen, Zora Neale Hurston, Alice Walker, Toni Morrison, Gloria Naylor, etc. have all made references to Africa, at deeper or superficial levels, affirmatively or ambiguously. In Zora Neale Hurston, for an instance, it is "If ah never see you no mo' on earth, Ah'll meet you in Africa" (*Their Eyes Were Watching God*, p.148); in Toni Morrison's *The Bluest Eyes,* it is Mr. Soaphead Church's African ancestry, which his family had progressively rejected for anglo-saxonism; in Alice Walker, it was the letters from Africa that informed Celie about her children, inheritance, and a description of the Olinka people's culture in *The Color Purple;* in Gloria Naylor's *Women of Brewster Place*, it is the radical Kiswana Brown who retained her African nationalism and identity. In numerous other works by African-Americans, Africa is evoked, sometimes sympathetically, while at others demagogically. In Countee Cullen's "Heritage" (Bontemps, 1974: 83-86) for an instance, there is an ambivalent attitude toward Africa in "I belong to Jesus Christ/preacher of humility/heathen gods are naught to me" (p. 85). In Weldon Johnson's *The Autobiography of an Ex- Colored Man*, it was the African blood in Ex-Colored Man's veins that was, to a large extent, a great source of his marginalism; if he could have only gotten rid of that African blood, he would not have had to be ashamed of belonging to a race, members of which could be lynched with impunity; he would not have had to abandon his mother's people for his white father's race and ruling class. Mr. Ex-Colored Man abandoned the 'dreams' of being a great black composer to settle down as an ordinary white man, because Blackness entailed syndromes or disadvantages.

Melvin Dixon (1979: 33) states that Edward Brathwaite has distinguished four kinds of New World Literature that evoke the African presence: (1) a rhetorical literature, which uses Africa as a mask and only says the word 'Africa' or invokes a dream of the Congo, Senegal, Niger, and other place names; (2) the literature of African survival, which 'deals quite consciously with African survivals in Caribbean society' but does not reconnect them with the great tradition of Africa; (3) the literature of African expression, 'which has its root in the folk, and which attempts to adapt or transform folk material into literary experiment'; and (4) the literature of reconnection by writers who have lived in Africa and the New World and who 'are consciously reaching out to rebridge the gap with the spiritual heart land'.

African-American writers could be put into each of the above categories; while Langston Hughes and Countee Cullen could be put into the first type, Zora Neale Hurston belongs to the second and third types, and Alice Walker in the fourth type. Terry McMillan continues the tradition of evoking Africa in all of her three novels so far, and can be categorized in the first and third types. In the first category, "a rhetorical literature, which uses Africa as a mask and only says the word 'Africa'...and place names" (Dixon, p. 33), we find Phyllis, the protagonist's daughter's cousin in *Mama*, wearing Afro, talking about Malcolm X and watching "...documentaries about wild life and everything about Africa..." (p. 116). The radical Phyllis of the 1960's was conscious enough to be concerned about Africa and attempted to influence Freida in that light. In *Waiting to Exhale*, we find Gloria's son's name as Tarik, perhaps named after the victorious African (Moor), Tarik, over king Roderick of Spain (Jackson, 1970: 174-175). Bernadine's daughter's name is Onika and there is an interest in "...various crafts...kinte cloths...Nelson and Winnie Mandela..." (p. 165). This interest in African aesthetic and persons is continued in McMillan's *Disappearing Acts* (1990); in the abortion room where Zora had 'found herself', there "...was a beautiful dark-skinned girl in a burgundy recliner. She couldn't have been more than eighteen. She looked African-Senegalese, maybe?" (p. 152). Zora was soon relieved when she found out that the girl was indeed Senegalese.

In addition to naming things and people of Africa, the first type in Brathwaite's paradigm (Dixon, p. 33), Terry McMillan also utilizes Brathwaite's third paradigm, in which black writers in the West use "the literature of African expression, which has its root in the folk, and which attempts to adapt or transform folk material into literary experiment" (p. 33). In this context, McMillan utilizes the traditional African literaray form of expression of call-and-response in her *Disappearing Acts*, in which Franklin Swift, alienated in his room, calls for an understanding black woman, to which Zora Banks answers and they meet on the stage, an apartment building, where Franklin works, in which Zora got an apartment to rent; on that stage, from that day on, they began their love affair, Jeremiah is born, conflicts arise and a denouement is approximated. This call-and-response, a 'literature of African expression', depicted in African and African-American tradition, especially in the orator of the black church, is 'experimented' with in McMillan's *Disappearing Acts*. Even though thousands of miles away, the same call-and-response literary form of expression is used in the Ugandan writer, Okot P'Bitek's *Song of Lawino and Song Ocol*, in which the husband responds to his wife's accusations about him abandoning the traditional ways of the tribe in favor of European manners, culture, and 'forest of books' (p. 113). As Lawino and Ocol attempt to iron out their differences in their own traditions in Africa, so also did Zora and Franklin in theirs in the United States. Terry McMillan is indeed a black woman writer who has continued the traditions of her African and African-American ancestors, and has been able to transform those traditions in her own local culture. Metaphorically, she is "...a separate river remembering its source" (Dixon, p. 26).

If African American literary artists have not totally abandoned their African roots, African American preachers have also continued significant African traditions in their African American churches, have continued to function as intermediaries between God and man and between the European American and the African American racial and ethnic groups; this, then, will be our main focus in the next chapter.

**References Chapter VIII.**

Angelou, Maya. 1970. *I Know Why The Caged Bird Sings. New* York: Bantam Books.

Bontemps, Arna. (ed.) 1990. *American Negro Poetry: Anthology*. New York: Farrar, Struas and Giroux. pp. 83-86.

Braithwaite, Ronald L. 1981. "Interpersonal Relations Between Black Males and Black Females," pp. 84-97, in Lawrence E. Gary (ed.) *Black Men*, Beverly Hills and London: Sage Publications.

Dixon, Melvin. 1979. "Rivers Remembering Their Source: Comparative Studies in Black Literary History- Langston Hughes, Jaques Roumain, and Negritude,"pp. 25-43, in Dexter Fisher, et. al.. (eds.) *Afro-American Literature: The Reconstruction of Instruction*. New York: The Modern Language Association of American.

Hemenway, Robert E. 1977. *Zora Neale Hurston: A Literary Biography*. University of Illinois Press.

Hurston, Zora Neale. 1985. *Spunk: The Selected Stories of Zora Neale Hurston*. Beverly, California: Turtle Island Foundation

_____. 1990. *Their Eyes Watching God*. New York: Harper & Row.

Jackson, John G. 1970. *Introduction to African Civilizations*. Secaucus, New Jersey: The Citadel Press.

Johnson, Weldon James. 1986. *The Autobiography of a Ex-Colored Man*. New York: Hill and Wang.

Lyons, Douglass C. 1993. "Where the Men Are: The Ten Best Cities." *Ebony*, 7: 30,32, 34.

McMillan, Terry. 1987. *Mama*. New York: Washington Square Press.

_____. 1990. *Disappearing Acts*. New York: Washington Square Press.

_____. 1992. *Waiting To Exhale. New* York : Viking.

_____. 1993. "Looking for Mr. Right," pp. 557-559, in Gerald Early (ed.) *Speech and Power, Vol., 2*. Hopewell, N.J.: ECO Publishers.

Mill, John Stuart. 1978. *The Subjection of Women. Cambridge*, Mass.: The M.I.T. Press.

Morrison, Toni. 1970. *The Bluest Eye*. New York: Washington Square Press.

Naylor, Gloria. 1982. *Women of Brewster Place*. New York : Penguin Books.

P'Bitek, Okot. 1984. *Song of Lawino and Song of Ocol*. Heinemann.

Shange, Ntazake. 1975. *For Colored Girls Who Have Considered Suicide When The Rainbow is Enuf*. New York : MacMillan.

Walker, Alice. 1977. "Zora Neale Hurston: A Cautionary Tale and a Partisan View," pp. xi-xx, in Robert E. Hemeway, *Zora Neale Hurston: A Literary Biography*. University of Illinois Press.

_____. 1982. *The Color Purple. New* York: Washington Square Press.

_____. 1983. *In Search of Our Mothers' Gardens*. New York: Harcourt, Brace, Jovanovich.

Wright, Richard. 1945. *Black Boy: A Record of Childhood and Youth.* New York: Harper & Row, Publishers.

_____. 1987. *Native Son.* New York: Harper and Row.

***Note:** This essay, "There was a Zora Neale Hurston Before Alice Walker," first appeared in Working Papers: The Black Women, Challenges and Prospects for the Future (pp. 29-42): The Proceedings from the Conference on the Black Women: Challenges and Prospects for the Future, May 1988, Columbus, Ohio; it's reprinted here by permission from the Ohio Department of Black Studies, Community Extension Center, 905 Mt. Vernon Avenue, Columbus, Ohio 43203.

# Chapter IX

## Black Preaching in the Global Village Context

Before examining Black Preaching in the context of the global village, I wish to confess that I am a product of three major religions and their corresponding cultures: The Islam, the traditional African and the Western. As we've seen in Chapter V, this triple culture is what Ali Mazrui (1986: 63-113) has termed Africa's triple heritage; it is the same thing Nkrumah referred to as constituting the African personality or philosophical consciencism. One of the major characteristics that this triple heritage or philosophical consciencism has imbued me with is *tolerance for diversity*. Naturally, to live in and to be educated for a polyglot, multi-religious and multi-tribal society, it is inevitable that one could be imbued with tolerance, flexibility and some eclecticism. But as man' s history has shown including recent and current world events, one man's tolerance may be significant but insufficient. Man's inhumanity to man, tribalism, sexism, ethnocentricism, imperialism, extreme nationalism and the other confocal-isms have caused major as well as minor wars, between seemingly intimate individuals as well as antagonistic groups.

In the twenty-first century, however, only a few persons could possibly ask for less tolerance, more bigotry, more sexism and less open-mindedness. The negative consequences of intolerance, closed mindedness are too glaring in the global arena of politics, in large urban centers as well as in rural areas in the West, Africa and the Middle-East, just to mention a few places. We certainly are no longer secure in our tribal cocoons, eurocentricisms or other particularisms. We are now, more than ever before, exposed to and conscious of many more cultural, technical, economic and social forces that cannot be brushed aside as simply unique, incidental, irrelevant, or too particularistic.

This chapter examines at some length the place of Black preaching in this impending global village. But what is Black preaching, and what are some of the major forces at work here that Black preaching must contend with, or respond to in this modern global zeitgeist? Above all, what should Black religion and Black preachers of the gospel focus on in this impending new world order?

It certainly seems not an enviable task to attempt to deal with justice, in a short chapter as this, the Black tradition of preaching that is rooted in the shores of Africa, and yet such a topic must be approached with labor of love. In the words of the African-American historian Vincent Harding (1981:102-103), 'Who has ever stopped the river of struggle?'

Black preaching has been and continues to be like a river of struggle, traveling across vast tracks of land, swamps, valleys, on the sides of mountains, meandering its way to the Lord, the ultimate truth, aiming for the ocean of humanity and the global community free from man's inhumanity to man based on class, sex, race, nationality or religious affiliation.

The concept of freedom has been central to Black preaching. The freedom that has been sought in Black preaching can be graphically put on a continuum. When African-Americans were physically in bondage Black preaching emphasized physical freedom; when they were politically in bondage, it demanded political freedom, and when the Bible was used to justify their bondage, Black preaching utilized the same text to argue for freedom. When African-Americans were segregated in Euro-American churches, they formed their own free African societies and churches in order to realize a community they could claim as their own. Thus, the advent of Black Theology in the 1960's was essentially the continuation of the river of struggle in search for the ocean of humanity and humanism free from forces that corrupt the truth, the word of the Lord, the religion of Jesus Christ.

African exhorters, spiritualists, and diviners on the West Coast of Africa were respected members of their communities. They were intermediaries between the spirit-world and the world of humanity. They exhorted, healed, interpreted signs and soothed their brethren to deal with the uncertainties of life and living. The Black men and women who terminated their lives by jumping into the Atlantic Ocean, rather than face an uncertain future, were not a people without a religion, knowledge of God, or theology.

The religion that the Africans brought with them remained as the bedrock upon which Western Christianity was built; the African conjurers, elders, wisemen and women among the slaves continued their roles as exhorters to their brethren in an outlandish environment, where they often felt like motherless children. John Blassingame (1972:41-76) in his classic *The Slave Community*, substantiates that the Africans on the plantation retained their African 'imponderables' whenever they were in their own communities, away from The Big House. In these communities of their own, the place of their conjurers, or the wise men and women, was highly valued. These early unlettered Black preachers had some valuable skills, spiritual as well as medicinal, that put them above the rest of their brethren, and were thus accorded respect. W.E.B. DuBois (1903:104) recognized and described these early rural Black preachers as leaders, orators, politicians and idealists.

Without religion, life for the African slaves in America would have been terrifyingly nightmarish. The separation of their families in an alien environment had its own human consequences, but life itself would not have been worth living for a whole host of Africans had there not been Black exhorters on the plantations, in the community of brethren in bondage. It must have simply been comforting to know that there were at least African elders and exhorters to administer to the wary. Paul Lawrence Dunbar (1896:26-29), the great plantation poet, had this as a sermon to his wary brethren:

> We is gathahed hyeah, my brothahs,
> In dis howlin' wildaness,
> Fu' to speak some words of confo't
> To each othah in distress.
> An' we chooses fu' ouah subjic'
> Dis-we'll 'splain it by an' by;
> "An' de Lawd said, 'Moses, Moses,'
> An' de man said, 'Heah am I.'"
>
> Now ole Pher'oh, down in Egypt,
> Was de wuss man evah bo'n,
> An' he had de Hebrew chillun
> Down dah wukin' in his co'n;
> 'T well de Lawd got tiahed o' his foolin',
> An' sez he: "I'll let him know-
> Look hyeah, Moses, go tell Pher'oh
> Fu' to let dem chillun go."
>
> "An' ef he refuse to do it,
> I will make him rue de houah,
> Fu' I'll empty down on Egypt
> All de vials of my powah."
>
> *I will pause right heah to say,*
> *Dat I'm still a-preachin' ancient,*
> *I ain't talkin' 'bout to-day.*
> But I tell you, fellah christuns,
> Things'll happen mighty strange
> Now, de Lawd done dis fu' Isrul,
> An' his ways don't nevah change,

An' de love he showed to Isrul
Was n't all on Isrul spent;
*Now don't run an' tell yo' mastahs*
*Dat I's preachin' discontent.*

'Cause I is n't; I'se a-judgin'
Bible people by deir ac's;
But I think it would be bettah,
Ef I'd pause again to say,
*Dat I'm talkin' 'bout ouah freedom*
*In a Bibleistic way.*

But de Moses is a-comin',
An' he's comin', suah and fas'
We kin hyeah h's feet a-trompin'
We kin hyeah his trumpit blas'.
*But I want to wa'n you people,*
*Don't you git too brigity;*
*An' don't you git to braggin'*
*'Bout dese things, you wait an' see.*

Paul Lawrence Dunbar's "Ante-Bellum Sermon" clearly emphasized the preacher's stand about the freedom of his brethren "in a Bibleistic way" (29) with subversiveness. He warned his fellow Africans to "wear the mask" (167) for the meanwhile, but at the same time promised them deliverance as Moses did for the Israelites. Mitchell (1970:30) states that when the Black plantation preachers preached 'to steal away to Jesus' they meant an escape to Freedom; to tell the old Pharaoh 'to let my people go' was also to speak of freedom, and that to preach 'I ain't got long to stay here' was the code language of the gospel of self-liberation. Furthermore, to preach to the slaves to humble themselves was the language of survival in the face of adversity, but only a temporary capitulation to the status-quo, in which hope was not given up. The Biblical knowledge and example that they will one day be liberated from bondage kept their hopes alive. After all, it had been foretold that the freedom of the oppressed was guaranteed and that it was just a matter of time before "Princes shall come out of Egypt," and that "Ethiopia shall soon stretch forth hand unto God" (*Psalm 68:31*).

The enslavers could not have their cake and eat it too; they could not have the Bible and slavery at the same time; they certainly could not have the Bible in the Black preachers' hands and insist that the servants should obey their masters, for in so doing, they shall be blessed abundantly (*Ephesians 6:5; 6:8*). Jupiter Hammon, the African-American poet, was also subversive when he wrote "A Dialogue Entitled the Kind Master and the Dutiful Servant" as follows:

Master.

My Servant, Heaven is high above,
Yea, higher than the sky:
I pray that God would grant his love,
Come follow me thereby.

Servant.

Dear Master, now I'll follow thee,
And trust upon the Lord;
The only safety that I see,
Is Jesus' holy word.

Master.

My Servant, follow Jesus now,
Our great victorious King;
Who governs all both high and low,
And searches things within.

Servant.

Dear Master, I will follow thee,
When praying to our King;
It is the Lamb I plainly see,
Invites the sinner in.

Master.

My Servant, we are sinners all,
But follow after grace;
I pray that God would bless thy soul,
And fill thy heart with grace.

Servant.

Dear Master, I shall follow then,
The voice of my great King;
As standing on some distant land,
Inviting sinners in. (Miller 1971:31,32)

In addition to Hammon's subversive poetry, the Bible in the hands of Nat Turner, Gabriel Prosser, Denmark Vesey, Gullah Jack, David Walker, Frederick Douglass and other African-Americans who educated themselves in the face of the status-quo's insistence on their compulsory ignorance, showed clearly the contradictions between the doctrines and practices of the religion of Jesus Christ relative to the sons and daughters of Africa. From where Nat Turner stood, "The first should be last and the last shall be first" and "Seek ye the Kingdom of Heaven and all these things shall be added unto you" (*Luke 12:31*), took on immediate earthly meanings relative to him and his brethren in bondage.

After Nat Turner's revolt, Black preaching was stigmatized with subversiveness; Black preachers were constrained in their labors to their flock, but the river of struggle, in the view of Vincent Harding, could not be stopped. David Walker (1829:75), who insisted that his *Appeal* had God's blessings, asserted that the man who did not fight for his liberation was fit to be in bondage forever. Frederick Douglass (1968), on the other hand, (as we've seen in chapter 7) eloquently pointed out the contradictions between Western Christian doctrine and practice relative to African-Americans in this way:

> The man who robs me of my earnings at the end of each week meets me as a class-leader on Sunday morning, to show me the way of life, and the path of salvation. He who sells my sister, for purposes of prostitution, stands forth as the pious advocate of purity. He who proclaims it a religious duty to read the Bible denies me the right of learning to read the name of the God who made me. He who is the religious advocate of marriage robs whole millions of its sacred influence, and leaves them to the ravages of wholesale pollution. The warm defender of the sacredness of the family relation is the same that scatters whole families, - sundering husbands and wives, parents and children, sisters and brothers, - leaving the hut vacant, and the hearth desolate. We see the thief preaching against theft, and the adulterer against adultery. We have men sold to build churches, women sold to support the gospel, and babes sold to purchase Bibles for the poor heathen! All for the glory of God and the good of souls! The slave auctioneer's bell and the church-going bell chime in with each other, and the bitter cries of the heart-broken slave are drowned in the religious shouts of his pious master. Revivals of religion and revivals in the slave-trade go hand in hand together. The slave prison and the church stand near each other. The clanking of fetters and the rattling of chains in the prison, and the pious psalm and solemn prayer in the church, may be heard at the same time. The dealers in the bodies and souls of men erect their stand in the presence of the pulpit, and they mutually help each other. The dealer gives his bloodstained gold to support the pulpit, and the pulpit, in return, covers his infernal business with the garb of Christianity. Here we have religion and robbery the allies of each other - devils dressed in angels' robes, and hell presenting the semblance of paradise. (121)

Even when some Black preachers took the pacifier path, in obedience to their masters to rely on a preferred biblical text, the African-American congregation knew better and sympathized with such preachers. Charles V. Hamilton, in his seminal *The Black Preacher in America* (1972), states that the Africans on the plantation always knew the difference between the pacifying preacher and the real exhorter and often understood the delicate position of Black preachers who painted the picture of a glorious hereafter. Preachers such as Nat Turner could not acquiesce with the dichotomy between Africans' lack of freedom and the biblical insistence on freedom and justice. Other Black preachers, however, took the less violent route by preaching to their flock to keep the faith, that the end of their bondage was at hand, for even the almighty himself had decreed so.

The second major event that radically affected Black preaching in the United States was the proclamation about the physical liberation of African-Americans which culminated into the reconstruction period, within which attempts were made to redress some of the major grievances of the African American condition. The physical liberation of African-Americans did not translate into equality for them in the macro-American social and religious institutions. The reconstruction period was short-lived and rapid attempts were made to keep the sons and daughters of Africa in their place, determined for them by their ex-masters. Black codes, defacto and de jure laws to 'intimidate' aspirant African-Americans for social equality were put in place. These intimidations, however, did not deter Black preaching; they did not and could not stop the river of struggle for the ocean of humanism; Black preaching merely adapted itself to the prevailing forces in order to combat the new evils of society that were destined, if unrestrained, to further deny the humanism of African people in the American wilderness.

As can already be deduced, physical liberation was significant but insufficient for the African humanity; the freedom to learn, to be enlightened about one's maker from where one stood and to be a native son in proclamations as well as in deeds became the new concern of the Black exhorter, or preacher to his people. What was the Black preacher to preach in this context, under these new circumstances of physical freedom, but not social, political, economic and religious equality?

In response to the prevailing forces of Jim Crowism, de facto and de jure segregation, the Black church became not only a place of worship in the late 1800's but also a classroom for the young and old, not only to acquire the rudiments of Western learning and Christianity, but also to refine one's moral and temporal conducts, to be in associations and in churches one could call one's own, where one was treated as a brother and a sister, but not an incidental, or a particular-ism. In response to the zeitgeist of the late 1800's the river of Black struggle divided itself into two major tributaries; in one, the Black preacher took up the issue of African-American colonization seriously, in the other, the 'home mission.' Bishop Henry Turner (1834-1915) was adamant about the former.

Although Bishop Turner was not formally educated, he was highly conscious of the impediments against African people in the late 1800's and the early 1900's. After the 'fruitlessness' of the hasty reconstruction period, Bishop Turner, after much experience in politics and the church, was convinced that the African-American could not hope to gain social and economic equality in the macro-American system and as such he advocated that they return to Africa where their color would not determine their social status. Turner envisioned Africa as a continent "where Black men could have their own high officials, dignitaries, artisans, mechanics, corporations, railroads, telegraphs, commerce, colleges, ...," and he dreamed "of the glory that would accrue to the whole race from such a seat of power and influence" (Redkey, 1978:232). Turner's preaching was both religious and nationalistic; he reasoned that it was God's desire and plan to have American Blacks return to Africa to redeem and develop it economically and spiritually. He advocated taking the good news of the gospel to his benighted brothers and sisters in Africa; the political, spiritual, moral and economic redemption of Africa and African people globally were central to his agenda. For African-Americans to have a nation as a base from which to proclaim their peoplehood was one of Bishop Turner's foci, as well as others such as Marcus Garvey, Malcolm X, and Kwame Nkrumah after him.

Although Turner's paradigm for African-American redemption by colonizing Africa offended a host of Northern Black laity and clergy who advocated for the home mission, he hardly abandoned his stance on the moral, political, economic and religious advancement of African people. It is important to note that most of the forces that opposed Bishop Turner were still present in the 1920's and were the ones that also opposed Marcus Garvey's movement for the redemption of the African masses in Africa as well as in the United States of America. In the meanwhile, the cultural, political, social and economic forces that kept the sons and daughters of Africa as marginal people were still in operation in the 1940's and the 1960's. About thirty years after Turner's African dream, Richard Wright (1944:13) could still write:

> Culturally the Negro represents a paradox: Though he is an organic part of the nation, he is excluded by the entire tide and direction of American culture. Frankly, it is felt to be right to exclude him, and it is felt to be wrong to admit him freely.

Twenty years later, Martin Luther King and a host of other African-American radicals, conservatives and liberals alike, could agree with Richard Wright of 1944, with Marcus Garvey of the 1920's and Bishop Turner of the late 1800's and the early 1900's.

This continual ambiguous position of the African people in America was to surely lead to their church and religious separation from mainstream America. Black religious separation (or particularism) accentuated as African-Americans increasingly found themselves rejected by their American 'father'; and if their American father was not going to religiously and politically liberate them according to the demands of the times, African-Americans by the 1960's were more than prepared to do it for themselves through their own schools, colleges, churches and their own preachers. Black churchmen such as Adam Clayton Powell, some of whose "...Sunday morning sermons were clearly political speeches, and no attempt was made on his part to make them seem or be otherwise" (Hamilton, 1972:112), and the Civil Rights Churchmen of the 1960's were simply continuing the historic river of struggle that still aimed for the ocean of humanism.

Clearly, Black preaching and African-American political and economic zeitgeist have had historic connections beginning with the capture of Africans on the West African coast, into the plantations, and through the reconstruction and great migration periods; Black churchmen have not only been exhorters and preachers, but also educators, community organizers, national and inter-national spokespersons against the dehumanization of African-Americans and other oppressed peoples in Azania, Southwest Africa, South America, and Vietnam. In the Civil Rights Movement of the 1960's, for instance, '"King was severely criticized by some secular and sectarian leaders for combining civil rights with foreign policy" (125). But this did not stop the tide of the river of struggle for liberation.

The third major cultural, intellectual and religious movement for the struggle of the African-American came into vogue in the 1960's with the demand and the assertion of Black theology as the theology of liberation. This demand and assertion of African-American theologians such as James H. Cone and Gayraud S. Wilmore also represented a continuation of the river of struggle for the recognition and acceptance of the African-American religious tradition, the tradition of self-definition, self-acceptance and the assertions of one's manhood and humanism. Like the previous historic struggles of African-Americans, the publication of *A Black Theology of Liberation* in 1970 shook the religious status-quo of the Euro-American Christian tradition that had monopolized the religion of Jesus Christ. The tradition of using Christianity as a weapon for sexism, colonialism, imperialism, segregation and ethnocentricism was bitterly exposed. In the footsteps of Nat Turner, Gabriel Prosser and other African-Americans of the past,

James Cone asserted that "knowing God means being on the side of the oppressed, becoming one with them and participating in the goal of liberation" (124). When Black liberation theology finally joined hands with the Black power movement to address the global religious and political predicaments of African people, understandably, Western religious traditions reacted with some reservations and predictable skepticisms. Black theology was viewed as too radical, too exclusive and particularistic, from the point of view of the mainstream society; from where the Black masses stood, however, Black liberation theology was timely in cognizance of the global domination of African people by Western religious, cultural, economic, political and intellectual institutions.

It is interesting to note a global phenomenon here: When Black liberation theology was being advocated and asserted in the United States, virtually all oppressed peoples of the world were in arms against Western cultural, political and economic domination. Indeed, immediately after World War II, the Atlantic Charter, the independence of India in 1947, the Bandung Conference of 1955 and the Ghanaian Independence in 1957, African people globally were becoming more and more fully conscious of their lowly place in the global arena of politics, peoplehood and ideas. More than all the other previous struggles for physical and political liberation, Black liberation theology called for an intellectual and philosophical liberation and saw the religion of Jesus Christ as a liberation theology that sided with the oppressed against the mighty and the powerful oppressors of the weak. Black Liberation theologians in the 1960's saw Christianity in the context of Black liberation in the political, spiritual and cultural senses of freedom; it was a freedom to be unlike one's oppressors who could not culturally, politically and religiously identify with the oppressed without shedding off some of their own ethnocentricisms. Black theology in the 1960s was a radical challenge to the well established Euro-American theologians to refocus their traditional concerns relative to the Black group that had been historically viewed as completely unlike themselves. James H. Cone was insistent that

> there is only one principle which guides the thinking and action of Black theology: an unqualified commitment to the Black community as that community seeks to define its existence in light of God's liberating work in the world. This means that Black theology refuses to be guided by ideas and concepts alien to Black people. (Cone, 1970:33)

In retrospect, Black liberation theology might have appeared too combatant, particularly focused and insistent on the active involvement of the nationalistic political ideas of the 1960s' political zeitgeist, which demanded that African people, their religions, political institutions and personhood be taken, in words and deeds, as integral parts of the American cultural mosaic. But because it was deemed insistently singular, particularistic and determined to unseat traditional ideas and the Euro-American ethnocentric emphasis in Christianity, it encountered temporary obstacles, as must have been expected, for even the religion of Jesus Christ itself had been dealt with as a threat to the well established norms of its time.

Black liberation theology, however, was timely and inevitable in cognizance of African-Americans' history of struggle. In the hands of Black preachers and scholars, Black liberation theology made its platform crystal clear and by the 1980's it was already an accepted phenomenon in theological schools and the general, social, cultural and academic climate. Black liberation theology has now pertinently asserted itself, as it must in an ever changing global village that requires changes in ideas, ideologies and paradigms of thought, actions and institutions.

The 1990's and beyond, however, confront us with new sets of ideas that have had their roots in the past and are now fruits of the evolutionary imperative of civilizations and human society. "There is no place (now) for sheltered piety. Who can 'pray' when all hell has broken lose and when the gut of human existence is (still being) trampled underfoot by evil forces?" (234).

In this 'new' context, Black preaching has new clients, prospects and concerns that go beyond particularism. Preaching against oppression, for an instance, must now include many more clients. At the same time, Black preaching has lessons for the new world order. One of the lessons Black theology and preaching has to offer the world include sermons about how it actually feels to live in a world where one is depersonalized and despised for simply being different, and how to survive and even flourish in such an environment. Another is how to survive and even flourish in an environment in which one is an object of hate over which one has no control except to rely on the religion of Jesus Christ. Yet another lesson that Black preaching has to offer humanity is how to live and propagate oneself in an entity where one often feels like a motherless child. Indeed, Black preaching can help a whole group of diverse humanity to keep the hope alive, to keep the candles lit in a storm bent on dehumanizing urban environments, hopelessness in the age of over-indulgence in materialism and self-aggrandizement, in an age in which God is secularized (Postman, 1993) and the Ten Commandments are ridiculed (Leo, 1996:16).

Intellectually, culturally and religiously, then, these cannot be easy times. How do we now look at forces we had always thought, from where we stood, were irrelevant, too emotional, too radical, unimportant, but which, as though all of a sudden, are now all too important and cannot be pushed aside as irrelevant? In the 1960's Black intellectuals could boast that

> By the grace of God and the whip of history, Black people, in the main, have not completely assimilated those values that (were) driving Western man to social and spiritual suicides: acquisitiveness, for example, numbness of heart and machine idolatry. To the extent that these things are foreign to the Black experience, to that extent the Black man is uniquely qualified to take the lead in recasting the human values of our civilization. (Mitchell,1970: 142).

But sadly enough, African people in Africa as well as in the United States are no longer unacquisitive to any significant degree; they are now part and parcel of the Western 'machine idolatry' and suffer from Western 'numbness of heart'; the African-American is no longer a completely separate entity to be easily shunned or wished away. Since the 1970's, for instance, classes within the African-American ethnic group have (practically) entrenched themselves, and radical Black politicians in the 1960's have changed their tones to cooperation, ecumenism and now advocate a new mainstream that includes *them.* In this context, as before, "...the Black preacher must understand and identify with the Black masses. But he must also possess a certain sophistication regarding the white culture which constantly surrounds and impinges on the Black experience" (142).

The 'new' Black experience is in the context of pluralism, a "pluralism understood as a combination of the new gender diversity, age diversity and ethnic diversity..." (Hough, 1991:8). How should Black theology and preaching respond to this new diversity? In this diversity, can Black preaching remain particularistic, emphasizing mostly the problems of the oppressed Black, or should it not be inclusive with respect to sexism, classism, and even intra-racism? In the impending global village, can Black preaching remain oblivious to sexism, classism, intra-racism and still claim universalism? *Can* any religion claim universalism in the new global context by simply abandoning certain racial, ethnic, or nationalistic particularisms?

The answers to these series of questions are self-evident; but for sure, positions that were infallible yesterday are today dubious; European Christianity that was yesterday the norm has now been greatly challenged by the new pluralism, secularization and the pursuance of the individual good life.

In the past, and even at present, Black preaching has emphasized physical freedom from bondage and the liberty to practice one's religion in relative security and has continued this struggle for an unquestionable freedom into the 21st century. This tradition of struggle of Black preaching for an unquestionable liberty, of taking the side of the oppressed, the least powerful, the despised, the mules of the world, in words and deeds, must be inclusive, and remains the greatest contribution to the religions of the global village. As Robert A. Bennett (1972:185) has observed, "Each generation and school of faith responds to God's word in its own way while yet in the old or new conventional relationship. Black preaching's insistence on the Jesus of Justice for the poor, powerless, oppressed and despised shall know no cultural, racial, ethnic or sexual boundaries." This then is the challenge and contribution of Black preaching to the impending global village in which classism, sexism, ethnocentricism and man's inhumanity to man still knows no bounds, but must be subdued, as contemporary Black women writers have been quick to point out in the previous chapter.

In the next chapter, we reflect on the relative position of African people in this global village.

## References Chapter IX

Aptheker, Herbert. 1966. *Nat Turner's Slave Rebellion: Including the Full Text of Nat Turner's 1831' Confessions.* New York: Humanities Press.

_____. (ed.) 1965. *One Continual Cry: David Walker's Appeal to the Colored Citizens of the World.* New York : Humanities Press.

Bennett, Robert A. 1972. " The Black Experience in the Bible, " pp. 176-189 in Martin E Marty and Dean G. Peerman (eds.) *New Theology,* No. 9. New York: The Macmillan Company.

Blassingame, John. 1972. *The Slave Community: Plantation Life in the Antebellum South.* New York: Oxford University Press.

Cone, James H. 1970. *A Black Theology of Liberation.* New York: J.B. Lippincott Company.

Douglass, Frederick. 1968. *Narratives of The Life of Frederick Douglass.* New York: American Library Inc.

Dunbar, Paul Laurence. 1954. *Lyrics of Lowly Life.* New York: Citadel Press.

*Ephesians 6:5, 6-8.*

Hammon, Jupiter. 1970. " A Dialogue Intitled[sic] The Kind Master and the Dutiful Servant," pp. 26-30 in Benjamin Brawley (ed.) *Early Negro American Writers.* New York : Dover Publications, Inc.

Hamilton, Charles V. 1972. *The Black Preacher in America.* New York : William Morrow and Company, Inc.

Harding, Vincent. 1986. *There is a River: The Black Struggle for Freedom in America.* New York: Vintage Books.

Hough, Joseph C. 1991. "Theological Education, Pluralism and the Common Good," *Theological Education.* Vol. XXVII, No. 1: 9-20.

Leo, John. 1996. "Thou Shall Not Command." *U. S. News & World Report.* December 18:16.

*Luke 12:31.*

Mazrui, Ali A. 1986. *The Africans: A Triple Heritage.* Little, Brown, and

Company.

Mitchell, Henry H. 1970. *Black Preaching*. New York: J.P. Lippincott Company.

Nkrumah, Kwame. 1970. *Consciencism: Philosophy and Ideology for De-Colonization*. New York: Monthly review Press.

Postman, Neil. 1993. *Technopoly: The Surrender of Culture to Technology*. New York: Alfred A. Knopf.

Redkey, Edwin S. 1978. "Bishop Turner's African Dream," pp. 227-246, in Randall K. Burkett and Richard Newmar (eds.), *Black Apostle : Afro-American Clergy Confront the Twentieth Century*. Boston: J.P. Hall and Company.

Wright, Richard. 1944. *American Hunger*. New York: Harper and Row, Publishers.

Weinberg, Meyer (ed.). 1970. *W.E.B. Dubois Reader*. New York: Harper and Row.

# Chapter X:

## Reflections on African People in the Global Village

The masses of African people in the contemporary global village are undoubtedly at the bottom of the educational, economic, technological, health and medicine, housing and road reconstruction ladder in comparison to other world regions. Some might view this long list of deficiencies with alarm, pessimism, and even defeatism. However, African people must not sit around waiting for handouts from the World Bank, the International 'Ministry of Finance' (IMF), or the Paris Club.

Certainly, a good number of African American and African individuals in the west and in Africa have benefited greatly from African independence and the Civil Rights movement in the United States of the 1960's. The masses of African people, however, have and might continue to be, for a very long time, the hewers of wood and drawers of water for everybody else, both in Africa and elsewhere. The ghettorized African people in the central cities of the United States, the segregated African people in Columbia, South America, Brazil, London, Mauritania, and countless other nations, cities, and entities are not and cannot be coincidences; they all have their roots in African continental powerlessness, which should have been 'grasped' in the 1960's and even much earlier, before the days of Kwame Nkrumah.

For an African born in the early 1950's, these cannot be happy times anywhere, in that contemporary African political problems seem dwarfing, daunting, and so overwhelmingly mountainous that it is often easier to throw in the towel and call it quits. It also seems very easy to blame most of Africa's problems on African leaders for their inability to make Africa into a Korea or Japan (Ayittey, 1993); if it only were not for their kleptocracisms (kleptocratic governments), Africa would have been developed by now, and African people around the world would not be so blatantly mistreated and suffer from low self-esteems. Compared to other groups in this global village, African children remain victims of some diseases that have been eliminated elsewhere in the world. Any African would have to be completely blind not to see that African people are not taken seriously in the world. Even those African people who have made it in the United States are not as respected as their white counterparts or colleagues (Cose, 1994; Massaquoi, 1996: 56-58, 60). The 1960's promised a lot to the world, blacks in the Diaspora and the African masses in Africa; these were the years of rising expectations in which African economies and societies were to be revolutionized; "backward, never; forward forever," were the slogans of the day. African people's pride, educational systems, economies, political institutions, etc. were all to be revolutionized to culminate into a united Africa. Pan-Africanism, African Socialism, Negritude, Afro-Marxism and other 'vibrant' ideologies were to redeem Africa's daunting problems. But like the post-1865 African-Americans, the Africans of the 1960's obtained their freedoms with minimal economic, scientific, administrative, entrepreneurial skills to effect their economic development. Thus, despite the natural, tangible wealth in Africa, in minerals and hydroelectric potentials, Africans had not been adequately prepared with the intangible resources-skills and know-hows to manufacture, or add-value to those natural resources in Africa's bosom. The North, or the developed regions of Europe, Canada, and North America had the technical know-how and the fiscal resources necessary to develop Africa's "buried" potentials, and were unwilling to give up that know-how for 'free' for Africa's development; there was to be no free lunch! Africans and their ex-colonizers had to find a new way to address each other, a new way of dealing with each other, at a new dinner table, where once one was the server and the other the served.

Indeed, how does the ex-slave see his ex-master? How does the ex-master view his former slave or colonial? Would both see each other as equals, now that they were both 'free' persons? How does a man with weapons see another without weapons, in the battlefield of political-economy? How does the former colonial master with money, military weapons, technological know-how, educational and linguistic power, etc. view his former colonial without money, military weapons, technology, educational institutions, and speaking in the language of his former master?

Most Africans were simply politically free in the 1960's, and therefore remained bound in fundamental ways - economically, linguistically, and social-psychologically to their former masters. They remained tied to the west in standards of beauty, aphorisms, variables relative to development, political nuances and research paradigms. Those African leaders who attempted to step out of those bounds established by the West and those today who make 'fun' of Western norms were, and are, readily dealt with in more ways than one. Those African leaders who disobeyed their 'ex-bosses' by 'flirting' with the then USSR were punished by being disqualified for financial, military, or educational assistance. Those who remained 'good ex-colonials' received 'tremendous' assistance, even if momentarily, and were individually handsomely rewarded.

By the 1990's, however, Africa had become a continent of micro-states, each living on 'hand-outs' (akin to the American welfare recipients, given just enough to survive but nothing more). The World Bank, the International Monetary Fund, and the Paris Club became central social welfare offices that handed out 'monthly' checks, after all types of embarrassing questions had been asked, and all types of restrictions had been spelled out as to how the welfare checks are to be used, effectively blocking the way of the recipients entering the political kingdom of plenty. In the words of Ravenhill and Callaghy (1994), the Africans were 'hemmed in' with practically no way out of the labyrinth of global capitalism.

The defeat of Russian Marxism in the late 1980's and the early 1990's effectively left the African leaders, the masses and their intellectuals, holding the bag; counter-arguments against global capitalism became ludicrous: Marxist, Maoist, and Nkrumahist arguments against capitalism sounded hollow and politically incorrect. Japan, which had borrowed lavishly from the West, and Korea, which had also lavishly borrowed from Japan, emerged to challenge Western dominance in technology and manufactured goods, especially in electronics and automobiles. Nonetheless, the West, and especially the United States, remained atop the global village. Thus Huntington (1993:39) could state unequivocally, that

> The West is now at an extraordinary peak of power in relation to other civilizations. Its superpower opponent has disappeared from the map. Military conflict among Western states is unthinkable, and Western military power is unrivaled. Apart from Japan, the West faces no economic challenge. It dominates international political and security institutions and with Japan international economic institutions. Global political and security issues are effectively settled by a directorate of the United States, Germany and Japan, all of which maintain extraordinarily close relations with each other to the exclusion of lesser and largely non-Western countries. Decisions made at the UN Security council or in the International Monetary Fund that reflect the interests of the West are presented to the world as reflecting the desires of the world community. The very phrase "the world community" has become the euphemistic collective noun (replacing "the Free World") to give

> global legitimacy to actions reflecting the interests of the United States and other Western powers. Through the IMF and other international economic institutions, the West promotes its economic interests and imposes on other nations the economic policies it thinks appropriate.

Huntington goes on to assert that

> Civilization identity will be increasingly important in the future, and the world will be shaped in large measure by the interactions among seven or eight major civilizations. These include Western, Confucian, Japanese, Islamic, Hindu, Slavic-Orthodox, Latin American and *possibly African civilizations.* The most important conflicts of the future will occur along the cultural fault lines separating these civilizations from one another. (25)

Was Africa an afterthought in Huntington's paradigm? What does Huntington mean by "possibly African civilizations"? Is the "fault line" between Africa and the West the largest, in comparison to the other major "civilizations"? Has that fault line between Africa and the West not narrowed in cognizance of the long presence of the West in Africa and Africans in the West? By listing Africa last, Huntington must have been signifying Africa's "unimportant" position in the contemporary global village, in which Africa is the least able to counter-act the West, as, say "Confucian" civilization. It is therefore, perhaps, not an accident that Huntington mentions Africa last, because in contemporary global capitalism, a borderless world, as Kenichi Ohmae (1990) has argued, African people are at the bottom of the developmental pile in terms of educational attainment, economic development, science, health and technology, housing, road construction, longevity, political stability, freedom of the press, and the other popular indexes that measure "civilizations". It also is therefore not an accident that both Whitaker (1988) and Davidson (1974) have wondered whether Africa would at all survive.

Even highly educated Africans and African-Americans (the so-called fortunate few) are not unreminded daily of their lowly place in this global village and that, despite their educations, they still belong to a lower people, unequal therefore to their European counterparts (Cose, 1993; Wright, 1987; Morrison, 1990; and Mabrey, 1995). These African people and their fellow 'Africans' they write about might have received their educations in some of the finest universities in the West, in Africa or elsewhere, but they continue to experience status discrepancy between their achieved and their ascribed status; they are not "fully" respected because they are an African people whose original land remains the poorest of the poor in terms of the number of telephones, televisions, hospital beds to a given population, the number of engineers, dentists, computer scientists, psychologists, medical doctors, infinitum; Africans are synonymous with the "Information Have-nots" (Gibbs, 1995:12b, 14). In these days of 'technopoly' (Postman, 1993), African people are still struggling with achieving basic literacy in terms of simply learning how to read and write; they lack significant research institutes that are globally respected; to do significant research, one must go north, publish in northern journals and magazines, cite northern writers and authorities, be affiliated with northern universities, colleges, or research outfits.

Those Africans who can, do migrate to the north to study, teach, write and/or do research and work. This brain drain starkly states that African societies are "inhospitable" economically and culturally to productive talent. One would wish that these academicians would return and bring tropical medical knowledge to tropical Africa, where it is developmentally needed the most. They remain in the north where they are not really respected or tolerated, but accumulate a lot of mess of pottage. These Africans work harder in the north than they would for Africa, to which they often return to show-off their northern lifestyles. Some of these Africans will never return to Africa; their tastes have been irrevocably changed; in the north, they attempt to cling to anachronistic Africanisms - during sermons, burial ceremonies, weddings, and/or drinking parties. Many marry northern women without love, in feign love, basically for exploitative reasons, so that they can continue to live the good life developed by the northerners, who do not actually appreciate them.

Brimelow (1995) is alarmed by the number of non-European immigrants to the United States from 1965 to the 1990's. Though most of these immigrants have been "from Latin America and the Caribbean, ...Asia," (77), Mr. Brimelow is more upset because these new immigrants are mostly colored, and do not look like him (British)(58). These new waves of immigrants are not from Western or Eastern Europe; some are Africans, completely different, with problematic cultural and intellectual traditions, "a black inflow, both from Africa itself and from the Caribbean" (61). Mr. Brimelow 'zeros' in on the Nigerians:

> David Simlox, a senior fellow at the Center for Immigration Studies, reported that U.S. law enforcement officials estimate an incredible 75 percent of the 100,000 Nigerians now in the United States are involved in an impressive and innovative variety of fraud schemes using extensive countrywide networks...Nigerian specialists: immigration and citizenship fraud: bank and credit card fraud, welfare fraud, insurance fraud, heroin.

> Interestingly, Nigerian criminals come from their country's privileged classes.(186)

Mr. Brimelow seems nostalgic for the pre-1965 U.S. immigration policies that favored European immigrants, when there were not so many colored peoples, especially from the Caribbean and Africa; he fears his son will have to grow up in a U.S. society that would have lost its European dominance.

Mr. Brimelow might have been over-reacting in 1995, but he must have been speaking for a good number of northerners who fear that the North could be overwhelmed by the darker races of mankind, especially blacks from Nigeria, Algeria, and the Caribbean islands, etc., who run away from their depressed economies and political instabilities to rejoice in Northern opulence. Instead of these Africans returning home to make a Korea out of Nigeria, Kenya, Uganda, Cameroon and elsewhere in Africa, they remain in societies in which Africanness remains a badge of inferiority; this badge will not transform itself until Africans compete technologically, industrially, and politically in the global market of ideas and manufactured goods.

Africa's dependence on Western manufactured goods has had disastrous effects on African economies, politics, and societies. Perhaps, above all, it has taught the least African intellectual that Africans are still peons in this global village, and this trend has not been fully challenged beyond rhetoric. The African masses, those who cannot hop on the plane to Lisbon, London, Paris, Washington D.C., or New York City, were betrayed by the 1960's African leaders (Ayittey, 1992); they were not able to make a Korea out of any African region in more than thirty-years. They instead became kleptomaniacs and international beggars to the World Bank and the International Monetary Fund, which we have likened to the welfare offices in the United States, 'giving' money to the poor with one hand, while the landlords collect from the other; the poor benefit the rich.

## The Positive Functions of African Poverty in the Global Village

Gans(1979:69-75), writing specifically about the positive functions of poverty in American society, describes fifteen ways by which the poor in America benefit the larger society. "First, the existence of poverty makes sure that (the) 'dirty work' gets done" (70). Furthermore, the poor

2. Subsidize the affluent;
3. Poverty creates jobs;
4. The poor buy goods others do not want and thus prolonging their economic usefulness;

5. The poor can be identified and punished as deviants or as alleged deviants;
6. The deserving poor provide the rest of the society with emotional satisfactions - pity, compassion, charity, thus allowing those who help them to feel that they are altruistic, moral, and practicing the Judo-Christian ethic;
7. The poor offer affluent people vicarious participation in uninhibited sexual, alcoholic, and narcotic behavior;
8. Poverty helps to guarantee the status of those who are not poor;
9. The poor also assist in the upward mobility of the nonpoor;
10. The poor help the aristocracy keep busy;
11. The poor perform several cultural functions;
12. The low culture of the poor is often adopted by the more affluent;
13. The poor are a political constituency;
14. The poor can be made to absorb the economic and political costs of change and growth in American society, and finally, because the poor vote in the political process, but participate less than other groups, the political system has been free to ignore them. (70-73)

It is easy to see that we can borrow all of these variables and apply them to African poverty in the global village, all the way from African people doing the filthy jobs in Africa and in the United States, to the wealthy in this global village using Africans as scapegoats for diseases, crime, environmental degredation, immigration problems, refugee assistance, a battle ground for contending ideologies, pleasures of the Safari, use of surplus food as charity, Jazz music and African dancers for tourists, primitive art in metropolitan museums, infinitum.

African poverty has enhanced the standard of living of a good number of Western and Northern professionals, all the way from World Bank officials to teachers, politicians, professors, singers, lobbyists, economists, travelers, novelists and peacemakers, just to mention a few. Africa seems to be a convenient place to dump old technologies, used clothing, textbooks, surplus food, medicines, 'tired' diplomats and many other specialists.

African poverty is so much so that the poor in the West feel better-off in comparison. If one thinks that the poor in the United States and Europe are poor, one has not yet seen African poverty! Some poor persons in the U.S. are wealthier than some of the wealthy in Africa, especially if they are European, and therefore smarter too [Murray and Heinstein (1994)] ! The poor in the West or North are at least in the bosom of wealth; they have all the modern technologies, even if those technologies might be ten years old or behind the latest electronic gadgets.

In the politics of the United Nations, no African nation (not Nigeria or Kenya) is yet represented in the Security Council; they have no veto power. As Huntington (1993:39) has reminded us, "decisions made at the UN. Security Council or in International Monetary fund that reflect the interests of the West are presented to the world as reflecting the desires of the world community". Africa remains a political constituency whose vote is sought only at exigent points in time, by the World's leading politicians from the North, when they need Africa's vote for their own schemes.

If the poor do not behave according to the rules of the wealthy, they can be punished. Thus, after the collapse of the former USSR, African politicians were urged to promulgate multi-party systems; those who remained recalcitrant in their old ways saw their financial pockets shrink. Sekou Toure of Guinea was perhaps the first well-known African leader to suffer the wrath of France for his failure to join the French community in 1958; others were to follow, notably Nkrumah and Lumumba. By the 1990's those African leaders who wished to remain in power had to 'play' by the multi-party rule of the powerful North (Perlez, 1991: 10). Bonner (1997: E5) states that

> All the new Congolese President Laurent Kabila had to do to get the money was become a democrat and free market capitalist. Reinforcing that message, Commerce and Treasury officials were along, dangling financial lures. The World Bank and International Monetary Fund were close behind.
>
> "Bribery," some critics sneer, but diplomats prefer to call offers of aid "carrots" - as opposed to "sticks," the economic sanctions and public condemnations of human rights abuses that have been applied in Iran, Iraq, Libya, Cuba and Burma.

Conversely, no African leader could choose an American leader for his positive foreign policy platform toward Africa. "The poor, being powerless, can be made to absorb the economic and political costs of change and growth in American society" (Gans, 1977: 72). Thus, the changes that were necessary due to the collapse of the former U.S.S.R. affected Africa negatively; aid that could have gone to Africa was used to aid Central Europe, the former Soviet satellite states; Asia, instead of Africa, commanded more attention from multinational corporations and Northern governments. French (1995: Al) tells us that

> For the three decades that constituted the infancy of African independence, Washington and its allies preached the virtues of democracy to this continent while

> supporting many of its most corrupt one-party regimes, invoking the strategic considerations of the cold war.
>
> Now, with the Soviet Union no longer the opponent that justified this policy, democratic systems have taken root for the first time in a score of countries across Africa. But as these sub-Saharan countries face grave crises of debt, population growth, poverty and religious militancy, leaders in Washington and in the capitols of Western Europe are increasingly telling African governments that they will have to rely on their own meager resources to solve the continent's problems. . .a round of budget cuts hit Africa more than any other continent, the United States Agency for International Development closed 8 of its African missions, leaving 27.

In this way, while Africa remains poor, the other world regions advance in converse to African economic and social stagnation. While the U.S. could then pay more attention to its own regional concerns such as the North Atlantic Free Trade Agreement (NAFTA), West European unity, and South East Asian integration, Africa is left holding the bag as the abandoned beggar. The beggar has to be kept poor for fear that he might become a formidable competitor. As Gans again (1973-74) observes,

> The role of the poor in the upward mobility of the other groups could be maintained without their being so low in income. However, if their incomes were raised above subsistence levels, they would begin to generate capital so that their own entrepreneurs could supply them with goods and services, thus competing with and perhaps rejecting "outside" suppliers. *...increases in income are generally accompanied by increases in power as well.*

Thus, we should not expect the wealthy North to help the poor (Africa) develop, for fear of another powerful competitor in the global market. Japan and Korea are already competitors; China is also becoming a problematic competitor in the global village against the West. In the view of racists and some ex-colonizers, Africa should not be allowed to compete; it should remain dependent or abandoned in the race for technological advancement. Should it develop, a host of Western theorems regarding African capacities would be shattered overnight, and this could disappoint a host of Westerners who have rejoiced, and continue to pinpoint Africa as the epitome of incapacity. Indeed, the poor in the global village have too much to offer the wealthy, for the latter to contribute to the former's advancement, which will then compete with some vivacity. As it should be now clear,

Africa's poverty is decidedly beneficial to the wealthy in the global village, psychologically, politically, and economically. Africans themselves must recognize this and do for themselves what the Japanese, the Koreans, the Americans, and the West have done and are doing for themselves; they must put their eggs in one basket in order to effectively compete in this global village; the days of micro-nations are over; the global village is now a borderless world, and we must all be prepared for that reality.

Kenichi Ohmae (1985, 1990, 1995) has persuasively argued that the powers of Japan, Europe and America have been unrivaled in the global village. This triad power utilizes its human, technological and commercial might to pervade the global village. Africa is not yet an equal participant in this global village; she is not as yet an insider. In this borderless world, depressed economies are attractive to businesses because they provide cheap laborers, take advantage of poor working conditions relative to safety and the absence of laws that protect workers. In this borderless world,

> natural resources are no longer the key to (development of) wealth. We have to accept that national borders have little to do any longer with the real flows of industrial activity. We have to accept that information and knowledge - a trained and literate population, not military hardware - are the real sources of strength. The better informed people are, the more they know what is going on elsewhere in the world, the more they will want for themselves all those things that make life pleasant and enjoyable. And the more they will want to make their own choices among them. (Ohmae, 1990:193)

In this borderless world, the remotest African village has been 'visited' by at least the Coke bottle, an epitome of Western consumerism. Africa cannot delink itself, even if it wants to; the power of the four I's: Investments, Industry, Information, and Individual Consumers (Ohmae, 1995:4) have rendered it impossible for any sector of the global village to remain immune to the contemporary global zeitgeist. Africa is a major component of that global village and cannot remain peripheral to Western technology, science, manufactured goods, techniques, and conspicuous consumption.

The traditional African states and those artificial states left by the former colonial powers in Africa are anachronistic in the contemporary global village; global consumers are becoming more and more alike, irrespective of their locations geographically, and even culturally (28). "Children and teenagers are, at deep levels of sensibility and world views, becoming much more like their counterparts in other societies similarly influenced than they are like the older generations within their own cultures" (30). Pride in one's nation is no longer sufficient to prevent individuals from migrating to where the action is, or is perceived to be. If one's nation of birth is comparatively poor, out-migration is urged by the pervasive media that have inundated even the bushmen of the Kalahari in Africa; traditional political units are no longer functional, in terms of preventing ideas from aliens or other nations.

According to Ohmae (89) the region state is what is now in vogue.

> Region states...are economic not political units, and they are anything but local in focus. They may lie within the borders of an established nation state, but they are such powerful engines of development because their primary orientation is toward-and their primary linkage is with-the global economy. They are, in fact, among its most reliable ports of entry.
>
> Region states welcome foreign investment. They welcome foreign ownership. They welcome foreign products. In fact, they welcome whatever will help employ their people productively, improve their quality of life, and give them access to the best and cheapest products from anywhere in the world. And they have learned that such access is often best and easiest when the products are not produced at home. (Singaporeans, for example, enjoy better and cheaper agricultural products than do the Japanese, although Singapore has no farmers-and no farms-of its own.) Region states also welcome the chance to use whatever surplus these activities generate to ratchet up their people's quality of life still further, not to fund the civil minimum or subsidize outmoded industries. Their leaders do not show up somewhere in the world trying to attract factories and investment and then appear on TV back home vowing to protect local companies no matter what. In a word, they consistently put global logic first.
>
> Region states make such effective ports of entry to the global economy because the very characteristics that define them are shaped by the demands of that economy.

Ohmae's region-state in Africa could be an economically dynamic Nigeria, Kenya, Ghana, Ivory Coast, or Gabon or strategic regions of these countries, that could stimulate the outlying economies.

> They must, for example, be large enough to provide an attractive market for the brand development of leading consumer products. Hence, they tend to be between 5 and 20 million people in size. The range is broad, but the extremes are clear: not half a million, not 50 or 100

> million. That is because they must be small enough for their citizens to share interests as consumers, but still of sufficient size to justify economies not of scale (which, after all, can be leveraged from a base of any size through exports to the rest of the world) but of service - that is, the infrastructure of communications, transportation, and professional services essential to participation in the global economy. (They must have, for example, at least one international airport and, more than likely, one good harbor with international-class freight- handling facilities.) (89)

Africa must become a 'region state' within this global village; she must throw herself into this global village permanently and compete with all the resources at hand, her people, minerals and rivers, forests and the deserts, mountains and valleys, swamplands and drylands, expatriates and native intellectuals and scientists; the wealthy may not want the poor to be wealthy, but this choice cannot be left to the affluent North; the poor South itself must do what it must to 'free' and develop itself.

## The African Masses

The African masses in this global village have seen and have experienced 'enough' oppression and are not about to continue being the hewers of wood and drawers of water for the North and members of the higher classes in Africa. They've been made to fight in foreign, European wars, mine diamonds, iron ore, gold, bauxite and others for multinational corporations and European factories and luxuries; they've grown cotton, coffee, tea, cocoa and other crops; they've been enslaved in Africa, Europe, the United States, the Caribbean Islands, Iraq, and Saudi Arabia, for the comforts of the haves, while they have consistently remained the have-nots, to the extent of starvation, large scale famine, malnutrition, and the experience of hell-on-earth.

The African masses include those who "know" no other place in which to live but Africa. They may not be highly educated, are not professors, teachers, nurses, pilots, engineers; and even if they are all these, they would rather live in Africa; they like African culture, music, traditions, lifestyles and want to see Africa develop, like any other world region, with the mark of Africanisms. They want justice for all, including themselves. They are tired of kleptomaniac African leaders and bureaucrats and foreign exploitation, directly and indirectly. They are also tired of the military and police forces that have contributed to Africa's downward spiral from the 1960's to the 1990's.

The African military take power for the sake of taking power without improving the conditions of the African masses - those who cannot afford to take the plane to London, Paris, Lisbon, Washington D.C. or New York city because of the depressed African economies. They've become the victims of civil wars, starvation, shanty towns in Kenya, Nigeria or the Ivory Coast, police and military intimidations, inflation, poor education, short lifespans, and numerous diseases that are already anachronistic in the other world regions.

The African masses include African women, most of whom remain the poorest of the poor in the contemporary global village. They are victims of global capitalism, peripheral African capitalism, African, Islamic and Christian traditions, each of which oppress women in multiple ways. African women are oppressed by Islam and animism in their polygamous traditions and their negative attitudes toward the female sex. Wife beatings, forced and arranged marriages, and the illiteracies of a host of African women have continued to hold down half of the African population. They are the least represented in African governments, high schools, colleges and the universities in Africa, both as students and as staff members. They remain objects of sexual gratifications for the well-to-do Africans, Europeanized Africans, European and American tourists. They entertain African leaders and their bureaucrats as dancers and singers, servants and lovers.

Several African leaders such as Julius Nyerere and Amilar Cabral did their utmost to elevate the status of women in Tanzania and Guinea-Bissau respectively (Ladner and Urdang, 1983: 107-139). They promulgated laws and formed national women's organizations to facilitate women's participation in their nations' governments. They implemented mass education and training programs that addressed the cultural and political economy of the African masses. Nonetheless, traditional masculine prejudices are not revamped overnight, by the stroke of a pen, or a mesmerizing speech about the necessity to elevate African women, who still remain less than *second class citizens*. They remain the food preparers and processors, child rearers, food distributors in the market places, sellers of consumer goods for immediate consumption, hewers of wood and drawers of water, and not considered "beautiful" by Western standards.

In addition to this strict sex-role segregation, classes in Africa have already entrenched themselves. There is really no use fooling ourselves that classes did not exist in Africa and, here, we are not speaking in Marxist terms; to explicate ourselves, we borrow from Michael Lind (1995:99), who states that

> Today, class analysis tends to be associated with Marxist pseudo-science and discredited by that association. This is unfortunate, because class analysis is much older than Marxism, and is not, in itself, linked to socialist or even liberal politics. Ideas about class conflict are integral elements of the political theories of

> Montesquieu and Aristotle, to name only two examples. In the United States, the authors of the Federalist Papers based their defense of the Constitution of 1787 on an analysis of class that presumed a permanent conflict of interest between the propertied and the propertyless.

Safely then, we can talk about African classes without the boogie label of *Marxism*. We aver that classes of persons have always existed in Africa; in traditional Africa, the family of chiefs, kings, and emperors enjoyed exclusive privileges. In *ancient Egypt*, the clergy and the Pharaohs enjoyed enormous privileges to which the African masses and slaves remained peripheral; with the imposition of Islam and colonialism, class stratification became even more pronounced. The Islamic clergy, the European colonizers and the African bureaucrats became powerful; with Western education, numerous professions came into vogue, further stratifying African societies based on those who are literate versus the rest of the society; university graduates versus high school drop-outs; military men versus civilians; those who studied abroad versus those who studied at home; top civil servants versus lower level management sectors, and infinitum.

The contemporary privileged African has been 'consumed' by Western style consumerism, especially of things Africa cannot, and does not at the moment produce directly; these privileged Africans use consumer goods to enhance their social, political and psychological positions against the African masses. This African "over-class" (Lind, 1995: 100) has not invested in Africa; it keeps its monies abroad, further depressing African economies, and therefore the 'well-being' of the African masses. These powerful Africans "and their clients operate almost with impunity. A bank clerk can demand payment before he will transact business, a teacher before exams, doctors or nurses before dispensing medicine. The general public is forced to subsidize the wage-bill" (*African Confidential,* 1988: 7). A clerk in the passport office would 'get his own cut' before he stamps the official seal; the policeman would accept bribes, readily, to allow too many passengers into a taxi, van or Mommy Truck. "An official position (in Africa) offers lucrative opportunities for graft" (Ibid.). In the former Zaire, "the directors of the big import houses of Kisingani, the commercial and administrative center of (Upper Congo), who allocate quotas of scarce manufactured goods to local retailers, are spoken of as 'les grands seigneurs' of the city because of their wealth'" (Ibid.).

Some African leaders are among the wealthiest of the world even though they govern the poorest of the poor, the least educated and the least adequately housed citizens in this global village: in their rapacity, some African leaders have 'totally' been numbed to the degrading conditions of their people. They've built monuments to themselves, raised armies for their own protection, and mismanaged national resources for their own aggrandizements (Ayittey, 1993).

However, the African masses who go homeless are becoming irrevocably numerous all over the African continent; they are also becoming more and more aware of their depravity in the global village, as they are increasingly coming in contact with richer lifestyles from within and outside of Africa. They are knowledgeable about modern African history with regards to the promises of the 1960's that African lives were to be improved under African leadership; housing, education, roads, medical facilities, jobs and the general improvement of the lives of the African masses were supposed to be effected under black African leaders; the African masses instead reaped bitter fruits from the trees of African independence.

The population of the African common man is getting larger and larger to include disgruntled African civil servants, and even some professionals, who have not been able to eke out a livelihood from their 'monthly' salaries, so to speak, to own homes, cars, and other rewards and amenities for a lengthy government service for African governments that are neither for, by, or of the people. To add African school drop-outs to this scenario would certainly suggest uneasiness of the masses across the continent.

Thus far, the African masses have been victims of oppression in traditional Africa, colonial and post-colonial Africa; they are now at the mercy of global capitalism that has spread its tentacles, as it were, to the most remote African village, and it will not relax this grip globally. Western technology, as evidenced in the 1980 comic movie - "The God's Must be Crazy" - has attacked Africans in urban centers as well as in the rural areas. It has now, more than ever before, inundated the African land, social, cultural, political, and educational spheres; there is no use hoping for a miracle that this inundation, deluge, as it were, will evaporate in thin air. The bush man in "The Gods Must be Crazy" might have, as he believed, thrown away the Coke bottle off the end of the earth, but his stories will never be the same again because in his sojourn to get rid of 'that evil thing', the Coke bottle, he encountered more and more of Western technology; he had no more place to hide, not even behind his nakedness, primitive social organization, or his traditional means of subsistence; he will not wipe away, no matter how much he wished for such, the Europeans in Africa, their languages, their trucks, schools, medicines, airplanes, prisons, laws, telescopes, vehicles, weapons, systems of government, infinitum.

## The Next African Nation

What then should be hoped for these transitional Africans? They cannot go back to the old, their most recent past under colonialism, or the post-colonial nightmare of the 1990's. The military, as well as the civilian governments, from the 1960's to the 1990's, failed the African masses stupendously, as Ayittey (1993) has adequately addressed.

As we've seen in chapter two, Africans have not been without their own contributions to medicine, theology, science, warfare, monument building, leadership, art, literature, writing, explorations, and the other elements of civilization. From ancient Egypt down to the twenty-first century, Africans in Africa and elsewhere have had their say about almost every subject, and will continue to do so in this global village according to the zeitgeist.

This, indeed, does not minimize the terrible defeats of Africans by the Arabs and Europeans in Africa and the long domination of African people in Brazil, the United States, South Africa, Iraq, India, Australia, England and elsewhere. Unequivocally, no other race of persons has been so despised, and for such a long time, by especially the Europeans, who didn't only enslave Africans but also divided the African continent into bits and pieces with all manner of rapacity. Had it not been for the African climate and the discovery of the Americas, it is certainly not far-fetched to reason that Europeans would have made out of Africa what they accomplished in Australia and North America; we must also acknowledge Africans' love of freedom that compels them to resist at all cost, including death, banishment, and long prison terms.

Some writers on Africa have divided African history into (a) Ancient Africa; (b) Pre-colonial; (c) Colonial; and (d) Post-colonial Africa, and have described how each has contributed to civilizations.

Nonetheless, it is quite clear that contemporary Africa has inherited what Ali Mazrui has termed "Africa's triple heritage" (Mazrui, 1986); to this heritage has been added the contemporary global zeitgeist of technopoly (Postman, 1993), a global village which Keniche Ohmae (1990) has termed "a borderless world", dominated by a *Triad Power* of Japan, Europe, and North America (Ohmae, 1985).

In his book, *The Next American Nation: The New Nationalism and the Fourth American Revolution,* Michael Lind (1995: 11) averred that the United States had gone through three major 'revolutions': (a) Anglo-America (1767-1861); (b) Euro-America (1875-1957), and multicultural America (1972-1990's). He opines that the twenty-first century America will be a trans-national America. A trans-racial America will be achieved around certain aesthetic and moral conformities (243). If Anglo and Euro-Americas were dominated by West Europeans, multicultural America overwhelmed the United states from the 1960's to the 1990's; Mr. Lind envisions that multicultural United States will come to pass to culminate into a transracial America, that will not be divided into white, Asian, Hispanic, Native and Black America; all of these Americas will eventually be "assimilated" to produce a transracial America that will have commonalties, a common public memory, a national language, and common culture (369). Mr. Lind took a biracial Frederick Douglass as one of the first transAmerican nationalists who opposed racism, sexism, and emphasized the common America foundation. Even though black skinned Americans will find it difficult to be accepted into this Lindian Trans-Amerca, Mr. Lind seems to have captured the spirit of globalism in which the various races, tribes, ethnicities, and sexes would have to live. Global capitalism and technopoly have brought and will continue to bring diversities not only into contact, but also into amalgamation. There will continue to be inter-racial love, sex, marriages, and multi-racial children, whether the 'Luddites' and the KKKs like it or not!

Brimelow, in his *Alien Nation* (1995), fears that the United States has already been too wide open to non-Europeans and that his son would have to live in a society where whites are no longer the "majority" in the United States. Mr. Brimelow seems to underestimate the power of American popular culture to fuse together a diverse group of people; he also seems to under-estimate the globalization of the world by technopoly (Postman, 1993), and the irreversible market forces that know no boundaries (Ohmae, 1985, 1995). The fundamental belief in scientism, family, peace and stability, consumerism and the "Californization" of the globe are becoming universalistic. Mr. Brimelow's nostalgia for the pre-1965 United States is, impressionistically, simply that, a nostalgia. Similarly, it seems simply nostalgic for Africans to wish for a return to the days before the Europeans 'invaded' Africa.

How then should Africans arm themselves to be competitive constitutes in this global village? If African-Americans can never 'go back to Africa,' and if Africans on the continent and elsewhere cannot delink themselves from this global capitalistic village, how must they live in this global phenomenon aside from being the drawers of water and hewers of wood for everyone else ?

"Anyone who practices the art of cultural criticism", writes Neil Postman (1993:181), "must endure being asked, what is the solution to the problems you describe?" We shall here not satisfy everyone or be bombastic, but simply observe that, in the contemporary global zeitgeist of mergers of a greater North America, South East Asia, Western Europe, China, and the rest of Asia, etc., Africans would have to be extremely myopic not to be radically Pan-Africanistic. A united Western Europe, a greater North America (USA, Mexico, Canada and possibly the whole of South America), North and South Korea, China and Hong Kong, etc., will dwarf balkanized Africa several times over. These political-economic groups are not only already advanced, but will also become much more sophisticated technologically, economically, and administratively.

For the African continent to face these formidable groupings, balkanized, would be the greatest of follies, and also 'suicidal'. They too, Africans, must form their own forces for an effective competition in this global village.

There might one day be a Euro-Africa, an Afro-Euro-Asia, or an Afro-Eurasia and a global government, but there should never be a Euro-Africa and a global government in which African people, of all shades of color and educational attainment, remain the hewers of wood and the drawers of water for the West and 'Westernized' Africans. In this context, Africans can do their part, for their own upliftment, in this global village, by uniting their economic, political, technical, and fiscal forces to be able to compete anywhere and at any time; Africans must face the global village from a competitive economic and political base; this base cannot be dreamed or hoped for; it must be planned and implemented.

Africans cannot continue to go snail-pace toward African political and economic integration while the other world regions zoom, with Concord/Jet speed, toward their own regional integrations. Pan-Africanism or Trans-national Africa is the next stage in African development. The time for micro-nationalisms has become anachronistic, obsolete, and dangerous. As Julius Nyerere observed in the 1960's, "the choice is not between change or no change; the choice for Africa is between changing or being changed - changing our lives under our own direction, or being changed by the impact of forces outside our own control" (Nyerere, 1966: 24). Continental African unity and integration is a change from within Africa, advocated by Africans, for the benefit of Africans wherever they are; it will not solve all our problems, but it certainly is the correct step toward a global village in which Africans, especially black Africans, will be treated as ineluctable members of the human society and humanity. Lastly, without a powerful continental African government, *a single African currency, and a union citizenship,* "Ethiopia" will not be able to "stretch forth her hands unto God."

## References: Chapter X


*Africa Confidential,* 1988:7.

Ayittey, George B.N. 1993. *Africa Betrayed.* New York: Saint Martins Press.

Brimelow, Peter. 1995. *Alien Nation: Common Sense About America's Immigration Disaster.* New York: Random House.

Callaghy, Thomas M. and John Ravenhill (eds.). 1994. *Hemmed In: Responses to Africa's Economic Decline.* New York: Columbia University Press.

Cose, Ellis. 1993. The *Rage of a Privileged Class.* New York: Harper Collins Publishers.

French, Howard W. 1995. "In Africa, West Can Pay Now, or Later." *New York Times*, Feb. 26: E3.

Gans, Herbert J. 1977. "The Positive Functions of Poverty." pp. 69-75 in Peter Wickman (ed.), *Readings in Social Problems: Contemporary Perspectives* (1977-78). New York: Harper and Row Publishers.

Gibbs, W. Wayt. 1995. "Information Have-Nots: A Vicious Circle Isolates Many Third World Scientists." *Scientific American.* 272/5: 12B, 14.

Herrnstein, Richard J. and Charles Murray. 1994. *The Bell Curve: Intelligence and Class Structure in American Life.* New York, New York: The Free Press.

Huntington, Samuel P. 1993. "The Clash of Civilizations." *Foreign Affairs*. Summer, pp. 22-49.

Ladner Joyce. 1981. "Tanzanian Women and Nation Building," pp. 107-117 in Filomina Chioma Steady (ed.). *The Black Woman Cross-Culturally.* Rochester, Vermont: Schenkman Books Inc.

Lind, Michael. 1995. *The Next American Nation: The New Nationalism and the Fourth American Revolution.* New York: The Free Press.

Mabry, Marcus. 1995. *White Bucks and Black-Eyed Peas.* New York, New York: Scribner.

Morrison, Toni. 1993. "On the Backs of Blacks." *Time.* Fall, p. 57.

__________. 1993. *Playing in the Dark: Whiteness and the Literary Imagination.* New York: Vintage Books; (see also Nathan Irvin Higgins, *Harlem Renaissance.* Oxford University Press, 1971, pp. 244-301).

Nyerere, Julius. 1969. *Nyerere on Socialism.* Dar es Salaam: Oxford University Press.

Ohmae, Kenichi. 1995. *The End of the Nation State: The Rise of Regional Economies.* New York: The Free Press.

__________. 1990 *The Borderless World: Power and Strategy in the Interlinked Economy.* New York: Harper Business.

__________. 1985. *Triad Power: The Coming Shape of Global Competition.* New York: The Free Press.

Perlez, Jane. 1991. "U.S. Reveals Sum of Aid it Withheld from Kenya." *New York Times,* Dec. 1:10.

Postman, Neil. 1993. *Technopoly: The Surrender of Culture to Technology.* New York: Alfred A Knopf.

Robinson, Lori. 1996. "An African Abyss." *Emerge.* March, Vol. 7, N 5:16.

Small, Stephen. 1994. *Racialized Barriers: The Black Experience in the United States and England in the 1980s.* London and New York: Routledge.

Urdang, Stephanie. 1981. "The Role of Women in the Revolution in Guinea-Bissau," pp. 119-139 in Filomina Chioma Steady (ed.). *The Black Woman Cross Culturally.* Rochester, Vermont: Schenkman Books, Inc.

Wright, Bruce. 1993. *Black Robes, White Justice.* New York: Carol Publishing Group.

# Bibliography


Abrahams, Peter. 1989. *Mine Boy*. Heinemann Educational Books.

Achebe, Chinua. 1990. *Things Fall Apart*. New York: Ballantine Books.

Adewoye, O. 1971. "Nationalism in Kenya, 1920-1963." *Tarikh*, 4/1:28-40.

*Africa Confidential*, 1988:7.

*Africa Report*. 1963. 6/9-13.

*African Research Bulletin*. 1994. "Economic Groupings: Casablanca Economic Summit." 31/10(Oct. 16-Nov. 15) pp. 11889-11890.

Afrifa, A.A. 1966. *The Ghana Coup, 24th February 1966*. New York: Humanities Press.

Allman, William F. 1989. "The First Humans: Scientific Detective Work Yields a Radically New View of Early Man." *U.S. News and World Report*.. February 27:52-59.

________. 1990. "The Mother Tongue." *U.S. News and World Report*. November 5:60-70.

Aluko, Olajide. 1976. *Ghana and Nigeria: A Study in Inter-African Discord*. New York: Harper and Row.

Andrews, William L. (ed). 1994. *Classic Fiction of the Harlem Renaissance*. New York: Oxford University Press.

________. (ed.). 1987. *Frederick Douglass: My Bondage and My Freedom*. Urbana and Chicago : University of Illinois Press.

Angelou, Maya. 1969. *I Know Why The Caged Bird Sings*. New York: Bantam Books.

Anonymous Author. 1975. "Why I hate the Negro," (By a White Man), pp. 15-16 in Robert A. Hill (compiler), *Marcus Garvey: The Black Man, A Monthly Magazine of Negro Thought and Opinion*. Millwood, New York:Kraus-Thomson Organization Limited.

Appiah, Kwame Anthony. 1992. *In My Father's House: Africa in the Philosophy of Culture*. New York: Oxford University Press.

Aptheker, Herbert. 1966. *Nat Turner's Slave Rebellion: Including the Full Text of Nat Turner's 1831' Confessions*. New York: Humanities Press.

________. (ed.) 1965. *One Continual Cry: David Walker's Appeal to the Colored Citizens of the World*. New York : Humanities Press.

Arifalo, S.A. 1982. "Pan-Africanism and the Organization of African Unity," pp. 127-149, in Richard Olaniyan (ed.). *African History and Culture*. Nigeria: Longman.

Armah, Ayi Kwei. 1968. *The Beautyful (sic) Ones Are Not Yet Born*. Heinemann Educational Books.

Asante, Molefi. 1981. "Black Male and Female Relationships: An Afrocentric Context," pp. 75-82, in Lawrence E. Gary (ed.) *Black Men*. Beverly Hills, CA: Sage Publications.

________. 1987. *The Afro-Centric Idea*. Philadelphia, Penn.: Temple University Press.

________and Kariamu Welsh Molefi Asante. 1993. *African Culture: The Rhythms of Unity*. Trenton, N.J.. Africa World Press, Inc.

Ashby, Eric. 1964. *African Universities and Western Tradition.* Cambridge, Mass: Harvard University Press.

Ayittey, George B.N. 1991. *Indigenous African Institutions.* New York: Transnational Publishers, Inc.

________. 1993. *Africa Betrayed.* New York: St. Martin's Press.

Baldwin, James. 1984. *Notes of a Native Son.* Boston, Massachusetts: Beacon Press.

Behm, Ronald and Salley Columbus. 1988. *What Color is Your God: Black Consciousness and the Christian Faith.* Secaucus, New Jersey: Citadel Press.

Belasco, Milton J. et. al. 1967. *Basic Review of World History.* N.Y. Bronxville: Cambridge Book Company, Inc.

Bell, Derrick. 1992. *Faces at the Bottom of the Well.* New York, Basic Books.

Ben-Jochannan, Josef A.A. 1971. *Africa: Mother of Western Civilization.* Baltimore, MD. Black Classic Press.

Bennett, Lerone. 1990. "Inaugurating the Future." *Ebony.* Vol. XLV, No. 6 April: 28.

Bennett, Robert A. 1972. " The Black Experience in the Bible, " pp. 176-189 in Martin E Marty and Dean G. Peerman (eds.) *New Theology,* No. 9. New York: The Macmillan Company.

Bernal, Martin. 1987. *Black Athena: The Afroasiatic Roots of Classical Civilization.* Vol. I. New Brunswick, N.J.: Rutgers University Press.

Berry, Mary Francis and John Blassingame. 1983. *Long Memory: The Black Experience in America.* New York, New York: Oxford University Press.

Beteille, Andre. 1968. "Race and Descent as Social Categories in India," pp. 166-185 in John Hope Franklin (ed.), *Color and Race.* Boston, Mass. Houghton and Mifflin Company.

Blassingame, John. 1972. *The Slave Community: Plantation Life in the Antebellum South.* New York: Oxford University Press.

Blyden, Edward. 1994. *Islam, Christianity and the Negro.* Baltimore, Maryland. Black Academic Press.

Boateng, Felix. 1983. "African Traditional Education: A Method of Disseminating Cultural Values." *Journal of Black Studies.* Vol. 3:321-336.

Bohannan, Paul and Philip Curtin. 1988. *Africa and Africans.* Prospect Heights, Illinois: Waveland Press, Inc.

Boley, G.E. Saigbe. 1983. *Liberia: The Rise and Fall of the First Republic.* London: MacMillan Publishers.

Bone, Robert. 1986. "Richard Wright and the Chicago Renaissance." *Callahoo* . Vol.9. No. 3: 446-468.

Bontemps, Arna. (ed).1990. *American Negro Poetry.* New York: Farrar, Straws and Siroux.

Braithwaite, Ronald L. 1981. "Interpersonal Relations Between Black Males and Black Females," pp. 84-97, in Lawrence E. Gary (ed.) *Black Men,* Beverly Hills and London: Sage Publications.

Brimelow, Peter. 1995. *Alien Nation: Common Sense About America's Immigration Disaster.* New York: Random House.

Britt, Donna. 1990. "Randall Robinson Continues to Fight for Africa's Freedom." *Democrat and Chronicle.* Rochester, New York.March 20:46.

Brooke, James. 1994. "Long Neglected, Columbia's Blacks Win Changes," *New York Times.* March 29. p. A3; See also Charles Whitaker, "Blacks in Brazil: The Myth and the Reality," *Ebony*, February 1991: 59-60, 62,64.

Brooke, James. 1994. "U.S. Blacks Find Study in Brazil Bittersweet Experience," *New York Times*, January 12:A17.

Brown, Leon Carl. 1968. "Color in North Africa," pp. 186-204 in John Hope Franklin (ed.), *Color and Race.* Boston, Mass. Houghton and Mifflin Company.

Brown, William Wells. 1989. *Clotel or the President's Daughter.* New York: Carol publishing group.

Brunt, Peter A. 1974. "Work and Slavery," pp. 36-46, in Allan Mitchell and Istvan Deak (eds.) *Every Man in Europe: Essays in Social History; The Preindustrial Millennia Vol. I.* Englewood Cliffs, N.J.: Prentice-Hall, Inc.

Budge, E.A. Wallis. 1923. *The Book of the Dead.* New York: Viking Penguin Inc.

Callaghy, Thomas M. and John Ravenhill (eds.). 1994. *Hemmed In: Responses to Africa's Economic Decline.* New York: Columbia University Press.

Chee-Mooke, Robert A. 1980. "White Indentured Servitude and the Atlantic Slave Trade." *Negro History Bulletin.* Vol. 43, no. 1. Jan-March. pp. 20-22.

Chimezie, Amusie. 1984. *Black Culture: Theory and Practice.* Shaker Heights, Ohio: The Keeble Press.

________. 1983. "Afro-centricity and Ethnicity: Definitive Concepts of Culture." *Western Journal of Black Studies.* Vol. 7, No. 4: 216-228.

Chinweizu. 1987. *The West and the Rest of Us.* Lagos, Nigeria: Pero Press.

Cleage, Albert B. 1987. *Black Christian Nationalism: New Directions for the Black Church.* Detroit, Michigan: Luxor Publishers of the Pan-African Orthodox Christian Church.

Cone, James H. 1970. *A Black Theology of Liberation.* New York: J.B. Lippincott Company.

Conton, William. 1960. *The African* . Heinemann Educational Books

Cose, Ellis. 1993. *The Rage of a Privileged Class.* New York: Harper Collins Publishers.

________. 1995. "One Drop of Bloody History: Americans Have Always Defined Themselves on the Basis of Race." *Newsweek* 2/13:70-71.

Crumwell, Alexander. 1962. *The Future of Africa.* New York: Charles C. Ribner.

________. 1860. "The Relations and Duties of Free Colored Men in America to Africa," pp. 63-71, in Okon Edet Uya (ed.). *Black Brotherhood: Afro-Americans and Africa.* Lexington, Mass: D.C. Heath and Company.

Davidson, Basil. *The African Past: Chronicles from Antiquity to Modern Times*. London: Longman.

________. 1969. "Africans Before Columbus?" *West Africa*. June 7:641.

________. 1974. *Can Africa Survive? Arguments Against Growth Without Development*. London: Heinemann.

________. 1989. *Modern Africa: A Social and Political History*. London and New York: Longman.

Dathorne, O.R. 1975. *African Literature in the Twentieth Century*. Minneapolis, Minnesota: University of Minnesota Press.

de Anda, Diane. 1984. "Bicultural Socialization: Factors Affecting the Minority Experience." *Social Work*. March-April: 101-107.

Decosta-Willis, Mariann. 1991. (Co-editor) *Double Stitch: Black Women Write About Mothers and Daughters*. New York: Harper Perennial. pp. 131-138.

deGraft-Johnson, J.C. 1986. *African Glory: The Study of Vanished Negro Civilizations*. Baltimore, Maryland: Black Classic Press.

Dixon, Melvin. 1979. "Rivers Remembering Their Source: Comparative Studies in Black Literary History- Langston Hughes, Jaques Roumain, and Negritude,"pp. 25-43, in Dexter Fisher, et. al.. (eds.) *Afro-American Literature: The Reconstruction of Instruction*. New York: The Modern Language Association of American.

Douglass, Frederick. 1968. *Narratives of The Life of Frederick Douglass*. New York: American Library Inc.

Drake, St. Clair. 1987. *Black Folks Here and There, Vol. I*. Los Angeles, California: Center for Afro-American Studies.

DuBois, W.E.B. 1989. *Souls of Black Folk*. New York: Penguin Books, Inc.

Dunbar, Paul Laurence. 1984. *Lyrics of Lowly Life: The Poetry of Paul Lawrence Dunbar*. New York : Citadel Press.

Durning, Alan B. 1990. "Ending Poverty," pp. 135-153, in Brown, Lesser R., et. al. *State of the World 1990*. New York: W.W. Norton & Co.

*East African Institute of Social Research*. 1963. "Attitudes of Makerere Students Toward East African Federation." Uganda: EAISR.

Ellul, Jacques. 1978. *The Betrayal of the West*. New York, NY: The Seabury Press.

Emecheta, Buchi. 1974. *Second Class Citizen*. New York: Braziller.

Esedebe, P. Olisanwuche. 1971. "The Independence Movement in Sierra Leone." *Tarikh*.
Vol. 4, No. 1, pp. 15-27.

________. 1968. *Pan-Africanism: The Idea and Movement 1776-1963*. Washington, D.C.: Harvard University Press.

Esen, Akpan. 1973. "The Care Syndrome: A Resource for Counseling in Africa." *Journal of Negro Education*. 2:205-211.

Etzioni, Amitai. 1994. "Incorrigible," *The Atlantic Monthly*, Vol. 274, No. 1 (July), pp. 14, 16.

Fanon, Franz. 1968. *The Wretched of the Earth*. New York: Grove Press, Inc.

Farley, D.W. and Watson, T. 1966. "Education in Tanganyika Between the Wars: Attempts to Blend Two Cultures." *The South Atlantic Journal.* Vol. XLV, No. 4: 471-490.

Farnsworth, Clyde H. "Australians Resist Facing up to Legacy of Parting Aborigines from Families," *New York Times.* 6/8:18.

Feit, Edward. 1968. "Military Coups and Political Development: Some Lessons from Ghana and Nigeria." *World Politics.* XX/2:179-193.

Finch, Charles S. 1982. "The African Background of Medical Science," pp. 8-24 in Ivan van Sertima (ed.), *African and African-American Science and Invention.* New Brunswick, N.J. Rutgers University Press.

Fisher, Allen G.B. & J. Humphrey. 1971. *Slavery and Muslim Society in Africa.* Garden City, NY: Doubleday and Company Inc.

Forbath, Peter. 1977. *The River Congo: The Discovery, Exploration and Exploitation of the World's Most Dramatic River.* Boston, Mass: Houghton Mifflin Company.

Fredrickson, George M. 1982. *White Supremacy: A Comparative Study in American and South African History.* Oxford University Press.

Friedman, Thomas L. 1994. "Asia Pacific Group Has Upbeat Start," *New York Times*, March 21:A10.

French, Howard W. 1995. "In Africa, West Can Pay Now, or Later." *New York Times.* Feb. 26:E3.

Gans, Herbert J. 1977. "The Positive Functions of Poverty," pp. 69-75 in Peter Wickman (ed.) *Readings in Social Problems: Contemporary Perspectives (1977-1978 edition*). New York: Harper & Row, Publishers.

Gaiter, Leonce. 1994. "The Revolt of the Black Bourgeoisie" *New York Times Magazine*, June 26, pp. 42-43.

Garvey, Amy Jacques. 1971. *Garvey and Garveyism.* New York, New York: Collier Books.

Gates, Henry Louis, Jr. (ed.). 1987. *The Classic Slave Narratives.* New York, New York: Penguin Books, Inc.

Gibbs, W. Wayt. 1995. "Information Have-Nots: A Vicious Circle Isolates Many Third World Scientists." *Scientific American.* 272/5: 12B, 14.

Glicksberg, Charles I. 1972. Quoted in Kenneth Kinnamon. *The Emergence of Richard Wright; A Study in Literature and Society.* The University of Chicago Press. p. 119.

Gregg, N. Taylor. 1984. "Hagi: Where Japan's Revolution Began." *National Geographic.* 16516:751-772.

Griffin, John Howard. 1960. *Black Like Me.* New York: Penguin Books.

Hacker, Andrew. 1992. *Two Nations: Black and White, Separate, Hostile, Unequal*: New York: Ballantine Books.

Hadjor, Kofi Buenor. 1987. *On Transforming Africa: Discourse with African Leaders.* Trenton, NJ: Africa World Press, Inc.

________. 1997. *Another America: The Politics of Race and Blame.* Boston, Mass.: South End Press.

Haley, Alex. 1992. *The Autobiography of Malcolm X.* New York: Ballantine Books.

________. 1976. *Roots: The Saga of an American Family*. New York: Dell Publishing Co., Inc.

Hallstein, Walter. 1962. *United Europe: Challenge and Opportunity*. Cambridge, Mass: Harvard University Press.

Hamilton, Charles V. 1972. *The Black Preacher in America*. New York : William Morrow and Company, Inc.

Hammon, Jupiter. 1970. " A Dialogue Intitled[sic] The Kind Master and the Dutiful Servant," pp. 26-30 in Benjamin Brawley (ed.) *Early Negro American Writers*. New York : Dover Publications, Inc.

Hancock, Graham. 1989. *Lords of Poverty: The Power, Prestige and Corruption of International Aid Business*. New York: The Atlantic Monthly Press.

Hansberry, William Leo. 1960. "Ancient Kush, Old Aethiopia, and the Balad Es Sudan." *Journal of Human Relations*. Vol. 8, No. 3 and 4 (Spring and Summer), pp. 357-387.

________and E. Harper Johnson. 1964. "Africa's Golden Past: Part I." *Ebony*, Vol. XX, No. 1, Nov., pp. 30-32, 34, 36, 38-39.

Harding, Vincent. 1981. *There is a River: The Black Struggle for Freedom in America*. New York, NY: Vintage Books.

Harris, Joseph E. 1987. *Africans and Their History*. New York: New American Library.

________. 1971. *The African Presence in Asia: Consequences of the East African Slave Trade*. Evanston, Illinois: Northwestern University Press.

Hemenway, Robert E. 1977. *Zora Neale Hurston: A Literary Biography*. University of Illinois Press.

Heron, G.A. 1976. *The Poetry of Okot p'Bitek*. Heinemann Educational Books.

Herrnstein, Richard J. and Charles Murray. 1994. *The Bell Curve: Intelligence and Class Structure in American Life*. New York, New York: The Free Press.

Herskovitz, Melville J. 1967. *The Myth of the Negro Past*. Boston, MA: Beacon Press.

Heyneman, Stephen H. 1990. "Education in the World Market." *The American School Board Journal*. Vol. 177, No. 3: 28-30.

Hodder-Williams, Richard. 1984. *An Introduction to the Politics of Tropical Africa*. London: George Allen and Unwin.

Hooker, J.R. 1975. *Henry Sylvester Williams: Imperial Pan-Africanist*. London: Rex Collins.

Hough, Joseph C. 1991. "Theological Education, Pluralism and the Common Good," *Theological Education*. Vol. XXVII, No. 1: 9-20.

Hountondji, Paulin. 1990. "Scientific Dependency in Africa Today." *Research in African Literatures*. Vol. 21, no. 3. Fall 1990, pp. 5-15.

Hughes, Langston. 1963. *The Best of Simple. New* York: Hill and Wang.

________. 1965. *Simple's Uncle Sam*. New York: Hill and Wang.

Hughes, Thomas. 1963. *Tom Brown's School Days*. London and Glasgow: Collins.

Huntington, Samuel P. 1993. "The Clash of Civilizations." *Foreign Affairs.* Vol. 72, No. 3 (Summer), pp. 22-49.

Hurston, Zora Neale. 1985. *Spunk: The Selected Stories of Zora Neale Hurston.* Beverly, California: Turtle Island Foundation.

________. 1990. *Their Eyes Watching God.* New York: Harper & Row.

Italiander, Rolf. 1961. *The New Leaders of Africa.* Englewood Cliffs, N.J.: Prentice-Hall.

Iyasere, Solomon D. 1978. "Narrative Techniques in *Things Fall Apart.*" pp. 92-110, in C.L. Innes and Berntt Lindfors (eds.); *Critical Perspectives on Chinua Achebe.* Washington, D.C.: Three Continent Press.

Jackson, John G. 1970. *Introduction to African Civilizations.* Secaucus, New Jersey: The Citadel Press.

________. 1985. *Christianity Before Christ.* Austin, Texas: American Atheist Press.

James, C.L.R. 1963. *The Black Jacobins.* New York: Vintage Books.

________. 1977. *Nkrumah and the Ghana Revolution.* Westport, CT: Lawrence Hill and Co.

James, George G.M. 1976. *Stolen Legacy.* San Francisco, California: Julian Richardson Associates, Publishers.

Jennings, James. 1973. "Pan-Africanism Reconsidered." *Pan-African Journal.* VI/3:321-340.

Johnson, Weldon James. 1986. *The Autobiography of a Ex-Colored Man.* New York: Hill and Wang.

Jordan, Winthrop D. 1974. *The White man's Burden: Historical Origins of Racism in the United States.* Oxford University Press.

Kaggia, Bildad. 1975. *Rcots of African Freedom 1921-1962.* Nairobi, Kenya: East African Publishing House.

Kaplan, Robert D. 1994. "The Coming Anarchy." *The Atlantic Monthly.* Vol. 273, No. 2 (Feb.) pp. 44-46, 48-49, 52, 54, 58-60, 62-63, 66, 68-70, 72-76.

Kaunda, Kenneth. 1963. *Zambia Shall Be Free: An Autobiography of Kenneth Kaunda.* New York : Praeger.

Kenyatta, Jomo. 1965. *Facing Mount Kenya.* New York: Vintage Books.

Kesey, Ken. 1962. *One Flew Over The Cuckoo's Nest.* New York: The Viking Press.

Kilborn, Peter T. 1994. "New York Police Force in Recruitment of Black Officers," *New York Times,* July 17:A1, 26.

King, James C. 1971. *The Biology of Race.* New York, NY: Harcourt Brace Jovanivich, Inc.

Kinnamon, Kenneth. 1990. "Native Son." pp. 60-72, in *Major Literary Characters: Bigger Thomas,* Harold Bloom (ed.) . New York and Philadelphia: Chelsea House Publishers.

Klitgaard, Robert. 1990. *Tropical Gangsters: One Man's Experience with Development and Decadence in Deepest Africa.* Glenview, IL: Basic Books.

Kup, Alexander Peter. 1975. *Sierra Leone: A Concise History.* New York: St. Martins Press.

Kwamena-Poh, et. al. 1982. *African History in Maps.* Longman Educational Books.

Labation, Stephen. 1994. "Denny's gets a Bill for the side orders of Bigotry," *The New York Times*, May 29:4E; see also Howard Kohn, 1994; "Service With a Sneer," *New York Times Magazine*, Nov. 6, Section 6, pp. 43-47; 58, 78, 81.

Ladner Joyce. 1981. "Tanzanian Women and Nation Building," pp. 107-117 in Filomina Chioma Steady (ed.). *The Black Woman Cross-Culturally.* Rochester, Vermont: Schenkman Books Inc.

Lapidus, "A Review of Islam and the West." 1993. *New York Times Book Review*. May 30:8.

Larsen, Nella. 1971. *Passing*. New York: Collier Books.

Laye, Camara. 1954. *The Dark Child: The Autobiography of an African Boy*. New York: Hill and Wang.

Lefkowitz, Mary. 1996. *Not Out of Africa: How Afrocentrism Became an Excuse to Teach Myth as History.* Basic Books.

Leo, John. 1996. "Thou Shall Not Command." *U. S. News & World Report.* 11,18:16.

Lewis, Bernard. 1971. *Race and Color in Islam*. New York. Harper and Row Publishers.

________. 1993. *Islam and the West.* Oxford University Press.

Lincoln, Eric E. 1984. *Race, Religion, and the Continuing American Dilemma*. New York: Hill and Wang.

Lind, Michael. 1995. *The Next American Nation: The New Nationalism and the Fourth American Revolution.* New York: The Free Press.

Lisizkey, Gene. 1947. *Thomas Jefferson.* New York, NY: The Viking Press.

Lugard, Lady. 1965. *A Tropical Dependency.* New York: Barnes and Nobles, Inc.

Lyman, Stanford, M. 1972. *The Black American in Sociological Thought: New Perspectives on Black America.* New York Times: G.P. Putnan's and Sons.

Lyon, Bryce, Herbert H. Rowen, and Theodore S. Hamerow. 1970. *A History of the Western World, Vol. 1: Prehistory to 1715.* Chicago, Illinois: Rand McNally and Company.

Lyons, Douglass C. 1993. "Where the Men Are: The Ten Best Cities." *Ebony*, 7: 30,32, 34.

Mabry, Marcus. 1995. *White Bucks and Black-Eyed Peas.* New York, New York: Scribner.

Manniche, Lise. 1987. *City of the Dead: Thebes in Egypt.* Chicago, Illinois: The University of Chicago Press.

Marah, John K. 1987. "Educational Adaptation and Pan-Africanism: Developmental Trends in Africa." *Journal of Black Studies.* Vol. 17, No. 4: 460-481.

________. 1989. *Pan-African Education: The Last Stage of Educational Developments in Africa*, Lewiston: The Edwin Mellen Press.

Masland, Tom et. al. 1992. "Slavery." *Newsweek.* May 4,:30-32, 37-39.

Massay and Denton. 1994. *American Apartheid: Segregation and the Making of the Underclass.* Cambridge, Mass: Harvard University Press.

Mathabane, Mark. 1987. *Kaffir Boy: The true story of a Black Youth's Coming of Age in Apartheid South Africa.* New York: New America Library.

Mazrui, Ali A. 1980. *The African Condition.* Cambridge University Press.

________. 1986. *The Africans: A Triple Heritage.* Boston, MA: Little Brown and Co.

________. 1971. "On the Concept of 'We Are All Africans,'" pp. 42-58, *Pax-Africana: A Study of Ideology and Ambition.* The University of Chicago Press.

________. 1967. *Towards a Pax-Africana: A Study of Ideology and Ambition.* Chicago, Illinois: The University of Chicago press, pp. 42-58.

Mbiti, John S. 1970. *African Religions and Philosophy.* New York: Anchor Books.

M'bow, Amadou-Mahtar. 1984. *Where the Future Begins.* UNESCO.

McGray, Walter Authur, Rev. 1990. *The Black Presence in the Bible and the Table of Nations, Genesis 10:1-32.* Chicago, IL: Black Light Fellowship.

________. 1990. *The Black Presence in the Bible: Teacher's Guide.* Chicago, IL: Black Light Fellowship.

McKay, Claude. 1990. "If We Must Die." p.31 in Arna Bontemps, *American Negro Poetry.*
New York: Farrar, Straus and Giroux.

McKay, John P, Bennett D. Hill, and John Buckler. 1991. *A History of Western Society, Vol. I.* Houghton Mifflin Company.

McMillan, Terry. 1990. *Disappearing Acts.* New York: Washington Square Press.

________. 1993. "Looking for Mr. Right," pp. 557-559, in Gerald Early (ed.) *Speech and Power, Vol., 2.* Hopewell, N.J.: ECO Publishers.

________. 1987. *Mama.* New York: Washington Square Press.

________. 1992. *Waiting To Exhale. New* York : Viking.

Memmi, Albert. 1991. *The Colonizer and The Colonized.* Boston: Beacon Press.

Mill, John Stuart. 1978. *The Subjection of Women. Cambridge*, Mass.: The M.I.T. Press.

Miller, Judith. 1992. "The Islamic Wave." *The New York Times Magazine.* 5/31:22-26, 38, 40, 42.

Mitchell, Henry H. 1970. *Black Preaching.* New York: J.P. Lippincott Company.

Morrison, Toni. 1970. *The Bluest Eye.* New York: Washington Square Press.

________. 1993. "On the Backs of Blacks." *Time.* Fall, p. 57.

________. 1993. *Playing in the Dark: Whiteness and the Literary Imagination.* New York: Vintage Books; (see also Nathan Irvin Higgins, *Harlem Renaissance.* Oxford University Press, 1971, pp. 244-301).

________.1981. *Tar Baby.* New York: New American Library.

Moses, Wilson J. 1975. "Civilizing Missionary...." *The Journal of Negro History.* 1512:229-51.

Mumford, W. Bryant. 1970. *Africans Learn to be French.* New York: Negro Universities Press.

Naylor, Gloria. 1982. *Women of Brewster Place.* New York : Penguin Books.

Nkrumah, Kwame. 1963. *Africa Must Unite.* London: Heinemann.

________ 1970. *Consciencism: Philosophy and Ideology for De-Colonization.* New York: Monthly Review Press.

________. 1968. *Dark Days in Ghana.* New York: International Publishers.

________ 1957. *Ghana: Autobiography of Kwame Nkrumah.* New York: Thomas Nelson and Sons.

________. 1965. *Neo-Colonialism: The Last Stage of Imperialism.* New York: International Publishers.

________. 1973. *Revolutionary Path.* New York: International Publishers.

________. 1962. *Towards Colonial Freedom: Africa in the Struggle Against World Imperialism.* London: Panaf Books, Ltd.

________. 1950. *What I Mean by 'Positive Action.'* Accra, Ghana: Ministry of Information and Broadcasting.

Ngugi, James. 1986. *Decolonizing the Mind: The Politics of Language in African Literature.* Heineman Educational Books.

________. 1982. *Devil On The Cross.* Heinemann

________. 1964. *Weep Not, Child.* Heinemann

Nyerere, Julius. 1969. *Nyerere on Socialism.* Dar es Salaam: Oxford University Press.

________. 1968. *Ujamaa: Essays on Socialism.* New York: Oxford University Press.

Odetola, T.O. 1982. *Military Regimes and Development: A Comparative Analysis of African States.* London: George Allen and Unwin.

Ohmae, Kenichi. 1995. *The End of the Nation State: The Rise of Regional Economies.* New York: The Free Press.

________. 1990 *The Borderless World: Power and Strategy in the Interlinked*
*Economy.* New York: Harper Business.

________. 1985. *Triad Power: The Coming Shape of Global Competition.* New York: The Free Press.

Olaniya, Richard (ed.). 1982. *African History and Culture.* Longman, Nigeria, pp. 1-11.

Osofsky, Gilbert. 1966. *Harlem; The Making of a Ghetto.* New York, New York: Harper & Row.

Oyo, Olatunde J.B. 1980. "Nigeria and the Formation of ECOWAS." *International Organization.* 34/4:571-604.

Padmore, George. 1972. *Pan-Africanism or Communism.* New York: Doubleday and Co., Inc.

Parker, George. 1995. "Communication by Gun Powder: The British and the Asante Were Much Alike, Except for the Machine Guns." *New York Times Book Review.* 2/12:13.

P'Bitek, Okot. 1984. *Song of Lawino and Song of Ocol. Heinemann.*

Perlez, Jane. 1991. "U.S.Reveals Sum of Aid it Withheld from Kenya." *New York Times* 1/12: 10.

Postman, Neil. 1993. *Technopoly: The Surrender of Culture to Technology.* New York: Alfred A. Knopf.

Poussaint, Alvin. 1972. *Why Blacks Kill Blacks.* New York: Emerson Hall.

Randall, Dudley. 1968. "Booker T. and W.E.B." pp. 470-471, in Abraham Chapman (ed.) *Black Voices: An Anthology of Afro-American Literature. New* York: New American Library.

Redkey, Edwin S. 1978. "Bishop Turner's African Dream," pp. 227-246, in Randall K. Burkett and Richard Newmar (eds.), *Black Apostle : Afro-American Clergy Confront the Twentieth Century.* Boston: J.P. Hall and Company.

Reeves, Jay. 1994. "Fire Destroys School Involved in Race Dispute." *Buffalo News,* Sunday, August, p. A9.

Robinson, Lori. 1996. "An African Abyss." *Emerge.* March, Vol. 7, N 5:16.

Rodgers, Harrell R. 1987. "Black Americans and the Feminization of Poverty: The Intervening Effects of Unemployment." *Journal of Black Studies.* Vol. 17, No. 4: 402-417.

Rogers, J.A. 1972. *World's Great Men of Color, Vol. I.* New York, New York: Collier Books.

Rooney, David. 1988. *Kwame Nkrumah: Political Kingdom in the Third World.* New York: St. Martin's Press.

Safire, William. 1990. "Those Defining Moments." *New York Times Magazine.* 23 September: 20.

Sandbrook, Richard. 1985. *The Politics of Africa's Economic Decline.* Cambridge University Press.

Scobie, Edward. 1982. "The African Popes," pp. 84-95, in Ivan van Sertima (ed.) *African and African American in Science and Invention.* New Brunswick, New Jersey: Rutgers University Press, 1982.

Shange, Ntazake. 1975. *For Colored Girls Who Have Considered Suicide When The Rainbow is Enuf.* New York : MacMillan.

Shipman, Pat. 1994. "Facing Racial Differences Together". *The Chronicle of Higher Education,* August 3, pp. B1-B2; see also Ref (1994) *The Evolution of Racism: Human Differences and the Use and Abuse of Science.* New York, NY: Simon and Schuster.

Sklar, Richard L. 1967. "Political Science and National Integration." *The Journal of Modern Africa Studies.* 5/1:1-11.

Small, Stephen. 1994. *Racialized Barriers: The Black Experience in the United States and England in the 1980s.* London and New York: Routledge.

Snowden, Frank M. 1983. *Before Color Prejudice: The Ancient View of Blacks.* Cambridge, Mass: Harvard University Press.

Solanke, Julayemi. 1982. "Internal African Migrations and the Growth of Cultures." pp. 13-37, in Richard Oloniyan (ed.) *African History and Culture.* Lagos, Nigeria: Longman Nigeria Limited.

Spiro, Herbert J. 1962. *Politics in Africa: Prospects South of the Sahara.* Englewood Cliffs, N.J. Prentice-Hall, Inc.

Sowell, Thomas. 1981. *Ethnic America: A History.* New York: Basic Books.

Stockwell, John. 1978. *In Search of Enemies.* New York: Norton.

Stride, G.T., Caroline Ifeka and J.F. Ade Ajayi. 1971. *Peoples and Empires of West Africa: West Africa in History 1000-1800.* New York, NY: Africana Publishing Corporation.

Takaki, Ronald. 1993. *A Different Mirror: A History of Multicultural America.* Little, Brown, and Company.

Thomas, Laurence. 1990. "In My Next Life, I'll be White". *Ebony* (December), p. 84.

Thompson, Vincent Bakpetu. 1969. *Africa and Unity: The Evolution of Pan-Africanism.* London and Harlow: Longman.

Thurman, Wallace. 1996. *The Blacker The Berry.* New York : Simon And Schuster.

Tischler, Henry L. (ed.). 1990. *Introduction to Sociology.* New York, NY: Holt, Rinehart & Winston, Inc.

Tordoff, William. 1984. *Government and Politics in Africa.* Bloomington, IN: Indiana University Press.

Thorpe, Earl E. 1977. *The Mind of the Negro: An Intellectual History of Afro-Americans.* Westport, CT: Greenwood Press.

Urdang, Stephanie. 1981. "The Role of Women in the Revolution in Guinea-Bissau," pp. 119-139 in Filomina Chioma Steady (ed.). *The Black Woman Cross Culturally.* Rochester, Vermont: Schenkman Books, Inc.

*U.S.A. Today,* 1997. "Inclusion, Not Rejection, Will Spur Racial Harmony." 6/30:18A.

Uya, Okon Edet (ed.). 1971. *Black Brotherhood: Afro-Americans and Africa.* Lexington, Mass: D.C. Heath and Co.

Van Sertima, Ivan. 1976. *They Came Before Columbus.* New York, New York: Random House.

Valentine, Charles A. 1971. "Deficit, Difference, and Bi-cultural Models of Afro-American Behavior." *Harvard Educational Review.* Vol. 41, No. 2: 137-157.

Van Loon, Hendrik. 1972. *The Story of Mankind.* New York: Garden City Publishing Company, Inc.

Wai, Dustan M. 1982. "Crisis in North-South Relations." *Africa Report.* March-April: 20-26.

Wallbank, Walter T. and Alastair M. Taylor. 1942. *Civilization: Past and Present, Vol. I.* Scott, Foresman and Company.

Walker, Alice. 1982. *The Color Purple. New* York: Washington Square Press.

________.1983. *In Search of Our Mothers' Gardens.* New York: Harcourt, Brace, Jovanovich.

________. 1977. "Zora Neale Hurston: A Cautionary Tale and a Partisan View," pp. xi-xx, in Robert E. Hemeway, *Zora Neale Hurston: A Literary Biography.* University of Illinois Press.

Walton, Hanes Jr. 1985. *Invisible Politics: Black Political Behavior.* Albany, NY: State University of New York Press.

Washington, Booker T. 1963. *Up From Slavery. New* York: Bantam Books.

Wayas, Joseph. 1979. *Nigeria's Leadership Role.* London: The MacMillan Press.

Webster, J.B. and Boahen, A.A. 1970. *A History of West Africa: The Revolutionary Years - 1815 to Independence.* New York: Praeger Publishers.

Weinberg, Meyer (ed.). 1970. *W.E.B. Dubois Reader.* New York: Harper and Row.

West, Cornel. 1993. *Race Matters.* Boston, Massachusetts: Beacon Press.

Wheatley, Phillis. 1971. "On Being Brought From Africa to America." p.34, in Ruth Miller (ed.) *Black American Literature.* Encino, California: Glencoe Publishing Company, Inc.

Whitaker, Jennifer Seymour. 1988. *How Can Africa Survive?* New York: Council of Foreign Relations Press.

White, Joseph L. 1984. *The Psychology of Blacks: An African-American Perspective.* Englewood Cliffs, N.J. : Prentice Hall.

White, Walter. 1948. *A Man Called White: The Autobiography of Walter White.* New York: Viking Press.

Wiesner, Merry E., et. al. 1989. *Discovering the Western Past: A Look at the Evidence, Vol. I to 1715.* Boston, Mass: Houghton Mifflin Company.

Wiesner, Samuel (Translator). 1988. *Egyptian Mysteries.* York Beach, Maine: Samuel Weiser, Inc.

Williams, Barry. 1968. *Emerging Japan.* New York, McGraw-Hill Book Company.

Williams, Chancellor. 1974. *The Destruction of Black Civilization: Great Issues of a Race From 4500 B.C. to 2000 A.D.* Chicago, IL: Third World Press.

Williams, George Howard. 1995. *Life on the Color Line.* New York, New York: Dutton.

Willis, Christopher. 1994. "The skin we are in." *Discover: The World of Science.* 15/11:76-81.

Wilson, Allan C. and Rebecca L. Cann. 1992. "The Recent African Genesis of Humans: Genetic Studies Reveal that an African Woman of 200,000 Years Ago Was Our Common Ancestor." *Scientific American.* April, pp. 68-73.

Wilson, William, Julius. 1980. *The Declining Significance of Race.* The University of Chicago Press.

________. 1987. *The Truly Disadvantaged.* Chicago, IL: University of Chicago Press.

________. 1996. *When Work Disappears: The World of the New Urban Poor.* New York: Alfred A. Knopf.

Wiltse, Charles M. (ed.). 1915. *David Walker's Appeal....* New York, NY: Hill & Wang.

Wiseman, John A. 1990. *Democracy in Black Africa: Survival and Revival.* New York: Paragon House Publishers.

Woodson, Carter Goodwin. 1972. *The Mis-Education of the Negro.* New York: AMS Press.

Wren, Christophers. 1992. "Pretoria Sees a New Unity with Africans." *New York Times*, 4/12:A21.

Wright, Bruce. 1993. *White Robes, Black Justice.* New York, New York, Carol Publishing Group.

Wright, Karen. 1990. "The Road to the Global Village." *Scientific American..* 3:83-94.

Wright, Richard. 1944. *American Hunger*. New York: Harper and Row, Publishers.

________. 1945. *Black Boy: A Record of Childhood and Youth*. New York: Harper & Row, Publishers.

________. 1974. *Black Power: A Record of Reactions in a Land of Pathos. Westport*, Conn.: Greenwood Press, Publishers.

________. 1987. *Native Son*. New York: Harper and Row Publishers.

________. 1964. *White Man, Listen*! New York: Anchor Books.

Wright, Robert. 1996. "Science and Original Sin." *Time*, 10, 28:76-77.

# INDEX

J



K



L



M



N

## V



## W



## Z